Studien zu Kinder- und Jugendliteratur und -medien

Volume 9

Series Editors
Ute Dettmar, Frankfurt am Main, Germany
Petra Josting, Bielefeld, Germany
Caroline Roeder, Ludwigsburg, Germany

Die Kinder- und Jugendliteraturforschung hat sich seit ihrer Etablierung an den Universitäten in den 1960er-Jahren zu einer eigenständigen Disziplin der Literaturwissenschaft entwickelt. Angesichts der (inter- und trans-)medialen Entwicklungen im Erzählen und der zunehmenden Adaptionen kinder- und jugendliterarischer Stoffe (Filme, Serien, Hörbücher, Apps etc.) ist insbesondere auch eine (inter-)disziplinäre Weiterentwicklung in Richtung Medienwissenschaften notwendig. Die kulturwissenschaftliche Wende in den Geistes- und Sozialwissenschaften erfordert eine methodische Weiterentwicklung und eine konzeptionelle Öffnung des Forschungsfeldes, die aktuelle theoretische Positionen und Diskurse aufgreift. Die Reihe widmet sich diesen Forschungsfragen in Monographien und Sammelbänden.

More information about this series at https://link.springer.com/bookseries/16241

Ute Dettmar · Ingrid Tomkowiak
Editors

On Disney

Deconstructing Images, Tropes and Narratives

Editors
Ute Dettmar
Institut für Jugendbuchforschung
Goethe Universität Frankfurt
Frankfurt am Main, Hessen, Germany

Ingrid Tomkowiak
ISEK – Populäre Kulturen
Universität Zürich
Zürich, Switzerland

ISSN 2524-8634   ISSN 2524-8642   (electronic)
Studien zu Kinder- und Jugendliteratur und -medien
ISBN 978-3-662-64624-3   ISBN 978-3-662-64625-0   (eBook)
https://doi.org/10.1007/978-3-662-64625-0

© The Editor(s) (if applicable) and The Author(s), under exclusive license to Springer-Verlag GmbH, DE, part of Springer Nature 2022
This work is subject to copyright. All rights are solely and exclusively licensed by the Publisher, whether the whole or part of the material is concerned, specifically the rights of translation, reprinting, reuse of illustrations, recitation, broadcasting, reproduction on microfilms or in any other physical way, and transmission or information storage and retrieval, electronic adaptation, computer software, or by similar or dissimilar methodology now known or hereafter developed.
The use of general descriptive names, registered names, trademarks, service marks, etc. in this publication does not imply, even in the absence of a specific statement, that such names are exempt from the relevant protective laws and regulations and therefore free for general use.
The publisher, the authors and the editors are safe to assume that the advice and information in this book are believed to be true and accurate at the date of publication. Neither the publisher nor the authors or the editors give a warranty, expressed or implied, with respect to the material contained herein or for any errors or omissions that may have been made. The publisher remains neutral with regard to jurisdictional claims in published maps and institutional affiliations.

Umschlagabbildung: Mad Tea Party, Disneyland, Anaheim, California. © Ingrid Tomkowiak

Responsible Editor: Oliver Schuetze
This J.B. Metzler imprint is published by the registered company Springer-Verlag GmbH, DE part of Springer Nature.
The registered company address is: Heidelberger Platz 3, 14197 Berlin, Germany

Preface

Disney—This name probably brings back, for most people, childhood memories of fairy-tale films, iconic characters such as Bambi, the Little Mermaid, and Jack Sparrow, or family visits to Disneyland or Disney World. The Disney Company can now look back on a thriving story that spans more than one hundred years: their productions are extremely popular worldwide and are among the formative media experiences of ever new generations, who grow up with the stories and later watch Disney films again together with their children—be it in the cinema or on the sofa, switching on the company's own streaming service Disney+.

It is, however, not only Disney's popularity that transcends generations, but also the criticism levelled at the company and their productions: criticism of its patriarchal corporate structure and capitalist business practices, of the entertainment industry as such and the related cultural globalisation, of the Americanisation of European culture and the conservative ideology inscribed in the films—criticism that is often summarised by the term 'Disneyfication' which is also used when Disney approaches and aesthetics are imitated, e.g. in contexts of urban planning and architecture.

An undifferentiated devaluation of this prime example of commercially successful popular culture, however, would be too simplistic. A decisive reason for Disney's success is the fact that throughout its history the company has always skilfully combined technical and aesthetic innovations on the one hand with tried-and-true narrative patterns on the other. This strategy also includes the fact that Disney has repeatedly responded to the *Zeitgeist* and virulent contemporary discourses by repositioning itself—for example on race, gender, diversity, body and human-animal relations—but without reinventing itself.

The aim of this volume is to take a closer look at this tension in historical, cultural and media contexts and to deconstruct images, tropes and narratives in different media and genres. It brings together scholars from several European countries to explore various dimensions that constitute 'Disney.' The volume sees itself as part of the now broad discussion of the Disney phenomenon from a media and cultural studies perspective, which is reflected in a large body of research literature.

The contributions are arranged in five chapters: The first chapter deals with **human-human and human-animal relations.** The relationship between culture and nature is negotiated in many Disney films and often fixed in sentimentalising images of an anthropomorphised animal world. But there are also representations that are ambiguous: Ingrid Tomkowiak examines the two *Dumbo* films focusing on the intersectional identity of the protagonist—as a child, an animal and a disabled person in the context of the cultural and social history of popular entertainment. Christine Lötscher analyses current documentary films and locates them in the field of tension between anthropomorphisation and animal agency.

The second chapter focuses on **gender and diversity,** central themes in the scholarly discussion of Disney. With a focus on a series of films made since the end of the 1980s (*The Little Mermaid, Mulan, Aladdin, The Princess and the Frog, Ralph Breaks the Internet, The Nutcracker and the Four Realms*), the contributions by Lies Wesseling, Yvonne Festl, Sara Van den Bossche, Claudia Sackl and Ute Dettmar ask, with reference to current cultural studies discussions, how representations of gender and diversity are shaped in the films and which representational strategies they pursue. They discuss how the films have responded to criticism about Disney's role in perpetuating racist and sexist stereotypes by changing, or at least superficially adapting, their representations of particular figures and social groups. The updating of images aimed at staging more diverse and progressive characters is critically reflected upon with reference to current research on gender, race and diversity. Film-specific dimensions (animation, live-action movie, transcultural and transmedial adaptation) are also included in these discussions.

The next chapter concentrates on how Disney has dealt with (European) **cultural heritage,** a central aspect of its production history. Emer O'Sullivan is concerned with a relatively unknown chapter in Disney history, the performances and representations of Irishness in the context of Irish-American culture and its popular traditions. Ludger Scherer undertakes a critical reflection on the 'Disneyfication' of European literary texts, myths, art and music, using the example of the animated film *Fantasia*.

Iconic characters and narratives are the subject of the following chapter: from dancing skeletons (in Julia Benner's contribution) to Robin Hood (in Anika Ullmann's) and Jack Sparrow (in Aleta-Amirée von Holzen's). These figures are discussed in the context of media techniques, media meta-reflection and myth adaptations.

In the final chapter on **immersive experience and reflexive engagement** Lincoln Geraghty and Natalie Borsy address transmedial and transfictional approaches to Disney's fictional worlds through theme parks and amusement parks, consumer culture, fan engagement and other participatory practices. Also in this context, Anna Sparrman explores Disney's visual legacy in a Swedish amusement park.

We thank all authors for their contributions to this volume and Eugenia Lao for her careful copy editing.

Frankfurt am Main and Zurich
in autumn 2021

Ute Dettmar
Ingrid Tomkowiak

Contents

HUMAN-HUMAN AND HUMAN-ANIMAL RELATIONS

Happy Pictures? Disney's *Dumbo* Films and the Entertainment Industry 3
Ingrid Tomkowiak

Animal Bodies, Human Voices, and the Big Entanglement. Disneynature's Documentary Series 25
Christine Lötscher

GENDER AND DIVERSITY

Curtailment in Mermaid Lore. Disney's *The Little Mermaid* (1989) 39
Lies Wesseling

"Be a Man". Gender and Body in Disney's *Mulan* (1998) 51
Yvonne Festl

Walking the Line. A Feminist Reading of Gendered Orientations and Voice in Disney's *Aladdin* Films (1992/2019) 67
Sara Van den Bossche

Screening Blackness. Controversial Visibilities of Race in Disney's Fairy Tale Adaptations 81
Claudia Sackl

From E.T.A. Hoffmann to Disney. Figurations of the Nutcracker in Changing Media and Culture 97
Ute Dettmar

ASPECTS OF CULTURAL HERITAGE

Walt O'Disney and the Little People. Playing to the Irish-American Diaspora 115
Emer O'Sullivan

ix

From the Old World. Disney's Transformation of European
Cultural Heritage in *Fantasia* (1940) 131
Ludger Scherer

ICONIC CHARACTERS AND NARRATIVES

Music in Their Bones. Play, Music and Materiality in Disney's
Dancing Skeleton Films 155
Julia Benner

"Taxing the Heart and Soul Out of the People". Disney's
Robin Hood (1973) as Conservative Fable 171
Anika Ullmann

Jack Sparrow—the Ultimate Adventurer 185
Aleta-Amirée von Holzen

IMMERSIVE EXPERIENCE, REFLEXIVE ENGAGEMENT

From Anaheim to Batuu. Fan Tourism and Disney's *Star Wars*:
Galaxy's Edge as Transmedia Playground 199
Lincoln Geraghty

Consuming Disney. Image Cultivation, Indoctrination and
Immersive Transmedia Storytelling in Disney Cookbooks 211
Natalie Borsy

The Social Aesthetics of Family Space. The Visual Heritage of
Disney in a Swedish Amusement Park 229
Anna Sparrman

Editors and Contributors

About the Editors

Ute Dettmar Prof. Dr., is Professor of Children's Literature Studies at Goethe University Frankfurt am Main, where she heads the Institute for Children's and Young Adult Literature Research. From 2007 to 2013, she was a junior professor at Carl von Ossietzky University Oldenburg. Main areas of work: Children's literature and media from the eighteenth century to the present; history, aesthetics and criticism of popular culture; seriality and transmediality.

Ingrid Tomkowiak Prof. Dr., University of Zurich, is professor emerita of popular literature and media. Also a specialist in children's and youth's media, she has written on children's classics and their film adaptations, as well as on bestsellers and blockbusters, and on material poetics in animation films. Current research deals with biopics about authors of children's literature.

List of Contributors

Julia Benner, Prof. Dr.; Institute of German Literature at the Humboldt-University, Berlin; history and theory of children's and young adult literature (and media), political aspects of children's and young adult literature, exile literature, constructions of childhood.

Natalie Borsy, MA; University of Zurich, Department of Social Anthropology and Cultural Studies—Popular Culture Studies; teaching and research assistant and administrative assistant. In her PhD project "Edible Fictions" she analyzes cookbooks that are based on fictional works of popular media and the trans-medial processes underlying the transformation of text to recipe. Her research focus lies on popular literature, media and genres, cookery writing, fictional cookbooks, nostalgia, and material aesthetics.

Ute Dettmar, Prof. Dr., is Professor of Children's Literature Studies at Goethe University Frankfurt am Main, where she heads the Institute for Children's and Young Adult Literature Research. From 2007 to 2013, she was a junior professor at Carl von Ossietzky University Oldenburg. Main areas of work: Children's literature and media from the eighteenth century to the present; history, aesthetics and criticism of popular culture; seriality and transmediality.

Yvonne Festl, BA, is a Master's student in Film Studies at Freie Universität Berlin. Her research interests include cinema, reality television, animation, special and visual effects, fantasy, the art of drag and the representation of gender.

Lincoln Geraghty, PhD, Professor of Media Cultures; School of Film, Media and Communication, University of Portsmouth, UK; my research focuses on media fandom and popular culture. I am particularly interested in contemporary media entertainment franchises and the relationships between fans, texts and industry. Recent publications have examined collecting, nostalgia and fandom. As well as *Star Wars*, my work on transmedia has included analysis on *Star Trek*, LEGO Batman and Pokémon.

Aleta-Amirée von Holzen, Dr. phil.; Schweizerisches Institut für Kinder- und Jugendmedien SIKJM, Zurich (Switzerland). Research focus: children's literature and media, comics, fantasy, adventure, pirates, masked superheroes and pulp heroes.

Christine Lötscher, Prof. Dr., is Professor of Popular Literature and Media at the University of Zurich. She obtained her PhD at the University of Zurich with a project on magic books in fantasy literature (*Das Zauberbuch als Denkfigur*, 2014) and her habilitation with a book on Lewis Carroll's Alice books and their influence on popular media (*Die Alice-Maschine. Figurationen der Unruhe in der Populärkultur*, Stuttgart 2020). Her research focuses on children's literature and media, popular genres, the fantastic in the arts, media theory and -aesthetics, new materialism and human-non-human-relations.

Emer O'Sullivan, Prof. Dr., Professor of English Literature, Leuphana University Lüneburg. She is the recipient of both the IRSCL Award for Outstanding Research and the ChLA Book Award. Areas of research: comparative literature, image studies, children's literature and translation studies.

Claudia Sackl, BA BA MA MA; Vienna; research assistant at STUBE—Studien-Beratungsstelle für Kinder- und Jugendliteratur, head of the adult education institution Literarische Kurse and editor of its annual correspondence course on literature *Fernkurs für Literatur*, PhD student at the Department of English and American Studies at the University of Vienna (working title *Afropean Imaginaries*: Diasporic Im/Mobilities in Twenty-First Century Anglophone and Germanophone Literature On and Off the Page); research focus: postcolonial and transcultural studies and literatures, critical race theory, children's and young adult literature and media, multimodal narratives.

Ludger Scherer, PD Dr. phil.; University of Bonn; former Lecturer, invited and stand-in Professor at the Universities of München, Graz, Köln, Innsbruck, Siegen, Paderborn, Aachen and Berlin (FU); teaching and research in Romance Philology (Italian, French and Spanish Literature from the beginnings until recent works, esp. Dante), Comparative Literature (Early Modern literature, Petrarchism, European Enlightenment, Poetics of the Novel, Intertextuality of Myths and Literary Themes, Post-Avant-gardes) and Children's and Young Adults' Literature and Media (fairy tales, inter-medial transformations, films).

Anna Sparrman, PhD, Professor at the Department of Thematic Studies—Child Studies, Linköping University, Sweden. She works at the intersection between visual culture, child consumption, child culture and child sexuality. She addresses how norms and values are enacted between children, adults and the material world in children's everyday life practices. Sparrman also has a special interest in visual methodologies and the productivity of research methods. Sparrman runs a large research project on visual digitization*Children's Cultural Heritage* (2021–2024).

Ingrid Tomkowiak, Prof. Dr., University of Zurich, is professor emerita of popular literature and media. Also a specialist in children's and youth's media, she has written on children's classics and their film adaptations, as well as on bestsellers and blockbusters, and on material poetics in animation films. Current research deals with biopics about authors of children's literature.

Anika Ullmann, MA. She is writing her PhD dissertation at Leuphana University Lüneburg on hackers as twenty-first century Robin Hoods. She also teaches literature at Goethe University Frankfurt. Her research focuses on the utilisation of digital media for the construction and performativity of young age in young adult novels and media. Her second field of attention is the intersection of age and queerness.

Sara Van den Bossche, Dr., Assistant Professor at Tilburg University. Research focus: Ethnic and cultural diversity, feminism, ideology criticism, cognitive criticism, canonisation, adaptation, literary criticism and text/image interaction in picturebooks.

Lies Wesseling, Prof. Dr., is professor of Cultural Memory, Gender and Diversity at the Faculty of Arts and Social Sciences (FASoS) of Maastricht University, the Netherlands. She is past president of the International Research Society for Children's Literature (www.irscl.com) and director of the Centre for Gender and Diversity at FASoS. She is a participant in the international research network COACC (Children as Objects and Agents of (Post-)Colonial Change).

HUMAN-HUMAN AND HUMAN-ANIMAL RELATIONS

Happy Pictures?

Disney's *Dumbo* Films and the Entertainment Industry

Ingrid Tomkowiak

> *But what's more Disney than Disney controlling the ways in which a filmmaker can critique Disney?*
>
> Katie Rife (2019)

Abstract This chapter analyses Disney's two *Dumbo* films, the 1941 animated film directed by Ben Sharpsteen and the 2019 live-action remake directed by Tim Burton. The discussion focuses on the intersectional identity of the protagonist as child, animal and disabled person, taking into account contextualising aspects from the cultural and social history of popular entertainment. It also considers the ways in which both *Dumbo* films address controversial aspects of labour in the entertainment sector. Sharpsteen's film paints an ambiguous picture of contemporary circus culture, referring to key moments in the prior history of entertainment culture that were pivotal in its development. Burton's film is set even earlier, in the period shortly after World War I, an era that can be regarded as a period of radical transformation for traditional popular entertainment. Not only does the film represent that historical reality, it also responds to aspects of the political agenda in the early twenty-first century.

Before the Show

On September 14, 1955 Walt Disney, in his television show *Walt Disney's Disneyland*, gave an introduction to the animated film *Dumbo,* directed by Ben Sharpsteen and released in 1941. In the show Disney first looked at a *Dumbo* picture book (Walt Disney Productions 1947), then closed it and turned to the audience:

I. Tomkowiak (✉)
University of Zurich, Zurich, Switzerland
e-mail: ingrid.tomkowiak@uzh.ch

© The Author(s), under exclusive license to Springer-Verlag GmbH, DE, part of Springer Nature 2022
U. Dettmar and I. Tomkowiak (eds.), *On Disney*, Studien zu Kinder- und Jugendliteratur und -medien 9, https://doi.org/10.1007/978-3-662-64625-0_1

> From time to time, people ask me which is the favorite of all the pictures that we've made. Well, it's the one that you're going to see right now on this program. The story of the little elephant with the big ears, Dumbo. From the very start, *Dumbo* was a happy picture. It really started with a very simple idea and like Topsy it grew. We weren't restricted by any set story line, so we could give our imaginations full play, in other words, if a good idea came to us, we'd put it in the story. It was really a happy picture, from the beginning to the end (Sharpsteen 1941, Bonus, 00:00:17–00:00:50).

The timing of the television broadcast was perfectly planned: Disneyland had opened in Anaheim just two months earlier on July 17, 1955, and the Dumbo Ride went into operation in August. But the fact that Disney describes the film *Dumbo* as a "happy picture, from the beginning to the end" requires explanation. The period during which the film was produced was anything but a happy time for Disney, and the story about the baby elephant with the exceptionally large ears— in spite of the happy spin Disney later put on it—is actually deeply sad.

When *Dumbo* was in production, Disney was in dire straits (cf. Barrier 2007, 151–181). The years of the Great Depression had hit the country. On September 1, 1939, the Second World War had begun in Europe and it had become extremely difficult, if not impossible, to distribute American films in Europe. Even after the box office success of *Snow White and the Seven Dwarfs* (1937) Disney had fallen well short of making a profit. The construction of the new studio in Burbank, which opened in 1939, had swallowed up a lot of money; the lavishly-produced animated films *Pinocchio* (1940) and *Fantasia* (1940) had not brought the hoped-for financial gain, and the ambitious project of producing *Bambi* (1942), which had been taken up in 1939, was very expensive. When production of *Dumbo* started at the beginning of 1941, Disney's instructions to Sharpsteen were clear: "simple and inexpensive" (quoted in Gabler 2006, 333).

But there was another complex knot of problems (cf. Barrier 2003, 306–309; id. 2007, 165–201; Sito 2006, 101–152; Platthaus 2001, 145–162; Zornado 2017, 119–123): due to the tight financial situation, Disney had dismissed a number of employees in 1940, which caused irritation among those remaining. In addition, there was growing displeasure among employees about suspended profit sharing, the opaque practice of bonus payments and privileges and the setting of wage levels, which differed widely among employees and was therefore criticised as unjust. At that time, many people in the entertainment industry, including those from the big animation studios like Warner Bros. and Fleisher, were already unionised. When Disney employees also tried to join the Screen Cartoonist Guild at the beginning of 1941, Walt Disney reacted with threats of termination and ultimately further layoffs. The situation worsened: on May 29, 1941 cartoonists and animators went on strike. It would last more than two months and had serious consequences. Walt Disney felt betrayed and responded with layoffs in large numbers.

During the production of *Dumbo,* Walt Disney was, unlike with previous Disney films, almost not involved at all. From August 17, 1941 on, during the final phase of production, he was on the so-called Goodwill Tour in South America; Disney travelled on behalf of the US government, which, in view of growing sympathy for the National Socialists in South America, was trying to improve relations between North and South America (cf. Gluck 2016; Barrier 2007, 174–175; id. 2003, 308).

Two weeks after his return, the film had its world premiere on October 23, 1941 and was a great success—*a happy picture* in the end.[1] And at the beginning? As far as acquiring film rights from the literary source was concerned (cf. Barrier 2011), Disney actually had a stroke of luck, for he got the rights to the story at the most favourable price of one thousand dollars (cf. Barrier 2011; Case 2002, 2014).

As already mentioned, the film tells a sad story. Its protagonist, a baby elephant named Jumbo Junior, lives in a circus. However, little Jumbo's integration into the circus community is hampered by the fact that he is discriminated against (called *freak* and *Dumbo*) because of his exceptionally large ears, and his mother, Mrs. Jumbo, who stands up for him, is declared mad and locked away. It is only with the help of other animals that the little elephant realises that his ears enable him to fly. In the end—as a new child redeemer—he saves his mother by becoming the new main attraction of the circus, and rises to become a nationally known and media-acclaimed star, even acquiring a fan following, as becomes clear at the end of the film.

This chapter will first analyse the animated film *Dumbo* with a focus on the character of Jumbo Junior, looking at his intersectional identity as a child, as an animal and as a disabled person. In doing so, contextualising aspects from the cultural and social history of popular entertainment will be taken into account. Against this background the article will also examine Disney's remake of *Dumbo*, directed by Tim Burton as a live-action film (with CGI elements) and released in 2019. Here the discussion will focus on this version's approach to dealings with the child/animal/disabled person nexus; on the choice to set the film in a different historical period; and on the representation of the entertainment business as well as the associated political message.

Both *Dumbo* films address controversial aspects of labour in the entertainment sector. The animated film released in 1941 paints a picture of contemporary circus culture (though the setting is in part peaceful and made fantastical by the presence of talking animals), thereby referring to key moments in the prior history of entertainment culture that were pivotal in its development. Burton sets his film even earlier, in the period shortly after World War I, an era that can be regarded as a period of radical transformation for traditional popular entertainment. Not only does the film represent that historical reality, it also responds to aspects of the political agenda in the early twenty-first century.

Ring Free! *Dumbo* (1941)

'Simple and inexpensive' was Disney's instruction for this film, and so unlike *Snow White* or *Bambi,* for example, the use of the multiplane camera was dispensed with altogether. Instead of depth effect and three-dimensional effects,

---

[1] However, the success was marred by Japan's attack on Pearl Harbor on December 7, 1941, which led to the United States' entry into World War II.

two-dimensional representation in watercolours dominates, often reminiscent of the aesthetics of the cartoon comedy short films that various animation studios had been producing since the 1930s. Moreover, the film featured rather caricatured depictions of many characters, which clearly followed neither Disney's goal of the *illusion of life* (cf. Thomas/Johnston 1995; Tomkowiak 2017, 125, 129) nor the principle of Disney formalism (cf. Pallant 2011, 35–54), which he had been aggressively pursuing at least since *Snow White*.

Nevertheless, the studio did not work entirely without live models, nor did it go completely against the prescribed orientation toward the techniques of realistic film. Thus animators drew inspiration from living models in the circus (cf. Thomas/Johnston 1995, 499, 522–524; Pallant 2011, 47), as is shown for example in the inside cover of a picture book edition of *Dumbo* (Walt Disney Productions 1941), depicting as it were a scene from a 'making of' documentary.

With its divergent elements, the film seems at first glance like a motley collection of different, incongruous styles, even like a "throwback to a style of caricature and broad comedy that Disney had been determined to move away from" (Zornado 2017, 124). By the 1930s, Disney had developed a form of animation that was rounder, softer, cuter than that of his competitors, and was favouring a style that made characters appear childlike and environments appear pastoral (cf. Sammond 2012, 4).

At second glance, however, the mixture in *Dumbo* is not quite as wild as it first seems. The animation has a system; Chris Pallant describes it as "aesthetic hybridity" (2011, 49). Right from the opening credits, which are based on the aesthetics of circus posters and which are accompanied by fast-paced music familiar from clown acts in the ring, the film positions itself in the genre of the circus film (cf. Richards 2020, 145–147; McIlroy 2019). As one might find in the dramaturgy of a circus performance, in the film fast scenes alternate with slow, loud scenes with quiet, garish colours with earth tones. In the words of Michael Charlton, who describes the film's patterning with reference to Mikhail Bakhtin, the film is "a planned, deliberate succession of individual bits and pieces that ultimately create a carnival atmosphere of joy and chaos [...] [,] then instantly goes from bleak to joyful and back again" (Charlton 2020, 106). For example, a tent-pitching scene is done in an impressionist style, while a dream sequence dreamt by a tipsy Jumbo Junior features a parade of *pink elephants* that looks to the expressive style of surrealism. Action scenes designed to heighten tension, produce shock and insert comedy in the sense of the "cinema of attractions" (Gunning 2006) are contrasted with scenes done in a naturalistic style that focus on sensation and pathos and are designed to arouse emotion and empathy. At the same time, these scenes counterbalance each other atmospherically, and the circus thus becomes an ambiguous place: on the one hand, the mother–child scenes with the animals present the circus as an indisputably idyllic place; on the other hand, we are shown the exploitation and de-individualisation of humans and animals, as well as the exclusion and exhibition of those declared to be different. And yet, those who are different are given the opportunity to become a star precisely because of their conspicuousness.

Thus the film offers "a story filled with sharp juxtapositions between the joyous and frightening aspects of the circus" (Charlton 2020, 110).

As Mark Langer (1990) has pointed out, two disparate animation traditions interact in *Dumbo*, an occurrence that is probably related to the fact that Walt Disney himself stayed out of the production: "While West Coast animation was more consistent with the codes of classic Hollywood cinema, the New York style violated those codes through its emphasis on the artificial quality of animation" (ibid., 306); it was "selfconscious of the image *as an image*" (ibid., 316 [emphasis in original]). Thus the cartoonesque, anarchic New York Style, which animators trained in New York had imported into the Disney Studio, was able to assert itself in various scenes as a *counterstyle* to the West Coast Style corresponding to the bourgeois values favoured by Disney. But not only that:

> These contrasts of style are central to DUMBO. As the film progresses, it becomes clear that Dumbo [i. e. little Jumbo] belongs to the mimetic world of West Coast style, but is prevented from succeeding within that world by his "cartoony" features. As a stylized character, Dumbo is excluded from the company of the more mimetic elephants. [...] Dumbo has become a clown (ibid., 315).

In the end, however, everything falls into place, in the West Coast manner that was to become typical of the golden era of Disney animation: "its project to purvey conservative, nostalgic, restorative fantasy in aid of the political and ideological status quo" (Zornado 2017, 123).

Central to this is the self-assertion of the individual. And so, Langer concludes:

> Dumbo realizes his identity through the achievement of self-knowledge. With his talent restated in terms of psychological naturalism, Dumbo escapes the "cartoony" life of a clown by demonstrating his ability to fly [...].
> The New York solution presented by the Pink Elephants is normalized by the West Coast ending of the "Success Montage". DUMBO's conclusion is not only a celebration of the typical restoration of family and prosperity [...] it also celebrates the triumph of the West Coast style. The anarchism of "Pink Elephants" is recouped into an American success story (1990, 317–318).

Let us now turn to the little elephant Jumbo Junior himself, on whom Langer applies his interpretation of the correspondence of form and content, aesthetics and message.

Jumbo Junior: Child/Animal/Disabled Person

Twenty years after Charlie Chaplin's *The Kid* (1921), one of the first feature-length films with a child protagonist, and at the tail-end of the Great Depression, when audiences were warmed by child stars like Shirley Temple, the animated little elephant Jumbo Junior once again put a *child* at the centre of cinematic attention. This was not simply an anthromorphised young animal among other anthropomorphised animals; this protagonist was explicitly conceived of as a young child (cf. Barrier 2003, 313–314). As such, he does not manage to speak a single time throughout the film, but nevertheless learns, despite his tender age, that conformity and obedience, as well as hard and also dangerous work, are expected of a circus child who really is supposed to earn a living. But in order to be perceived positively as an individual, Jumbo Junior must first learn to accept himself as he is. Eventually, with the help of Timothy the mouse and the friendly crows,[2] he recognises his supposed flaw as an advantage and literally soars to become the star of the circus. However, there are limits to the (self-)empowerment and emancipation of this elephant child: Timothy, as his manager, signs a contract with Hollywood, but at the end of the film it is clear that Jumbo Junior will remain in the service of the circus.[3] The wild parade of pink elephants that Jumbo saw in his dream also turned into nothing but pink clouds in the end (cf. Langer 1990, 316). And so, as Siegfried Kracauer concluded in a review written at the time of the film's release: "[Y]oung Dumbo, instead of flying off towards some unknown paradise, chooses wealth and security and so ends up as the highly paid star of the same circus director who once flew his mother Jumbo" (2012, 140).

In this film, the circus appears as a place of deep security (especially in the mother-and-child scenes) just as much as one of extreme terror: "It is a symbolic playground where children are cherished and indulged as well as cast aside and punished" (Charlton 2020, 110). Charlton reads the film's narrative as a child's attempt "to work through psychological issues and anxieties around abandonment and being a social outsider [...]. Like many children, he matures into confidence only by first facing fear and anxiety" (ibid., 111).

Stephen Watt sees *Dumbo* as a social and political allegory of American values in the Depression era. For him, Jumbo is "the virtuous, defenseless underdog who struggles against arbitrary forces, bucks up his courage, finds his way to productive work, and ultimately joins with other marginalized figures to overcome their oppressors" (Watt 1997, 90). This, however, goes a little too far. The film's conclusion does nothing to change the social structure of the circus world, which is characterised by the cruel and irresponsible exercise of power (in which a mother who vigorously defends her child against insults is declared insane, isolated and locked away, and this child is forced to perform life-threatening and humiliating acts). Thus, Jumbo's triumph in the ring is not about breaking up, breaking out or overcoming the oppressors, but, as Joseph Zornado argues, about submission and voluntary persistence in captivity—where the first class carriage is an illusory

---

[2] The accusations of racism towards the depiction of the crows will not be addressed here, cf. Wainer [not dated]; Sammond 2005, 8–9, 12–15; Gregory 2012, 195, note 54; Glassmeyer 2013, 108; alexandc 2015; Zornado 2017, 128; Perea 2018, 5–6; Meeusen 2019, 347; Charlton 2020, 109, 111.

[3] Cf. the circus film *The Greatest Show on Earth* (de Mille 1952), made in cooperation with Ringling Bros. and Barnum & Bailey's Circus, with its staff of 1400 people as well as hundreds of animals, including, of course, the show's elephants.

paradise. Jumbo Junior is put on sale to the audience by the Ringmaster for profit, as a child labour slave with privileges (cf. Zornado 2017, 126) or, in terms of capitalist self-commodification, as a unique product that values itself and becomes valuable to others (cf. Sammond 2012, 13).

In his study *Babes in Tomorrowland: Walt Disney and the Making of the American Child, 1930–1960*, Nicholas Sammond examines the emergence and development of the Disney canon in the context of changing child-rearing theories and practices. This change coincides with Disney's rise and the appreciation of his products by child education experts as positive media. Indeed, in contrast to earlier criticism of films as harmful to children, films were now thought to contribute to children's moral growth. Disney took advantage of this assessment. Once it had been identified as a positive influence, the company deliberately cultivated this image. Walt Disney himself—because of his past, his work ethic and his status as a self-made man—would come to be understood in the late 1930s and early 1940s as a prototype of the kind of person that a child's upbringing should produce. Disney characters embodied the qualities that had made Disney what he was, and children, by watching Disney films, thereby imbibed those qualities as well, according to the widespread assumption of the time (cf. here and below Sammond 2005, 1–134; id. 2012; Glassmeyer 2013, 106–113).

The child-rearing practices of the 1930s, Sammond argues, emphasised conformity and parental regulation of needs and drives with the aim of having children internalise their parents' favoured values. On the other hand, he notes, films such as *Pinocchio*, *Dumbo* and *Bambi* were informed by Depression-era emphasis on the need to develop autonomy and self-management or self-government. Sammond shows that Disney's films disseminated these values to a wide audience and functioned, as it were, as surrogate training manuals for parents. This involved portraying the normalised child and also balancing conformity with individualism. From 1940 on and during the production of *Dumbo,* the discourse on child-rearing (to which Walt Disney Productions had become increasingly attuned in the 1930s) shifted away from behaviourist, management-based models and towards what would later become known as the 'child-centred' or 'permissive' model, according to which the properly reared child would be allowed to find his or her own inner talents and strengths without undue interference from authority figures.

At first glance, the plot of *Dumbo* seems to be a celebration of individualism, a paean to the very qualities that seem embodied in the life story of Walt Disney himself. A closer look suggests a slightly different message: Jumbo Junior triumphs only after he accepts his uniqueness. But instead of setting up his own business (like Walt Disney), he puts his talents in the service of the same circus that had treated him and his mother so cruelly. For the United States, about to enter World War II and vacillating between two opposing ideals of child-rearing—behaviourism and neo-Freudian 'permissiveness'—the circus world in which Jumbo Junior was to find his place combined the discipline of domestication with the adventure of self-discovery.

Even with the focus on *animals* (but in the context of the circus, always anthropocentric), an ambiguous picture emerges: Captivity and hard labour under the dictatorship of the ringmaster are juxtaposed with idyllic scenes intended to give the audience the impression that it is cosy and spacious in the animals' wagons. For example, the entry into the city and the erection of the tent was modelled on harsh contemporary reality[4]: Both elephants and anonymous human 'roustabouts,'[5] portrayed as people of colour, have to toil hard. Counterbalancing this are the animal family scenes so typical of Disney, showing us a pastoral ideal and presented in a highly emotionalised key. At times the animals even look as if they were happy to be living in cages and performing dangerous tricks in the ring for the sake of satisfying the ringmaster (cf. Stanton 2021, 128–141). This contrasts sharply with the human workers, who demand wage increases, just as Disney employees did in real life.

On the subject of animal labour, however, we should consider yet another reality.

In the original *Dumbo* (Pearl/Pearl 1939) the largest elephant in the circus is given the name Jumbo. This name in fact refers to a historical elephant by the same name: Jumbo (1860–1885) was one of the first animal international superstars of entertainment culture, and his story, marked by human exploitation, tells only one of the many sad fates of circus animals (cf. McClellen 2014): Born in Sudan, the one-year-old boy elephant fell into captivity after his mother was killed. He was transported to Suez and shipped to Trieste, sold to the Kreutzberg travelling menagerie in Germany, then kept in the Jardin des Plantes in Paris and finally transferred to the London Zoo in 1865, where—under the name Jumbo—he became the main attraction because of his extraordinary size and because he let children ride him. Despite great protests from the public, the animal was sold in 1882 to New York (cf. Fig. 1). The circus entrepreneur Phineas Taylor Barnum, who had been running Barnum and Bailey's Circus together with James Anthony Bailey since 1881, initially exhibited Jumbo in Madison Square Garden. The arrival of the then already famous elephant in the United States launched a 'Jumbo Mania', complete with advertising, merchandising products, postcards, advertising pictures, etc. Everything that had to do with the elephant Jumbo was extremely popular. Jumbo, who had not learned any circus tricks, was then sent on a three-year tour of the US and Canada with P.T. Barnum's Greatest Show on Earth, a travelling menagerie, serving as its icon. He died in a train accident in Ontario in 1885.

---

[4] See, for example, the documentary *Circus Day in Our Town* (by Encyclopaedia Britannica Films, 1949) at https://vimeo.com/358492576. Accessed: 23. May 2021.

[5] The accusations of racism regarding the portrayal and characterisation of the 'roustabouts' will also not be addressed in detail here, cf. Langer 1990, 314; Charlton 2020, 107. The term 'roustabout' refers to unskilled workers who were employed to erect circus tents and showmen's stalls at fairs. Both the crows and the 'roustabouts' are designed in such a way that the scenes, instead of being read as racist and discriminatory, can be read as exposing precisely this view.

Happy Pictures?

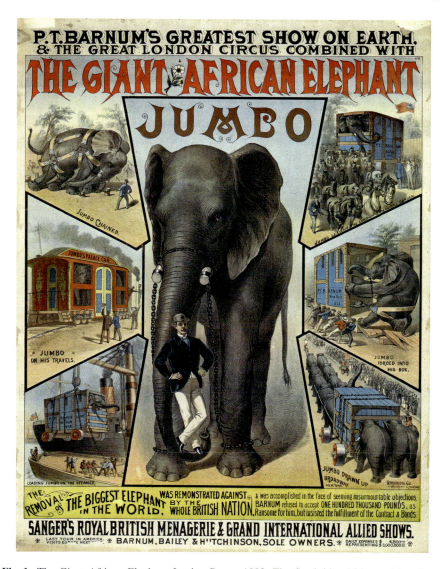

Fig. 1 The Giant African Elephant Jumbo. Poster 1882. The Strobridge Lithographing Company. (© State Historical Society of Wisconsin, Circus World, CWi 15,239)

As Disney was to later become, Barnum was a storyteller as well, and so he proclaimed Jumbo's death to be a heroic one: the elephant had given his life to save a baby elephant. Even his remains initially served business interests; the animal was immediately taxidermied, continued to travel with the circus and was exhibited in various places before being given to Tufts University to be put on display in its newly built Barnum Hall (Barnum Museum of Natural History).

Jumbo eventually became the university mascot, remaining popular in this role to this day. Even after the preserved elephant was destroyed by fire in 1975, Jumbo's posthumous fame endured. According to Andrew McClellan, his greatest legacy, however, may be his role in the cultural history of America in the late nineteenth century:

> Jumbo's story weaves together important strands of nineteenth-century history: the emergence of new vehicles of public education and entertainment—museums, zoos, and the circus—and the expansion of their exhibits in the wake of colonial exploration; the development of steamship travel and the railroad; the explosion of commercial products and advertising (2014, 7).

In an interview on Jumbo, he adds to this list, as it were, "the rise of popular entertainment, mass entertainment [...], of celebrity itself" (in Hacker 2014, 13:54–14:08).

Of course, there is no direct mention of any of this in the animated *Dumbo*, which is set in 1941. At the time the film was made, The Greatest Show on Earth was just working its way out of the Great Depression; the elephants were still the main attraction, and a fundamental questioning of the disenfranchisement, imprisonment and exploitation of animals in the circus was still a long way off.

Last but not least, *Dumbo* is about the production of celebrity in an ambiguous context. Because his fame rested on physical difference, we shall now focus on Jumbo Junior as a *disabled person*. *Dumbo* was released almost ten years after Tod Browning's controversial film *Freaks* (1932). The latter, though widely perceived as a horror or exploitation film, characterised disabled people in a more humane way than usual (cf. Williams 2017, 39–47; Church 2011, 7, 11–12, 14). At the same time as the Nazis were carrying out Aktion T4 (1940–1941, cf. Klee 2010), the systematic mass murder of people with physical, mental and psychological disabilities, for which they laid the groundwork with unprecedented propaganda, *Dumbo* presents a decidedly different ethos. It depicts the construction of otherness (othering) and the mechanisms of exclusion, and promotes empathy with the little elephant. To the anthropomorphised elephant community (a caricature of human behaviour), Jumbo Junior is "cute," "sweet," "adorable," "a darling"— as long as his big ears are not visible (Sharpsteen 1941, 00:09:36–00:10:12). But when they are unfolded, the reactions are negative and grow in intensity until, as a result, the community refuses to recognise his status as an elephant at all. First the elephant ladies (except for the mother Mrs. Jumbo) are shocked by the sight; then they ask if this is even possible and if there is not a mistake; then the ears are deemed "funny" and someone declares, "who cares about her precious little Jumbo," at which point the baby is given the discriminatory name Dumbo (drawn from dumb), a sobriquet which amuses the elephant ladies very much (ibid., 00:10:13–00:10:57). From the physical difference, mental weakness is inferred; his identity as Jumbo and his dignity are denied and he is subjected to ridicule. For the fact that his mother defended him against mockery and is therefore locked away as a 'mad elephant,' the elephant ladies blame Jumbo Junior himself:

> It's all the fault of that little—F-R-E-A-K. Yes, him with those ears that only a mother could love. [...] Don't forget that we elephants have always walked with

dignity. His disgrace is our own shame. [...] Well, frankly, I wouldn't eat at the same bale of hay with him. [...] Here he comes now. Hmm. Pretend you don't see him. (Ibid., 00:20:32–00:21:20)

This seals his exclusion from the elephant community in the circus. But the humiliation does not stop there. After Jumbo has failed in the big elephant act and has been demoted to a clown for the new act, the elephant group declares that he no longer belongs to their race: "Oh, the shame of it. Let us take the solemn vow. From now on, he is no longer—an elephant" (ibid., 00:33:33–00:33:48).

In contrast, Timothy the mouse defends the little elephant and tries to teach him strength. In this way Timothy turns Jumbo's physical difference into a positive attribute and builds the child up to be a star:

It ain't nobody's fault you got them big ears. [...] I think your ears are beautiful. Sure. As a matter of fact, I think they're very decorative. You know, lots of people with big ears are famous. Ho-ho, boy. All we gotta do is build an act. Make ya a star. A headliner! Dumbo the Great! (Ibid., 00:23:35–00:24:06)

And later he sees it clearly in front of him, including a coping strategy for the little elephant that turns the *disabled* into an *enabled* person: "Your ears. Just look at 'em, Dumbo. Why, they're perfect wings. The very things that held ya down are gonna carry ya up and up and up! I can see it all now. Dumbo, the Ninth Wonder of the Universe! The world's only flyin' elephant!" (Ibid., 00:52:10–01:01:16).

What is presented here is the cultural construction of a 'freak' as it has occurred many times in the contemporary reality of human society (not only in the National Socialist context) and as it has manifested in the entertainment industry from around 1840 to 1940 as the so-called freak show or side show (cf. in the following Bogdan 1990, 1–116; Adams 2001; Williams 2017, 17–33; Goodall 2020, 18–30). Staring at people with physical abnormalities in public was for a long time not only socially acceptable, but was a popular family entertainment, especially among the middle class, a practice that thrived on curiosity and wonder as well as on fright, fear, disgust and contempt of others. For P.T. Barnum, the real-life Jumbo was not the only such vehicle for his success: Barnum had previously based his popularity primarily on the commercial enterprise of exhibiting, on a large scale, people who were either considered curiosities or whom he had made into such by fraudulent means. Many of them had been forced into this kind of existence as objects of mass entertainment from childhood onwards, and their working conditions were harsh. On the other hand, this context was probably their sole means for obtaining a regular income; some performers achieved fame and became sought-after stars. In their heyday, originally initiated by Barnum, freak shows were part of museums, menageries and vaudeville, but above all it was an essential part of circus entertainment, especially at The Barnum & Bailey Greatest Show on Earth (cf. Fig. 2) and its successors.

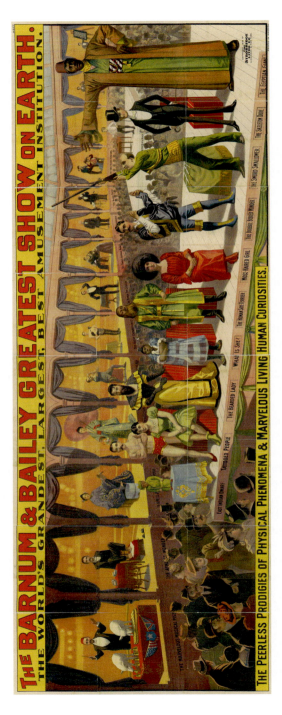

Fig. 2 The Peerless Prodigies of Physical Phenomena & Marvelous Living Human Curiosities. Poster 1899. The Strobridge Lithographing Company. (© Library of Congress, CC-BY-SA-4.0, https://hdl.loc.gov/loc.pnp/ppmsca.55200. Accessed: 12. July 2021)

Happy Pictures? 15

In *Dumbo*, too, the audience is invited to attend a show described in similar terms, and this show too includes an exhibition of 'freaks':

> Step right up and get your tickets. Hurry, hurry now. Hurry to the big sideshow. That's why you go under the big top. Fifteen big attractions that you can't see anywhere else in the world! The greatest collection in the entire world. The greatest congress of freaks[6] ever assembled (Sharpsteen 1941, 00:17:45–00:18:01).

When the viewers see Jumbo Junior, they react with an attitude that indicates their sense of entitlement to such amusement: "Ain't that the funniest thing you ever saw? Look at his ears. […] You can't hide him from us. […] Come on! We wanna see him! We wanna laugh. Sure, that's what we came for" (ibid., 00:18:01–00:18:32).

With the decline of the traditional circus as entertainment from the 1920s onwards—due to competition from cinemas, amusement parks and radio—and increasingly from the early 1940s onwards, such freak shows in North America experienced a decline, and by 1950 they had all but disappeared. The reasons for this were also medical progress and more widespread knowledge about physical deformities and their pathologisation, so that what had been an attitude of amazement at the anomalies on display in the freak shows came to be replaced by a sense of pity for the sick. It was felt that these people should no longer be directly exposed to the public gaze, and instead they became objects of care (cf. Church 2011, 3–5). Media-mediated attractions were cheaper and more accessible, and so the media took over the role of live freak shows, but without abandoning their binary and hierarchical patterns of explanation and presentation. Even ambivalent reactions "of denial *and* recognition, disgust *and* empathy, exclusion *and* identification" (Margrit Shildrik quoted in Church 2011, 4; emphasis in original) ultimately confirmed the cultural superiority of the viewer (cf. Williams 2017, 5, 32). And finally, an ethical debate began about human rights or disability rights, about the cultural perception of difference and the associated view of human bodies as broken, pitiable, monstrous, dangerous or otherwise undesirable (cf. ibid., 6).

'Freak,' according to the cultural studies perspective taken in disability studies, is a normalising concept of performative identity that needs a spectacular narrative and an audience (cf. ibid.): "'Freak' is a frame of mind, a set of practices, a way of thinking about and presenting people" (Bogdan 1990, xi) or, as Williams puts it: "all freaks are freaks of culture" (2017, 9; cf. Waldschmidt 2017). We see this represented in *Dumbo* as well.

At the End: A Beginning? *Dumbo* (2019)

Disney's 'remake' of *Dumbo* (Burton 2019), realised as a live-action film, takes a very different path from the original in many aspects. Above all, it tells a very different story, and tells the familiar story quite differently.

---

[6]Congress of freaks was a term used, for example, by Ringling Brothers with Barnum & Bailey Combined Circus, cf. https://static.wixstatic.com/media/a27d24_61b753ea7a8742b49c1c4763a-da4e4a8~mv2.jpg. Accessed: 8. June 2021.

The action is set in 1919. The First World War and the Spanish flu are still present, and the small Medici Bros. Circus has obviously seen better days. The few circus wagons travelling overland by train are in a pitiful state; the advertising for the attractions and their stars is faded or already peeling off. Animals are few and far between. There are no talking animals in the film—little Jumbo is only weakly anthropomorphised—and so the focus is really on the human beings. In particular, the half-orphans Milly and Joe, the autonomous and creative acting children of the one-armed war veteran Holt take centre stage and drive the plot. Baby Jumbo, the only 'real freak' among the 'fake freaks'[7] in the Medici Circus freak show (as the ringmaster declares, with little pleasure, at the sight of the little elephant, cf. Burton 2019, 00:14:05–00:14:11), is seen as inferior because of his large ears and is separated from his protective mother, just like in the first film, but in this film the circus employees—outsiders like him—feel compassion for him and are on his side.

Only eighteen minutes into the film Milly, Joe and the film audience already know that Jumbo can fly, and after thirty-eight minutes the staff and circus audience have also already witnessed the phenomenon; from this point on the original storyline proceeds to unfold along a whole new arc for the remainder of the film's one-hundred-and-twelve minute running time. The capitalistically unscrupulous entertainment magnate Vandervere, owner of the gigantic Dreamland in New York City, arrives on the scene. In order to incorporate the new star of the Medici Circus—the flying baby elephant Jumbo—into his superlative amusement park and make him the main attraction (including Disney-like merchandising tie-in products), he gets the opportunistic ringmaster Max Medici to merge with his company under false pretences. Vandervere plans to betray him by dismissing the circus staff and having Jumbo's mother killed. At the instigation of the children, Milly and Joe, and with the help of the little elephant, victory is finally achieved over Vandervere, whose Dreamland perishes in an infernal conflagration. Mother Jumbo, on the other hand, can be freed, goes with her son on board a ship to India, and arrives in a paradise-like elephant habitat, while Medici once again roams the country with his small travelling circus—now (almost) without animals: "Welcome to the Medici Family Circus! Where we believe no wild animals shall be held in captivity" (Burton 2019, 01:35:49–01:35:57). Meanwhile, Milly, who has always made it clear that she does not want to exhibit herself, demonstrates the flying elephant as an animated film on a praxinoscope—a self-referential element in the film—in the World of Wonders attraction.

The task of transforming the animated film, which in many respects had become outdated, into a live-action film for an all-ages mass audience of the twenty-first century was not an easy one. Director Tim Burton and screenwriter Ehren Kruger found and implemented solutions by drawing from tropes already well-established in popular culture. Hence the plot of this would-be blockbuster features, once again, not only the pathos of destruction and a heroic, action-packed final battle against evil (here the capitalist-organised entertainment industry), but it also

---

[7] On the notion of 'born freak' versus 'made freak' cf. Williams 2017, 137–138.

incorporates the trope of rescuing children as well as a love story. At the same time, the family theme, which can hardly be avoided at Disney, is reinforced by setting up human beings as foils for the elephants. The mechanisms of the production of otherness and its discrimination, which were prominently shown in the original version of 1941, are weakened here and replaced by the presentation of inclusion in an empathetic multicultural circus community. This alteration must be seen as a reduction in thematic complexity, especially in view of the extra-filmic, racially-charged social present.

By omitting the scenes with the 'roustabouts' and the crows, which had been criticised as racist, the film maintains a political correctness that serves contemporary concerns, as it also does when it refrains from depicting the circus as a place that makes a practice of exhibiting people with congenital deformities (even though 'freak shows' still existed in 1919). In fact the film remains politically correct to the end, for it concludes by actively demonstrating the rejection of keeping wild animals in the circus. In reality, it was only in the 1970s, when a debate about the circus arose, that people started to demand an end to the captivity, exposure and dressage of wild animals; this reduction has been expanding since the 1990s and has been partially implemented.[8] The animal rights organisation PETA (People for the Ethical Treatment of Animals) had already intervened in the run-up to the production of the new *Dumbo* film. Ever since 2014, their website has stated:

> The iconic movie *Dumbo*, released in 1941, was ahead of its time in showcasing how baby elephants in circuses are torn away from their mothers, beaten into submission, and sentenced to a life in chains and boxcars when they aren't being forced to perform dangerous tricks. Fast-forward to Disney's upcoming live-action version, and PETA is asking producers to tweak the endearing film's ending to allow the baby elephant to retire from entertainment altogether. [...] In Disney's original film, Dumbo jumps from the "frying pan" of the circus to the "fire" of the movie industry. Elephants forced to perform in films and television suffer, just as elephants in circuses do. (O'Connor 2014/2017)

After Ringling Bros. and Barnum & Bailey Circus announced in 2015 that they were abandoning their iconic elephant act in The Greatest Show on Earth,[9] PETA reiterated its position in an open letter to Tim Burton: "We're hopeful that in your adaptation of *Dumbo,* the young elephant and his mother can have a truly happy ending by living out their lives at a sanctuary instead of continuing to be imprisoned and abused in the entertainment industry," wrote PETA senior vice president Lisa Lange, also referring to the abuse of animals by the film industry (quoted

---

[8] Cf. Brando 2015, 432–436; Kompatscher [et al.] 2017, 91–94; https://www.stopcircussuffering.com/circus-bans/. Accessed: 10. June 2021.

[9] After legal disputes and demands from various animal rights organisations, Ringling Bros. and Barnum & Bailey Circus initially stopped circus work with the elephants only in 2016 (cf. Huval 2011; Milman 2016; Zalkind 2016); Donald Trump tweeted: "@RinglingBros is retiring their elephants–the circus will never be the same.—Donald J. Trump (@realDonaldTrump)" (quoted by Milman 2016). In 2017 Ringling Bros. gave the final performances of The Greatest Show on Earth (cf. Reuters 2017). In the same year its creator P.T. Barnum was honoured with the completely uncritical biopic-musical *The Greatest Showman* (Gracey 2017).

by Vlessing 2015). In Burton's mix of live-action film and CGI, there are indeed hardly any living animals; at any rate there are no elephants. But Burton would not be Burton if he did not also invite a subversive reading here and there, which gives his film greater complexity.

It is worth noting, then, that the CGI elephant sanctuary in India seems like a distant utopia, and the animal-free Medici Family Circus seems less than viable, especially since the film performance towards the end of *Dumbo* clearly points to the media future of entertainment that was already foreseeable in the late 1910s. Medici's merger with the big businessman Vandervere is treated as an unwelcome alternative to remaining an independently-owned and operated small circus enterprise. Here it is worth taking a closer look at the transfer of the setting to 1919. The alteration is not accidental, as evident from the indirect references to P.T. Barnum in the 1941 film. Burton's visual style tells us that in 1919 the era of the small travelling circus was already over: this can be seen in the patina that covers not only the circus wagons themselves, but which overlays the imagery as a whole, which together create an artificially generated aura of the past. In the extra-filmic reality, the merger of Barnum & Bailey's Greatest Show on Earth with the Ringling Bros. World's Greatest Shows took place in 1919. However, since a fictional film like this is not concerned with historical accuracy, this merger is linked to another development relevant to twentieth-century mass entertainment: the perpetuation of the circus in a stationary, partially industrialised and electrified context, in gigantic amusement parks such as Steeplechase Park, Luna Park and Dreamland on Coney Island, New York. Coney Island, which plays a central role in Burton's film, had already fallen victim to a major fire in 1911, but in *Dumbo* it stands as a metaphor for all the amusement parks of the twentieth century that professionalised and commercialised circus-like entertainment:

> The size of a city block, Dreamland was lit up like Coney Island; New York's famous seafront attraction being the key inspiration for the mix of theme park, circus and world fair, purposefully designed with the exaggeration of a cartoon. [...] The fictional year is 1919 and this is the future of entertainment. [...] The intention too was for something grand and old-fashioned, aglow with the sunset radiance of a dream. (Nathan 2019, 181)

From the 1950s to the present day, Disney's theme parks are also among the great amusement parks, and like their founder, they are repeatedly criticised. Various reviewers of the film (cf. Schweizerhof 2019; Zylka 2019; Rose 2019; Rife 2019) therefore raise, not without justification, the question of whether the figure of the unscrupulous big businessman Vandervere ("the emperor of enchantment [...] the architect of dreams [...] the Columbus of Coney Island," Burton 2019, 00:40:26–00:40:31), whose lucrative Dreamland empire is suspiciously reminiscent of Disneyland, stands not for circus entrepreneurs like Ringling, Bailey or Barnum, but rather for Walt Disney or the Disney exploitation machine itself. When Dumbo and his comrades-in-arms finally rebel against Vandevere and his sinister machinations, the film in a sense celebrates resistance against its own superfather and the mass entertainment he stands for: the idea is that along with the purely capitalist Dreamland, Disneyland is supposed to go down in flames as well.[10] Katie Rife formulates this film message most clearly:

> Tim Burton's live-action *Dumbo* bites the corporate hand that feeds it. [...] Basically, the movie offers a metaphor for the evils of corporate mergers, with villainous circus mogul V.A. Vandevere (Michael Keaton) standing in for Disney itself. [...] Of course, it's almost certainly a coincidence that *Dumbo* is coming out one week after the Disney/Fox merger was finalized. But what else are we to think of when [...] [t]he P.T. Barnum-esque Vandevere likes to buy up other operations, then pair off their star attractions with his own [...]. The metaphor tracks, though it's anyone's guess how it survived its trip down the corporate line. (Rife 2019)

To answer this question, some critics accuse Burton of conformism: He had to make concessions to the Disney corporation in order to be allowed to send out his subversive message (cf. Zylka 2019). Thus of all his films, *Dumbo* least of all bears his signature (cf. Krekeler 2019). Rife finally draws the bitter conclusion

> of an auteur long since absorbed into the Hollywood system: [...] And yes, these are all symptoms of the same relentless conformist drumbeat the film is critiquing in its script. But what's more Disney than Disney controlling the ways in which a filmmaker can critique Disney?

While filmmaker Burton—under Disney's umbrella—relies on the alienation effect of historicisation for his reckoning with the capitalist-oriented excesses of the entertainment industry, which ends in a flaming inferno, and works with innuendo and fabric softener in relation to the abuses of the past ('freak shows' and animal cruelty), the artist Banksy, in 2015, took the more direct—albeit pedagogical and thus hierarchically structured—path of Critical Art, with his post-apocalyptic-looking, politically engaged theme park Dismaland Bemusement Park in order to, "uncover the ugly underbelly of modernity" (Moser 2017, 1027; cf. Koutras 2018; Pimentel Biscaia/Marques 2020).

In fact, the early amusement parks at Coney Island confronted their visitors with controversial topics (like the Boer War, the Galveston Flood, the Fall of Pompeii, the gates of hell), whereas theme parks like Disneyland that emerged from the 1950s onwards avoided anything on the glittering surface that might offend or alienate the general public (cf. Freitag 2017, 925–926). Burton's interpretation of *Dumbo* follows this line, even if Dreamland bursts into flames spectacularly. At the end of the story—and here perhaps lies what is actually subversive about this 'remake'—only unrealistic utopias remain.

---

[10] An interpretation based on the biography of the former Disney employee Burton is dispensed with here, cf. on this Rose 2019.

References

Primary Sources

Books

[Pearl, Helen/Harold Pearl] (1939): *Dumbo, the Flying Elephant*. Syracuse NY.: Roll-A-Book Publishers, Inc. [missing]. Cutout: https://www.cnyhistory.org/wp-content/uploads/2014/10/dumbo-roll-a-book-1939.jpg. Accessed: 29. March 2021

Walt Disney Productions (1941): *Walt Disney's Dumbo. The Story of the Little Elephant with the Big Ears. Suggested by the Story, "Dumbo, the Flying Elephant," by Helen Aberson and Harold Pearl*. New York: Winkler & Ramen. [2010 edition online: http://cowancollectionanimation.blogspot.com/2010/04/. Accessed: 29. March 2021]

Walt Disney Productions (1947): *Walt Disney's Dumbo*. Denver: Western Publishing

Films

Browning, Tod, dir. (1932): *Freaks*. MGM

Burton, Tim, dir. (2019): *Dumbo*. Walt Disney Studios Home Entertainment 2019. DVD

Chaplin, Charlie, dir. (1921): *The Kid*. Charles Chaplin Productions

de Mille, Cecil B., dir. (1952): *The Greatest Show on Earth*. Paramount Pictures

Gracey, Michael, dir. (2017): *The Greatest Showman*. 20th Century Fox

Sharpsteen, Ben, dir. (1941): *Dumbo*. Disney Special Collection 2010. DVD

Secondary Sources

Adams, Rachel (2001): Sideshow U.S.A. Freaks and the American Cultural Imagination. Chicago [et al.]

alexandc [Alexander, Christopher] (2015): Walt Minstry: Dumbo's Jim Crow. Music 345: Race, Identity, and Representation in American Music. [Rolvaag Library, Northfield MN.] https://pages.stolaf.edu/americanmusic/2015/04/27/walt-minstry-dumbos-jim-crow/. Accessed: 17. March 2021

Barrier, Michael (2003): *Hollywood Cartoons. American Animation in Its Golden Age*. New York

Barrier, Michael (2007): *The Animated Man. A Life of Walt Disney*. Berkeley

Barrier, Michael (2011): The Mysterious Dumbo Roll-A-Book. http://www.michaelbarrier.com/Essays/DumboRollABook/DumboRollABook.html. Accessed: 11. January 2021

Bogdan, Robert (1990): *Freak Show. Presenting Human Oddities for Amusement and Profit*. Chicago [et al.]

Brando, Sabrina (2015): Zirkus. In: *Lexikon der Mensch-Tier-Beziehungen*, eds. Arianna Ferrari/Klaus Petrus, Bielefeld, 431–436

Case, Dick (2002): The Long Flight of Dumbo. *The Post Standard*, 05.05.2002. [Reposted by Sean Kirst in:] https://www.syracuse.com/kirst/2015/10/the_tale_of_dumbo_from_dick_case_the_little_elephant_took_off_in_syracuse.html. Accessed: 31. January 2021

Case, Richard G. (2014): The Creation of Dumbo and His Syracuse Connection. Onondaga Historical Association. https://www.cnyhistory.org/2014/10/dumbo/. Accessed: 31. January 2021

Charlton, Michael (2020): *Dumbo* and the Circus of Childhood. In: *The Big Top on the Big Screen. Explorations of the Circus in Film*, ed. Teresa Cutler-Broyles, Jefferson NC., 103–113

Church, David (2011): Freakery, Cult Films, and the Problem of Ambivalence. In: *Journal of Film and Video*, Vol. 63, No. 1, 3–17. https://www.jstor.org/stable/https://doi.org/10.5406/jfilmvideo.63.1.0003

Freitag, Florian (2017): Critical Theme Parks: Dismaland, Disney and the Politics of Theming. In: *Continuum: Journal of Media and Cultural Studies*, Vol. 31, No. 6, 923–932. https://doi.org/10.1080/10304312.2017.1310180

Gabler, Neal (2006): *Walt Disney. The Triumph of the American Imagination*. New York

Glassmeyer, Danielle (2013): Fighting the Cold War with *Pinocchio, Bambi* and *Dumbo*. In: *Diversity in Disney Films. Critical Essays on Race, Ethnicity, Gender, Sexuality and Disability*, ed. Johnson Cheu, Jefferson NC., 99–114

Gluck, Keith (2016): Walt and the Goodwill Tour. *The Walt Disney Family Museum*, 09.08.2016. https://www.waltdisney.org/blog/walt-and-goodwill-tour. Accessed: 8. April 2021

Goodall, Jane (2020): Engineers of Curiosity: The Barnum Era. In: *Circus, Science and Technology. Dramatising Innovation*, ed. Anna-Sophie Jürgens, Cham, 15–32. https://doi.org/10.1007/978-3-030-43298-0_2

Gregory, Sarita (2012): Disney's Improvisation. New Orleans' Second Line, Racial Masquerade and the Reproduction of Whiteness in *The Princess and the Frog*. In: *Contemporary Black American Cinema. Race, Gender and Sexuality at the Movies*, ed. Mia Mask, New York [et al.], 175–199

Gunning, Tom (2006): Attractions: How They Came into the World. In: *The Cinema of Attractions Reloaded*, ed. Wanda Strauven, Amsterdam, 31–39

Hacker, Steffan, dir. (2014): Jumbo: Marvel, Myth & Mascot. Tuft Digital Communications. https://now.tufts.edu/multimedia/jumbo-marvel-myth-mascot. Accessed: 26. May 2021

Huval, Rebecca (2011): Ringling Bros. Circus Hit with Largest Fine Ever. *Mother Jones*, 29.11.2011. https://www.motherjones.com/politics/2011/11/ringing-bros-usda-fine-elephant-abuse/. Accessed: 19. March 2021

Klee, Ernst (2010): „Euthanasie" im NS-Staat. Die „Vernichtung lebensunwerten Lebens". Frankfurt/M.

Kompatscher, Gabriela/Reingard Spannring/Karin Schachinger (eds.) (2017): *Human-Animal Studies. Eine Einführung für Studierende und Lehrende*. Münster [et al.]

Koutras, Konstantinos (2018): Democratic Art / Art démocratique. In: *esse arts + opinions*, No. 92, 14–23. http://id.erudit.org/iderudit/87245ac. Accessed: 24. March 2021

Kracauer, Siegfried (2012): *Dumbo* (1941). In: *Siegfried Kracauer's American Writings. Essays on Film and Popular Culture*, eds. Kristy Rawson/Johannes von Moltke, Berkeley CA., 139–140

Krekeler, Elmar (2019): Elefanten können gar nicht fliegen. In: *WELT*, 27.03.2019. https://www.welt.de/kultur/kino/article190887859/Trailer-Kritik-Tim-Burtons-fliegender-Zirkus-Film-Dumbo.html. Accessed: 28. March 2019

Langer, Mark (1990): Regionalism in Disney Animation. Pink Elephants and Dumbo. In: *Film History*, Vol. 4, No. 4, 305–321. https://www.jstor.org/stable/3815059

McClellan, Andrew (2014): JUMBO. Marvel, Myth, and Mascot. Medford MA.

McIlroy, Brian (2019). *The Big Top on Screen: Towards a Genealogy of Circus Cinema*. [Conference paper at the Film Studies Association of Canada annual conference at University of British Columbia on June 5th, n. p.]. https://open.library.ubc.ca/collections/facultyresearch-andpublications/52383/items/1.0388272. Accessed: 24. March 2021

Meeusen, Meghann (2019): Power, Prejudice, Predators, and Pets: Representation in Animated Animal Films. In: *The Palgrave Handbook of Children's Film and Television*, eds. Casie Hermansson/Janet Zepernick, Cham, 345–361. https://doi.org/10.1007/978-3-030-17620-4_19

Milman, Oliver (2016): Ringling Bros and Barnum & Bailey Circus Will Retire All Elephants by May. In: *The Guardian*, 11.01.2016. https://www.theguardian.com/us-news/2016/jan/11/ringling-bros-barnum-and-bailey-circus-elephants-retire-may-2016. Accessed: 19. March 2021

Moser, Keith (2017): Exhuming the "Dismal" Reality Underneath Banal Utopian Signs: Banksy's Recent Parody of the Disneyfication of the Modern World. In: *The Journal of Popular Culture*, Vol. 50, No. 5, 1024–1046

Nathan, Ian (2019): *Tim Burton. The Iconic Filmmaker and his Work*. London

O'Connor, Jennifer (2014/2017): Dumbo: Old Movie, New Twist? *PETA*, 29.07.2014, updated 05.04.2017. https://www.peta.org/blog/dumbo-old-movie-new-twist/. Accessed: 24. February 2021

Pallant, Chris (2011): *Demystifying Disney. A History of Disney Feature Animation*. New York

Perea, Katia (2018): Touching Queerness in Disney Films *Dumbo* and *Lilo & Stitch*. In: *Social Sciences*, Vol. 7, No. 225, 1–11. https://doi.org/10.3390/socsci7110225

Pimentel Biscaia, Maria Sofia/Lénia Marques (2020): Dystopian Dark Tourism: Affective Experiences in Dismaland. In: *Tourism Geographies*, 1–20. https://doi.org/10.1080/14616688.2020.1795710

Platthaus, Andreas (2001): *Die Welt des Walt Disney. Von Mann und Maus*. Berlin

Reuters in New York (2017): 'Greatest show on Earth': Ringling Bros Circus Bows out after 146 Years. In: *The Guardian*, 22.05.2017. https://www.theguardian.com/stage/2017/may/22/ringling-bros-barnum-bailey-circus-final-show-new-york-146-years. Accessed: 19. March 2021

Richards, Ruth (2020): The Circus and Technologies of Animation. In: *Circus, Science and Technology. Dramatising Innovation*, ed. Anna-Sophie Jürgens, Cham, 143–158. https://doi.org/10.1007/978-3-030-43298-0_8

Rife, Katie (2019): Tim Burton's Live-Action *Dumbo* Bites the Corporate Hand that Feeds It. *AV Club. Pop culture obsessives writing for the pop culture obsessed*, 26.03.2019. https://www.avclub.com/tim-burton-s-live-action-dumbo-bites-the-corporate-hand-1833553819. Accessed: 10. June 2021

Rose, Steve: Grounded? How Disney's Dumbo flop could threaten its master plan. In: The Guardian, 27.03.2019. https://www.theguardian.com/film/2019/mar/27/grounded-how-disney-dumbo-flop-could-threaten-its-master-plan-tim-burton. Accessed: 28. March 2019.

Sammond, Nicholas (2005). *Babes in Tomorrowland. Walt Disney and the Making of the American Child, 1930–1960*. Durham

Sammond, Nicholas (2012): *Dumbo*, Disney, and Difference: Walt Disney Productions and Film as Children's Literature. In: *The Oxford Handbook of Children's Literature*, eds. Lynne Vallone/Julia Mickenberg [New York 2011, 147–166], 1–21. https://doi.org/10.1093/oxfordhb/9780195379785.013.0008

Schweizerhof, Barbara (2019): Er fliegt wieder, hach! In: *ZEIT Online*, 27.03.2019. https://www.zeit.de/kultur/film/2019-03/dumbo-neuverfilmung-tim-burton-walt-disney?print. Accessed: 28. March 2019

Sito, Tom (2006): *Drawing the Line. The Untold Story of the American Unions from Bosko to Bart Simpson*. Lexington KY.

Stanton, Rebecca Rose (2021): *The Disneyfication of Animals*. Cham

Thomas, Frank/Ollie Johnston (1995): *The Illusion of Life: Disney Animation*. Disney Editions, New York

Tomkowiak, Ingrid (2017): Capture the Imagination—100 Jahre Disney-Märchenanimationsfilme. In: *Märchen im Medienwechsel. Zur Geschichte und Gegenwart des Märchenfilms*, eds. Ute Dettmar/Claudia Pecher/Ron Schlesinger, Stuttgart, 121–141. https://doi.org/10.1007/978-3-476-04593-5_7

Vlessing, Etan (2015): Live-Action *Dumbo*: PETA Asks Tim Burton to Change Ending. *The Hollywood Reporter*, 11.03.2015. https://www.hollywoodreporter.com/news/general-news/live-action-dumbo-peta-asks-tim-burton-change-ending-780664/. Accessed: 19. March 2021

Wainer, Alex [n. d.]: Reversal of Roles: Subversion and Reaffirmation of Racial Stereotypes in *Dumbo* and *The Jungle Book*. In: *Jim Crow Museum of Racist Memorabilia*. Ferris State University, Big Rapids MI. https://www.ferris.edu/HTMLS/news/jimcrow/links/essays/reversal.htm. Accessed: 17. March 2021

Waldschmidt, Anne (2017): Disability Goes Cultural. The Cultural Model of Disability as an Analytical Tool. In: *Culture—Theory—Disability. Encounters between Disability Studies and Cultural Studies*, eds. Anne Waldschmidt/Hanjo Berressem/Moritz Ingwersen, Bielefeld, 19–29

Watt, Stephen (1997): *The Magic Kingdom. Walt Disney and the American Way of Life.* Boston

Williams, Jessica L. (2017): *Media, Performative Identity, and the New American Freak Show.* Cham

Zalkind, Susan (2016): 'The End of an Era': Ringling Bros Circus Closes Curtain on Elephant Shows. In: *The Guardian*, 02.05.2016. https://www.theguardian.com/stage/2016/may/02/ringling-brothers-elephants-circus-final-show. Accessed: 19. March 2021

Zornado, Joseph (2017): *Disney and the Dialectic of Desire. Fantasy as Social Practice.* Cham

Zylka, Jenni (2019): Sind so große Ohren. In: *SPIEGEL online*, 27.03.2019. http://www.spiegel.de/kultur/kino/dumbo-von-tim-burton-filmkritik-sind-so-grosse-ohren-a-1259719-druck.html. Accessed: 28. March 2019

Animal Bodies, Human Voices, and the Big Entanglement

Disneynature's Documentary Series

Christine Lötscher

Abstract How can stories about animals be told in a way other than by treating them as human protagonists? How can animals be treated as characters with their own agency? These are the questions that have been raised ever since Harriet Ritvo announced the animal turn in 2007, in which she called for a new perspective on the past and present of human/non-human relations. At first sight Disney's animal documentaries, produced and distributed by the Disneynature studio, seem to give us quite the opposite of animal agency, for these films represent animals anthropomorphically, as individuals that live in human-like family structures and go through fable-like conflicts. At the same time video producers, directors and camera operators make a point of saying that Disney is all about commitment to the planet and raising children's awareness of the environment: Disney actually wants to send home the message, 'we're not separate from nature, we're part of it.' This chapter focuses on the ambiguous nature of Disneynature documentaries, which create 'assemblage'-like spaces where on the one hand animals develop their own agency at their own pace, and on the other are treated to classic anthropocentric storytelling. Disney attempts the impossible: to create a world where animals and humans merge on a material and narrative level—as a kind of new, potentially utopian team of species capable of saving the planet.

Their names are Oscar, Mai-Mai, Jomo, Amber or Steve, and they live in very different landscapes and social structures around the world. They are the main characters in the animal documentaries released by Disneynature between 2009 and 2020 and have one thing in common: they are all animal children. Oscar is a chimpanzee, Mai-Mai a panda, Jomo an African elephant, Amber a brown bear from Alaska and Steve an Adélie penguin from Antarctica. But hang on a minute: How does a nature documentary even get to have a main character? The explanation is

---

C. Lötscher (✉)
University of Zurich, Zurich, Switzerland
e-mail: christine.loetscher@uzh.ch

© The Author(s), under exclusive license to Springer-Verlag GmbH, DE, part of Springer Nature 2022
U. Dettmar and I. Tomkowiak (eds.), *On Disney*, Studien zu Kinder- und Jugendliteratur und -medien 9, https://doi.org/10.1007/978-3-662-64625-0_2

quite simple. Disneynature's films are actually hybrids of documentary and fiction. They personalise and anthropomorphise the animals in order to tell stories that human viewers can easily relate to. Disneynature, Disney's animal-documentary studio founded in 2008, thus chooses a common denominator and a familiar narrative for most of its films: family and coming of age. In this respect Disneynature remains true to the values we are familiar with from Disney's animated films. The studio's decision to highlight the animals' everyday lives and the care they receive from their parents has resulted in an innovative approach to storytelling which is a characteristic, even a unique, selling point for the series. A journalist sums it up in a collective review of Disneynature movies:

> Now we start to get into what Disneynature does best: squeezing a narrative out of the most amazing nature photography you've ever seen. This isn't to suggest the filmmakers are manipulating events or getting overly tricky with the editing, but when you start naming the "characters" this represents a red line that some purists won't cross. Well, those purists can take a hike. These stories are riveting (Hoffman 2019).

Before we take a hike, let us first consider the work of cultural animal studies scholar Roland Borgards, who suggests that there are three ways to read stories with animal protagonists: the anthropocentric, the theriocentric and the decentralising reading (Borgards 2017, 52–55). An anthropocentric reading would quickly dismiss Disneynature documentaries as mere allegory, much too keen on seeing animal life through a human lens (ibid., 52). A theriocentric point of view would point out that there is too much human narrative; this distracts from the animals and their reality, and thereby disregards the epistemological problem that always comes with filming animals (cf. Nessel 2012). A decentralised reading would be more productive. As a "third gaze" (Borgards 2017, 63) it would not attempt to read the stories entirely in terms of humans or entirely in terms of animals; rather, it would focus on the moments where there is a constitutive blending of the two realms. The point of a decentralised reading is to find a way to analyse the ways in which the films organise the relationship between animals and humans—indeed between animals, humans and technology, with man/woman "as an actor among actors, a companion among companions" (Borgards 2015, 157).

While other documentaries—especially Richard Attenborough's highly popular *Our Planet* series (UK 2019) produced for Netflix—adopt an explicitly eco-critical perspective on the endangered planet and its beauty as an ecosystem, emphasising at every turn the responsibility that humans possess, Disneynature films seem to tell stories about animal individuals. Little Oscar for example (cf. Fothergill/Linfield 2012), the chimpanzee, suffers the same fate as Bambi, one of the early animated Disney heroes from 1942, as well as that of many other animal children: his mother dies. For the rest of the movie, the poetics of affect rely entirely on Oscar's more and more desperate search for a foster parent. In the end, Freddy, the alpha male of the group, surprisingly adopts Oscar and cares for him like his mother used to. This twist, the narrator explains, is highly improbable within chimpanzee societies. But viewers familiar with Disney's recent films might see the happy ending as part of Disney's queering agenda, which has been widely discussed not only among fans but also in the media ever since the release of *Frozen* in 2013 (cf. for example Nikolas 2014). The queering agenda can be observed in productions like *Maleficent* (2014) and *Maleficent: Mistress of Evil* (2019), where love between two women who choose each other as family is stronger than romantic heterosexual love and blood bonds of any kind (cf. Lötscher 2020, 75).

At this point we might ask whether the films are about animals at all or rather about humans. This paper argues that they are actually about both: they're about all the kinds of relationships and "contact zones" (Haraway 2008, 205) that exist between animals and humans. Donna Haraway locates "material-semiotic nodes or knots in which diverse bodies and meanings co-shape one another," and explains: "For me, figures have always been where the biological and literary or artistic come together with all of the force of lived reality" (ibid., 4). What happens in Disneynature films is similar to what Haraway describes when she talks about researchers and birds: "[T]he specific practices of observation, narration, and the liveliness of the birds were far from independent of each other" (Haraway 2016, 128). And she goes on: "What scientists actually do in the field affects the ways 'animals see their scientists seeing them' and therefore how the animals respond" (ibid.). The same could be said of the relationship between camera teams with their narratives and animals in the field.

Accordingly, in this paper I shall unpack the way these "material-semiotic knots" work in Disneynature films, focusing especially on *Chimpanzee* (Fothergill/Linfield 2012) and *Wings of Life* (Schwartzberg 2011). Again, Oscar provides me with an argument. From the point of view of reception, it seems that the plot must have been intended from the beginning. But that's not the case. Only during research did I learn that actual drama was involved, as well as animal agency. Christian Moran, whose book relies on interviews with stakeholders of *Chimpanzee*, reproduces what Alastair Fothergill, the director of the film, told him:

> [T]he filmmakers almost had to cancel production altogether when the mother of the young chimp they were documenting died. Fothergill went so far as to say that he was ready to call Disney to tell them that they did not have a movie. Fortunately, an adult male chimpanzee took it upon himself to rescue the motherless ape and raise it as best he could, a behavior never before witnessed amongst the species. This bond between the two became the crux of the film (Moran 2017, 130).

The conditions of production, with the difficulties they had in creating footage and then assembling it into a thrilling story, point clearly to Bruno Latour's actor-network theory (cf. Latour 2004). Cameras, animals, the weather etc. all played their part in the storytelling. In the end, it was the plot that had to be adapted to the footage, not the other way around. The process they described can be read as a variety of "staying with the trouble" (Haraway 2016, 4) and the "practice of tentacular thinking" (ibid., 5) in mainstream popular culture. According to Haraway, tentacular thinking is what shapes a multispecies understanding of 'becoming-with' that insinuates the field of human/animal/tool relations (cf. ibid., 128). In the Diseneynature films themselves, such tentacular concepts are fused with a seemingly traditional way of storytelling and are never directly addressed; the audience is free to just have fun with Oscar, Steve and Mai-Mai or to accept the offer to be part of a reflection on the material-semiotic terrain.

In trailers, however, for individual films or the series as a whole and in extensive educational materials found online (cf. Disneynature. Learn and Discover), there is quite an explicit message. "On this planet everything is interconnected. It's beautiful," says Jane Goodall in the trailer welcoming visitors on Disneynature's website, gesturing dreamily as if she were drawing string figures in the air, as a tribute to Donna Haraway. The famous ape scholar's comment is framed by a rapid succession of images that conjure up her own research among chimpanzees as well as scenic views of land- and seascapes vibrating with biodiversity (cf. Disneynature). In a video released to celebrate ten years of Disneynature, cinematographer Sophie Darlington emphasises an aspect of the films perhaps more important for production than reception: "Making these Disneynature films is such a unique experience because you get to spend a huge amount of time with the animals. You see their highs and their lows and share all of that with them" (Celebrating 10 Years of Disneynature 2019, 00:01:05–00:01:15). The edited footage with its powerful storytelling relies on the endless hours that cinematographers have spent with the animals in the field in participant observation.

Thus even though the films are set in remote areas uninhabited by humans, and even though Disneynature's approach to animals seems to be extremely anthropomorphising, an in-depth analysis building on a set of theoretical assumptions from cultural animal studies can shed new light on this approach to non-human and human animals, plants and technology. My hypothesis is that Disney's films are not only hybrids between documentary and fiction but that they can also be read as a popular way of storytelling related to Donna Haraway's concept of cross-species communities.

Analysing Disneynature's animal films as contact-zone stories allows the viewer to discover a complex texture of storytelling, where the familiar Disney plot is just one film element out of many. What makes these films especially interesting from a cultural animal studies perspective is that storytelling and highly sophisticated technology seem to depend on, or at least to be entangled with, animal agency.

The Disneynature Concept

Disneynature, located in Paris, was founded in 2008 as an independent Disney studio and a nature conservation project. It has since released an event film every year on Earth Day, with each release accompanied by a conservation campaign (cf. Molloy 2013, 173–174). Each campaign has a key theme and a related activity. For "Earth" (2009) it was tree-planting, for "Oceans" (2010) coral reef protection, for "African Cats" (2011) protection of migration corridors (cf. ibid., 174). Claire Molloy quotes Disneynature's first press release, which states that the aim of the films is to "contribute to a greater understanding and appreciation of the beauty and fragility of our natural world" (Disneynature 2008, cited in Molloy 2013, 174).

Disneynature takes inspiration from the True-Life Adventure series Walt Disney created in 1949, which consisted of fourteen documentaries produced up to 1960. The studio claims that its projects have the spirit as that of Walt Disney himself, who expressed his ideas on nature in statements like this: "What I have learned from the animal world, and what anyone will learn who studies it, is a renewed sense of kinship with the Earth and all of its inhabitants" (quoted in Moran 2017, 138). Christian Moran, who wrote a rather laudatory history of True-Life Adventures for Theme Park Press, a publisher specialising in non-fiction on Disney addressed to a wide audience, states that the first set of Disney documentaries exercised a strong influence on all nature films produced ever since its very first, *Seal Island* (1949). He even goes as far as to state that all nature films since then "have been a direct descendant of the True Lifes" (Moran 2017, 101). Furthermore, the True Lifes are said to have functioned as a stepping stone into theme park projects such as Disney's Animal Kingdom (cf. ibid.). But most of all, and this seems quite obvious with regard to Disney's animated films as well as their live-action film remakes such as *The Jungle Book* (1967/2016), *Lady and the Tramp* (1955/2019) and *The Lion King* (1994/2019), the True Life films are said to have inspired the makers of feature films at Disney to particularly focus on animals as protagonists:

> Today these programs, which were once shot on 16mm film, are now produced using 4K ultra-high definition digital cinema cameras, allowing us to view our natural world like never before. […] This doesn't only concern the way animals move in animation films and the materiality of their bodies, but extends to the style of storytelling which is very characteristic for Disneynature films today (Ibid., 101–102).

Steve's Romantic Moment and Disneynature's Epistemological Anthropomorphising

But Disneynature is not just about storytelling. Before I explain in more detail what they are really about, let me describe the way the stories are told. The films are made in a way so that they highlight one particular fact: that the stories the narrators tell about 'Oscar' or 'Mai Mai' or 'Steve' are made up; they are a human addition to the footage, and there is something very artificial and funny about the often exaggerated way the storytellers anthropomorphise the animals. Especially when the scenes are supported by music, it is obvious in an almost ironic way that the films are using human aesthetic strategies to make sense of what the animals are doing. Thus the films self-consciously reflect on human projections and even deconstruct them. In *Penguins* (Fothergill/Wilson 2019) narrator Ed Helms comments on teenage-penguin Steve's quest for a partner in a comedic style by attributing imaginary dialogue to the character. When Steve crosses a field full of much larger penguins, Helms says: "Hey, any of you see a half a million penguins about my height? Similar build … No? … Okay …" (ibid., 00:05:48–00:05:58). Steve seems to have some difficulties finding a mate at first. But when he actually meets a female, music swells to put the scene into a romantic perspective. While the first bars of R.E.O. Speedwagon's 1984 hit *Can't fight this feeling*—quite popular in coming-of-age films—are played, Helms explains that Steve finally found Adeline (ibid., 00:17:23–00:17:42). Kevin Cronin starts singing about true love and about bringing the ship into the shore while the two penguins perform their courtship ritual. At the end, the pile-up of heteronormative stereotypes will be topped by a sunset and a brief blackout (ibid., 00:17:44–00:17:59). That, we assume, is when the sex takes place—probably the only animal activity which is never visible in any of the Disneynature films. This scene is too cheesy to be taken seriously, but the question is if all the fun doesn't distract the viewers from the fascinating dance the two penguins perform. Strangely, it does and it doesn't. In any case, it makes you want to watch the scene all over again, this time focusing on the animals, because human romantic cheesiness doesn't help explain what is happening on screen in the least.

There is a similar scene at the beginning of *Chimpanzee*. After a rather contemplative beginning, the mood suddenly changes. A swing tune—Caro Emerald's *That Man* (2010)—accompanies scenes showing the mischief the chimpanzees are up to. Even more than Steve and Adeline's courting dance, it is the equivalent of the musical or dance scenes common in Disney's animated films.

Obviously, in Disneynature films, the entanglement of human genre poetics and animal footage does not make the actual animals disappear behind the human features that the storytelling suggests they stand for. That's what happens when we see animals as symbols in traditional fables and children's books. Susan McHugh calls it the "disappearing animal trick" (McHugh 2009, 24): "Reading animals as metaphors, always as figures of and for the human, is a process that likewise ends with the human alone on the stage" (Ibid.). But Disneynature documentaries don't allow the animal to vanish, because it's always clear that what we see isn't necessarily what we're told. The films constantly prompt the audience to wonder if what the narrator says is what is actually happening among the animals or if it is all just fantasy. Moreover, the narrators' voices are not anonymous at all. They belong to actors like Meryl Streep (*Wings of Life*), Samuel L. Jackson (*African Cats*) or Natalie Portman (*Dolphins*), or to celebrities like Meghan, Duchess of Sussex (*Elephants*), all figures with enough star power to call up their actual selves in the viewer's imagination.

In Disneynature films, the narrators' voiceovers as well as the musical accompaniment are not there to make the animals vanish behind human interpretations of the world, but rather they are there to render the ineluctable entanglement between human aesthetics, popular culture, technology and animals living in their habitats more visible. Watching a Disneynature film, we realise that the only way we can think about animals is with our human minds and through our human knowledge; we acknowledge the omnipresence and agency of non-human animals and deconstruct our human gaze. This is what scholars of cultural animal studies call "epistemological anthropocentrism" (Borgards 2017, 53). Because there is no way to escape the human perspective, the question is not whether anthropomorphism can be avoided, but whether it is reproduced naively or done in a critical or, as in Disneynature films, even in a creative way (cf. ibid.). In the end, it is this approach that allows us to marvel even more at what we see. In playfully exaggerating anthropomorphising strategies, the films avoid othering the animals and instrumentalising them for didactic purposes.

A Double Sense of Wonder: Nature's Beauty and Media Technology

The first and favourite word that Disneynature trailers use to advertise their films is actually "wonder": the video Celebrating 10 Years of Disneynature (2019) starts with dramatic images of clouds, the ocean, mountains and flashing lightning, accompanied by the heading: "Ten years of wonder, majesty, magic," drum rolls and swelling strings (00:00:00–00:00:14). "Disneynature really gives the audience a view into nature that we don't see," says Roy Conli, producer of *Born in China* (2016): "The story of each of these animals touches our heart in a way that Disney can only do" (ibid., 00:00:33–00:00:44). Alastair Fothergill, director and producer of eight Disneynature films, says: "One of the great joys of these movies is when those eyes look out from the massive screen. There is meaning in those eyes, we as human beings connect with them" (Ibid., 00:00:45–00:00:53). The few scientific articles on Disneynature films emphasise the power of the wonder they project as well. Claire Molloy rightly points out that one can find a double sense of wonder in them. She stresses that "the marketing for Disneynature event films also highlights the spectacle and aesthetic value as well as drawing attention to the 'dazzling technology' (Disneynature 2008) used in the production of each film" (Molloy 2013, 174). I do agree with Molloy that this double sense of wonder accounts for the films' success. The viewers are amazed not only by the beauty of the animals and the biospheres they live in, but also by the cinema technology and camera work that allow us, in the first place, to glimpse into the realms of wild animals living in remote spaces. The fact that the documentaries refer to Disney's first series of nature films, True-Life Adventures, even increases the impression that the more elaborate technology is, the more closely we experience how animals live. The making-of films as well as the trailers distributed by Disneynature emphasise "how incredibly difficult it is to get the footage" (Born in China—Trailer, 01:01–01:05) and promise "pure cinematic magic" (ibid., 01:23).

Chimpanzee, filmed in the jungles of the Ivory Coast's Tai National Park (cf. Moran 2017, 129), starts with a self-referential scene that makes us marvel at the beauty and magic of life in the forest and at the same time addresses wonder as a product of media technology and storytelling. We recognise the classic

Disneynature opening, where we are abducted, as it were, and taken to a realm of enchantment—but this signature entrance is made even more wondrous by the implication that this place is perfectly real, a miracle in itself. A panoramic shot gives us a view of the misty forest from above while narrator Tim Allen takes up and riffs on the initial formula of fairy tales: "Once, not long ago, in deepest Africa, a great rain forest, a wild, magical land, barely touched by humankind" (Fothergill/Linfield 2012, 00:00:30–00:00:47). The sentence remains unfinished and the camera zooms in on the trees; the epic horns that accompany the first shots are replaced by delicate xylophone sounds, reminding us of drops of water or light (ibid., 00:00:47–00:01:00). Hidden behind the leaves and illuminated by the sun, the face of a chimpanzee appears, marvelling not at the camera—the ape is not aware of its presence—but at something mysterious we can't see (ibid., 00:01:13–00:01:22). A special installation of cables in the canopy of the rainforest allowed Fothergill and his team to smoothly run cameras through the rainforest, thus producing shots that seem to flow through the trees in the forest (cf. Moran 2017, 131). The editing suggests that the object of wonder is a tiny baby asleep in his mother's arms, but this is what triggers the spectators' sense of wonder, not the chimpanzee's. The few seconds we spend watching them marvelling strike us as a moment captured for the purpose of drawing attention to the power of wonder itself, as an ability both humans and non-humans share. According to Nicola Gess, wonder has been popularly looked upon as an experience especially prominent in children because both wonder and childhood seem to contain moments of 'seeing for the first time.' The chimpanzee and the human viewer of the film both adopt this childlike position, which marks the beginning of the process of acquiring knowledge. The concept of the 'wondering child,' however, is not an anthropological given, but a figure which emerges from the convergence of literary, epistemological and educational discourses beginning in the eighteenth century (cf. Gess 2019, 22–23). By drawing on such tropes as the wondering animal/child/film-viewer, Disneynature does not merely reproduce, but even exposes, the nature/culture entanglement. The process of entering a closed entity, of getting on the inside of something hitherto unseen—in an intrusive and yet at the same time non-invasive manner—is something that the rhetoric of wonder can produce in specific genres (cf. ibid., 147). In the poetics of wondering, writes Gess, feeling wonder is much more than simply enjoying spectacular images, for it is an "epistemic emotion" (ibid., 30). Wonder provokes curiosity, the desire to to find out and know more.

To some degree Molloy is right when she writes that "the aesthetic qualities of Disneynature wildlife films have more in common with those of the blockbuster in the sense that they foreground technology and spectacle" (Molloy 2013, 175). But as Gess's considerations make clear, a filmic experience that features spectacular scenes that inspire wonder does not necessarily mean an absence of complexity. Thus I disagree with Molloy's conclusion that "environmental and conservation messages are subordinated to the spectacle of nature in event movies which are intended to be used in the cross-promotion of other Disney interests and aimed at the family audience" (ibid.). The fact that the Disneynature films do not have an overt environmental message does not necessarily mean that they are "relatively 'message-free'" (ibid.)—quite the contrary, considering the way it draws attention to the presence of the human perspective and the use of media.

Assembling Science Fabulation through Animal Agency

There is one film in the Disneynature series that in particular aims to present the non-human perspective even more radically. Louis Schwartzberg's *Wings of Life* (2011) tells the story of pollination, bees, bats, hummingbirds, butterflies and flowers. With respect to tentacular thinking and the 'becoming with' approach, it is the most interesting documentary produced by Disneynature so far. Not only does Schwartzberg utilise spectacular time-lapse photography (a technique in which he specialises), but he also incorporates an innovative storytelling style, which is swathed in metacinematic reflection on the possibilities that technology and storytelling can offer to the effort of understanding animals and plants in human terms. Like all Disneynature films, *Wings of Life* begins by situating us in a context: the camera reveals a panoramic view of the ecosystem we are about to enter and get to know more closely. This time, it's a tropical rainforest of deep green colours, with a giant waterfall roaring in the background. On the soundtrack, intra- and extradiegetic sound is mixed in a way that suggests we are about to enter an entirely different world. A soft carpet of strings mixes with the sounds of the forest, the rippling water and chirping birds; the gentle voice of storyteller Meryl Streep seems to be part of it as well. Further, it should be stressed, the sense of wonder with which these films begin is always and explicitly committed to epistemological anthropomorphism (cf. Borgards 2017, 53).

The film's motto, "Life depends on little things we take for granted" (Schwartzberg 2011, 00:00:25), raises the expectation that the film will feature mindfulness and a lifestyle connected to sustainability—inevitably, it influences the spectators' approach to the images they will see in the next ninety minutes. But in fact, this film once again turns out to be all about wonder, drama and fun—the three crucial elements of Disneynature's productions. The studio's films systematically transform keystones of the ecocritical agenda into popular metaphors, using cinematic techniques compatible with mainstream cinema. The narrator turns the idea of connectivity into mystery: "I live in forests like this, but then I live almost everywhere" (ibid., 00:01:55–00:02:02), or: "Everything is related to everything—that's the 'great enterprise of life'" (ibid., 00:05:43). The same thing happens when we are given the pleasure of peeping below the surface—what really happens in nature is as exciting as solving a case in a thriller. Drama enters the stage through music, but also when the narrator speaks of beauty as a strategy and seduction as a tool of survival (ibid., 00:05:22). We witness how a bucket orchid cleverly traps a bee with its perfumes in order to spread its pollen. When the bee finally escapes, the orchid says: "I glue two pollen sacks to his back, each filled with tens of thousands of pollen grains. These are the only pollen sacks I will ever produce, so I won't let him go until the glue is dry. This one bee now carries my legacy" (Ibid., 00:09:40–00:10:14).

All in all, the film is what Anna Tsing would call an assemblage—a vibrant, open, ever-changing relation of entities of all kinds (cf. Tsing 2015, 22–23). Moran asserts that the film allows us to see the world from the point of view of non-human beings. He describes this remarkable possibility as the result of technological progress and insight:

> I think it's transformational to be able to witness life growing and dying in front of your eyes. Going through portals of time and space. That is a different, immersive experience than the twenty-four frames per second that is human reality. It's like dreams, it's like movies. Being able to see the world from the point of view of a bee or a butterfly is so much different than seeing it from the point of view of a redwood tree and a flower. It's like basically, every species, every organism has their own frame rate, and being able to look at the world through their metabolic frame rates (2017, 142).

But this is not the point. The film does make us marvel at the entanglement, the beauty and the strangeness of everything that's alive, but it doesn't create the illusion that humans are able to see reality through the eyes (or other sensory organs) of other creatures. It rather creates an assemblage of an ecosystem constructed by human narratives, human knowledge, technology, a concept of time—and all the material and sensual elements we still cannot fathom. There is a gap between the narrator's explanations and what we see and hear. The fact that Meryl Streep's voice should belong to a flower, or every single flower that ever existed on the planet, and, paradoxically, to the very idea of a flower, all at the same time, makes the experience even stranger. The concept of flower that the film unfolds is an assemblage in itself: flowers are pollinators, fruit, living water tanks (Schwartzberg 2011, 00:18:20), traps for insects, partners in most unusual alliances with partners of all kinds. They appear as metaphors and material beings at the same time, and thus *Wings of Life* can be interpreted as a reflection on the flower as a material-semiotic node. Life, we learn, could be something completely different from what we think it is.

References

Primary Sources

Born in China—Trailer. https://nature.disney.com/born-in-china. Accessed: 28. June 2021
Celebrating 10 Years of Disneynature (2019). https://www.youtube.com/watch?v=pTI7Ag-DLVKQ. Accessed: 5. April 2021
Disneynature. https://nature.disney.com. Accessed: 10. April 2021
Disneynature. Learn and Discover. https://nature.disney.com/educators-guides. (Accessed: 5. April 2021)
Fothergill, Alastair/Jeff Wilson, dir. (2019): *Penguins*. Disney
Fothergill, Alastair/Mark Linfield, dir. (2012): *Chimpanzee*. Disney
Schwartzberg, Louis, dir. (2011): *Wings of Life*. Disney

Secondary Sources

Borgards, Roland (2017): Märchentiere. In: *Macht und Ohnmacht. Erfahrungen im Märchen und im Leben*, eds. Harlinda Lox/Sabine Lutkat, Krummwisch, 49–71

Borgards, Roland (2015): Introduction: Cultural and Literary Animal Studies. In: *Journal of Literary Theory*, Vol. 9, No. 2, 155–160

Gess, Nicola (2019): *Staunen. Eine Poetik*. Göttingen

Haraway, Donna (2008): *When Species Meet*. Minneapolis

Haraway, Donna (2016): *Staying with the Trouble. Making Kin in the Cthulhucene*. Durham

Hoffman, Jordan (2019): All 13 Disneynature Movies, Ranked. https://www.thrillist.com/entertainment/nation/best-disneynature-movies. Accessed: 10. April 2021

Latour, Bruno (2004): *Politiques de la nature. Comment faire entrer les sciences en démocratie*. Paris

Lötscher, Christine (2020): Der Feminismus steckt im Ornament. In: *Märchenfilme diesseits und jenseits des Atlantiks*, ed. Ludger Scherer, Berlin, 75–87

McHugh, Susan (2009): Animal Farm's Lessons for Literary (and) Animal Studies. In: *Humanimalia*. A journal of human/animal interface studies, Vol. 1, No. 1, 24–39

Molloy, Claire (2013): Independent nature: Wildlife films between Hollywood and indiewood. In: *American Independent Cinema. Indie, indiewood and beyond*, eds. Geoff King/Claire Molloy/Yannis Tzioumakis, Abingdon-on-Thames, 165–176

Moran, Christian (2017): *True-Life Adventures: A History of Walt Disney's Nature Documentaries*. [s.l.]

Nessel, Sabine (2012): Animal medial. Zur Inszenierung von Tieren in Zoo und Kino. In: *Der Film und das Tier. Klassifizierungen, Cinephilien, Philosophien*, eds. Sabine Nessel/Winfried Pauleit [et al.], Berlin

Nikolas, Akash (2014): "It's not just Frozen. Most Disney Movies Are Pro-Gay". https://www.theatlantic.com/entertainment/archive/2014/04/its-not-just-frozen-disney-has-always-been-subtly-pro-gay/361060/. Accessed: 10. April 2021

Tsing, Anna Lowenhaupt (2015): *The Mushroom at the End of the World. On the Possibility of Life in Capitalist Ruins*. Princeton/Oxford

GENDER AND DIVERSITY

Curtailment in Mermaid Lore

Disney's *The Little Mermaid* (1989)

Lies Wesseling

Abstract This chapter explores the long-lasting Western fascination with the legendary mermaid character, focusing on the Disney animation of Hans Christian Andersen's fairy tale *The Little Mermaid* (1837). The enduring appeal of the mermaid trope derives from the cultural ambivalences it evokes. On the one hand, it is a subversive trope, destabilising foundational Western binaries such as reason vs. nature/ mind vs. body/ reason vs. matter/ rationality vs. animality/ reason vs. emotion/ man vs. woman, etc. On the other hand, the plot structures in which the mermaid has become implicated in Western narratives effectively neutralise the subversive potential of the mermaid trope. I explore how this tension between subversion and repression plays out in Disney's animation of Andersen's tale.

Tails in Tales

This chapter explores the enduring Western fascination with the legendary mermaid character, focusing on the Disney animation of Hans Christian Andersen's fairy tale *The Little Mermaid* (1837).

The mermaid has a very long tail. It reaches back all the way to classical antiquity and beyond. Hybrid beings who can live (and breathe) in water and on land can be traced back to the Babylonian fish god Ea/Oannes, Lord of the Waters, who was worshipped around 5,000–4,000 BC. Ea was represented as a creature half human down to the waist, and half fish from the waist down. He may be regarded as the first merman to appear in the history of culture. Mermaids likewise originate from pre-Judaic religions, such as the Semitic fish-tailed goddess Derceto, and the water nymphs and deities in semi-fish form who figure in the Vedas. Greek mythology also had its fish-tailed deities, such as the tritons and the

---

L. Wesseling (✉)
Maastricht University, Maastricht , Netherlands
e-mail: lies.wesseling@maastrichtuniversity.nl

© The Author(s), under exclusive license to Springer-Verlag GmbH, DE, part of
Springer Nature 2022
U. Dettmar and I. Tomkowiak (eds.), *On Disney*, Studien zu Kinder- und
Jugendliteratur und -medien 9, https://doi.org/10.1007/978-3-662-64625-0_3

sirens. The latter were originally depicted as bird-women, with the head and bust of a woman and the body and claws of a bird. It was Homer who turned them into sea-enchantresses, although he left us to guess what they looked like, precisely. The seductive sirens who lure unsuspecting sailors to a sure death with their irresistible singing voices famously appear in Homer's *Odyssey,* in which Odysseus barely escapes from the usual lethal fate because of his extraordinary cunning. Gradually, the sirens acquired their fish-like features during the Hellenistic period from 300 BC onwards (cf. Benwell/Waugh 1961, 23–51). From that point onwards, the siren or mermaid was here to stay, imagined, in an ever-expanding collection of myths, legends, folk- and fairy tales, novellas, theatre plays, films and TV productions, as a highly eroticised being that wields magical powers over life and death (cf. Donder 1992).

Sure enough, the mermaid also entered the world of children's media through Hans Christian Andersen's fairy tale *The Little Mermaid.* Andersen married the rich cultural genealogy of the mermaid to the fairy-tale plot, which is often about the trials and tribulations of growing up, a process in which the young hero or heroine confronts antagonists and has recourse to helpers, whose services always come at a price. Andersen's tale inspired a great many adaptations in a wide array of media, which continues to this day (cf. Hayward 2017). The most widely distributed of these adaptations is undoubtedly Disney's animated film *The Little Mermaid* (1989).[1]

Nancy Easterlin explains this long-lasting fascination with the part-human, part-animal mermaid as follows:

> Probably based in the self-other distinction and underlying much of human epistemology, cultural organization, and symbolism, binary thinking pervades human life yet functions ironically in dynamic relationship with the emotional ambivalences and cognitive ambiguities it was perhaps intended to resolve. Since the origins of culture 10,000 years ago, humans have more and more "successfully" actualized the division between the human and the natural; but the awareness that this division fragments experience and, if accepted too fully, proves maladaptive because it is ultimately illusory, informs all our negotiations of this particularly problematic binary. Myths and tales of animal transformation are one means of psychologically reconnecting what culture has worked hard to separate (2001, 261).

In short, mermaid tales are rife with the ambivalences and ambiguities they are meant to exorcise. As constant reminders of humankind's watery animal origins, they work both within and against the Cartesian dualisms that have driven the Western domination of the natural world, such as reason vs. nature/mind vs. body/ reason vs. matter/rationality vs. animality/reason vs. emotion/man vs. woman, etc. These binaries function as gendered hierarchies, with the first terms carrying the connotations of superiority and masculinity. The suggestive trope of the mermaid

---

[1] The 1989 movie was definitely not the first time the Disney corporation tried its hand at the adaptation of Andersen's tale. There are earlier versions of varying lengths, and after the immense commercial success of the 1989 film, several prequels and sequels were produced. For a complete overview, cf. Hayward 2017, 21–51.

unsettles the Western dichotomies that pit humans against nature, but the plot structures in which she is implicated generally reinstate them, conjuring them up and away as a kind of homeopathic remedy for the blurring of boundaries between humans and super-humans. Mermaid lore thus manifests both subversive and repressive features, ultimately restoring temporarily destabilised gendered hierarchies. This chapter analyses how this tension between subversion and repression plays out in the Disney animation of Andersen's tale.

Mirror Worlds in Andersen's Fairy Tale

Andersen's mermaid is the youngest of six daughters living together with their widowed father, the sea king, and their grandmother in a world under water that mirrors the human world above but for subtle differences. The water is as blue as a clear blue sky, but it is traversed by fish rather than birds. This subaqueous domain has its kings and castles too, replete with lush gardens, albeit containing scentless flowers. The sun also shines on the world below, but from far, far away.

The youngest daughter differs from her elder sisters in that she is not fully at home in what is supposed to be her element. Her keen awareness of another world above water has developed into an obsession with all things human, which is epitomised by her constant doting on the marble statue of a handsome boy in the midst of her red 'rose' garden. When she is finally allowed to rise up to the surface the moment she turns fifteen, she becomes completely enthralled by the wonders of the human world. Soon enough, she falls desperately in love with a beautiful young prince, who somehow reminds her of the marble statue presiding over her garden. When the mermaid learns from her grandmother that humans have an immortal soul, unlike her own kind, which vanishes into sea foam after a life span of three hundred years, her fascination with humankind acquires a transcendental glow. And all the more so when she is told that if she succeeds in gaining a human marriage partner whose love for her will surpass the love for his parents, she will become likewise endowed with this much-prized immortal soul. Aspiring to immortality, the mermaid braves the terrifying abode of the sea witch and is even willing to pay the price of the irreparable loss of her mermaid world, the painful transformation of her beautiful tail into 'two props' called legs and the violent removal of her tongue, which silences her beautiful singing voice. To top it all off, she faces the impending threat of the untimely curtailment of her young life if she fails to ensnare the prince.

Sadly, by the end of the tale the worst is set to come true, but the 'daughters of the air' take pity on her and take her up into their company. The mermaid's second metamorphosis, from a human being into an invisible air spirit, tentatively suggests that her transcendental desire for an immortal soul might be satisfied after all, even though her love interest came to naught. If she performs good deeds for three hundred years, this will eventually be her reward.

In Andersen's tale, the tension between subversion and repression is played out by conjuring female agency up and then away. The ambitious and powerful grandmother, whose influence on her six granddaughters vastly exceeds that of their father; the even more powerful sea witch in her unmistakably phallic abode who assists the youngest daughter's aspiration to rise above her station; the united front of the five sisters who dare to launch a murderous attack on a human prince to save their sister from a sure death: these are all frightening forebodings of what would happen if power passes into the hands of women, revealing how male authorities would be ruthlessly dethroned. However, the impending threat of female agency is warded off through the violent castration of the most ambitious of them all, who becomes upwardly mobile at the cost of typically agential features such as her capacity to move around freely and to express herself.

Andersen tames the dangerously seductive mermaid of myths, legends and folktales by flipping her over as it were. Rather than fatally attracting hapless men, this mermaid is lured to her near doom by a human prince. Instead of causing death by drowning, she saves the life of her love object during a shipwreck, bringing him safely to shore and jeopardising her own life in the process by falling in love with him. What is more, Andersen christianises mermaid lore by sacrificing romance to a transcendental plot, in which sexual fulfilment is sublimated by the promise of spiritual fulfilment. Good girls go to heaven indeed, and they remain quite harmless over there. All in all, the little mermaid gets more than she had bargained for, not just in shedding her animal part to become a full human being, but even in moving beyond her human shape towards complete disembodiment. Thus, the plot reinstates the time-honored hierarchies of mind over matter, and spirituality over animality after a brief spell of momentary destabilisation. The close resemblances between the mirror worlds under and above water and the heroine's cross-species mobility suggest that the audience should take the moralising lesson of the mermaid's life story to heart rather than shrug it off as mere fantasy, and aspire towards mortification of the flesh as well, however painful it may be.

Adapting *The Little Mermaid* to Animation

Produced a century-and-a-half after Andersen's literary rendering of mermaid lore, the Disney movie modernises the heroine's aspirations by turning it into teenage rebellion. The little mermaid, now called Ariel, wants to break free from the control of her domineering father by exploring the world above, where he is not in charge. Interestingly, Ariel's obsession with all things human precedes her infatuation with a human male. Her longing for a higher life is visualised very powerfully in the towering grotto/museum's collection of manmade artefacts salvaged from shipwrecks. The impressive structure rises up high to end in a round dome of light that directs the gaze upwards. Ariel wants more than the safe and predictable life of perfect contentment that the world under the sea offers. She cannot rest content with mere relics and gadgets from the human world. Ariel wants to become part of the living, breathing human world that has produced all this splendid artifice. Her first song, *Part of that World*, does not include a single word about love. Rather, Ariel is attracted to the world above through its promise of freedom, the freedom to explore unknown phenomena such as the burning sun, or to gather knowledge about whatever piques your curiosity: "Up where they walk, up where they run/ Up where they stay all day in the sun/ Wanderin' free, wish I could be/ Part of that world" (Clements/Musker 1989, 00:16:51).

Falling in love is for a later episode, when prince Eric enters into the picture, and only then does Ariel concede to curtailment. In keeping with the strictures of the romance plot, her initially transgressive desire to become 'part of that world' is suddenly toned down to the much more conventional romantic longing to become "Part of your World" (ibid., 00:25:55). Seeking the aid of the sea witch Ursula, Ariel now has to meet even stricter terms than her counterpart in Andersen's tale, as Ursula grants her only three days to seduce the prince. Even though various sea creatures do what they can to assist Ariel, she nevertheless fails in her daunting assignment because Ursula intervenes as well, in the shape of the seductive Vanessa, who is in possession of Ariel's mesmerising voice—the faculty that the hapless mermaid had passed over to the sea witch as part of the deal. After an agonising battle between her helpers and antagonists, Ariel finally regains her voice and the prince to boot.

As these things go, the Disney adaptation avails itself of a series of significant shifts, omissions and additions. Just like in Andersen's tale, the tension between subversion and repression also plays out in the film in the frightening spectacle of female agency, but this version tells the tale in a completely different key. The harshly punitive and moralising tone of Andersen's tale gives way in the Disney version to a light-hearted musical comedy. Although the film still has its agonising moments, various characters provide comic relief on a regular basis, most notably the crab Sebastian, as in the slapstick scenes in which he is pursued by a French chef, or in Ursula's drag queen performance of *Poor Unfortunate Souls*.

Secondly, the cast of characters has changed. The band of sisters moved by murderous intent at the end disappears entirely. It is now a motley crew of diverse sea creatures who come to Ariel's rescue, the most notable being Sebastian, who gives a colonial twist to the tale (as does, incidentally, the heroine's new name, which refers back to Shakespeare's *The Tempest*). Sebastian, with his strong Caribbean accent and Caribbean musical idiom, embodies the colonialist caricature of the happy-go-lucky, innocently idle native or noble savage, whose exotic world is presented as a pastoral idyll. The world of natural beauty under the sea has a perennially temperate climate, nobody has to work for a living, there are neither predators nor prey, just perfect harmony amongst all its inhabitants—all this is on display in the scene in which Sebastian performs *Under the Sea* with all the sea creatures playing their parts in perfect unison, like musicians in a pan-maritime orchestra. Strikingly, none of their musical instruments have been crafted. Instead, the musicians make do with whatever the sea has to offer them. This creates a stark contrast between the worlds above and under water. As Sebastian puts it in *Under the Sea*: "Up on the shore they work all day/ Under the sun they slave away/ While we devotin'/ Full time to floatin'/ Under the sea" (ibid., 00:29:51). Humans transform the raw into the cooked and natural resources into artefacts, while the indigenous nations populating the sea just take it as it comes. The question of how they find nourishment is not addressed at all. In the animated adaptation, land and sea are not only contrasting, but even antagonistic worlds, for humans prey on Sebastian and his friends as seafood: "Under the Sea/ Nobody beat us/ Fry us and eat us/ In Fricassee" (ibid., 00:30:24). In other words, if the sea creatures fail to avoid contact with the upper world, they will be enslaved and exploited as well, faring no better, but rather even worse, than the human labourers who slave away under the scorching sun. These contrasting worlds resonate with the projections and exploitations of colonial history. This is another significant departure from Andersen's tale, where the two worlds largely mirror each other.

Furthermore, even if some characters carry over from one version to another, they play different roles. Ariel's father is a much more active and dominant presence in the Disney version, actively occupying himself with the upbringing of his daughters and eventually even sacrificing himself for the rescue of his rebellious daughter, as opposed to Andersen's version, where he does nothing at all. Ursula also meddles much more actively in Ariel's life by sabotaging her love affair with Eric in order to keep her from meeting the terms Ursula herself has imposed on the unfortunate mermaid. This blows the sea witch's evil nature all out of proportion. Ursula's counterpart in Andersen's tale is terrifying for sure, but not unfair: she sticks to the terms of her contract and acts as a helper of sorts, albeit a demanding one, but that is nothing new in fairy tales. What is more, there are even subtle points of resemblance between the mermaid and the sea witch, who is, after all, her aunt. The bleached, white bones of drowned men with which Ursula has built her witch's den echo the deadly white marble statue in the mermaid's garden of Andersen's tale. The two characters both cultivate aspirations beyond their station: Ariel wants to become like humans while Ursula wants to exercise power to counter male rule. In the Disney version, however, the two are worlds apart, and the upshot is that Ursula has to be destroyed utterly before full paternal authority can be restored to both prince and king.

The most significant shift of all, however, is the early abandonment of the transcendental plot that dictates the ending of Andersen's tale. In the Disney version, this plot line is superseded by the romance plot as soon as Ariel casts her eye on Eric, an experience which leads Ariel to exchange her masculine ambition quite effortlessly for the conventional feminine position of wife and mother-to-be. Complete fulfilment is attainable in the human world, the animated film suggests. Indeed, the Disney version is full of sexual innuendo. The artwork for the cover of the movie's video cassette edition shows a picture of Eric's castle with a steeple that is quite similar to a penis; Sebastian's song *Under the Sea* claims "Darling it's better/ down where it's wetter" (ibid., 00:29:40) and "That's why it's hotter/ Under the water" (ibid., 00:32:08); Ariel enters Ursula's domain through a *vagina dentata*, while the polyps and snakes surrounding Ursula are as phallic as in Andersen's tale. Ursula's appearance is pretty phallic as well, given her visualisation as part woman, part octopus, with gigantic tentacles flopping about at her nether end as if she were an inverted murderous Medusa. She presents herself as the helper of the 'poor unfortunate souls' who are incapable of fulfilling their desires on their own; they depend on Ursula's dark aphrodisiacs, which tend to degrade them to an even more unfortunate state. Overall, the Disney version gives its audience to understand that females easily let go of their lofty aspirations as soon as they find the right man, and that seems to be all they need for complete happiness and fulfilment. There is no need here for the sublimation of desire into a higher form of spiritual fulfilment. This world will do.

Is Disney's adaptation of mermaid lore a typical example of 'Disneyfication' then, (among other things) defined as the simplification of moral ambiguities into clear-cut good-evil oppositions, and their unwarranted resolution in saccharine happy endings that reinforce dominant patriarchal and capitalist value systems (cf. Sayers 1965; Schickel 1985)? Many a critic has answered this question in the affirmative (cf. McReynolds 1974; Zipes 1979, 93–128; Hastings 1993; Bendix 1993; Murphy 1995). They argue that the rather complex multi-layered story of Andersen's tale has been simplified into a one-dimensional romance plot, with the Disney adaptation largely sanitising Anderson's tale of its disturbing elements, most notably the traumatic, violent 'castration' of the mermaid. In the Disney version, the transformation of Ariel's tail into a pair of legs is fairly painless, while the silencing of her voice does not involve cutting her tongue. Rather, it is spirited away and preserved quite safely in a shell adorning Ursula's neck, from where it is eventually returned to its rightful owner unscathed. According to Hastings, Disney animation in general and this film in particular depict a Manichean universe, with clear oppositions between good guys and bad guys, the latter usually being females:

> The film encourages a pervasive world view that sees malignant evil, not human fallibility, as the chief source of conflict; a similar world view can be seen in former President Reagan's characterization of the (pre-glasnost) Soviet Union as the "Evil Empire" or President Bush's more recent transformation of the Gulf War from a geopolitical conflict into a crusade against the person of Saddam Hussein. In a Manichean world, one party to any conflict must always be "bad", the other "good"; … In this Disneyfied world, there is no reason for diplomacy; the proper way to deal with an Ursula is to destroy her, not to negotiate (1993, 90).

In a similar vein, Patrick Murphy argues that the prospect of a trans-species union is 'Disneyfied' through the total assimilation of Ariel to the human world and by her concomitant loss of agency, which eradicate all traces of her exotic origins. Assimilation to patriarchal human society requires the severing of all ties to the natural world, as represented by Triton's realm, and to the indigenous nations that populate it. In Murphy's vocabulary, Ariel is subjected to both "denaturalization" and "deculturation" (Murphy 1995, 133). And Regina Bendix argues that shifts in the *dramatis personae* and plot in the Disney adaptation of Andersen's tale solidify stereotypical notions of gender roles, sexuality, family relationships and ethnicity that underpin Disney's corporate worldview (cf. Bendix 1993, 281).

However, there is also the occasional voice of dissent, most notably that of David Whitley, whose monograph *The Idea of Nature in Disney Animation* (2012) makes a sustained effort to forestall an all too hasty and facile identification of

Disney animation with 'Disneyfication,' through detailed analyses of the representations of nature in Disney's animated films. Whitley argues that the movies respond quite sensitively to changing conceptualisations of and attitudes towards nature in society at large, suggesting that they are anything but escapist or simplistic wish-fulfilment fantasies. Rather, he demonstrates quite convincingly that Disney films resonate with the acute environmental awareness of its cultural context. Whitley's interpretation of *The Little Mermaid* is included in a chapter called "Healing the Rift," (ibid., 39–61) a title that already gives the gist of his argument away. First of all, Whitley defends the movie against feminist critiques by dwelling on the differences between Ariel and the heroines in previous Disney fairy tale adaptations, such as Snow White, Cinderella and Sleeping Beauty. Whereas the latter are firmly anchored in domestic spaces, where they subordinate natural forces to the performance of homemaking, the somewhat rootless Ariel is intent on leaving her domestic environment behind to cross the divide between her own natural world and human culture. He observes that the feisty and ambitious Ariel was designed so as to make this heroine palatable to a new generation of mothers who had taken second wave feminism to heart and were not going to buy into yet another Snow White or Cinderella.

Taking issue with Murphy, Whitley argues that critiques of 'Disneyfication' pass over the comic elements in the movie entirely. In a Manichean universe, there is no place for the subversive rhetorical effects of slapstick humour, drag queen burlesque and so on. As Whitley sees it, the repeated reminders in the movie that Ariel's companions are liable to end up on a plate in the world above, and that human beings are the predators par excellence, imply a critical view of Western consumerism. The final scene in which poor Sebastian is harassed once again by the eager French chef while the movie is reaching its romantic closure provides a sobering counterpoint to the sugary resolution of the romance plot, according to Whitley. This indicates that the ending is not as one-dimensional as critics of 'Disneyfication' have made it out to be. It stands as a critical reminder of human exploitation of the natural world: "The human world is envisaged as embracing the natural not only in an act of love but through its ongoing need for consumption. The conventional harmony of comedic closure is thus counterpointed by an uneasy sense of issues unresolved" (ibid., 44). This ending compels us to face up to our role as predators, which is generally obscured by Western consumerism. Thus, Whitley attributes an element of critical self-reflection to the movie: "In terms of sentiment, the romantic plot certainly dominates, but the comedic elements inflect the film in more complex ways with the texture of conflicting stories we currently tell ourselves about our place in nature" (ibid.). He regards this lingering sense of unease as in keeping with eighties environmental thinking, which had to swallow the rather bleak lessons of the Club of Rome. In contrast to the postwar period, when European and North American societies were mostly concerned with expanding their food production to feed their growing populations through agro-technological innovations such as synthetic manure and pesticides, the seventies and eighties were forced to face up to the fact that nature's resources are far from infinite, and that consumerist societies continue to exploit them in an industrial manner at their own peril. As Whitley sees it, then, this movie does not deserve to be bashed by critical feminist or eco-critical perspectives.

While Whitley's voice is a welcome and novel addition to the chorus of Disney critics, and has helped to pave the way for successor projects such as animal studies and posthumanist inquiries into the shifting borders between nature and culture in children's media, I nevertheless beg to disagree. Whitley's sophisticated interpretations tend to focus on setting rather than plot, and they also pass over the narrative genres informing plot, with the result that he neglects the fact that Ariel's masculine ambitions and upwardly mobile aspirations are nothing new in stories about female maturation, even though she may be a refreshing departure from the heroines of fifties' Disney fairy-tale adaptations. Tomboy stories have allowed their heroines to spread their wings or flap their tails since their inception in the nineteenth century, but only for a while. As Shawna McDermott argues, the storyline of Disney's mermaid takes its cue from the literary tomboy tradition, i.e. *Bildungsromane* about and for adolescent girls. Their leading characters are transformed from unruly gender benders into proper women who are finally prepared to occupy their rightful place in society. While tomboy stories always start out with subversive (and often humorous) episodes that mark the period in which the heroine has not yet learned to play her part, patriarchal order is reinstated all the more forcefully at the end:

> The disappointing truth of tomboy texts is that they're an elegant trap: they teach readers first how to dream of more and then how to succumb to the reality that those dreams won't come true for them. These texts teach that womanhood, the end of the road after girlhood, is about learning to manage and live with constant disappointment, all while keeping alive the faint flame of hope that one's Prince Eric or Friedrich Bhaer will come along with feminine completion and happiness in tow. The truth, in short, is that in taming their heroines, tomboy tales seek to tame their readers as well (McDermott 2019, 150).

McDermott's argument from literary history may be further reinforced by insights from eco-feminist theory, which has illuminated how the oppression of non-normative 'others' such as women, queers and persons of color, is rooted in the Western masculinist project of 'mastering nature,' more specifically, in the one-dimensional conceptualisations of nature that have driven this project. The instrumentalisation and exploitation of nature is premised on a sharp contrast between the human world and the natural world, the latter either being degraded into mere inanimate matter devoid of awareness, volition or agency, or idealised, in a reactionary escapist fantasy, as the realm of pure pastoral innocence and harmony, where food is freely available without any need for labour (cf. Plumwood 1993). Given the fact that the category of the 'human' has proved to be an extremely tenuous one, to which only a select category of human beings has been granted full access, non-normative others such as Sebastian and Ariel will have no other option but to undergo exploitation or full assimilation, as long as these fundamental dualisms remain in place.

Queering the Mermaid

Do we have to conclude then that mermaid ta(i)les will always be curtailed sooner or later? Can mermaid lore ever depart from the familiar narrative pattern of momentary subversion followed, ultimately, by repression? To use Ursula's words in *Poor Unfortunate Souls*: "Yes indeed!" (Clements/Musker 1989, 00:41:00), with the queer witch herself pointing the way. Since 1989, much has been happening in mermaidology, mainly because of the increasing visibility of transgender persons in public space and cultural imaginaries, including transgender children. Significantly, a British organisation assisting gender-diverse children has called itself Mermaids (www.mermaidsuk.org). Sally Campbell Galman's arts-based ethnographic study of transgender and gender-diverse children between 3 and 10 years old has revealed that these children frequently portray themselves as mermaids (cf. Galman 2018), a phenomenon also observed by Nat Hurley, who claims that transgender children "are obsessed with mermaids" (Hurley 2014, 258; see also Hayward 2017). These children are mostly familiar with Disney's Ariel, but in all likelihood, they have been enabled to capitalise on the mermaid's queer potential through the well-known example of Jazz Jennings, a media-personality and transgender teen, who frequently portrays herself as an Ariel-style mermaid, for example in her children's book *I am Jazz* (2014). Sally Campbell Galman's research subjects are definitely not alone in this. Quite a few twenty-first century mermaid narratives have appeared in diverse media, such as the picture book *Julián is a Mermaid* (2018) by Jessica Love, the early readers novel *Ik ben een zeemeermin (maar dat is geheim*, or *I'm a Mermaid [but That's a Secret]*) (2018) by Sabine Wisman with illustrations by Annet Schaap, and Annet Schaap's highly acclaimed children's novel for more advanced readers *Lampje* (*Lampie*) (2019), which has been translated into sixteen languages, including English, German, French, Spanish, Italian and Russian, or Maya Kern's webcomic *How to Be a Mermaid* (2012), for all ages. These books discard the heteronormative romance plot completely, including dualistic assumptions about what is natural and what is human. The love interest is either absent altogether here, or radically queered. In the process, they also enable alternative figurations of humans, animals, artefacts and the elements, most notably the sea. Precisely how they do so, however, is a subject for another article.

References

Primary Sources

Andersen, Hans Christian (2010): The Little Mermaid. In: *Fairy Tales by Hans Christian Andersen*, Auckland: Floating Press, 555–586 [1837]

Jennings, Jazz (Auth.) and Jessica Hertel (Ill.) (2014): *I am Jazz*. New York: Dial Books for Young Readers

Kern, Maya (2012), *How to be a Mermaid.* https://www.deviantart.com/mayakern/art/how-to-be-a-mermaid-1-328117812. Accessed: 2. June 2021

Love, Jessica (2018): *Julián is a Mermaid.* Somerville MA.: Candlewick Press

Schaap, Annet (2019): *Lampje.* Amsterdam: Querido

Clements, Ron/Musker, John, dir. (1989): *The Little Mermaid.* Walt Disney Pictures

Wisman, Sabine (Auth.) and Annet Schaap (Ill.) (2018): *Ik ben een zeemeermin (maar dat is geheim).* Amsterdam: Leopold

Secondary Sources

Bendix, Regina (1993): Seashell Bra and Happy End: Disney's Transformations of *The Little Mermaid.* In: *Fabula,* Vol. 34, No. 3/4, 280–290

Benwell, Gwen/Arthur Waugh (1961): *Sea Enchantress. The Tale of the Mermaid and Her Kin.* London

Galman, Sally Campbell (2018): Enchanted Selves: Transgender Children's Persistent Use of Mermaid Imagery in Self-Portraiture. In: *Shima: The International Journal of Research into Island Cultures,* Vol. 12, No. 2, 163–180, http://dx.doi.org/https://doi.org/10.21463/shima.12.2.14

Donder, Vic de (1992): *De lokroep van de zeemeermin.* Antwerpen

Easterlin, Nancy (2001): Hans Christian Andersen's Fish out of Water. In: *Philosophy and Literature,* Vol. 25, 251–277

Hastings, A. Waller (1993): Moral Simplification in Disney's *The Little Mermaid.* In: *The Lion and the Unicorn,* Vol. 17, No. 1, 83–92

Hayward, Philip (2017): *Making a Splash . Mermaids (and Mer-Men) in 20th and 21st Century Audiovisual Media.* Bloomington IN.

Hurley, Nat (2014): The Little Transgender Mermaid: A Shape-Shifting Tale. In: *Seriality and Texts for Young People,* eds. Mavis Reimer, Nyali Ali, Deanna England, Melanie Dennis Unrau, London, 258–280

McDermott, Shawna (2019): The Tomboy Tradition: Taming Adolescent Ambition from 1869 to 2018. In: *Children's Literature Association Quarterly,* Vol. 42, No. 2, 134–155

McReynolds, William (1974): Disney Plays 'The Glad Game.' In: *Journal of Popular Culture,* Vol. 7, 787–796

Murphy, Patrick (1995): 'The Whole Wide World Was Scrubbed Clean': The Androcentric Animation of Denatured Disney. In: *From Mouse to Mermaid. The Politics of Film, Gender, and Culture,* eds. Elizabeth Bell, Linda Haas, Laura Sells, Bloomington IN., 125–137

Plumwood, Val (1993). *Feminism and the Mastery of Nature.* London

Sayers, Frances Clarke (1965): Walt Disney Accused. In: *Horn Book,* Vol. 41, 602–611

Schickel, Richard (1985): *The Disney Version. The Life, Times, Art and Commerce of Walt Disney.* New York

Whitley, David ([2]2012): *The Idea of Nature in Disney Animation. From* Snow White *to* WALL-E. London [[1]2008]

Zipes, Jack (1979): *Breaking the Magic Spell. Radical Theories of Folk and Fairy Tales.* New York

"Be a Man"

Gender and Body in Disney's *Mulan* (1998)

Yvonne Festl

Abstract The animation of (gendered) bodies has long been central to Disney's style, but one specific Disney film puts gender and body at the forefront of its story as well: *Mulan* (1998). A detailed analysis of the film's animated images reveals a multitude of ideas concerning body and gender that are far more complex and challenging than it may at first appear. The body of the titular heroine is the site of constant and effortless transformation—a potentially subversive quality that is only matched by the animalistic body of the villain Shan Yu, with which Mulan's is covertly aligned. Transgressive and 'wild,' Mulan and Shan Yu are a threat to the static power relations upheld by the 'male' characters of the training camp, whose bodies are shown as stable and fixed. While it can be argued that the film's narrative ultimately reinforces traditional gender roles, the film's visual elements provide a unique look at the constructedness of the gendered body.

Disney and the Gendered Body

Beautiful princesses, dashing heroes, cloak-sweeping villains, silly sidekicks and "painfully thin, rule-bound" bureaucrats (Bell 1995, 120)—Disney is famous for its arsenal of recurring character types. Of course, when telling stories through the art of animation, Disney is not only creating characters, but animated bodies that are meant to tell the audience immediately who a character is, what their personality traits are and what role they are meant to play in the narrative. And by creating images of bodies, Disney is also creating images of gender: "The Walt Disney Company's emphasis in animation constantly forces the studio to consciously fashion and control bodies—drawing characters that somehow represent images of 'men' and 'women'" (Griffin 2000, 5). The representation of body and gender in

---

Y. Festl (✉)
Freie Universität Berlin, Berlin, Germany
e-mail: yvonne.festl@googlemail.com

© The Author(s), under exclusive license to Springer-Verlag GmbH, DE, part of Springer Nature 2022
U. Dettmar and I. Tomkowiak (eds.), *On Disney*, Studien zu Kinder- und Jugendliteratur und -medien 9, https://doi.org/10.1007/978-3-662-64625-0_4

Disney's animated feature films has been an ongoing topic of scholarly discussion for some time now. Scholarship examining this subject tend to describe the bodies of the hero and the heroine as presenting heteronormative standards of gender and beauty, while the body of the Disney villain is seen as transgressing conventional notions of gender (cf. Li-Vollmer/LaPointe 2003; Putnam 2013): Disney therefore 'naturalises' certain performances of gender while demonising others. However, as Sean Griffin's analysis in *Tinker Belles and Evil Queens* shows, the enjoyment of Disney films was never limited to an exclusively heteronormative audience: Disney's construction and animation of gendered bodies has always opened up possibilities for queer and camp readings, and thus for queer audiences to enjoy and relate to Disney films (cf. 2000, 71–77).

One specific Disney film that puts gender and body at the forefront of its narrative is *Mulan* (Bancroft/Cook 1998). In this film set in a fictionalised Imperial China, the titular heroine struggles with the gender expectations placed upon her by society and family, feeling that she will never be able to fulfil the role of the 'perfect bride.' When the Huns, led by Shan Yu, invade China, Mulan decides to disguise herself as a man in order to join the army in her father's place. By focusing on gender roles and the expectations and limitations that come with them, *Mulan* also brings to the fore themes that, it can be argued, have always been at the heart of animation: the construction and performativity of gendered bodies. However, these themes are not necessarily dealt with on the narrative level. As is the case with the queer readings Griffin explores in his book, one has to look at the animation itself—that is, at the visual elements of the film and the design of the characters. Sometimes one has to read between the lines and against the grain to find a multitude of different, complex and challenging ideas about gender and body in *Mulan*—ideas that may sometimes contradict the narrative itself.

On a narrative level, according to Gwendolyn Limbach, *Mulan*'s outwardly progressive message of female empowerment does not hold up (cf. 2013, 115): ultimately, Limbach argues, the film establishes and reinforces the idea of gender as a binary, where femininity is perceived as passive and masculinity as active and inherently more valuable (cf. ibid., 119–121). As Limbach notes, boundary-crossings, both literal and figurative, are thematised in *Mulan*: the heroine crosses genders, the Huns cross state borders, men attempt to 'cross over' from being recruits to becoming full-fledged soldiers. These themes could have been used to call into question patriarchal power structures, but, Limbach argues, the film's narrative successfully contains these potentially subversive forces (cf. ibid., 115–116, 125–126). Mulan's 'cross-dressing,' for example, is framed as an inevitable and burdensome necessity (nothing Mulan would 'actually' desire to do) (cf. ibid., 121–122) and—as if to prevent any actual blurring of gender lines—Mulan "is constantly redesignated as female to the audience" (ibid., 123). Limbach's essay is undoubtedly effective in describing the strategies used to contain the disruptions presented by the story's boundary crossings. However, what exactly are these disruptive forces in the first place? What are they made of and what makes them so very threatening?

Undoubtedly *Mulan* presents us with a society where it seems that the path one must follow in order to perform one's gender 'correctly' is very narrow indeed. One of the early scenes shows two little boys playing with swords, while a little girl is playing with her doll. Their play is accompanied by the lyrics: "We all must serve our Emperor who guards us from the Huns, a man by bearing arms, a girl by bearing sons" (Bancroft/Cook 1998, 00:07:22–00:07:32). Obviously, this scene establishes a culture that rigidly defines gender roles from a very young age and demands that they be obeyed and respected; this is, then, the culture that forms the background against which all the characters are placed. Yet while the narrative may be cautious in its critique of gender roles—more often reinforcing than questioning these societal norms—the film's visuals and the animation of its characters' bodies are more ambiguous and complex. By analysing Mulan's power of metamorphosis (never addressed by the narrative), Shan Yu's creature-like physique, and the variety of 'male' bodies in the film (instead of analysing masculinity as something that is only represented monolithically) we can see cracks and tears that open up possibilities for more subversive readings of gender and body than we might at first expect.

Mulan's Body—a Story of Transformation

Mulan's bodily appearance is marked by an interesting fluidity that none of the other characters in the film even come close to possessing. This is manifested in the slight but telling change in character design that occurs as soon as Mulan is masculine-presenting. The actual process of transformation from feminine- to masculine-presenting is told in ten relatively short shots (cf. ibid., 00:18:48–00:19:08). While these are part of a longer sequence in which Mulan decides to leave her home and join the army in her father's place, the main focus of this segment is on the actions Mulan takes in order to change her appearance: cutting her hair and donning her father's armour. Most of the time Mulan's face stays hidden, as detail shots (e.g. of Mulan's hair falling to the ground) and rear-view shots (e.g. as she puts her hair up) dominate the segment. However, two close-ups of Mulan's face do appear—one at the very beginning, one at the very end of the process. These shots serve as a kind of framing device: the first close-up shows Mulan's face as she was introduced in the beginning of the film; the final close-up simply shows a face that, while still recognisable as Mulan's, has subtly changed. When the two shots are compared, small but significant differences emerge in the design of Mulan's face: before the transformation, Mulan's upper eyelid is drawn significantly darker and broader than the rest of her eye, extending beyond the outer edge to suggest thick eyelashes that end in a little curve. Furthermore, a fine line can be seen just above her eye to indicate the eyelid crease. This line, as well as the curvy lash line, are omitted once Mulan is transformed. Additionally, the outline of the upper eyelid is noticeably thinner when Mulan is masculine-presenting. Colour also underscores the change: before her transformation, Mulan's lips are a soft pink, and her cheeks have a rosy tint. After the transformation, her face has an almost uniform skin tone, with her lip colour only a shade darker than the rest of her face. Even the shape of Mulan's face is slightly modified, as her jawline becomes a bit more angular after the transformation.

Interestingly, these changes are introduced with no explicit narrative commentary. Rather, they just appear as soon as the other external signifiers of femininity with which Mulan is marked—long hair, narrow waist and a slightly curved line that indicates breasts—disappear. (In this case, 'disappear' should be construed quite literally, for the suggestion that these physical features could be found 'under the armour' ignores the fact that as Mulan is an animated figure, her body is literally re-created in every frame.) As suddenly as they disappear however, they reappear—but only after Mulan is uncovered as a woman. Before this incident, there are two scenes that show Mulan alone—or rather, only in the presence of Mushu and Cri-Kee, who are in on her secret. But even though none of the other recruits are near her, Mulan's face remains 'masculine' (cf. ibid., 00:34:47–00:36:10, 00:42:05–00:42:36). However, Mulan's face changes back immediately as soon as she is perceived as female by the other characters. As Captain Shang, shocked by the news, enters the hospital tent where Mulan lies wounded, Mulan's face is transformed: back are the more rounded contours of her jawline, the curvy lash line, the soft pink lips and rosy cheeks. This (re-)transformation happens (again) without any diegetic explanation; it just coincides with the way Mulan is perceived by the characters in the story.

Mulan's body, it seems, can change quite effortlessly. This ability is based, of course, on the power of animation. In the world of Disney, the absence or addition of just a few lines or a few brushstrokes has the potential to change a character's perceived gender, to turn a figure perceived as female into one perceived as male and vice versa.[1] It is precisely this freedom to transform, this power of metamorphosis, that Griffin sees as one of animation's "founding conceptions" (2000, 57). In Disney's earliest (pre-1930) cartoons, this capability was used freely and joyfully—bodies would be created that were far from stable and coherent, but rather would change their shape or be taken apart in a cheerfully carnivalesque fashion: "[T]he very early Disney product seems to revel in […] the potentiality of the body in every frame of film. […] The body is not a sacred temple with a sturdy foundation; it is a polymorphous sight of pleasure and excess" (ibid., 6). During the early to mid-1930s, however, the Disney studio began to develop the so-called 'illusion of life' style, which was concerned with introducing a sort of stylised version of 'realism' and 'laws of nature' into animation. Griffin argues that this and other changes in Disney's animation style and in content that developed at the same time effectively controlled and regulated animated bodies in a

---

[1] This potentially subversive quality has not gone unnoticed by fans, who seem to find a certain satisfaction in how easily the perceived gender of a Disney character can be changed. The internet is full of drawings and compilation videos that show Disney characters who have been given a gender swap, in some cases by making only minor changes to their appearance.

way that was congruent with (and ultimately profited from) an emerging social attitude that called for everything deemed immoral to be prohibited (or in the case of films censored) (cf. ibid., 12–23). Bodies that had the power to transform were not completely omitted from Disney's later work but were often legitimised and rationalised in the narrative by being ascribed to the realm of fantasy (cf. ibid., 58, 62).

Mulan's powers of metamorphosis are never explained or rationalised in this way, for she is not portrayed as a magical character.[2] Rather, there seems to be some kinship between the figure of Mulan and the polymorphous bodies of early Disney animation, in that both are able to transform physically simply because they want to, or because the situation requires it of them. When Mulan's new face is revealed in close-up, the image visually harkens back to the shot showing Mulan's 'old' face shortly before her transformation. Both times her father's sword plays an important role in the staging: in the initial shot, the sword is drawn from its scabbard, and Mulan's face is shown as only a reflection on the shiny blade (cf. Bancroft/Cook 1998, 00:18:48). In the later shot Mulan's face is suddenly revealed as she turns the sword she was initially holding in front of her face sideways (cf. ibid., 00:19:07). Both times the shot is framed so that Mulan's face is cut in half, visually hinting at her duality. But only the first shot uses the symbolism of the reflection, thus harkening back to the musical number *Reflection*, where Mulan's body and face is reflected multiple times on different surfaces (cf. ibid., 00:11:53– 00:13:34). Even after Mulan wipes off the bridal make-up that had been put on her earlier (which highlights and exaggerates exactly those facial features that vanish once she is masculine-presenting), she still asks herself the question, "When will my reflection show who I am inside?" (ibid., 00:13:14–00:13:28). While Mulan's initial face is marked by the symbol of reflection, her new face is presented in quite a different way.[3] Now the shiny surface of the sword is no longer used as just

---

[2] As a matter of fact, in the live-action remake (Caro 2020), Mulan is indeed portrayed as a magical character: she wields the power of 'chi'—depicted in the film as a magical force that when possessed by men is valued and encouraged but vilified when possessed by women. However, this magical power does not help Mulan to transform her body or to pass as a man. Whereas in the original film Mulan's bodily transformation happens with ease, the remake actually focuses on the difficulties the transformation gives Mulan, especially the pain of binding her chest. The viewer is told that Mulan's disguise weakens her 'chi.' Only once she leaves her disguise behind can she be at her most powerful. Thus, while in the original Mulan's greatest strength is her ability to transform, the remake portrays this as a hindrance for her actual magical powers. Comparing these two versions of Disney's *Mulan* and their configurations of gender and identity would make a fascinating topic for future research.

[3] This is true not only for the shot that introduces her new face but for the rest of the film. When Mulan is masculine-presenting, the reflection symbolism is supplanted: even when Mulan is bathing in a lake, her reflection does not really appear on the water's surface; her body only throws a vague shadow in a slightly darker shade of blue (cf. Bancroft/Cook 1998, 00:42:06– 00:44:36). The reflection symbolism is only reintroduced when Mulan is uncovered as a woman and 'returns' to her former facial design. Using her helmet as a mirror, she once again is disappointed by what she sees (cf. ibid., 01:02:38–01:03:00). The theme of self-alienation seems to surface only when Mulan's body wears the markers of femininity. While masculine-presenting,

another mirror, implying a difference between Mulan's sense of self and the reflection she sees. This time, instead of having a change imposed on her by someone else, it is Mulan who instigates the change herself. This enables us to read Mulan not just as a person who 'cross-dresses,' but as a person whose very body is fluid, capable of metamorphosis. This ability of hers brings into question the stability of categories like identity and the gendered body.

And yet Mulan's powers of metamorphosis are not independent of the world around her: when she is revealed as a woman, her physical re-transformation coincides with the change in how the outside world perceives her. This again stresses that her bodily transformation is deeply connected to gender. On the one hand, it could be argued that by gendering physical features like eyelashes, eyelid crease[4], and lip colour, *Mulan* naturalises "the idea that male and female humans aren't just different, they're opposites" (Cohen 2015 [n. p.]). On the other hand, these are subtle, easily modifiable markers that are very different from the kind of extreme exaggeration of gender dimorphism that can often be seen in animation. For example Philip N. Cohen calls attention on his blog to what he calls "Disney's dimorphism" (2013 [n. p.]), focusing mainly on overexaggerated differences in body height and mass, and especially hand and wrist size when it comes to 'female' versus 'male' characters in animation, most prominently as seen between romantic couples (cf. ibid.).

Mulan's own fluidity seems to be more closely related to older conventions in animation. More (seemingly) subtle features have long been used to communicate gender to the audience: since the earliest days of Disney animation, eyelashes were a shorthand signifier for femininity. After all, Mickey Mouse's partner Minnie is basically just Mickey with eyelashes:

> [I]t didn't take much to see that there weren't very many differences between Mickey and his girlfriend Minnie. [...] Minnie was the *same* design. All the animators did was put Mickey in pumps with a polka-dot skirt and three long eyelashes, and presto!—he was now a she. The obvious similarities between the two expose gender considerations as an issue of costume [...] (Griffin 2000, 69–70, emphasis in original).

By highlighting the importance that costume, make-up, gesture and movement play in constructing a gendered animated character,[5] animation has the potential

---

the question "When will my reflection show who I am inside?" never arises, either in dialogue or visually.

[4] There are also racial implications to this, since the presence of an eyelid crease is perceived to be a Western attribute. (Kind note from Eugenia Lao.)

[5] This is something the animators at Disney seemed very much aware of. In his analysis of Minnie Mouse, character animator Fred Moore describes how he relies solely on attire and gesture to convey Minnie's 'femaleness.' Moore's phrasing and tone also speak to the effort that was put into achieving and maintaining Minnie's gender performance: "Drawn same as Mickey, *substituting a skirt and lace pants* for his pants, and *high-heeled slippers* in place of his shoes with addition of a small hat and *eye-lids and lashes*. Minnie's *poses and mannerisms* should be definitely feminine. This means, too, her *expressions*, *reactions*, etc. [...] In order to make Minnie *as feminine as possible*, we should use everything in her make-up to achieve this end. [...] Her

"Be a Man"   57

to make visible the many ways in which gender relies on performance (cf. ibid., 70–71). With the character of Mulan this potential is realised:[6] not only are the differences between Mulan's character designs minute (only a few slight alterations are needed to be 'effective'), but they also seem to be heavily influenced by society's expectations of how a 'female' body looks, as opposed to a 'male' one. Contrary to Limbach's interpretation of the film's narrative message (cf. 2013), the fluidity in Mulan's design implies that there are only minor, rather than fundamental, differences between masculinity and femininity, and that these differences are socially constructed and dependent on our perception of the world.

Mulan, in short, seems to be designed to be as 'neutral' and as open to different gender connotations and attributes as possible. When she is introduced in the film she wears, tellingly, quite gender-neutral clothing, a grey ensemble of shorts and a tank top (cf. Bancroft/Cook 1998, 00:03:04–00:03:47). In this respect she stands out, for the film does not endow all its characters with such quasi-subversive tendencies. A completely different set of rules seems to apply to those bodies that are solely marked as masculine.

Of Captains and Recruits—Strict Hierarchies of Masculinity

Yvonne Tasker writes that a hero's transformation is often told through the body— an inner journey is both accompanied by and signalled through a physical transformation: in women's fiction the central character's journey is often emphasised and illustrated "through changes in the heroine's appearance—weight loss, new clothes, hairstyle and so on" (1993, 137). The physical transformation of the bodybuilder action hero works in a similar way, as it reflects and solidifies their new position of power in the world (cf. ibid.). Likewise, for the Disney heroes Hercules and Tarzan, the first step on their way from awkward outsider to respected, confident individual is to get themselves a big, muscular body. This transformation process is told in both films through musical sequences that are structurally and functionally reminiscent of *Mulan*'s *I'll Make a Man Out of You* (Bancroft/Cook

---

eyelids and eyelashes *could help very much* in keeping her feminine [...]" (1981, 553, emphasis added).

[6]As the film *Mulan* heavily relies on the principles and rules set by the 'illusion of life' paradigm, one could argue that this potential is *only* realised *within the boundaries* of this style. According to Griffin the 'illusion of life' style quelled animation's inherent ability to expose the constructedness of identity and therefore gender when it attempted to base animation on some form of 'realism' and to animate bodies that move and look 'natural.' However, readings that went against the grain by focusing on the constructedness of the animated figures became even more satisfyingly rebellious (cf. 2000, 71–72).

1998, 00:37:42–00:41:05). They all share a repetitive structure that depicts the hero(ine) initially failing at a particular task, only to eventually master and succeed at the same (or a very similar) task.[7] However, when these montages are compared with each other, it becomes clear that *Mulan*'s version differs in an important way: the protagonist's journey to skill and mastery is decisively *not* told through the body. Unlike Hercules or Tarzan, neither Mulan nor her fellow recruits undergo a physical change that signals their process of maturation.

At the training camp the recruits' supervisor, Captain Li Shang, is the only male character whose body is presented as strikingly muscular. The film further emphasises Shang's muscularity by contrasting his body with those of the recruits in a shot/reverse shot. As Shang takes off his shirt in preparation for training, the back of his upper body is 'revealed': the outlines of his shoulders, triceps and biceps are all rounded and bulging, conveying the plasticity of his muscular back; sharp, curved lines on his back indicate shoulder and back muscles. In the reverse shot Mulan, impressed, can be seen peeking out from behind the round bellies of two nameless recruits, and framed in the background by Chien Po's massive body. Mulan's own body is not visible; from the neck down she is hidden behind the other recruits (cf. ibid., 00:36:37–00:36:46). As the staging of this shot implies, it is not Mulan's body that is relevant here, but rather the men's: one specific type of masculinity, which is worthy of admiration (as Mulan's facial expression implies), is juxtaposed with other types of masculine physique. These in turn are marked, by the staging of the three nearly identical bellies, as quite unremarkable. Additionally, because the new recruits are lower in rank and weaker in battle than the Captain, they are also marked as subordinate to him on a narrative level. This hierarchy is not only introduced but legitimised in this scene, as the recruit Yao fails miserably in his attempt to ridicule Captain Li Shang (cf. ibid., 00:36:47–00:37:09). When Yao tries to call out Shang's performance of power ("Oh, tough guy," ibid. 00:36:47–00:36:51), Shang answers in a way that not only positively reinforces his status but effectively humiliates the provocateur: he uses his skills (as he points his arrow at Yao) and his rank (as he orders Yao to bring the arrow back) to demonstrate the hierarchy between them while strengthening it at the same time. As a last resort, Yao tries to level the playing field by mocking the Captain's looks, muttering under his breath: "I'll get that arrow, pretty boy, and I'll do it with my shirt on" (ibid., 00:37:02–00:37:09).

According to Christian Hißnauer and Thomas Klein (cf. 2002, 28–31), this sort of bald comparison, as well as the implication that one type of masculinity is superior to others, is a typical strategy used to present masculinity in cinema: in film, masculinity is usually defined by contrasting it to what it is not. In search of a productive method for analyzing masculinity in film, Hißnauer and Klein argue, there is never only one kind of masculinity; rather they are always portrayed in relation to each other. The kind of idealised, favoured masculinity is termed—in

---

[7] In *Hercules* (Clements/Musker 1997) the musical number referred to is *One Last Hope* (00:28:20–00:31:20); in *Tarzan* (Buck/Lima 1999) it is *Son of Man* (00:22:44–00:25:25).

accordance with the influential research of sociologist R. W. Connell—
'hegemonic.' As a construct of the cultural imagination, 'hegemonic masculinity'
is an effective tool for legitimising patriarchy; it is an ideal that is constantly culturally (re-)produced by institutions such as the state or media.

In *Mulan*, Captain Li Shang represents this film's version of hegemonic masculinity. This is conveyed via the portrayal of his physique, his abilities and his
social status, all of which are rendered as positive and desirable. In contrast, the
other masculinities represented in the training camp are constantly associated with
being feminine and childlike. The film marks these features as negative, as characters constantly use these descriptors to mock and insult each other: the bureaucrat, Chi Fu, is ridiculed by the recruits, because he "squeal[s] like a girl," while
Chi Fu himself dismissively calls the new recruits "those boys" (Bancroft/Cook
1998, 00:46:52, 00:44:44). According to Hißnauer/Klein (cf. 2002, 29) and Tasker
(cf. 1993, 95), these are typical patriarchal strategies used to discredit certain types
of masculinity within male hierarchical relations. The hierarchy between the male
characters is never really questioned or challenged in the film: by belittling each
other regularly, the other male characters are shown to also accept and uphold a
hierarchy that denigrates masculinities perceived as 'less manly' (i.e. associated
with 'femininity'). The idea of one 'perfect' form of masculinity is thereby legitimised. The fact that neither Mulan nor the other recruits have acquired a muscular body by the end of *I'll Make a Man Out of You* merely underscores Shang's
untouchable position of power—quite out of reach for anyone who does not perform masculinity the way he does. Yao, Ling and Chien Po have no chance of
coming any closer to this image of ideal masculinity constructed by the film, for
even their attempts to do so only expose their failure: when Ling exits a lake, his
armour, being fully soaked with water, gives the impression of enormous muscularity. After he strikes some poses, however, the water escapes his armour with a
squeal, leaving Ling standing there, soaking wet and with his usual thin figure—
thus strikingly emphasising the contrast between the physique he aspires to and
the one he actually possesses (cf. Bancroft/Cook 1998, 00:48:37–00:48:41).

The animation of Mulan's body, which works in tandem with the presentation
of her performance of gender, lend themselves to a radical reading of the film as
one that presents a social constructionist view of gender, that is, the view that gender is dependent on cultural understanding. Yet the film also shows rigid power
structures that are not only based on but also justified through a hierarchisation
of masculinities, constructing as well as idealising a form of masculinity against
which all others are judged. While most of the male characters in the camp aspire
to approximate this ideal, thus legitimising and upholding the power structure
through their compliance, the antagonist Shan Yu by contrast threatens its very
core.

Shan Yu—the Beast in Man

The film presents Shan Yu through a few recurring patterns that repeatedly associate him with two distinct qualities: destructive nature and excessive masculinity. This becomes clear from a scene that shows the Huns on Chinese soil for the first time: the very first shot of this scene establishes a firm distinction between nature and culture, associating the people of China with the latter and the Hun Army with the former. An establishing shot shows gentle blue hills framed by trees in the foreground. The staging and colouring is consistent with the concept and style usually used in the film to depict scenery (mostly as backdrops) in *Mulan*'s fictional China. However, the destroyed village upon the hills, still in flames, disrupts the image of the harmonious landscape. The village is a clear sign of warfare and devastation—a devastation that is immediately linked with the Huns, as Shan Yu's pet falcon hovers over the scenery. As the camera follows the bird, the background style changes drastically: jagged mountains replace the gentle hills, and the (previously bluish) colours of the background are replaced by colours similar to the bird's, namely grey and brown. As the falcon descends, Shan Yu and his army enter the frame, following the bird on horseback at full gallop. The falcon then flies out of sight, and the camera descends even further until it reaches the ground, below the hooves of the Huns' horses, a camera angle that puts the viewer in the position of being trampled (cf. ibid., 00:25:25–00:25:35). The Hun soldiers are featured in the same shades of grey, brown and black as their leader's falcon— even their skin colour is tinted grey. This creates a stark contrast with the Chinese characters, who are depicted with a much larger section of the colour palette. The invaders seem to bring with them not only destruction but darkness, dull colours and a harsh, inhospitable nature; their arrival erases everything that is bright and soft. The village is burning down; the hills vanish. Visually the Huns are identified with nature in its frightening aspect—and the most frightening of the Huns is of course their leader Shan Yu.

This characteristic is again conveyed through the body's appearance, and this time the body looks barely human. Sharpened instincts, superhuman strength and immense speed—these are all qualities that Shan Yu is repeatedly shown to possess. All Shan Yu needs in order to conclude that Imperial scouts are hiding close by is a rustling sound, and he is able to hear so soft a sound, it seems, while riding at full gallop (cf. ibid., 00:25:36–00:25:50). Shan Yu is able to easily break a flagpole with his bare hands (cf. ibid., 00:02:08), to lift a full-grown man (cf. ibid., 00:26:28), to cut down massive wooden pillars with a single stroke of his sword (cf. ibid., 00:13:41). Shan Yu often enters the frame abruptly, either by jumping into the frame from below or by letting himself fall from above. With these characteristic entrances Shan Yu literally invades the space of the screen, without warning confronting everyone—viewer and characters alike—with his enormous body. For example in the scene where the Imperial scouts detected by Shan Yu are brought before him, Shan Yu enters the frame abruptly from above: the first thing to appear are his heavy black boots, indicating that he has jumped down from his horse. A tracking and tilting shot then reveals the rest of Shan Yu's body, which bears many animalistic markers. First we see the furs in which he is dressed, then his ungloved right hand as it lifts his fur hood. The transition from clothing to hand suggests that the animal skins merely conceal Shan Yu's own animality, for the exposed parts of his body are then revealed as even more animalistic than what's covered in furs: his hands end in claws, his canine teeth are extremely pointed, and as he lifts his hood, yellow eyes that resemble those of his pet falcon are revealed (cf. ibid., 00:26:00–00:26:13).

Associating villains with predators has long been a tradition in Disney films. Patrick D. Murphy writes that Disney typically positions female antagonists outside of culture and cultural norms, identifying them with nonhuman, 'wild' nature. Murphy believes that the construction of a hierarchical dichotomy between culture and nature is based on the fact that in patriarchal society both women and nature are believed to be subordinate to men. The domesticated woman is preferred to the rebellious; the domesticated/anthropomorphised nature to the uncontrolled/ nonhuman. The Disney villainess combines the very qualities of independence and uncontrolled/nonhuman nature that pose a threat to patriarchal norms; meanwhile the 'good' female character is often associated with domesticated nature (cf. 1995, 125–129). The fact that *Mulan*'s male villain Shan Yu is presented in a similar way—as 'wild' and 'inhuman'—puts an interesting spin on this character type.[8]

According to Murphy, Disney films tend to portray culture as static, timeless and stable, while wild nature (and therefore change and process) is entirely excluded from human society (cf. ibid., 125–126). This nature/culture dichotomy is also central to *Mulan*. Here, a culture is constructed whose primary strength lies in essentially influencing and controlling both its members' gender and the gendered body. Shan Yu's body, however, emphatically marked as animalistic and presented as untameable and uncontrollable, represents the antithesis. His body threatens the static hierarchy of masculinities that the film establishes through its 'good' male characters in the training camp, whose bodies never have the opportunity to transform (even when it would be diegetically plausible). When the scouts gaze at Shan Yu, a moment of tension is created where the villain's body is presented as capable of shattering the existing masculine power relations.

---

[8] It is important to note that *Mulan* not only places its characters on different sides of the culture/ nature or human/nonhuman dichotomy, but in doing so simultaneously creates and defines these very categories. As Donna Haraway reminds us, there is nothing self-evident about any of those dichotomies; they are always constructed and highly specific: "Remember, however, that what counts as human and as nonhuman is not given by definition, but only by relation, by engagement in situated, worldly encounters, where boundaries take shape and categories sediment. If feminist, antiracist, multicultural science studies—not to mention technoscience—have taught us anything, it is that what counts as human is not, and should not be, self-evident" (1994, 64).

Shan Yu—the Epitome of Masculinity

Again, it is through a shot/reverse shot that the significance of a specific body is conveyed in *Mulan*. After we see the scouts' faces in an over-the-shoulder shot looking horrified at the sight of Shan Yu, we are then shown the reason for their horror: Shan Yu's body is revealed in an extremely stylised way. The camera work marks his body as a spectacle worth beholding: first the camera moves forward towards Shan Yu in symbiotic accompaniment to his walk; then it tilts up from below and pans over his entire body, slowly revealing his face. The unfolding of this spectacle is intercut with a shot showing the terrified scouts, pointedly registering the fear and terror that this body causes (cf. Bancroft/Cook 1998, 00:25:56–00:26:13). As if describing this very scene, Steve Neale writes:

> We are offered the spectacle of male bodies, but bodies unmarked as objects of erotic display. [...] We see male bodies *stylized* and fragmented by close-ups, but our look is not direct, it is *heavily mediated by the looks of the characters involved.* And these looks are marked not by desire, but rather *fear*, or hatred, or aggression (1993, 18, emphasis added).

Using Laura Mulvey's influential essay on the male gaze as a reference point, Neale adds that in mainstream film not only the female but also the male body can be marked as the object of the erotic gaze. Only the gaze's potential eroticism is not exploited but is on the contrary repressed and denied (cf. ibid., 13–14, 16–19). Shan Yu's body is presented in a way that could invoke fetishisation, but the implied erotic potential is defused and transformed into a threat through the scouts' gaze. However, both the potential for eroticism and for intimidation seem to originate from the same source: Shan Yu's hypermasculinity.[9]

Not only do Shan Yu's enormous muscles (*supposedly* obvious signs of masculine power, cf. Dyer 1982, 68, 71[10]) connote hypermasculinity—his bicep is the size of his head—but so does his face: his eyebrows, ears, nose, cheekbones and his horseshoe moustache are all angular. Shan Yu's eyes are especially remarkable in this regard, as they are triangular.

---

[9] As already argued in a previous essay, a new kind of Disney villain emerged during the 1990s who was a departure from the tall, thin and graceful villains that dominated earlier Disney films. This new villain is marked as excessively masculine—towering height, enormous hands and extreme muscularity being his most striking features. In my analysis of Gaston in *Beauty and the Beast* (Trousdale/Wise 1991), I termed this kind of villain 'hypermasculine' (cf. Festl 2019, 3). Shan Yu is another example of this type of Disney antagonist. In contrast to Gaston, he is not portrayed as particularly vain or narcissistic (cf. ibid., 14–17). Whereas most of the time Gaston is presented as somewhat comedic in his villainy, Shan Yu is always unironically presented as a menace. His hypermasculinity is never the object of ridicule.

[10] 'Supposedly' because, as Dyer notes, while "[t]he potential for muscularity in men is seen as a biological given," visible muscularity—and extreme muscularity especially—reveals the muscular male body as something that is far from 'natural,' but intentional and achieved (1982, 71). While Gaston revels in his own muscularity, always showcasing it, but never 'legitimising' it through activity (cf. Festl 2019, 17–24), Shan Yu hides his muscles under furs: he only shows off his physical abilities, never his body.

The design of his face may seem arbitrary at first, but when set against the design of Mulan's (transformed) face, new readings and meanings emerge. When discussing the aesthetic of the pin-up, Dyer argues that "hard lines and angular shapes" are culturally considered to be masculine, while soft, round shapes are associated with femininity (cf. ibid., 71). When the shape of Mulan's jawline changes from round to slightly more angular, her transformation draws exactly from this cultural idea. Of course, the face of Captain Li Shang—the character presented in *Mulan* as the masculine ideal par excellence—is also dominated by angular shapes: his nose, eyes and jawline all have sharp edges. But Shan Yu's face, defined entirely by angular shapes, is a grotesque version of this masculine ideal: the villain is not merely masculine, he epitomises the kind of masculinity that *Mulan* deems desirable; he is the visual representation of everything the song *I'll Make a Man Out of You* asks of a man:

"Be a man! You must be *swift* as a coursing river [...], with all the *force* of a great typhoon [...], with all the *strength* of a raging fire, *mysterious* as the dark side of the moon!" (Bancroft/Cook 1998, 00:39:27–00:39:48, emphasis added). The similes in the refrain, which associate desirable manliness with natural phenomena, are better suited to Shan Yu's untamed nature than to the 'good' male characters, who decisively belong with (static) culture. By framing manhood as something 'natural,' something that is not constructed by society, the lyrics have a vagueness that serve, as Limbach notes, to obscure what it is exactly that makes a man (cf. 2013, 120). However, the male character that is most closely associated with nonhuman nature is the film's villain. So, ultimately the film seems to fear what it praises: in *Mulan*, the attainment of the masculine ideal simultaneously transforms masculinity into a frightening thing; 'nature' overtakes and consumes what is 'human' in the body; strength and force degenerate into cruelty and brutality. Just as Disney villainesses overperform their femininity "to the point where the 'naturalness' of their gender can be called into question" (Griffin 2000, 73), Shan Yu overperforms hegemonic masculinity to the point where its constructedness becomes obvious. His body is stylised to the point of fetishisation; at the same time it is feared, because it reveals that the ideal of hegemonic masculinity on which patriarchal structures rely can never be reached: "While the ideal ego may be a 'model' with which the subject identifies and to which it aspires, it may also be a source of further images and feelings of castration, inasmuch as that ideal is something to which the subject is never adequate" (Neale 1993, 13).

Turning the villain into an exaggerated version of the film's ideal masculinity inevitably poses the question if this ideal is something worth striving for at all. And once the appeal and validity of the hegemonic ideal is questioned, patriarchy itself is at risk of being delegitimised.

Conclusion—Enemies or Allies

During the film's final confrontation, the viewer gets a glimpse of an intriguing connection between Shan Yu and Mulan, the film's two transgressive characters. As Limbach writes, there seems to be a special bond, a certain kind of unspoken agreement, between the two: Shan Yu is the only one who recognises Mulan's liminal status by addressing her with the gender-neutral term "soldier" (Bancroft/ Cook 1998, 01:13:09); he also treats her as an equal opponent (cf. 2013, 124). Limbach, however, does not elaborate on the fact that shortly before Shan Yu addresses Mulan in this way, Mulan gives him a brief but special glimpse into her fluidity and ambiguous status. Mulan, who at this point in the narrative has already been revealed as a woman, pulls back her hair—in order to, as Limbach writes, "resemble her former self" (ibid.). But she actually reveals herself to Shan Yu as much more than just 'the soldier': for a fleeting moment (and for the only time during the entire film) her face clearly signifies an in-between. Her eyes are drawn in the style that is marked as masculine—without the eyelid crease, dark outline and curvy lashes—but her lips and cheeks have a rosy tint (cf. Bancroft/Cook 1998, 01:13:07). This image lasts for only one shot as Mulan immediately changes back to her former appearance.

Although the two characters are enemies on the narrative level, the animation suggests on the visual level that there is a complicity between the film's 'wild' woman and 'wild' man: both threaten the film's patriarchal social structures.[11] It is therefore not surprising that Mulan's first attempt to kill Shan Yu by using a force of nature (the avalanche) is ultimately bound to fail. Only once she is symbolically placed on the side of culture can she defeat Shan Yu, which she accomplishes by using a rocket to send him into a tower filled with other explosive fireworks.[12] With Shan Yu dead and Mulan ready to return home, the status quo is re-established. By killing Shan Yu, Mulan effectively kills *two* forces that pose a danger to the film's patriarchal social structures: the creature-like hypermasculine villain as well as her own 'wildness' and fluidity, which she thereby surrenders to a culture that claims control over its members' (gendered) bodies. Nevertheless, by putting gender roles, gendered bodies and identity at the forefront, *Mulan* also makes visible the constructedness of these categories. The design of the heroine's body shows that her gender cannot be described as fixed or stable but as the site of constant transformation. Accordingly, the body of the villain is presented as the

---

[11] In the *Mulan* remake (Caro 2020) the male villain, Bori Khan, is accompanied by the witch Xianniang. Thus, in this version a 'wild' man as well as a 'wild' woman are featured as antagonists. The character of Xianniang is used primarily as a cautionary tale for Mulan as they are both women who wield the power of 'chi.' Yet, Xianniang has chosen to turn her back on a society that is punishing her for her powers, while Mulan ultimately strives to thrive in it.

[12] An element that was included in the film, according to producer Pam Coats, because fireworks as an invention represent one of ancient China's cultural legacies (cf. *Making of: Character Design* 2004, 00:02:41–00:02:55).

antithesis to static culture: it is untameable and 'wild.' But not only is Shan Yu threatening the construct of culture as stable and timeless, his body also questions the validity and virtue of the film's ideal of hegemonic masculinity as praised in the song *I'll Make a Man Out of You*. In this way the character complicates and questions what patriarchy demands of men. It is these disruptions, these moments of (gender) trouble and openness, that leave the viewer wondering, even as Mulan returns home.

References

Primary Sources

Clements, Ron/John Musker, dir. (1997): *Hercules*. Walt Disney Pictures. https://www.disneyplus.com/de-de/video/507f8810-a082-42c4-8022-84ce8f72a998. Accessed: 3. April 2021
Caro, Niki, dir. (2020): *Mulan*. Walt Disney Pictures
Bancroft, Tony/Barry Cook, dir. (1998): *Mulan*. Walt Disney Pictures. https://www.disneyplus.com/de-de/video/f401021b-47de-459a-a283-e2b9236b1e63. Accessed: 3. April 2021
Buck, Chris/Kevin Lima, dir. (1999): *Tarzan*. Walt Disney Pictures. https://www.disneyplus.com/de-de/video/25deeb7c-9ab5-42ce-ae9a-f282cc436a88. Accessed: 3. April 2021
Trousdale, Gary/Kirk Wise, dir. (1991): *Beauty and the Beast*. Walt Disney Pictures

Secondary Sources

Bell, Elizabeth (1995): Somatexts at the Disney Shop. Constructing the Pentimentos of Women's Animated Bodies. In: *From Mouse to Mermaid: The Politics of Film, Gender, and Culture*, eds. Elizabeth Bell/Lynda Haas/Laura Sells, Bloomington [et al.], 107–124
Cohen, Philip N. (2013): Disney's Dimorphism, 'Help! My Eyeball Is Bigger than My Wrist!' Edition. *Family Inequality* (blog). https://familyinequality.wordpress.com/2013/12/16/disneys-dimorphism-help-my-eyeball-is-bigger-than-my-wrist-edition/. Accessed: 22. February 2021
Cohen, Philip N. (2015): Herculean Dimorphism. *Family Inequality* (blog). https://familyinequality.wordpress.com/2015/01/04/herculean-dimporphism/. Accessed: 22. February 2021
Dyer, Richard (1982): Don't Look Now: Richard Dyer Examines the Instabilities of the Male Pin-Up. In: *Screen*, Vol. 23, No. 3–4, 61–73
Festl, Yvonne (2019): Rambo im Märchenland—Zur Darstellung von Hypermaskulinität in Disneys *Beauty and the Beast* (1991). In: *Zeitschrift für Fantastikforschung*, Vol. 7, No. 1, 1–31. https://doi.org/10.16995/zff.791
Griffin, Sean (2000): *Tinker Belles and Evil Queens: The Walt Disney Company from the Inside Out*. New York [et al.]
Haraway, Donna Jeanne (1994): A Game of Cat's Cradle: Science Studies, Feminist Theory, Cultural Studies. In: *Configurations*, Vol. 2, No. 1, 59–71. https://doi.org/10.1353/con.1994.0009
Hißnauer, Christian/Thomas Klein (2002): Visualität des Männlichen. Skizzen zu einer filmsoziologischen Theorie von Männlichkeit. In: *Männer—Machos—Memmen. Männlichkeit im Film*, eds. Christian Hißnauer/Thomas Klein, Mainz, 17–48

Limbach, Gwendolyn (2013): "You the Man, Well, Sorta": Gender Binaries and Liminality in Mulan. In: *Diversity in Disney Films: Critical Essays on Race, Ethnicity, Gender, Sexuality and Disability*, ed. Johnson Cheu, Jefferson NC. [et al.], 115–128

Li-Vollmer, Meredith/Mark E. LaPointe (2003): Gender Transgression and Villainy in Animated Film. In: *Popular Communication*, Vol. 1, No. 2, 89–109

Making of: Character Design. DVD: Disney DVD, Mulan—Special Collection, Walt Disney Meisterwerke, 2-Disc-DVD-Set, 2004

Moore, Fred (1981): Analysis of Mickey Mouse (Appendix). In: *The Illusion of Life: Disney Animation*, eds. Frank Thomas/Ollie Johnston, New York, 551–553

Murphy, Patrick D. (1995): "The Whole Wide World Was Scrubbed Clean": The Androcentric Animation of Denatured Disney. In: *From Mouse to Mermaid: The Politics of Film, Gender, and Culture*, eds. Elizabeth Bell/Lynda Haas/Laura Sells, Bloomington [et al.], 125–136

Neale, Steve (1993 [1983]): Masculinity as Spectacle: Reflections on Men and Mainstream Cinema. In: *Screening the Male: Exploring Masculinities in Hollywood Cinema*, eds. Steven Cohan/Ina Rae Hark, London [et al.], 9–20

Putnam, Amanda (2013): Mean Ladies: Transgendered Villains in Disney Films. In: *Diversity in Disney Films: Critical Essays on Race, Ethnicity, Gender, Sexuality and Disability*, ed. Johnson Cheu, Jefferson NC. [et al.], 147–162

Tasker, Yvonne (1993): *Spectacular Bodies: Gender, Genre, and the Action Cinema*. London [et al.]

Walking the Line

A Feminist Reading of Gendered Orientations and Voice in Disney's *Aladdin* Films (1992/2019)

Sara Van den Bossche

Abstract *Aladdin* (2019), Disney's live-action remake of its eponymous 1992 animation, attracted attention due to the female protagonist's fleshed-out role and its apparent attunement to feminist issues. Starting from the observation that its source was drenched in patriarchal ideology, which purportedly renders the adaptation dissimilar, this essay adopts a feminist approach to read the two films alongside each other. It scrutinises the phenomenological, gendered 'orientations' the narratives advance, and the cognitive 'cultural narratives' informing them. Applying the same theoretical concepts and methodological tools to both movies, it aims to gauge their feminist calibre. The analysis reveals that the animation enacts a decidedly patriarchal worldview entailing the entailment of female motility and voice. As for the remake, it demonstrates that the film explicitly engages with some of the antifeminist issues underpinning its source's ideology. However, because it ultimately merely reverses its predecessor's patriarchal constructs without dismantling them, the remake is better understood with the label 'postfeminist.'

Aladdin (Ritchie 2019), one of the latest in a series of live-action remakes of Disney animations,[1] met with varied reviews. Scores assembled on the portal "Metacritic.com" range between eighty and twenty-five percent, averaging out at fifty-three, and twenty-eight of fifty reviews are labelled 'mixed' (Metacritic 2021). It has been noted that this adaptation departs from the animated *Aladdin* (Clements/Musker 1992), adjusting some of its Orientalist stereotypes. With these remakes, critics have observed, Disney tackles "issues of the originals that don't stand up under a modern eye" (Radulovic

---

[1] Whenever I write "Disney," I use it as shorthand for The Walt Disney Company.

S. Van den Bossche (✉)
Tilburg University, Tilburg, The Netherlands
e-mail: s.vandenbossche@tilburguniversity.edu

© The Author(s), under exclusive license to Springer-Verlag GmbH, DE, part of Springer Nature 2022
U. Dettmar and I. Tomkowiak (eds.), *On Disney*, Studien zu Kinder- und Jugendliteratur und -medien 9, https://doi.org/10.1007/978-3-662-64625-0_5

2019, n. p.). Moreover, on the streaming platform Disney+, an advisory precedes the animated *Aladdin* stating that it "includes negative depictions and/or mistreatment of people or cultures" (The Walt Disney Company 2021). Disney condemns these "stereotypes" as "wrong," but instead of deleting it opts to "learn from it and spark conversation to create a more inclusive future" (ibid.). Thus, critics and Disney alike acknowledge viewing audiences' sensitivities and willingness to accept contested worldviews have changed drastically over the decades.

Apart from correcting racist tendencies, noted changes in the new *Aladdin* (2019) concern the role of female characters. The remake has received some cautious praise as a feminist revision of the animated film, mainly because Jasmine is granted "more three-dimensionality" (Romano 2019, n. p.) and "more agency and a story that is not entirely reliant on Aladdin" (Radulovic 2019, n. p.).[2] Nevertheless, some consider the female characters' parts questionable. Jasmine's two-part solo song *Speechless* has attracted particular attention. It champions women's voices explicitly, yet A.O. Scott for instance denounces it as "a ham-fisted attempt to paste some power-princess feminism into the film that feels [...] condescending" (2019, n. p.).

As the remake noticeably foregrounds Jasmine's part, and as the reception of precisely that revision proves divided, this aspect of the film begs further scrutiny. Therefore, I aim to examine female roles in the two versions of *Aladdin* from a feminist vantage point. I subscribe to the definition of feminism that Roberta Seelinger Trites proposes: "Feminism is the belief that all people should have equal rights under the law, regardless of race, gender, orientation, religion, ability, social class, ethnicity, or any other factor" (2018, xi). I study the nature of male/female relationships in both narratives, alongside the distribution of voice and power valences between male and female characters. As entry points I use cognitive 'cultural narratives' and phenomenological 'orientations' pertaining to possible trajectories in life. The latter I scrutinise because they function as shorthand for power, as opportunities granted in life are indices of one's positionality, which includes gender. Using orientations as lenses to read the films, I consider which types are available to male and female figures, which cultural narratives inform them, and if there is any room for disturbing them. Thus, I aim to lay bare the extent to which the films are feminist, if at all.

Aladdin (1992): A 'Pseudo Feminist' and 'Patriarchal' Tale

Scholars have addressed the role of women in the animated *Aladdin*, which notably features only one significant female character: Jasmine. The other women serve as mere set dressing. Jasmine is ostensibly depicted as a "strong woman,"

---

[2] Regarding these aspects, 2019's *Aladdin* seems to engage in a type of adaptation Julie Sanders (2006), with Deborah Cartmell, terms *commentary*, which usually concerns the source's cultural or political contents and is achieved through adjustments and/or additions. The audience's awareness of the association between source and commentary is stimulated by e.g. retaining plot elements or the same title, as in the case here.

but because "a highly patriarchal subtext" undercuts this characterisation, Marwan M. Kraidy categorises the narrative as "pseudo feminist" (1998, 51). The movie reaffirms the patriarchy as it casts the only female character as subsidiary to the men's interests. "[T]he patriarchs hold the ultimate say" (Artz 2004, 130), meaning Jasmine's father (the sultan), Jafar (his vizier) and Aladdin. Lee Artz aptly remarks, "Jasmine [...] is spunky, adventurous, and independent—although ultimately she needs male guidance, rescue and approval" (ibid., 127). As Artz implies, and I agree, Jasmine's indebtedness to men undermines her surface autonomy.

Jafar's part is particularly misogynist. He curtails Jasmine's voice when he notes, "You're speechless, I see. A fine quality in a wife" (Clements/Musker 1992, 01:04:28; cf. Kraidy 1998, 51). His observation is symptomatic of what Trites terms a 'cultural narrative,' that is a "cognitively-stored and culturally reinforced scrip[t] about status, power, and constructed social roles" (Trites 2014, 60).[3] Such ideas connect individuals and society and make the communal bleed into the personal. The present cultural narrative associates women with silence and obedience, and "an idiotizado [stupefied] role" (Madrigal Torres/Madrigal Torres 2015, 352). Moreover, Jasmine deceives Jafar by performing a seductive dance, deploying her body—the sole form of power she possesses. This scene is implicated in the trend of the "orientalization of women of color" that Celeste Lacroix detects in several Disney films, a harmful pattern that "represents racist imagery of women of color as sexualized beings" (2004, 227).

As previous studies have established that *Aladdin* perpetuates the patriarchy, I build on those findings by asking how the film manoeuvres the sole female character into subordination. What narrative mechanisms create this effect? My thesis is that the narrative enacts the patriarchy by imposing on the woman a gendered life trajectory, which is conflated with the curtailment of her bodily movement and voice—prominent issues within feminist criticism. I argue that *Aladdin* advances a prescriptive 'orientation' that reduces Jasmine to her body and is expressed through its containment and instrumentalisation through marriage to secure her family's reign. This thesis I prove by analysing the 1992 movie from a feminist theoretical standpoint, translated into a methodology borrowing from cognitive criticism and queer phenomenology. This analysis then serves as the basis for comparison in gauging the gender politics of the remake.

---

[3]Cognitive scholars define a script as "a predetermined, stereotyped sequence of actions that defines a well-known situation" (Schank/Abelson 1975, 151, in Trites 2014, 36–37), stipulating "how a sequence of events is expected to unfold" (Mercadal 1990, 255, in Trites 2014, 37). Recognisable examples are how to use public transport, or how to conduct oneself at a job interview. The unwritten rules for such occasions are stored as implied knowledge in our brains.

Key Theoretical Concepts: Orientations, the Family Line and Gendering

To explain my theoretical concepts, I take my cue from Jasmine's first scene, which introduces her and her father squabbling over her prescribed destiny. It defines Jasmine's narrative's arc, for as the sultan reminds her, "The law says you must be married to a prince [...] by your next birthday." The princess protests, "I hate being forced into this. If I do marry, I want it to be for love." The sultan finally explains, "I just want to make sure you're taken care of" (Clements/Musker 1992, 00:13:14–00:13:45). This conversation demonstrates that Jasmine cannot plan her life freely because of a legal obligation and sketches the outlines of the path she is expected to follow, namely marriage.

For my feminist analysis, I draw on Sara Ahmed's *Queer Phenomenology* (2006) to highlight the impact of gendered mental constructions on individuals' bodies. Ahmed's rationale concerns possible trajectories in life, which she refers to as *orientations*, thereby stressing that these routes are embodied. Ahmed writes, "'Life itself' is often imagined in terms of 'having a direction,' which decides from the present what the future should be" (2006, 20). Crucially, directions are prescriptive. Writing from the orientation of a queer feminist of colour, Ahmed's main argument is that the direction most individuals are being orientated toward is heterosexual reproduction. The chief route to be pursued is the family line. This is precisely what Jasmine and her father quarrel about. In citing the law, the sultan is "performing the work of alignment:" he is bringing Jasmine "into line" by assigning to her "a future that is 'in line' with the family line" (ibid., 83). He thus inscribes Jasmine into the family tree, the "hope" of which "is that the vertical line [of reproduction] will produce a horizontal line [a marital bond], from which further vertical lines will be drawn" (ibid.).

Jasmine and her father respectively take as orientating principles romantic love and the legal requirement. Both beliefs perform antifeminist work, serving to keep the princess 'in line.' The law echoes Adrienne Rich's notion of "compulsive heterosexuality:" a manifestation of "male power" that "convince[s] [women] that marriage [is] inevitable—even if unsatisfying or oppressive" (Rich 1993, 234; cited in Ahmed 2006, 84). This law does exactly that, coercing the princess into a marital bond that the sultan frames as inescapable. Furthermore, although marrying for love may seem a self-contained objective for a woman, Judith Fetterley points out that androcentric (male-centred) narratives—such as *Aladdin*—deploy "the mythology of romantic love in the maintenance of male power" (1978, xxiv), to subjugate females. Similarly, Lacroix argues that the marriage plot in Disney films undermines women's autonomy and positions them as secondary. Foregrounding the patriarchal charge of the plot device, she remarks, "many film and feminist critics have bemoaned the continued positioning of the female characters in passive roles that eventuate in marriage and thereby reinforce cultural logic regarding the natural fulfillment of a young woman's dream as continually defined by men" (2004, 225). That the family line Jasmine is inscribed into is patriarchal has several crucial effects that determine her narrative arc, which I will discuss in the following sections.

Curtailment of Female Agency and Voice

Firstly, the dominance of the patriarchy undercuts Jasmine's agency and voice. The princess's predicament becomes more apparent when Aladdin, disguised as prince Ali, presents himself as a suitor to the sultan and Jafar. Aladdin's courting endorses the cultural narrative that ordains a man to ask a woman's father for her hand, effectively circumventing her agency. Discussing the princess's failed courtships, the men are talking over her head, thus linking female gender with 'speechless[ness],' or lack of voice (cf. Beard 2018, 26). The sultan predicts, "*Jasmine will like* this one," Jafar "intercede[s] *on Jasmine's behalf*," and Aladdin claims, "I will *win* your daughter" (Clements/Musker 1992, 00:53:25–00:53:44; emphasis added). The princess enters the room unnoticed—underlining the men's neglect of her—and interrupts the conversation, thus appearing as a "strong woman" (Kraidy 1998, 51). Although she objects, "I am not a prize to be won" (Clements/Musker 1992, 00:53:51), that is exactly what she is: a valued possession, handed over from one man (father) to another (suitor), without getting a proper say.

Collectively these short scenes make Jasmine appear as hardly more than an appendage of the men around her. As their property, she is an "extension" of them, and in their trading of her, she is "annihilated as a separate person and is solipsized into [them]" (Fetterley 1978, 98). Overall she barely figures as a distinct individual; she is rather the sultan's daughter or the protagonist's love interest. The movie thus participates in a bias in androcentric literature that Fetterley discerns: a woman's position is only discussed "indirectly and primarily in terms of its effects on men" (ibid., 116). Such male-centred narratives treat women as the other, an "it" devoid of "personhood" (ibid., ix). Fetterley's view thus aligns with Simone de Beauvoir's notion of women as "being-other": "she is taught that to please, she must [...] make herself object; she must therefore renounce her autonomy. She is treated like a living doll and freedom is denied her" (De Beauvoir 2011, 305).

Curtailment of Female Motility

De Beauvoir's comment on relinquished independence points to a second issue: alignment with the patriarchy entails entailment of female bodies. Because Jasmine is a woman, her trajectory is male-centred and focused on her body, the political locus of male pursuit of power. Jasmine's orientation, then, is heavily gendered. Ahmed conceives of gendering as related to how bodies take up space, and of gender as "a bodily orientation" (2006, 60). Consequently, gender norms engender a "politics of mobility": they dictate "who gets to move with ease" and "be at home" in the world (ibid., 142). In an androcentric environment, men's bodies are at home and possess "motility" (ibid., 131–136),[4] women's do not.

For Jasmine, gendered body curtailment manifests literally, as she is locked up in the palace, a metonymy for the oppressive family line. Her confinement iterates the traditional distinction between the domestic realm as female and the public as male (cf. Ahmed 2006, 31; Beard 2018, 38–39; Fetterley 1978, 116; Nikolajeva 2010, 123). Confining women to the private and denying them access to the public serves the needs of a male-centred society. Indeed, no reason is given for the princess's detention other than the gendered orientation that accompanies her royal rank. When Jasmine laments never having left the palace, her father's reply, "But Jasmine, you're a princess" (Clements/Musker 1992, 00:14:02), aptly captures the oppressive nature of her gendered orientation, as if her status justifies everything. As there is no room for her to wander in the space she inhabits, she escapes. Fleeing captivity constitutes her veering "off course," encountering "that which is off the line" she ought to take (Ahmed 2006, 19), namely her meeting Aladdin. The successive plot twists give us reason to surmise that her detention is informed by the necessity to control her familial alignment, as her breaking quarantine leads her to her love interest and thus the means to slightly alter her prescribed orientation.

The city—the public domain—is men's territory. The streets of Agrabah figure male characters predominantly. Women are rare, and depicted either veiled or behind a window, with one group of women appearing to belong to a harem (an androcentric and acutely female-unfriendly space, cf. Lacroix 2004). Tellingly, Jasmine, accustomed to the private, moves uneasily in the public, male-orientated world. At the market, everyday scenes startle her, and she gets into trouble. Spotting a hungry street urchin, she unsuspectingly grabs an apple from a market stall, without realising she has to pay for it. As a result of her captivity, she is not financially mature—a position Mary Beard deems indicative of women being denied access to the public domain (cf. 2018, 26). The vendor accuses her of stealing and his "interpellation" makes Jasmine come across as "out of place," as she is "being stopped" in her tracks (Ahmed 2006, 139–141). She cannot roam the streets unnoticed, which proves she has no motility. The vendor's threat to cut off her hand cues saviour Aladdin, moved to rescue the princess by her good looks, hence reducing her to her body. He concocts a condescending lie about Jasmine being mentally ill and therefore erratic, thus reproducing the cultural narrative that associates women with hysteria (cf. Vorona Cote 2020). That Jasmine's rescuer is male is no coincidence. Indeed, a pivotal side effect of her captivity is that it makes her dependent on men, who do have motility. Even a low-status man such as Aladdin is more calibrated to the world than she as a high-ranking woman is.

---

[4] "Motility" is a scientific term for "the ability of plants, organisms, and very small forms of of [sic] life to be able to move by themselves" (Cambridge Online Dictionary).

Gendered Orientations

Thus this scene demonstrates that orientations in *Aladdin* are highly gendered, giving men more freedom. Also, as it corroborates the sultan's preoccupation with the idea that Jasmine needs to be 'taken care of,' it shows that women's dependence on men is a self-fulfilling prophecy, concomitant to their curtailment. Furthermore, whereas female gender binds Jasmine to the patriarchal family line and hence physically restricts her, for a male character, regarding orientations, the sky is the limit. The "riffraff" (Clements/Musker 1992, 00:07:54) Aladdin ends up the sultan's successor. As Kraidy notes, the narrative thus establishes "a movement of 'upward social mobility'" as his main storyline (1998, 49). Aladdin's association with the princess propels him uphill. This proves a point of Ahmed's, that "the relationship between mobility and privilege involves […] movement 'upward[:]' […] in lining up the body also moves up" (2006, 137). Alignment with the royal family allows Aladdin to climb the social ladder.

From their meet cute onward, Aladdin frequently takes the lead and makes Jasmine familiar with the world, most conspicuously in the well-known song *A Whole New World*. From a feminist perspective, the ballad epitomises Aladdin's role as superior guide (cf. Kraidy 1998, 53), predicated as it is on his familiarity with the public and Jasmine's restriction to the private. The opening line, "I can show you the world" (Clements/Musker 1992, 00:58:11), implies that a woman, by herself, cannot see the world, for want of access to it. As an effect of her entailment, she needs a motile man's guidance to gain admittance. The phrases, "I can open your eyes" (ibid., 00:58:26) and "don't you dare close your eyes" (ibid., 00:59:31), suggest that a woman, by herself, is blind to the world. Only by virtue of male motility can she access "a whole *new* world, a new *fantastic* point of view" (ibid., 00:58:42–47; emphasis added). The adjectives suggest that the male perspective is alien to the woman and, furthermore, splendid. These lyrics cast the woman as subordinate to and dependent on the man and glorify his support to escape confinement. In short, they corroborate the association of the masculine with ease in the world, and are thus exceedingly androcentric—and even andronormative.

Falling in love with Aladdin threatens the family line, however, as he is not of royal birth. Ahmed conceives of an orientation as an inheritance, passed down from generation to generation. One is born into a family line and automatically expected to perpetuate it, and, therefore "*required* to 'tend toward' some objects and not others as a condition of familial […] love" (2006, 85; emphasis in original). The family line might demand a particular kind of love interest. From the sultan, Jasmine inherits royal status. With that comes the obligation to marry a prince and not a "street rat" (Clements/Musker 1992, 00:07:54) like Aladdin. The obstacle of Aladdin's lowly birth is erased by his acquisition of the magic lamp and transformation into a prince, which is predicated on his being a "diamond in the rough" (ibid., 00:06:43). His morally sound nature cancels out the risk of his modest stature damaging the reputable family line.

The narrative suggests that because romantic love prevails, it means that Jasmine is granted a legal exception,[5] but we could also read this as a way of tricking her into being 'in line.' Ultimately the sultan gets what he wants: Jasmine walks 'the straight line,' which secures the family line. His permission is given as a last resort, as Jasmine had rejected every suitor and escaped. Ironically, meeting Aladdin returned her to the palace, after his arrest. So the sultan indulging Jasmine's craving for romantic love, initially a sign of revolt, ultimately brings her back in line.

To conclude, in the world of *Aladdin* (1992) orientations are heavily gendered. In the depicted society, ruled by and catering to men, women are orientated as unfit to encounter the world alone and requiring male guidance. Their prescribed orientation is to guarantee through marriage the continuation of men's power. In the next sections, I analyse how the remake treats the scenes and circumstances I identified as supporting the narrative's androcentric worldview. I will highlight similarities and differences between the two iterations, to show that, regarding female agency, voice and motility, the remake paints an ambivalent picture. Indeed, my analysis yields arguments for and against a feminist reading, which I will list below.

Aladdin (2019): An Ambivalent Tale

Nuances in Female Voice and Motility

The live-action film *Aladdin* introduces Jasmine in the city streets instead of behind palace walls. While the animated film frames her excursion as a desperate runaway's, the adaptation begins *in medias res*, without unveiling its reason. As it fails to portray Jasmine primarily as governed by laws dictating her relation to men, from a feminist standpoint, this scene does something entirely different from the pre-text. However, it is complicated by Jasmine and Aladdin's meet cute. Invoking the apple scene, Jasmine offers two poor children a loaf of bread, is accused of stealing and sees Aladdin appearing unexpectedly to save her. This scene reproduces the image of the economically immature, 'out-of-place' woman requiring male guidance, even if it omits the negative stereotyping of mental illness and substitutes the harem with a classroom.

Although she does not state this explicitly, Jasmine, posing as a handmaid and wishing to remain incognito, seems hesitant to disclose her identity. Although we first meet her outside, Jasmine is not free. This becomes apparent when Aladdin urges Jasmine to "tell the princess to get out more," and she replies, "They won't

---

[5]This interpretation ties in with what happens, according to Ahmed, when "we reach what is not expected[:] When bodies take up spaces that they were not intended to inhabit, something other than the reproduction of the facts of the matter happens" (2006, 62).

Walking the Line 75

let her. Ever since my… The queen was killed, the sultan's been afraid. So, she's kept locked away" (Ritchie 2019, 00:14:59–00:15:19). Invoking her father's apprehension about her safety perhaps garners understanding from the audience for her confinement. Although the sultan apologises for it, ultimately he still treats her like a possession, his to protect, not an autonomous person.

The suitors' courtship perpetuates this harmful image.[6] As Aladdin, posing as prince Ali, presents gifts to impress the royals, Jasmine asks, "what do you hope to buy"? Aladdin exclaims, "You!", to which the princess sharply retorts, "Are you suggesting I am for sale?" (ibid., 01:01:13–01:01:34). The phrase recalls the animated film's feminist statement, "I am not a prize to be won" (Clements/Musker 1992, 00:53:51). Similarly, Jasmine objects to prince Anders' reducing her to her looks. Clearly, she does not appreciate being objectified. These examples suggest Jasmine is attuned to feminist issues.

That feminist attitude certainly is no luxury, as men continue to subordinate her. In the animated film the failed courtships set the stage for the Sultan, Aladdin and Jafar talking over Jasmine's head. The remake, by contrast, grants Jasmine a voice, if a marginal one, as the unsuccessful courtships prompt a conversation with—and not just about—her. This discussion is pivotal for the main plotlines. Therefore I quote it almost in full:

Sultan:	My dear, I'm not getting any younger. We must find you a husband […].
Jasmine:	What foreign prince could love our people like I do? I could lead, if only…
Sultan:	My dear, you cannot be a sultan because it has never been done in the thousand-year history of our kingdom.
Jasmine:	I have been preparing for this my whole life. I have read…
Jafar:	Books? But you cannot read experience. […]
Sultan:	Jafar is right. One day you will understand.
Jafar:	Life will be kinder to you, Princess, once you accept these traditions and understand it's better for you to be seen and not heard. (Ritchie 2019, 00:21:52–00:23:10)

This conversation is important for several reasons. Firstly, it portrays Jasmine as a well-read woman exhibiting political ambition, an orientation inconceivable in the animated film. Secondly, instead of a law delineating Jasmine's destiny,[7] the sultan and vizier invoke as incentives the former's old age, and 'history' and 'traditions'—in other words, cultural narratives. Although ostensibly less coercive than citing a law, the implication that a marriage would preserve the kingdom's future nonetheless works to inscribe Jasmine into the family line. I should note that it

---

[6]This image also persists when Jafar punishes the sultan by "tak[ing] what you love most," by "marry[ing] your daughter" (Ritchie 2019, 01:43:41–01:43:45).

[7]At the end of the movie, Genie does refer to a law that requires the princess to marry a prince (Ritchie 2019, 01:54:30). Other than that, the term "law" is not used.

is not only men who try to keep her in line. Her handmaid, Dalia, participates in the men's efforts. She represents traditional womanhood, playing a subservient role, as handmaid, wife and mother, and as one who follows the conventional orientation of settling down with a husband and children. Most importantly, she is critical of Jasmine's political aspirations, questioning why she wants to become sultan. Jasmine feels she "was born to do more than marry some useless prince," an explanation Dalia undermines with mockery: "A handsome prince wants to marry you. Oh, when will life get easier?" (ibid., 00:26:19–00:26:22). This shows that women can uphold the patriarchy, too (just as men can dismantle it).

Finally, the exchange lays bare a central communicative dynamic in the story: the conflict between voice and silence. On the one hand, it displays a conversational shift, as Jasmine is no longer merely the object of the discussion but also a participant. On the other hand, although the men grant her voice some space, it is still only marginal since they dismiss her arguments. Moreover, Jafar emphasises that women ought 'to be seen and not heard,' a precept that effectively curtails their voice (cf. Beard 2018; Vorona Cote 2020). Whereas in the animation, the theme of female voice is evoked solely in Jafar's fleeting remark about speechlessness, the remake engages with the issue resolutely and repeatedly. Jafar's imperative is worded more elaborately and invokes the cultural narrative, *tais-toi et sois belle*,[8] coupling femininity with silence and beauty (cf. Vorona Cote 2020). Additionally, when Jasmine objects to the vizier's war plans, he shuts her down, saying, "I think we've heard enough from you, Princess. It's time you start doing what you should have done all along. Stay silent" (Ritchie 2019, 01:35:46–01:35:52). His response again thematises the inhibition of female voice.

Male Silencing and Female Voice

In both instances Jafar's silencing triggers the two-part song *Speechless*. As mentioned, the positive reception of the film's feminist calibre partly rests on this ballad. The lyrics voice how Jasmine condemns the restriction of her voice, with 'speechless' directly referencing Jafar's original misogynist comment. The first part Jasmine performs in the film's exposition. This position in the plot foregrounds her lack of voice. Ironically, Jasmine vents alone, without anyone around to hear her speak up. Thus, the song functions as a soliloquy, which undermines its impact. The ballad's second, more elaborate iteration occurs right before the narrative's climax, again highlighting the issue. Jasmine criticises cultural narratives, "written in stone // [...] centuries-old and unbending," that tell her, "stay in your place // better seen and not heard" (ibid., 01:36:41–01:36:51). Indicating, "now

---

[8] "Shut up and be beautiful." Significantly, the feminine inflection "belle" of the adjective "beau" points to the gendered nature of the expression, mainly directed at women.

that story is ending," she resolves to not give up her voice: "I won't be silenced // You can't keep me quiet // […] I won't live unspoken" (ibid., 01:36:52–01:37:39). In its entirety, *Speechless* explicitly engages with what Beard designates as the gendered politics of voice, bracketing women with silence (2018). The lyrics also invoke the essence of a feminist attitude Fetterley pinpoints: "the discovery/recovery of a voice, […] capable of cancelling out those other voices, […] which spoke about us and to us and at us but never for us" (1978, xxiii-xxiv). This time, the song is framed as a dream sequence, which again leaves Jasmine without an audience. The framing undercuts the effect of her resolve to not be speechless and virtually turns it into empty speech.

Significantly, the remake does not show Jasmine needing to rely on her body to seduce Jafar. Rather, her voice is instrumental in his defeat. Given the narrative weight of the theme of marriage, it is meaningful that Jasmine ultimately deceives Jafar during their wedding ceremony by strategically deploying her voice: she stretches the phrase "I do" to deflect attention from her hands stealing the lamp from Jafar's belt (Ritchie 2019, 01:45:50). Right then, Aladdin shows up on the magic carpet as a *deus ex machina* to help her escape—yet another last-minute rescue, closing the circle begun in the opening scene at the market. Although Aladdin provides the carpet, a means of escape that underlines his motility, Jasmine's intellect and voice were what initially created the opening to steal the lamp. Thus the emphasis on the male saviour's role is slightly weakened. That stress is restored in the movie's climax, however, when Aladdin tricks Jafar into trapping himself inside the lamp and frees Agrabah of him, while Jasmine is paralysed. Ultimately, the main female character cannot solve the predicament unaided. She merely provides assistance to the male protagonist's rescue efforts.

Female Substance versus Andronormativity

In addition to the substantial plot twists, the shift from beauty to brains is noticeable in minor details throughout the film. Unlike in the animation, Aladdin is not just impressed with Jasmine's looks, but also with her intelligence. He likes her because "[s]he is smart, and kind, and so beautiful" (ibid., 00:51:09). Furthermore, prince Ali's opulent arrival disturbs Jasmine while she is reading. When Aladdin breaks into the palace, he again finds her studying, a map this time. Handmaid Dalia offers as advice, "the way to her heart is through her mind" (ibid., 01:10:56). Taken together, the multiple hints of Jasmine's intelligence characterise her as somewhat of a scholar. She is shown having a "room of her own" (Ahmed 2006, 61), to put it in Virginia Woolf's famous words. This makes Jasmine appear intellectual and therefore potentially a "threat to the patriarchal system" (Fetterley 1978, 143).

Importantly, maps point to Jasmine's knowledge as well as her confinement. She offers, "Maps are how I see the world" (Ritchie 2019, 01:14:01), implying they are her main means to gather information about the outside world that she is not allowed to explore. Aladdin naively replies, "I thought a princess could go anywhere" (ibid., 01:14:04), which Jasmine contradicts. Aladdin then suggests, "you should see these places" (ibid., 01:14:40), which cues *A Whole New World*. The remake maintains the original song verbatim, thereby leaving the ballad's androcentric worldview intact.

The adaptation's dénouement diverges considerably from its source's. Granted, the finale likewise sees Jasmine marrying Aladdin and romantic love prevailing. However, instead of marriage making her the wife of the next sultan, she becomes sultan herself first, which gives her the power to alter the law so she can take Aladdin as her spouse. So, traditions are reformed, a woman obtains power, makes a man her dependant, and the patriarchal family line is broken. However, the changes' implications are ambivalent. Jasmine's first political act is to use her newly-acquired power to associate herself with a man. Hence, the conclusion slightly undermines her autonomy, as it frames her own goals as partly determined by a man. Moreover, she does not seem to make Aladdin her equal in a feminist spirit. By adopting a man's position and making a man her extension, she reproduces the patriarchy's uneven power relations, simply reversing the pattern without abolishing its principles. Finally, Jasmine's father makes her sultan to reward her conduct. He explains, "You have shown me courage and strength. You are the future of Agrabah" (ibid., 01:57:26–01:57:31). Although the result is that Jasmine acquires power, from a gender perspective, the rationale is rather fraught, as power is granted because she exhibits the qualities of vigour and valour typically associated with the ideal man, and valorised through that association. She gains her father's approval by abandoning the image of the "ideal woman" (Fetterley 1978, 143) as passive and non-aggressive. Thus, as male properties are valued more positively than female, andronormativity predominates, although the outcome superficially seems feminist.

Conclusion: From Antifeminist to 'Postfeminist'

As my analysis demonstrates, androcentrism in the animated *Aladdin* (1992) manifests in Jasmine's orientation, which entails captivity and a concomitant lack of bodily agency. Because she is a woman, unfit to rule herself, her voice is curtailed and she is reduced to her body, which serves to secure a marriage to ensure the continuation of her family's reign. Precisely by limiting the feminine faculties of voice and physical agency, the film epitomises the most prominent issues within feminist criticism. Significantly, Jasmine attempts to revolt but is eventually kept in line through her exceptional marriage to a common yet morally sound man whose background does not damage the family line. What is more, the sultan's intervention in the law to enable this exception participates in a pattern that Artz discerns in Disney films, where egotistical sovereigns do not care about their population's fate, which *Aladdin* exemplifies (2004, 116). The tendency entails that "[r]ulers are also responsive to the individual needs of their duly anointed successors, frequently revising rules that do not overturn the status quo" (ibid., 133). As a rule, in Disney films, "[i]ndividual happiness for elites never requires social change" (ibid., 135). This is exactly the case in *Aladdin*, as Jasmine is granted an exception, but the law generally remains unaltered. While Jasmine's fate is reformed, the plight of civilian women is not. It does not even come up, so there is no evidence of female cross-class solidarity. Thus, the plot resolution defies the very definition of feminism underlying this analysis. Overall, then, on a scale ranging from antifeminist to feminist, the animated *Aladdin* tends strongly toward the former.

The remake's position on that continuum is perhaps more moderate. Throughout, the film exhibits concern with feminist questions, a breach in the patriarchal line and a more developed female protagonist. That said, it also displays some particularly androcentric and even andronormative dynamics, such as Jasmine's confinement and the prominence of the male guide and saviour. Finally, although Jasmine shows a clear interest in the people, whether she will use her political power to ameliorate women's situation in her kingdom remains undecided. I can only speculate that it is perhaps slightly more likely than in the animation, as she demonstrates sensitivity to feminist issues. Generally, I deem the adaptation's engagement with feminist topics a matter of "would-be" feminism, as it "operate[s] in an 'ambivalent space' of opportunity, tension, and contradiction" (Tienari/Taylor 2019; cited in Hollowell 2020, 3). The narrative supplies ample opportunities to begin to challenge patriarchal circumstances, but ultimately does not relinquish the male-centred ideology. I am by no means implying the remake ought to rectify the antifeminism of its source. Rather, I am critical of the way the movie remedies surface issues, thereby appearing feminist, but neglects to address the fundamental inequity underlying them.

In conclusion, with Adam Hollowell, I would label the live-action *Aladdin* 'postfeminist' rather than feminist. As Hollowell explains,

> To call a Disney film postfeminist […] is to suggest that it advances women's empowerment at the level of the individual through a single female character's transformation of the self, but avoids feminism as an ethical imperative for structural change and collective liberation from a misogynist social order (2020, 3).

A 'postfeminist' ideology builds on a form of "liberation [that] operates only at the level of the empowered individual self," not of the entire population (ibid., 3). As far as I can judge, that applies to *Aladdin* (2019), which makes the label 'postfeminist' appropriate. As Hollowell indicates, "The 'post' in postfeminism marks the belief that feminism is no longer necessary" (ibid., 3). This is what the remake implies as well, whereas my analysis reveals that it is indeed very much needed still.

References

Primary Sources

Clements, Ron/John Musker, dir. (1992): *Aladdin*. The Walt Disney Company. Streaming
Ritchie, Guy, dir. (2019): *Aladdin*. The Walt Disney Company. Streaming
The Walt Disney Company (2021): Advisory. https://storiesmatter.thewaltdisneycompany.com.
　Accessed: 18. June 2021

Secondary Sources

Ahmed, Sara (2006): *Queer Phenomenology. Orientations, Objects, Others*. Durham [et al.]

Artz, Lee (2004): The Righteousness of Self-Centred Royals: The World according to Disney Animation. In: *Critical Arts*, Vol. 18, No. 1, 116–146

Beard, Mary (2018): *Vrouwen & Macht. Een Manifest*. Amsterdam

De Beauvoir, Simone (2011). *The Second Sex*. London

Fetterley, Judith (1978): *The Resisting Reader. A Feminist Approach to American Fiction*. Bloomington [et al.]

Hollowell, Adam (2020): Chief Tui Makes Way: Moana, Misogyny, and the Possibility of a Profeminist Ethic. In: *Men and Masculinities*, Vol. XX, No. X, 1–20

Kraidy, Marwan M. (1998): Intertextual Manoeuvers around the Subaltern. *Aladdin* as a Postmodern Text. In: *Postmodernism in the Cinema*, ed. Cristina Degli-Esposti, New York [et al.], 45–59

Lacroix, Celeste (2004): Images of Animated Others: The Orientalization of Disney's Cartoon Heroines from *The Little Mermaid* to *The Hunchback of Notre Dame*. In: *Popular Communication*, Vol. 2, No. 4, 213–229

Madrigal Torres, Berta Ermila/Rosalba Madrigal Torres (2015): Misogynist Phrases which Minimize the Woman and Create Stereotypes: A Proposal to Remove Them. In: *Weber Educational Research & Instructional Studies*, Vol. 1, No. 7, 350–354

Mercadal, Dennis (1990): *A Dictionary of Artificial Intelligence*. New York NY

Metacritic (2021): Aladdin. https://www.metacritic.com/movie/aladdin-2019/critic-reviews. Accessed: 24. June 2021

Nikolajeva, Maria (2010): *Power, Voice and Subjectivity in Literature for Young Readers*. New York [et al.]

Radulovic, Petrana (2019): Disney Finally Gets the 'Updated' Princesses Right with Aladdin's Jasmine. https://www.polygon.com/2019/5/25/18637301/aladdin-live-action-jasmine-disney-princess-character. Accessed: 17. June 2021

Rich, Adrienne (1993): Compulsory Heterosexuality and Lesbian Existence. In: *The Lesbian and Gay Studies Reader*, eds. Henry Abelove/Michèle Aina Barale/David M. Halperin. New York

Romano, Aja (2019): The Fraught Cultural Politics of Disney's New Aladdin Remake. https://www.vox.com/2019/5/24/18635896/disney-live-action-aladdin-controversy-history. Accessed: 17. June 2021

Sanders, Julie (2006): *Adaptation and Appropriation*. Abingdon [et al.]

Schank, Roger/Robert Abelson (1975): Scripts, Plans, and Knowledge. In: *Proceedings of the Fourth International Joint Conference on Artificial Intelligence*, 151–157. San Francisco CA

Scott, A.O. (2019): 'Aladdin' Review: This Is Not What You Wished For. https://www.nytimes.com/2019/05/22/movies/aladdin-review.html. Accessed: 21. June 2021

Tienari, Janne/Scott Taylor (2019): Feminism and Men: Ambivalent Space for Acting Up. In: *Organization*, Vol. 26, No. 6, 948–960

Trites, Roberta Seelinger (2014): *Literary Conceptualizations of Growth. Metaphors and Cognition in Adolescent Literature*. Amsterdam [et al.]

Trites, Roberta Seelinger (2018): *Twenty-First-Century Feminisms in Children's and Adolescent Literature*. Jackson, MS

Vorona Cote, Rachel (2020): *Too Much. How Victorian Constraints Still Bind Women Today*. New York [et al.]

Screening Blackness

Controversial Visibilities of Race in Disney's Fairy Tale Adaptations

Claudia Sackl

Abstract As far as its fairy tale adaptations are concerned, Disney has a fraught relationship to race. While its animated features have repeatedly been criticised for centring on *white* characters and perpetuating racist (and sexist) stereotypes, the studio has recently made efforts to reassure its audience of its inclusive and progressive philosophy by incorporating characters of colour in its princess line. In this article, I discuss Disney's representational strategies in relation to Black fairy tale characters on screen and the ways in which fan reactions on digital and social media have shaped Disney's storytelling practices. By investigating the historically specific, mediatised sociopolitical processes and conditions that allow for or hinder the construction of recognisable Black bodies and identities, I will illustrate that the emergent visibilities of race result from a multi-layered convergence between reality and imagination caught between online participatory culture and corporate fan service, fan activism and conservative backlash.

Drawing on Jack Zipes's notion that fairy tales "are informed by a human disposition to action" (2012, 2), in *Fairy Tales Transformed?* Cristina Bacchilega has argued that "[f]airy tales interpellate us as consumers and producers of transformation" (2013, 3). When considering media adaptations of fairy tales such as those of the Walt Disney Company in the context of contemporary convergence culture, where traditional distinctions between media producers and consumers have become increasingly blurred, this idea becomes even more multi-layered. As a "transnational media conglomerate rooted in American capitalist culture" (Anjrbag 2019, 152) that has produced more than forty animated and live-action movies inspired by fairy tales, all of which were drawn from a multiplicity of cultures and subsumed into its multimedia universe, Disney has a fraught relationship to race. While its animated features have repeatedly been criticised for centring

---

C. Sackl (✉)
STUBE – Studien-Beratungsstelle für Kinder- und Jugendliteratur, Wien, Austria
e-mail: c.sackl@stube.at

© The Author(s), under exclusive license to Springer-Verlag GmbH, DE, part of Springer Nature 2022
U. Dettmar and I. Tomkowiak (eds.), *On Disney*, Studien zu Kinder- und Jugendliteratur und -medien 9, https://doi.org/10.1007/978-3-662-64625-0_6

on *white*[1] characters and perpetuating racist (and sexist) stereotypes,[2] the studio has recently made efforts to reassure its viewers of its progressive, inclusive philosophy by incorporating characters of colour such as Tiana in *The Princess and the Frog* (Clements/Musker 2009) or Ariel in the upcoming live-action remake *The Little Mermaid* (directed by Rob Marshall) within its line of princesses. Though many have applauded these gestures towards diversification, others have criticised the company for "cash[ing] in on its racist past" (Breaux 2010, 399) while reinscribing racial hierarchies and distorting the sociopolitical historical context of the movies. More recently, the 2019 announcement that the African American actress and R&B singer Halle Bailey had been selected to play the live-action role of Ariel prompted digital fan protests decrying Disney's casting decision. One year earlier, Disney had already been harshly criticised by viewers on social media, albeit for very different reasons. After fans accused the production company of whitewashing princess Tiana in the trailer[3] for *Ralph Breaks the Internet* (2018), Disney actually redrew the character for the final film version.

In this article, I will discuss Disney's representational strategies in relation to Black fairy tale characters on screen and the ways in which fan reactions on digital and social media have shaped Disney's storytelling practices. I will illustrate that the emergent visibilities of race result from a complex, multi-layered convergence between reality and imagination caught between online participatory culture and corporate fan service, fan activism and conservative backlash.

Conditions of Recognition: Minority Subjects between Power and Visibility

In the course of the last few decades, visibility has developed into a significant political category within oppositional feminist, queer and antiracist rhetoric. Sociologists, grassroots initiatives, artists and producers of popular culture, emphasising the transformative potential of visibility for racialised minorities, have made arguments for inclusive practices of representation that provide figures of identification for people of all colour. As Linda Martín Alcoff notes, "[i]n our excessively materialist society, only what is visible can generally achieve

---

[1] In this article, the term "white" is italicised in order to mark its hegemonic role within racial hierarchies. In contrast, the term "Black" is capitalised in order to stress both its cultural constructedness and its use as a political identity.

[2] This criticism is by no means limited to Disney's fairy tale adaptations, but is also directed at the highly troubling images of Blackness purveyed in its animated movies such as *Dumbo* (1941) and *Song of the South* (1946). Disney has never released *Song of the South* on DVD in order to distance itself from the film's blatantly racist rhetoric.

[3] Although Disney removed the offensive trailer from the Internet, screenshots of the early images were posted on social media and featured in the news media coverage of the controversy, for example in Kai 2018b.

Screening Blackness 83

the status of accepted truth" (2006, 6), while Andrea Brighenti underlines that any "exercise of power is always an exercise in activating selective in/visibilities" (2007, 339). Indeed, as a category located at the intersection of politics and aesthetics (cf. ibid., 324), visibility is closely connected to empowerment and recognition, which Nancy Fraser (2006) and Judith Butler (2004, 2009) have described as a social practice that confirms and produces identity, i.e. makes subjects intelligible. Consumed by millions of people all over the world, cultural media productions, including those of the Disney studios, constitute important sites for negotiating and producing such recognition.

However, while public visibility of minority subject(ivitie)s is constitutive for empowerment and (socio)political recognition, Johanna Schaffer and scholars following her have stressed that the connectivities of power and visibility are more complex than the assertion, 'more visibility grants (socio)political recognition and, thus, more rights, resources and political power,' would suggest. Such simplified causal narratives disregard the conditions of representation, i.e. who is producing visibilities of whom, in what context and by what means, forms or structures (cf. Schaffer 2008, 12). If we conceive of representation, as Stuart Hall has suggested, as an "active work of selecting and presenting, of structuring and shaping: not merely the transmitting of an already-existing meaning, but the more active labour of making things mean" (1982, 64), it becomes clear that, especially for minority subjects, visibility can go both (and many more) ways, as it is also closely connected to spectatorship, disempowerment and a racialised as well as a racialising gaze—in other words, to processes of stereotyping, essentialism, exoticism and racism. As Martín Alcoff puts it, "[v]isibility is both the means of segregating and oppressing human groups and the means of manifesting unity and resistance" (2006, 7).

Because of these intricate interrelations of visibility and power, Schaffer calls for the category of visibility to be qualified in a way that takes into account the conditions in which images are made visible and intelligible, which are deeply permeated by norms (cf. 2008, 19). Along similar lines, Butler has discussed how dominant frames of recognisability are interrelated with different degrees of visibility, arguing that "[c]ertain faces must be admitted into public view, must be seen and heard for some keener sense of the value of life, all life, to take hold" (2004, xviii). While referring to affirmative forms of representation as 'recognizing visibility'[4] (cf. Schaffer 2008, 19), Schaffer also acknowledges the constraints placed on visibility. She introduces the concept of 'contingent recognition'[5] (cf. ibid., 21) in order to describe forms of recognition that are granted only under certain conditions via specific types of visibilities, while also producing specific forms of invisibilities. According to Schaffer, this form of recognition is

---

[4] In the German original, Schaffer refers to this concept as "anerkennende Sichtbarkeit" (2008, 19).

[5] Or, in Schaffer's words, "Anerkennung im Konditional " (2008, 21).

contingent either because its production of 'a sense of sovereignty' serves entirely different subject positions, or because the sense of sovereignty of the majority subject positions is not questioned in the first place (cf. ibid.).

As one of the world's leading producers and distributors of children's and family media, the Walt Disney Company plays an important role in shaping the public gaze via its onscreen representations and related franchises. Henry Giroux goes even so far as to argue that the impact of animated features such as Disney's has "exceeded the boundaries of entertainment," transforming them into "the new 'teaching machines'" (1996, 90). Additionally, the specific communicative architecture of social media platforms where fans discuss viewing experiences and express opinions facilitates the performative production of public spaces that are not necessarily determined by top-down structures. Allowing users to rapidly react to recent events and topics, these platforms can create what Axel Bruns and Jean Burgess have described as 'ad hoc publics' (cf. 2015, 14), which, in turn, can reach wider 'post hoc' public spheres via news media and the like. In the following, I will discuss how the representational and communicative practices involved in the production (and denial) of visibility and recognition come into effect in and in response to Disney's portrayal of Black fairy tale characters in *The Princess and the Frog* (2009), *Ralph Breaks the Internet* (2018), and *The Little Mermaid* (upcoming). Addressing the emergent power relations, available discursive structures and the representational strategies employed by Disney, I will investigate the historically specific, mediatised sociopolitical processes and conditions that allow for or hinder the construction of recognisable Black bodies and identities.

(Post-)Racial Stereotypes in *The Princess and the Frog*: Blackness between Inclusion and Erasure

With the creation of their first Black protagonist in a feature-length fairy tale adaptation, the Disney studios have not only catered to increasing calls to diversify their media productions, but also positioned themselves favourably so as to expand their marketability to new audiences. The movie's release in 2009 coincided with the first year of Barack Obama's first term as US President, marking what Sarah Turner has described as "a complex moment in a culture steeped in political correctness and an adherence to the politics of colorblindness" (2013, 83). The complex politics involved are evident both in Disney's treatment of race and in viewers' responses to the film. Most notably, the complexities of the movie's racial politics are illustrated by its paradoxical conditions of Black visibility. As the first Black Disney princess, Tiana and her Black body become "audaciously visible" (Moffitt 2019, 477), while being rendered "simultaneously invisible" (ibid.) by the fact that she appears as a green frog during most of the film as well as by the

Screening Blackness 85

movie's message of colour-blindness.[6] To put it in Turner's words, "[a]udiences must simultaneously 'see' her blackness and also overlook it in favor of her character and her desire to access the American dream" (2013, 84).

Set during the 1920s jazz age in New Orleans, *The Princess and the Frog* reimagines the Grimm brothers' fairy tale *The Frog Prince* by placing the transformative kiss at the beginning of the story, and by creating a narrative where the characters must search for a way to reverse their metamorphosis in order to fulfil their dreams. The disinherited foreign prince Naveen strives to restore his wealth by marrying a rich girl (Tiana's *white* friend Charlotte La Bouff), while Tiana wants to buy her own restaurant. The subsequent depiction of Tiana's transformation from rags to riches constitutes a colour-blind, historically distorted realisation of the American Dream. Conveniently disregarding the systemic oppression and racial tensions that African Americans faced in the early twenty-first century, when Jim Crow laws[7] were at their highest point, the colourful cityscape of New Orleans is imagined as a post-racial society. While obscuring the segregationist histories of the American South, the inspiring children's and family feature also disregards the socioeconomic disparities between Tiana's working-class family and her wealthy *white* friend Charlotte, against whom Tiana as a Black woman and as a modern Disney princess is defined (cf. Moffitt 2019, 481–484).

Unlike the classic (*white*) Disney princesses, wishing is not enough for Tiana, who is staged as a romanticised embodiment of the rhetoric of hard work and individual perseverance. The characters' dialogues and songs repeatedly reaffirm the dominant ideology of equal opportunities for upward social mobility in post-racial, colour-blind America. For example, in the lyrics of *Dig a Little Deeper*, the (both literally and metaphorically) blind (fairy god)motherly Voodoo witch Mama Odie erases class and race distinctions: "Don't matter what you look like. Don't matter what you wear. [...] Don't matter where you come from. Don't even matter what you are" (Clements/Musker 2009, 01:03:04–01:03:18). While most other female Disney characters have to work as a form of mistreatment or punishment (cf. England et al. 2011, 564), and *white* princesses are relieved of their burdens of labour after their happy endings (cf. Condis 2015, 26), Tiana is the only Disney princess who holds an occupation as a paid employee both before and beyond the filmic narrative. Moreover, it is her and her family's labour that render Charlotte's princess fantasies possible (cf. ibid., 39). Originally drafted as a maid called Maddy, which evoked images of Black women from the American South working in subservient roles (cf. Moffitt 2019, 479), Tiana was renamed and

---

[6] Described as the "central ideology of the post civil rights era" (Bonilla-Silva 2010, 2–3), discourses of colour-blindness disregard structural racial inequalities in favour of neoliberal individualism. Under the premise of 'not seeing race,' they aim to explain racial disparities through individual shortcomings, obscuring and thus perpetuating systemic racism and *white* privileges via the illusion of equal opportunities.

[7] From the late nineteenth century until 1965, the so-called Jim Crow laws served to enforce racial segregation in the South of the United States.

reconceptualised as a waitress after the studio received negative feedback from its cultural critics, including members of the NAACP (National Association for the Advancement of Colored People) and Oprah Winfrey, concerning this latent racism.

On a different level, the absence of discursive markers regarding Tiana's Black body and (feminine) beauty serves to further erase race from the narrative (cf. Turner 2013, 88–89). In contrast to her *white* friend Charlotte, whose extraordinary feminine beauty is repeatedly articulated, Tiana's physical attributes (as a human) largely remain unmentioned. As several scholars have suggested, within a feminist reading this could be interpreted as a progressive shift (cf. Moffitt 2019; Turner 2013); especially since the determined and independent Tiana is contrasted with the "buffoonish and superficial" (Moffitt 2019, 482) Charlotte, who is presented as a caricature of classic Disney Princesses. And indeed, to a certain extent, Tiana challenges the traditional damsel-in-distress motif by way of her unabated professional aspirations. However, from a postcolonial standpoint, the missing examination of Tiana's appearance as a Black woman suggests that in her social reality her racial(ised) identity and body are devoid of any noteworthy significance. Along similar lines, for Naveen, the poor brown-skinned prince from the fictional country of Maldonia, who remains "racial[ly] obfuscat[ed]" (Gehlawat 2010, 424) throughout the movie, race and cultural identity seem irrelevant. Unclear and ambiguous in origin, he carries an Indian name while employing a bizarre accent that blends Romance languages with different varieties of English.

The non-intimidating, colour-blind reading encouraged by the movie has been pointedly summarised by Sarah Turner: "Tiana didn't need affirmative action to succeed, just a good work ethic; such a portrayal of blackness appeals to all viewers—no one is alienated or threatened by Tiana or her gumbo restaurant" (2013, 86). Within the framework of visibility and recognition introduced above, it can be concluded that *The Princess and the Frog* produces an image of Blackness that only provides a contingent recognition of Black subjectivities as it leaves the dominant norms of *white* supremacy unchallenged. Despite Disney's efforts to "fix [their] past mistakes" (Condis 2015, 37), the racially hyper-sensitive, but all the more disturbing and contradictory "attempt to pass as an African American princess narrative" (Gehlawat 2010, 417) that invokes but simultaneously negates the milieu of 1920s New Orleans (ibid., 429) cements rather than destabilises familiar power dynamics. Albeit more modern in its setting, more progressive regarding its concept of femininity and more unconventional in terms of its narrative pattern, *The Princess and the Frog* remains restricted to a (rather uninventive) visualisation of race whose overt and covert stereotypes are infused with reassuring colour-blind politics. Investing in the innovativeness of including a Black leading character for the first time in a fairy tale adaptation, Disney thus managed to serve its corporate interests without risk of losing its majority viewers.

Indeed, it is hardly surprising that the colour-blind ideological underpinnings of the movie were embraced by an audience filled with the post-racial optimism that prevailed after the election of America's first Black president. Although studies have shown that merchandise featuring Tiana and Jasmine, the two princesses of colour included in the investigations, rank last in the list of the most popular Disney Princess merchandise, which is instead led by the *white* princesses Elsa, Cinderella and Snow White (cf. Friedman 2014; Dundes/Streiff 2016), *The Princess and the Frog*-related products were reported to be "flying off the shelves" (Frost 2009 [n.p.]) even weeks before the movie's release. The success of the film and its merchandise demonstrates not only that Disney's first Black princess was highly anticipated, but also that many fans who were buying into Princess Tiana (and who were familiar with Disney's storytelling formula[8]) were willing to set the bar for an 'inclusive' Disney animated feature rather low. It appears, however, that in the last years this has begun to change.

Fan Activism against *Ralph Breaks the Internet*: Mediating between Viewer and Corporate Interests

Today, the rhetoric of colour-blindness and post-racialism coexist and clash with a continually growing recognition of race as a "visible identity" (Martín Alcoff 2006, 102) and an "imagined concept" (Cole 1996, 449) that shapes social, economic and political realities. Increasingly, viewers of popular culture demand that representations of racial difference are not "emptied out and resignified as cultural commodities indicating mere 'lifestyles'" (Gray 2005, 142). What is more, Disney fans have indeed found effective ways to urge the studio to adjust how it "handle[s] cultural narratives in a collaborative way" (Anjrbag 2019, 173).

As part of the corporate marketing strategies that actively interpellate viewers as fans (cf. Busse/Gray 2011, 431), Disney released teaser material for the *Wreck-It Ralph*-sequel *Ralph Breaks the Internet* in August 2018, in which Tiana appears along with the other Disney princesses in a short sequence that features them as 'netizens' (virtual characters) of the website "Oh My Disney." A number of fans noticed that Tiana's physical features were significantly Europeanised when compared to her appearance in *The Princess and the Frog*. Making use of the digital networks available to them, fans circulated their protest on social media. Calling out the whitewashing of the only Black princess in the Disney franchise, users criticised how the newly released stills and trailer showed Tiana with lighter skin, slimmer lips, a smaller nose and less kinky, lighter hair:

---

[8] What Janet Wasko has termed the "Disney formula" (2001, 110–119) describes the narrative, aesthetic, and thematic components/patterns that form the core of the classic Disney aesthetic and determine viewer expectations.

> In today's edition of "you tried it," Disney decided to reinforce colorism[9] by lightening Princess Tiana's skin in #RalphBreaksTheInternet. Tiana was a dark skin Black woman in Princess and the Frog, now she has light skin and Eurocentric features. What happened to her wide nose? (@TheCaliNerd August 9, 2018).[10]

While several Twitter users juxtaposed Tiana's 2009 and 2018 appearances, others observed that she had looked more like her original self in a preview of *Ralph Breaks the Internet* that had been released some months earlier and had been taken from a different scene. Indeed, in the final film version Tiana seems to have sprouted two different versions of herself: There is the darker Tiana of the initial pre-released images, who is relegated to the background or the margins of the screen. Meanwhile, positioned at the centre of the image is a Tiana who, despite Disney's redrawing of her looks, has still lighter skin and hair than her first version.

Going back to August 2018, fan protests on social media were so widespread that the civil rights advocacy organisation Color of Change, which uses online resources to address issues of racial representation and political inequality, created a petition that called upon Disney to "Stop Whitewashing Their Black Characters," receiving widespread support. By engaging in different forms of digital activism by publicly voicing their criticism and supporting the online petition, Disney fans thus created spaces for resistance that allowed individual and collective counter-discourses to be put forward. As the 'ad hoc' protest by individual fans organised loosely on social media platforms was supported both by an experienced civil rights network that generated wider 'post hoc' public attention and by the subsequent media coverage that featured the online controversy, the outcry, it seems, became too loud for Disney to ignore. Consulting representatives from Color of Change and Anika Noni Rose, who voiced Tiana in *The Princess and the Frog* and *Ralph Breaks the Internet*, the studio finally redrew Tiana and removed the offensive trailer and images from online platforms. While Disney's willingness to put a substantial amount of additional time and money into 'correcting' the representation of Tiana's Black body was, at times, celebrated as a profound intervention into Disney's hegemonic representational strategies (as for example in a statement by Color of Change's Senior Campaign Director Brandi Collins-Dexter quoted in Kai 2018b [n.p.]), others have highlighted a troublesome aspect that remains. As Alicia Adejobi argues, the controversy "highlights the lack of diversity in the animation industry and perfectly shows exactly why it's important to have black animators, writers and producers in these influential positions" (2018 [n.p.]).

---

[9] Referring to a "form of skin tone bias" (Knight 2013, 546), colourism constructs a social hierarchy that attributes higher levels of acceptance to light skin than to dark skin. Frequently coupled with Eurocentric beauty ideals, it is related to both class discrimination and *white* supremacy (cf. ibid., 547).

[10] This tweet is no longer available on Twitter but has been quoted in several online articles covering the controversy (cf. Kai 2018a [n.p.]).

Recognising the need to diversify both productions and producers, Michelle Anya Anjrbag has analysed how the Disney corporation and many of its appropriations of other cultures continue to operate within neo-colonial and neo-capitalist superstructures (cf. 2019, 161). While, historically speaking, misrepresented groups had little to no means of "push[ing] back against the hegemonic dominance of the corporation in such a way that racist materials would never see the light of day" (ibid.), the fan protests surrounding *Ralph Breaks The Internet*—as well as other recent Disney franchises (cf. Anjrbag 2019)—have shown that viewers today can effectively write back to the centre of power that has produced (mis)representations of their identities and bodies for almost a century. In fact, recent fan strategies of "civic engagement" (Jenkins et al. 2020, 7) that make use of digital activism and social media have produced ad hoc public spaces of resistance, inducing Disney to create a "participatory culture" (Jenkins 2006, 3) in which fans contribute to the final media product via their critical feedback on pre-released production material, thus further blurring traditional distinctions and power relations between media producers and consumers.

Within fan studies, the creative potential of fans and fannish engagement, which has increasingly expanded into mainstream audiences in the last few years (cf. Busse/Gray 2011, 430), has been emphasised for a long time. While early adopters of (fannish) participatory culture were disproportionately *white* middle-class males (cf. Jenkins 2006, 23), today minority groups have established and subversively used their access to participatory cultures. Mobilising the democratic access and the expansive platforms that digital media provide to traditional, industry-driven, and casual fans, minority groups exert powerful influence on sociopolitical discussions and effectuate political and cultural change. As demonstrated by the struggles over Tiana's representation in *Ralph Breaks the Internet*, the media-specific architecture of digital networks not only facilitates "a range of peripheral participation that includes users' roles in *sharing* […] media content" (Florini 2019, 12, italics added), but also enables them to participate in *shaping* media content as it significantly increases the recognisable visibility of their objectives. It does so by making use of the following features: 1) The rapid pace of digital and social media allow for the circulation of protest activities in real time; 2) their technological and communicative structures encourage convergence, collaborative spaces and participatory practices; 3) their communicative strategies harbour the potential for reaching a wide public audience (cf. Bruns/Burgess 2015; Florini 2019).

At the same time, however, we should not let ourselves be lulled into the illusion that critical progressive fan voices will always be heard or that these grassroots achievements, laudable as they are, will inspire the Disney company to undergo large-scale structural changes. Henry Jenkins has already highlighted that not all the members of participatory cultures exert an equal amount of power (cf. 2006, 3). By catering to wide-ranging fan protests like those mentioned above, Disney also follows its corporate interests and what Jenkins has referred to as "affective economics" (ibid., 20). Capitalising on fan practices, the studio's decision to redraw Tiana mirrors their recognition of the "immense profitability of encouraging and exploiting fannish behaviors" (Busse/Gray 2011, 430). Taking fans and their concerns seriously ensures that they maintain (or develop) a positive attitude towards the Disney industry; Disney thus secures a "loyal audience base" (ibid.) while promoting an inclusive image of itself.

Nevertheless, with the decision to act on its viewers' criticism, Disney performatively revised the norms and conditions that, on the one hand, define who participates by means of what resources in the practices of producing representations (cf. Thomas/Grittmann 2017, 25), and that, on the other hand, enable individuals or groups not only to become visible, but also to be seen and heard (cf. ibid., 25–26). Thus interpellated as 'socially significant' (cf. ibid., 26), recognisable voices and "civic agent[s] capable of making change" (Jenkins/Peters-Lazaro/Shresthova 2020, 5), Black people (and their allies) achieved a small but well-earned and long overdue share of what Nancy Fraser refers to as 'participatory parity' (cf. 1996, 25), a framework in which members of society are equally enabled to participate in the structures of representation, recognition and redistribution.

White Fragility Facing *The Little Mermaid*: Viewer Reactions between Nostalgia and Normative *Whiteness*

In contrast to Jenkins and fan studies scholars who tend to view new media technologies under primarily optimistic parameters that highlight their empowering potential, digital media researchers like Sarah Florini have pointed out the constraints of the "emancipatory possibilities of digital and social media" (2019, 7). While the fan activism surrounding Tiana's Eurocentric makeover has shown that grassroots movements can not only "appropriat[e], remi[x], and redeplo[y]" popular culture (Jenkins et al. 2020, 3), but also directly influence its production processes and representation practices, the same platforms and mechanisms that enable the rapid and massive circulation of anti-racist discourses allow regressive, racist ideologies to be practised and disseminated to a global audience.

The fan protests surrounding Disney's casting of a Black Ariel constitutes a notable example of the duality of fan-driven social media campaigns. In July 2019 Disney announced that the African American actress and R&B singer Halle Bailey had been selected for the role of Ariel for the live-action remake of the 1989 animated classic *The Little Mermaid*. This prompted an outraged backlash on social media, where (mostly, but not exclusively[11] *white*) fans argued against what many of them considered a misguided intervention into their cherished childhood memories of their beloved *white* red-haired mermaid. These fans viewed the casting

---

[11] A considerable number of Hispanic users also expressed their racially motivated outrage over Disney's casting choice using the hashtag #NotMyAriel.

Screening Blackness 91

choice as a tokenistic move toward ethnic inclusivity that was motivated by an empty gesture of (commodified) political correctness. Reacting to the challenge to *white* centrality posed by a Black Ariel, the fans channelled their racial anxieties under the quickly trending hashtag #NotMyAriel, which created a global public discursive site that established a sense of community united by a common goal. Fuelled by a racialised nostalgic yearning for "a romanticized past" (DiAngelo 2018, 59) in which Ariel was/could only be *white*, *white* dominance could remain unquestioned and normative *whiteness* could remain invisible, Disney fans not only expressed their disapproval on social media but also created a (now deleted) Change.org petition to "Remove Halle Bailey as Ariel," gathering almost 11,000 signatures in only a few days (Guardians of Democracy 2019 [n.p.]).

As a manifestation of the recently resurgent anti-Black and *white* suprema-cist narratives that have re-entered mainstream discourses, the discursive strat-egies employed by the protesting fans are reminiscent of a condition that Robin DiAngelo has referred to as "white fragility" (2018, 2). "[T]riggered by dis-comfort and anxiety" while "born of superiority and entitlement" (ibid.), *white* fragility describes both a state of racial stress resulting from the disruption of internalised racial dynamics (cf. ibid., 103) and a set of response strategies that "work to reinstate white equilibrium" (ibid., 2) by restoring *white* racial comfort, centrality and dominance. Putting forward racist comments, memes and argu-ments, the users criticising Disney's casting decision exhibited a reluctance to accept a Black woman in a prominent role that until now had been coded, self-ev-idently, as *white*. Arguments used to support their criticism included the claim that they were simply advocating for staying true to the original (referring either to the Disney movie or to Andersen's fairy tale or to both) and the assertion that the casting choice constituted 'reverse racism' against red-heads (a supposition that conflates systemic racism with racial prejudice [cf. DiAngelo 2018, 21–22, 83]). Comments also included the crisis rhetoric of minority takeover and 'blackwash-ing,' as well as insulting remarks about Bailey's body, facial features and hair. For example, invoking the eponymous fairy tale by the Danish author Hans Christian Andersen as the 'origin' of Disney's 1989 version of *The Little Mermaid*, many users argued that, as a character inspired by Scandinavian mythology, Ariel surely was Danish, from which they concluded—disregarding the centuries-long history of Black presence in Europe—that she could not be Black. At the same time, many fans adhered to the colour-blind logics of post-racialism, conflating the act of addressing race with racism. Along similar lines and in defence of being accused of racist reasoning, a user wrote on Twitter:

> This is NOT RACIST! You are making it a race thing by PURPOSELY making sure Ariel is not White! THAT is a RACE thing!!! YOU made it about RACE, not us! Why go out of your way to make a Black woman feel included if she is ALREADY our EQUAL? #NotMyAriel (@GothianTh July 9, 2019).

Simultaneously employing the incompatible, but at the same time mutually consti-tuting ideological strategies of reverse racism and colour-blindness, which charac-terise *white* fragility rhetoric and work to restore the "retrotopia" (Bauman 2017, 5) of *white* supremacy, the above comment refuses to recognise the dominant status of *whiteness* as the (invisible) hegemonic standard even as it invokes "the power to choose when, how, and to what extent racism is addressed or challenged" (DiAngelo 2018, 109). As such, it is symptomatic of the (often heated) discussions, which erupted on social media in the summer of 2019 and extended well into 2020, between those who supported and those who opposed the #NotMyAriel movement.

Appropriating the racist hashtag, fans opposing the movement quickly redirected the ongoing conversations and critically intervened into the racist shitstorm, creating a platform where visibilities and relations of recognition were dialogically negotiated. Additionally, prominent voices like Jodi Benson, who voiced Ariel in the animated feature, or Auli'i Cravalho, who voiced Moana and starred as Ariel in the musical *The Little Mermaid Live!* (2019), spoke out against the racist backlash (cf. Abell 2019; Bailey 2019)—as did most of the media coverage, which frequently included lengthy pieces explaining why the racist logic of Bailey's opposers did not hold up (cf. Mahmood 2019; Trammell 2019). Joining these critical voices, Disney published an unequivocal statement that used humour, irony, history, science, fictionality, common sense and Bailey's talents to make a case for its casting choice:

> Yes. The original author of 'The Little Mermaid' was Danish. Ariel…is a mermaid. She lives in an underwater kingdom in international waters [...]. But for the sake of argument, let's say that Ariel, too, is Danish. Danish mermaids can be black because Danish *people* can be black. Ariel can sneak up to the surface at any time with her pals Scuttle and the *ahem* Jamaican crab Sebastian (sorry, Flounder!) and keep that bronze base tight. [...] (@FreeformTV July 7, 2019).

By releasing this statement and reaffirming their casting choice, the Disney corporation once again produced conditions of recognition that favoured those who argued for inclusive representations of race and dismissed colour-blind and *white* supremacist voices, thus ensuring that Halle Bailey would indeed become Disney's second Black princess.

Cultures of Participation—and Transformation?

As Stuart Hall has argued, popular culture constitutes "a battlefield where no once-for-all victories are obtained but where there are always strategic positions to be won and lost" (1981, 513). And indeed, a great deal is at stake in the struggle over representation and the efforts to make the systemic structures of race and (anti-Black) racism visible and recognisable. This is especially true in the contemporary context of resurgent *white* supremacist and prevailing colour-blind neoliberal discourses in the US and beyond, where (post-)racial stereotypes, colourism and whitewashing have determined people's social lives and cultural productions for centuries. Disney's children's and family entertainment media, which are consumed and negotiated all across the world, constitute one of the manifold terrains of these endeavours.

In the case of the fan protests surrounding the Disney princesses Tiana and Ariel, the collective and collectivising powers of fan cultures, social media and digital or hashtag activism are closely entangled with and reinforce one another. Revealing yet another layer—or, indeed, several interrelated layers—of Cristina Bacchilega's proposition, introduced at the beginning of this article, to read fairy tales as facilitators of transformation, Disney's use of participatory structures to negotiate viewer reactions to their recent fairy tale adaptations most literally "interpellate[s] us as consumers and producers of transformation" (2013, 3) on multiple levels. In the above, I have analysed some of the discursive and representational strategies employed in these processes.

With its reactions to the criticism put forward in online fan discussions (i.e. redrawing Tiana after consulting cultural critics, while standing by and standing up for their casting of Ariel), Disney contributed to a significant shift within the dominant conditions of visibility and recognition, which it had nonetheless perpetuated in its colour-blind movie *The Princess and the Frog*. But even as norms and resources have been (temporarily) revised, viewers familiar with Disney's persistent storytelling schemata and its investment in "hegemonic cultural representations" (Anjrbag 2019, 158), which have come to comprise the recognisable 'Disney formula' (cf. Wasko 2001; Anjrbag 2019), remain cautious in their expectations towards the studio's upcoming productions. Only by moving away from the rigid frames that define what the industry deems successful with their target audiences and, in turn, determine viewer expectations, will the Walt Disney Company be able to break with its vexed history of racialised essentialisms and racial comfortability. Certainly, a Black Ariel constitutes a promising and worthy opportunity for such a transformation.

References

Primary Sources

Films

Moore, Rich/Phil Johnston, dir. (2018): *Ralph Breaks the Internet*. Disney
Clements, Ron/John Musker, dir. (2009): *The Princess and the Frog*. Disney
Marshall, Rob, dir. (upcoming): *The Little Mermaid*. Disney

Social Media

@FreeformTV (2019): Twitter tweet, 07.07.2019. https://twitter.com/freeformtv/status/11476 47797732106240. Accessed: 20. January 2021
@GothianTh (2019): Twitter tweet, 09.07.2019. https://twitter.com/GothianTh/status/114862 5146174775296. Accessed: 18. January 2021

Secondary Sources

Abell, Bailey (2019): Halle Bailey, Auli'i Cravalho Respond to #NotMyAriel Backlash from "The Little Mermaid" Casting. *Inside the Magic,* 12.08.2019. https://insidethemagic.net/2019/08/halle-bailey-the-little-mermaid-response-ba1/. Accessed: 18. January 2021

Ajedobi, Alicia (2018): What Disney Did to Fix the Whitewashing Problem of Princess Tiana Exposes Another Glaring Problem. *Metro,* 28.09.2018. https://metro.co.uk/2018/09/24/what-disney-did-to-fix-the-whitewashing-of-princess-tiana-exposes-another-glaring-problem-7975103/?ito=cbshare. Accessed: 15. January 2021

Anjrbag, Michelle Anya (2019): Reforming Borders of the Imagination: Diversity, Adaptation, Transmediation, and Incorporation in the Global Disney Film Landscape. In: *Jeunesse: Young People, Texts, Cultures*, Vol. 11, No. 2, 151–176

Bacchilega, Cristina (2013): *Fairy Tales Transformed? Twenty-First-Century Adaptations and the Politics of Wonder*. Detroit

Bailey, Alyssa (2019): The Original Voice of Ariel, Jodi Benson, Spoke out against the Halle Bailey #NotMyAriel Casting Backlash. *Elle,* 09.07.2019. https://www.elle.com/culture/celebrities/a28334240/jodi-benson-halle-bailey-ariel-casting-backlash-response/. Accessed: 18. January 2021

Bauman, Zygmunt (2017): *Retrotopia*. Cambridge

Bonilla-Silva, Eduardo (³2010): *Racism Without Racists. Color-Blind Racism & Racial Inequality in Contemporary America*. New York

Breaux, Richard M. (2010): After 75 Years of Magic: Disney Answers Its Critics, Rewrites African American History, and Cashes in on Its Racist Past. In: *Journal of African American Studies*, Vol. 14, No. 4, 398–416

Brighenti, Andrea (2007): Visibility: A Category for the Social Sciences. In: *Current Sociology*, Vol. 44, 323–342

Bruns, Axel/Jean Burgess (2015): Twitter Hashtags from Ad Hoc to Calculated Publics. In: *Hashtag Publics. The Power and Politics of Discursive Networks*, ed. Nathan Rambukkana, New York, 13–28

Butler, Judith (2004): *Precarious Life. The Powers of Mourning and Violence*, New York.

Butler, Judith (2009): *Frames of War. When Is Life Grievable?*, New York

Busse, Kristina/Jonathan Gray (2011): Fan Cultures and Fan Communities. In: *The Handbook of Media Audiences*, ed. Virginia Nightingale, Malden, 425–443

Cole, Mike (1996): Race and Racism. In: *A Dictionary of Cultural and Critical Theory*, eds. Michael Payne/Meenakshi Ponnuswami/Jennifer Payne, Oxford/Cambridge, 449–453

Condis, Megan (2015): Applying for the Position of Princess: Race, Labor, and the Privileging of Whiteness in the Disney Princess Line. In: *Princess Cultures. Mediating Girls' Imaginations and Identities*, eds. Miriam Forman-Brunell/Rebecca C. Hains, New York, 25–44

DiAngelo, Robin (2018): *White Fragility. Why It's So Hard for White People to Talk about Racism*. Boston

Dundes, Lauren/Madeline Streiff (2016): Reel Royal Diversity? The Glass Ceiling in Disney's *Mulan* and *The Princess and the Frog*. In: *Societies*, Vol. 6, No. 4, 1–14. https://doi.org/10.3390/soc6040035

England, Dawn E./Lara Descartes/Melissa A. Collier-Meek (2011): Gender Role Portrayal and the Disney Princesses. In: *Sex Roles*, Vol. 64, No. 7–8, 555–567

Florini, Sarah (2019): *Beyond Hashtags. Racial Politics and Black Digital Networks*. New York

Fraser, Nancy (1996): *Social Justice in the Age of Identity Politics. Redistribution, Recognition, Participation*. The Tanner Lectures on Human Values, Stanford University, April 30–May 2, 1996. https://www.intelligenceispower.com/Important%20E-mails%20Sent%20attachments/Social%20Justice%20in%20the%20Age%20of%20Identity%20Politics.pdf. Accessed: 15. January 2021

Fraser, Nancy (2006): Mapping the Feminist Imagination: From Redistribution to Recognition to Representation. In: *Die Neuverhandlung sozialer Gerechtigkeit. Feministische Analysen und Perspektiven*, eds. Ursula Degener/Beate Rosenzweig, Wiesbaden, 37–52

Friedman, Megan (2014): Does Skin and Hair Color Affect Disney Princesses' Popularity? *Seventeen*, 04.11.2014. https://www.seventeen.com/celebrity/movies-tv/reviews/a25462/disney-princesses-most-popular-ebay. Accessed: 19. January 2021

Frost, John (2009): Princess Tiana Merchandise Already a Gig Hit. *The Disney Blog*, 03.11.2009. https://thedisneyblog.com/2009/11/03/princess-tiana-merchandise-already-a-big-hit/. Accessed: 15. January 2021

Gehlawat, Ajay (2010): The Strange Case of *The Princess and the Frog*: Passing and the Elision of Race. In: *Journal of African American Studies*, Vol. 14, No. 4, 417–431

Giroux, Henry A. (1996): *Fugitive Cultures. Race, Violence, and Youth*. London

Gray, Herman (2005): *Cultural Moves. African Americans and the Politics of Representation*. Berkeley

Guardians of Democracy Staff (2019): Racist Fans Sign Petition Urging Disney To Remove Black Actress From 'Little Mermaid' Remake. *The Guardians of Democracy*, 07.07.2019. https://theguardiansofdemocracy.com/racist-fans-sign-petition-urging-disney-to-remove-black-actress-from-little-mermaid-remake/. Accessed: 19. January 2021

Hall, Stuart (1981): Notes on Deconstructing 'The Popular'. People's History and Socialist Theory. Reprinted in: *Cultural Theory. A Reader*, ed. John Storey, Harlow, ⁴2009, 508–518

Hall, Stuart (1982): The Rediscovery of 'Ideology': Return of the Repressed in Media Studies. In: *Culture, Society and the Media*, eds. Tony Bennett/James Curran/Michael Gurevitch/Janet Wollacott, London, 56–90

Jenkins, Henry (2006): *Convergence Culture. Where Old and New Media Meet*. New York/London

Jenkins, Henry/Gabriel Peters-Lazaro/Sangita Shresthova (2020): Popular Culture and the Civic Imagination. Foundations. In: *Popular Culture and the Civic Imagination: Case Studies of Creative Social Change*, eds. Henry Jenkins/Gabriel Peters-Lazaro/Sangita Shresthova, New York, 1–30

Kai, Maiysha (2018a): Colorism, or Complete Makeover? Disney's Princess Tiana Has a New Look, and We Have a Question. *The Root*, 15.08.2018. https://theglowup.theroot.com/colorism-or-complete-makeover-disneys-princess-tiana-1828353805. Accessed: 15. January 2021

Kai, Maiysha (2018b): Color of Change: Remember the Outcry Over Princess Tiana's Makeover in Wreck-It Ralph 2? Disney Listened! *The Root*, 21.09.2018. https://theglowup.theroot.com/color-of-change-remember-the-outcry-over-princess-tian-1829226084. Accessed: 15. January 2021

Knight, Wanda B. (2013) Colorism. In: *Multicultural America. A Multimedia Encyclopedia*, ed. Carlos E. Cortés, Los Angeles, 546–549

Mahmood, Saira (2019): Yes, the #NotMyAriel Anger to "The Little Mermaid" Casting Choice Is Racist. *The Tempest*, 07.07.2019. https://thetempest.co/2019/07/07/entertainment/halle-bailey-ariel/. Accessed: 18. January 2021

Martín Alcoff, Linda (2006): *Visible Identities. Race, Gender, and the Self*, New York

Moffitt, Linda R. (2019): Scripting the Way for the 21st Century Disney Princess in *The Princess and the Frog*. In: *Women's Studies in Communication*, Vol. 42, No. 4, 471–489

Schaffer, Johanna (2008): *Ambivalenzen der Sichtbarkeit*. Bielefeld

Trammell, Kendall (2019): Yes, Black Mermaids Exist, Along with Many Others from Different Cultures. *CNN Travel*, 14.07.2019. https://edition.cnn.com/travel/article/little-mermaid-folklore-trnd/index.html. Accessed: 18. January 2021

Thomas, Tanja/Elke Grittmann (2017): Anerkennung und Sichtbarkeit. Impulse für kritische Medienkulturtheorie und -analyse. In: *Anerkennung und Sichtbarkeit. Perpektiven für eine kritische Meidenkulturforschung*, eds. Tanja Thomas/Lina Brink/Elke Grittmann/Kaya de Wolff, Bielefeld, 23–46

Turner, Sarah E. (2013): Blackness, Bayous and Gumbo. Encoding and Decoding Race in a Colorblind World. In: *Diversity in Disney Films. Critical Essays on Race, Ethnicity, Gender, Sexuality and Disability*, ed. Johnson Cheu, Jefferson, 83–98

Wasko, Janet (2001): *Understanding Disney: The Manufacture of Fantasy*. Cambridge

Zipes, Jack (2012): *The Irresistible Fairy Tale: The Cultural and Social History of a Genre*. Princeton

From E.T.A. Hoffmann to Disney

Figurations of the Nutcracker in Changing Media and Culture

Ute Dettmar

Abstract Disney's live-action movie *The Nutcracker and the Four Realms* (2018) is a twenty-first century iteration of a story that has enjoyed a successful international reception history ever since its inception in the nineteenth century as a *Kunstmärchen* by E.T.A. Hoffmann, *The Nutcracker and the Mouse King* (1816). This paper discusses Disney's version in the context of the transcultural and transmedial adaptation and popularisation of the Hoffmann tale. Disney's remediatisation of the fairy tale displays influences from current fantasy film conventions, but that is not all. Thematically, the film is particularly interesting in the way it handles gender constructions: Disney turns the children's fairy tale into a coming-of-age drama. This recoding will be considered in the context of Disney's efforts to re-stage femininity in recent years. An analysis of the seemingly progressive representation of gender and diversity in this film, a response to the criticism that has been formulated against Disney's productions, will be presented.

Fairy-tale Variations

"Let us tell an old story anew and see how well you know it," declares the narrator as he introduces the Disney movie *Maleficent* (2014). Based on Perrault's version of the fairy tale *The Sleeping Beauty* (*La belle au bois dormant*, 1697), *Maleficent* also makes intermedial reference to Disney's 1959 animated film *Sleeping Beauty*. Moreover, it tells the story from an unusual angle, namely that of the evil fairy (the title character). The rephrasing of the stock fairy-tale opening, the change of perspective, the references to Disney's previous fairy-tale productions and the way in which the movie plays with the audience's knowledge and expectations—all these

---

This article is partly based on Dettmar 2020a but has been fundamentally revised and extended.

U. Dettmar (✉)
Goethe University, Frankfurt am Main, Germany
e-mail: udettmar@em.uni-frankfurt.de

© The Author(s), under exclusive license to Springer-Verlag GmbH, DE, part of
Springer Nature 2022
U. Dettmar and I. Tomkowiak (eds.), *On Disney*, Studien zu Kinder- und
Jugendliteratur und -medien 9, https://doi.org/10.1007/978-3-662-64625-0_7

exemplify not only how considerably fairy stories alter as they undergo (global) popularisation and enter different media, but also how substantial a part Disney has played in the processes of retelling and reinterpretation. After Disney entered the fairy-tale business on a grand scale in 1937 with *Snow White and the Seven Dwarfs*, the first feature-length animated film,[1] a symbiotic, almost metonymic relationship evolved between the genre and the company. According to Zipes: "Disney identified so closely with the fairy tales he appropriated that it is no wonder his name virtually became synonymous with the genre of fairy tale itself" (1995, 28).

In many cases, Disney's fairy-tale films, as well as still images taken from them, are now probably better known than their literary urtexts: against the background of changing media, the films have obscured and recoded the written texts. As a result, the name Disney represents not just a global multimedia entertainment company with "corporate power" (Giroux/Pollock 2010, xiii), but also a specific expressive style: "Disney" means a recognisable repertoire of narrative modes, visual languages and narratives and, critically speaking, a specific ideology. The poetics/pedagogy of innocence, an icon of American culture and the Americanisation of European fairy tales (Zipes 1995, 40, uses the harsher term "colonization") are some of the buzzwords that academics have used to sum up this successful programme (cf. Bell/Haas/Sells 1995b; Zipes 1995; Giroux/Pollock 2010). The cultural dominance of the company's movies, and the subsequent 'Disneyfication' of fairy tales, have drawn criticism for some time. Zipes, for example, describes the allure of Disney as follows:

> [...] Walt Disney cast a spell on the fairy tale, and he has held it captive ever since. [...] The great "magic" of the Disney spell is that he animated the fairy tale only to transfix audiences and divert their potential utopian dreams and hopes through the false promises of the images he cast upon the screen (Zipes 1995, 21–22).

Given (and notwithstanding) the existence of Disney, and judging by current reception, fairy tales continue to be handed down from one generation to the next—the audience is not yet sated. The lively use of fairy-tale material and motifs is manifest in a wide array of media, from picture books and television series to apps and computer games. Disney movies are involved in these reinterpretations and repeatedly provide a point of reference whenever these cultural set pieces are reimagined. Texts and media draw on the reservoir of cinematic and musical motifs, narratives, characters and intermedial references created by Disney, whether through parody (for example in the *Shrek* films, with their allusions to other Disney films and the Walt Disney Company itself) or through postmodern referential play (such as in Benjamin Lacombe's adaptation of *Snow White* (2011)). Now-established forms of communication and participation in social media can also be found citing Disney as a reference. For example, images from

---

[1] Disney had already used fairy tale material in the *Laugh-O-Grams* and *Silly Symphonies* in the 1920s and 1930s, cf. Tomkowiak 2017.

Disney's famous fairy-tale productions are often seen in memes that employ collages of texts and images to comment on recent events (cf. Stemmann 2019).

Furthermore, Disney's style is so unmistakable in animation and live-action films that the company has been viewed as a source of unchanging "monolithic myths" (Bell/Haas/Sells 1995b, 5). One factor in their success—and this applies to popular culture in general (cf. Dettmar 2019)—is the flexibility with which their media productions have reacted to changing discourses and changing conditions of production and reception, the way they have modified their modes of presentation and narration, have referred to virulent images, and have adapted to the changing expectations of audiences and critics. According to Tomkowiak (2017, 121), the fact that throughout its history Disney has skilfully combined technical and aesthetic innovation on the one hand with tried-and-true narrative patterns on the other is a decisive reason for its success, which has now lasted for more than a century. Disney's productions have always been geared to contemporary taste, have responded to criticism, have absorbed other media and have even remoulded genre developments. Disney movies are thus always of their time; they feature gender discourses, concepts of age and body, of queerness and race. As Bell puts it when referring to changing concepts of gender, beauty and the body, traditional fairy-tale texts are "templates" onto which new layers of "contemporaneous popular images of feminine beauty and youth" (1995, 108–109) are continually superimposed.

Maleficent is an example of the mutability of these images. It's also one of a recent spate of Disney productions since the 1990*s* that have presented (or intended to present) gender, race and diversity differently—not least in response to the criticism that Disney has faced over the years. "Disney is, in fact, becoming more multicultural in its cinematic fare and its image," states Cheu (2013b, 1), citing films such as *The Princess and the Frog* (2009) and even going back as far as *Pocahontas* (1995), *Mulan* (1998) and *Aladdin* (1992). In addition, more recent animated films such as *Frozen* (2013) are considered examples of "Disney's New Woman" (Limbach 2013, 115), who is depicted as being more active and independent than her predecessors. However, far from rendering criticism of these representations obsolete, these reimaginings have themselves become targets of criticism, as evident from research on recent Disney films.[2]

In what follows I shall discuss the developments outlined above, using the example of the Disney live-action film *The Nutcracker and the Four Realms* (Hallström/Johnston 2018), exploring in particular how the film deals with gender and coming of age. I start by examining aspects of adaptation, cultural hybridisation, and intermediality in Disney's treatment of its explicitly credited sources, E.T.A. Hoffmann's 1816 fairy tale *The Nutcracker and the Mouse King,* and Marius Petipa, who composed the libretto and choreography for Tchaikovsky's world-famous ballet *The Nutcracker* (1892). I shall therefore begin with the

---

[2] Cf. Bell/Haas/Sells 1995a; Giroux/Pollock 2010; Cheu 2013a; Condis 2015; Tomkowiak 2017.

literary original, discussing its narrative potential, the history of its popularisation, and its transcultural and transmedial influence before Disney came along. My reference to the literary original and its adaptations should not be construed as a standard of assessment; recent adaptations and intermediality theory agree that fidelity to the original is not an appropriate yardstick,[3] especially when dealing with the narrative genre of the fairy tale, where retelling, translation and adaptation have always been constitutive elements of the process of dissemination and popularisation.[4] According to Zipes (2011, 8), fairy tales are "flexible" or "fluid text[s]"; they vary and hybridise in transcultural contexts, they develop intermedial entanglements, they find new aesthetic forms and they refer to changing social discourses and expectations. Texts of fairy tales are therefore interesting as palimpsests,[5] requiring examination of the ways in which stories and images are overlaid within them, just as much as the cinematic registers with which they are reimagined and remediatised should be examined too, each in their respective production and reception contexts.

Dance of Symbols: E.T.A. Hoffmann's Fairy Tale *The Nutcracker and the Mouse King* and Its Popularisation

E.T.A. Hoffmann's *Nutcracker*, Disney's urtext, is formally and thematically complex. Given its ironic tone, the artistic manner in which the frame story is connected to the internal narrative, the interplay between depicted reality and magical elements, and the intertextual play between fairy-tale and horror literature, this Romantic *Kunstmärchen* is an intricate text operating on multiple levels. Hoffmann's tale is based on Romantic poetics and the concept of childhood. Yet instead of presenting childhood as happy and carefree, emphasis is placed on its vulnerability to disaster. The scene in which Marie plays with her presents on Christmas Eve—her dolls and the nutcracker—is transformed into a nightmarish vision as the toys come to life and engage in a bloody battle with the Mouse King and his army when they invade the room. The young imagination—held in such high esteem in the Romantic period—is pushed by the story's straddling of dream

---

[3] Cf. Hutcheon/O'Flynn 2013.

[4] Referring to cinematic adaptations of fairy tales, Zipes points out: "Whatever the case may be, there is no authoritative hypotext or *Urtext* upon which a filmmaker does or can rely, and this is because literary fairy tales stem from oral folk tales and have a long history of variation and dissemination in an oral tradition up through the present. Many literary fairy tales are already adaptations because they are translations that comprise some kind of adaptation in language and references to different social context. [...] Numerous classic fairy tales and popular folk tales from the oral tradition have been translated, illustrated, and spread in diverse ways, but when published, they become so-called fixed texts—but only seemingly" (2011, 8).

[5] Regarding the concept and theory of the palimpsest, see Genette 1993.

and reality to venture into the realm of the uncanny, or as discussed by Freud in his famous essay on the uncanny (Freud 1999), to cross over into the semantically ambiguous *unheimlich*, which Freud explicates in part using an etymological justification. Indeed recent studies on Romanticism, critically responding to research that had tendentiously emphasised childhood innocence, point to depictions of childhood as a traumatic experience, as an act of fundamental injury running throughout a person's life or as an unconscious wound that controls their actions (Kremer/Kilcher 2015, 84).

The spatial semantics of this dualistic fairy tale can be interpreted in this context psychologically: dream and reality interact on the boundary of childhood, while the confusion inherent in the child's worldview is represented in the tale's alternation between the two worlds. The magical enchantment (the dreamlike, miraculous sequences in the interior narrative that take Marie and the nutcracker into the fairy-tale doll kingdom, a rococo-like fairyland full of unbelievable delicacies and sparkling magic) merges with the nightmarish distortion of the real world. The demands of reality, represented here by the parents (who don't believe Marie's fantastical adventures and dismiss them as a confused dream) start competing with her magical experience. Furthermore, Hoffmann's *Nutcracker* fairy tale uses a nested structure to transition between illusion and reality, encapsulating interior narration within the frame story. Some of the characters appearing in the different narrative spaces seem to operate in both worlds, such as Marie, her godfather Droßelmeier, and the nutcracker (Droßelmeier's nephew), and this dual role of theirs gives them all an impenetrable, ambiguous quality.

Marie, travelling back and forth between two worlds, between dream (or possibly nightmare) and reality, is thus caught in a dichotomous existence between the unconscious and the conscious. The narrative's gender constructions are also interesting in relation to the existential thematics. The two children, Marie and Fritz, conform to heteronormative gender roles that correspond to those found in the bourgeois family world in which the story is set; the attributes of childhood—the two children's toys, clothing and behaviour—are differentiated according to gender. These roles are sustained throughout the narrative and integrated into the dynamics of narrative and character development.

Hoffmann's fairy story has thus also been interpreted not just as a story of a child's development, but also as a story of female development beset by crisis. According to Schmaus (2015, 101), Marie's psychosexual development is metonymically and metaphorically accompanied by a trail of blood, illness and death-like states. Instinctual life is acknowledged in the form of the Mouse King bursting forth from beneath the floorboards of the living room, and has to be shaped in the interplay of genders via stages of latency, drive renunciation and sublimation (cf. also Neumann 1997).

However, part of the ambiguity of Hoffmann's text lies in the fact that these traces and signs of the initiation narrative are found in the framework of a child's fairy tale, and not in a narrative that features a literally adolescent protagonist—for

Marie, as we learn at the beginning of *The Nutcracker*, has only just turned seven (Hoffmann 1987, 67).[6]

We can discern two basic strands in the further reception and influence of the text. The story, which was not initially included in the canon of children's literature (it was thought inappropriate for children due to its narrative complexity), has long become a children's classic due to its literary qualities. For a long time, the narrative openness and complexity that have since come to be appreciated caused bewilderment, something that Hoffmann himself pondered over. In the frame narrative of the anthology *The Serapion Brethren* (the first volume of which was published in 1819), which included *The Nutcracker and the Mouse King*, Cyprian (one of the brethren) declares:

> Still, it must always be a risky undertaking to bring the utterly fanciful into the domain of everyday life, and clap mad, enchanted caps on to the heads of grave and sober folks—judges, students, and Masters of the Rolls—so that they go gliding about like ghosts in broad daylight up and down the most frequented streets of the most familiar towns, and one does not know what to think of his most respectable neighbours (Hoffmann (1886)).

Thanks to this narrative strategy, Hoffman's *Nutcracker* fairy story achieved significance in literary history, especially with respect to the history of genre and form. This dualistic fairy tale, which oscillates between reality and fantasy, and is structurally characterised by the tension between the magical-mythical and the modern conception of reality, is regarded as the precursor and forerunner of children's fantasy literature (cf. Ewers 1987 and Kümmerling-Meibauer 2012). As the nineteenth century progressed, this genre rose to prominence internationally, initially in Great Britain. Nevertheless, Hoffmann's venture into fantasy literature is more radical than that of many of his successors. In *The Nutcracker*, the fantasy world of make-believe and the realistically depicted world are not harmoniously connected, nor is the fantasy world envisioned as a compensatory, free or developmental space standing in lieu of the real world; instead, the two worlds permeate each other in a mysterious way and at the same time call worldview and characters into question.

However, the well-regarded complexity of the story isn't the only reason for its enduring popularity and presence. The intertextual and intermedial web in which the text is embedded was already at the time of its inception closely linked to scenarios from popular culture. Hoffmann's narrative refers to the popular form of the *féerie* (fairy play), a genre whose tropes he also ironically and satirically shatters. What's more, the grotesque motifs are clearly borrowed from horror literature, so

---

[6] Marie is hence not a girl in puberty, despite the claim by Neumann (1997, 154), who interprets Marie's story as that of the maturation of a girl into a woman (ibid., 142). Mediated through her godfather Droßelmeier, and embodied in the vivified figure of the nutcracker as an object of love and transition (ibid., 150), the complex constellations play out into childhood—or rather into the childish fantasies of the latency stage. Kümmerling-Meibauer (2012, 87–89) therefore sees in the change of Marie's world of play and fantasy a genuine development from symbolic play to role play typical of childhood.

From E.T.A. Hoffmann to Disney

the text isn't just the starting point of a transnational development in children's literature, but is itself positioned within—and is also inspired by—other literary, intertextual/intermedial and cultural contexts.[7]

The influence of Hoffmann's fairy tale continues to resonate, above all in its many adaptations in other media. Alexandre Dumas *père's The Nutcracker* (*Histoire d'un casse-noisette*), published in Paris in 1844 with woodcuts by Bertall, marks a crossroads in the history of its reception, for it is thenceforth that the story crosses over into different media and becomes popularised (cf. Dettmar 2020b). Dumas's work is an adaptation or, to use Genette's terminology, an imitation of Hoffman's story (cf. Genette 1993). Dumas's version sticks to the plot but changes its presentation: the gruesome events involving the Mouse King are described with far more restraint, emphasis is placed on the playful elements of make-believe and to some extent the linguistic signs of ambiguity disappear. Dumas's fantasy work is a narrative depiction that gives ample space to the child's imagination. In it, the narrative is brought to a happy end more clearly than in Hoffmann's work, for after Marie and Droßelmeier's nephew are married, they both move to Fairyland. Marie's parents grant their consent to the wedding in Dumas's version, whereas in Hoffmann's the status of the experience remains unresolved, hovering between delusion and magic.

Dumas's text paved the way for the international, intermedial triumph of the Nutcracker story, above all in Tchaikovsky's famous ballet (premiered in 1892; libretto by Marius Petipa, choreography by Marius Petipa and Lev Ivanov; cf. in more detail Brandstetter 1997), a firm favourite in the ballet repertoire to this day. As well as becoming influential in musical theatre, it also became a point of reference in adaptations to other genres, as for example in the Canadian animated film *The Nutcracker Prince* (1990) and the animated *Barbie in the Nutcracker* (2001). Even Disney, decades earlier, had drawn on Tchaikovsky's tour de force in its 1940 *Fantasia,* an animated feature film set to classical music in which animals, plants, mushrooms and fairies dance to the *Nutcracker Suite.*[8] The magic of Christmas Eve, toys coming to life, and choreographed dolls, all accompanied and embellished by music from Tchaikovsky's fairy ballet, has become an enduring intertextual and intermedial collection of images, staged year after year with much success. In the United States, performances by the New York City Ballet (based on George Balanchine's choreography) are popular, especially around Christmas—and this elaborate production is also a point of reference for Disney's live-action film adaptation, to which I shall now turn.

---

[7] Neumann (1997, 149–151) also points to allusions to Goethe's novel *Wilhelm Meisters Lehrjahre* (*Wilhelm Meister's Apprenticeship),* the myth of Pygmalion, Gozzi's play *Turandot* (itself based on a Persian fairy tale) and Fouqué's *Undine.*

[8] Disney also drew on the nutcracker material in the animated short *The Nutcracker* (*Mickey Mouse Works* 1999).

The Nutcracker and the Four Realms (2018)

Christine Lötscher (2017, 323) describes the impactful reimagination strategies of recent fairy-tale and fantasy films as the affect poetics of intoxication. The Walt Disney Company has involved itself in this recent development through live-action movies, especially through lavishly-produced films like *Maleficent* (2014) and *Beauty and the Beast* (2017). Another such movie was the big-budget *The Nutcracker and the Four Realms* (2018),[9] which had an all-star cast, including Keira Knightley, Helen Mirren and Morgan Freeman. The opening scene by itself emphasises that no expense or effort was spared to create spectacular images with technological wizardry. The camera flies towards Victorian London (where the story is now set) in breath-taking pans as we rush over Big Ben and enter the city illuminated by Christmas lights. The era and location were presumably altered to improve the film's international marketing prospects (Hoffmann's fairy tale was set in Berlin in the early nineteenth century), although it should be added that for the purposes of the movie, London—already established in literature and cinema as an enchanted city—has been reimagined here as one outfitted both in the magic of Christmas and in steampunk. Echoing literary and musical tradition, the plot takes place on Christmas Eve. But the intimacy of a family gathering is replaced by a large party in the palace owned by Clara's godfather Droßelmeier; the interior is richly decorated with chandeliers, and the guests are attired in magnificent costumes. The frame narrative, especially its audio-visual elements, is buttressed by the literary and musical mainstays of the nutcracker story: it is the popular musical themes, motifs, characters and scenes from the ballet that are primarily quoted in this part of the film. There are mechanical toys that come to life and large dancing mechanical puppets, for instance. And there are the ballet sequences, comprising a kaleidoscopic assortment of images that refer to the stage sets of the original production, and which are used to intradiegetically tell the backstory of the four realms and their erstwhile queen, Marie Stahlbaum.[10]

Given the assemblage of characters and the themes of the fairy tale, the transposition of the story to a different era is significant. The protagonist is named Clara as in Tchaikovsky's ballet, but here she is the *daughter* of Marie Stahlbaum, the central character of Hoffmann's tale (incidentally, Marie's siblings Fritz and Louise are now Clara's siblings in the film, making the time structure illogical). The movie thus presents itself as a sequel to Hoffmann's urtext, one that elaborates on the original story and continues it with the next generation. The themes of the original fairy tale are reproduced and shifted, with Clara's passage to the magical world now told in the context of a mother-and-daughter story. She follows the trail

---

[9] According to Wikipedia, the film's budget exceeded \$120 million: https://en.wikipedia.org/wiki/The_Nutcracker_and_the_Four_Realms. Accessed November 23, 2020.

[10] Cf. Goldhammer (2018): https://www.br-klassik.de/aktuell/br-klassik-empfiehlt/film/der-nussknacker-und-die-vier-reiche-film-kritik-100.html. Accessed November 23, 2020.

of her deceased mother, Marie, who was once queen of the four realms. Clara then embarks upon her own adventure in the magical land, and this journey becomes her personal heroic odyssey. She successfully braves the menacing Fourth Realm and saves the fantasy world and its inhabitants.

Another change concerns the protagonist's age: Clara is now a sixteen-year-old teenager. Thus the two worlds become a site for a coming-of-age drama, set in motion by Clara's entry into the fantasy, fairy-tale realm. Loose references to original elements—characters like the children's godfather Droßelmeier, the nut-cracker and Mouserinks (the Mouse King)—are worked into the story. These are intertwined with intramedial references to other movie adaptations of fairy tales and classics of children's fantasy literature. This is apparent in the very first scene, which opens, as *Maleficent* (2014) does, with a high-flying aerial shot. The gloomy presentation of the four realms is reminiscent of Tim Burton's dark version of *Alice in Wonderland* (2010), and when a winter wonderland opens up before Clara as she enters the fairy-tale realm, leaving her visibly flabbergasted, we're reminded of not only Tchaikovsky's ballet, but also of the way in which the transition to the fantasy world is depicted in Disney's adaptation of *The Chronicles of Narnia* (2005).

In Disney's version of *The Nutcracker*, this transition is shown as a passage through a long dark tunnel, inviting psychoanalytic interpretations. Reminiscent of a birth canal, this liminal moment is all the more fitting because the fantasy world in the film is clearly depicted as a motherland (another respect in which it is similar to Burton's *Alice* movie). Clara's mother Marie was once the revered queen of the Fourth Realm, who brought the toys to life with the help of a machine she herself designed and built. This technological marvel has now malfunctioned, and the key that could restart it has been lost. It's interesting that the film now uses the fantasy structure to tell its story, with its echoes of fairy-tale magic, along-side technological wizardry. The archetypal symbolic worlds of the film can be interpreted as an expression of children's fears and conflicts: Clara grieves for her mother, but by entering the fairy-tale world, she follows in her footsteps and comes closer to her again. At the same time, the journey—with all the trials Clara has to undergo—opens up a path for herself. The fantastical is now no longer a structural expression of the division of childhood. Instead, since it is a different world of experience, it becomes a space where she can cope with her grief, a place of healing and development. The external obstacles that Clara must overcome in order to save the fantasy world and herself also add a little of the heroic fantasy to the fairy-tale plot, but without the political allusions common in this genre. The film clearly shows that this is principally a story of self-discovery. "Everything you need is inside" (Hallström/Johnston 2018, 00:05:14), Marie writes in the letter that accompanies her parting gift to her daughter, a locked box in the shape of a silver egg. When Clara finally finds the key and opens what turns out to be a music box, a mirror flips open, showing her her own reflection. Here, the prominent motif of the mirror familiar from the *Alice* novels, which had symbolised in those books the potential for worlds and identities to become duplicated and fragile, now becomes a symbol of successful self-discovery.

Disney's *Nutcracker* is evidently intended as a story of female empowerment. Right from the start, Clara, who as Marie's daughter is a princess in the fairy-tale world, can be seen as a counter-image to Disney's customary princesses and teenage heroines. In the opening scenes, Marie is introduced as a technologically orientated, talented, 'clever girl.' Unlike her predecessor in Hoffmann's urtext, she doesn't bother with dolls, and instead is well-versed in science, technology and mechanics; she repairs complex apparatus and conducts experiments with mechanical systems, expertly incorporating the laws of Newton. She thus has all the qualifications required to save the fairy-tale world when it is turned upside down, and she takes on and defeats Sugar Plum, who has seized control of the machine for her own dark ends. The plot focuses on Clara's odyssey; a love affair with Captain Hoffmann, the 'nutcracker,' is hinted at but not played out. Instead of finding and marrying her Prince Charming—as intended in the "classic narrative about an adolescent girl's coming of age" (Sells 1995, 176)—Clara, richer in experience and self-confidence, returns to the old world, where she reconciles with her father.

This representation of a strong female character and an active heroine is consistent with other recent productions by Disney, which launched a "feminist reframing" (Condis 2015, 32) of the traditional princess role in the 1990s (the 'Eisner era'). Clara figures as one of the "seemingly rebellious, female characters: Disney's New Woman" (Limbach 2013, 115). It's also striking that all the other important characters are women: Mother Ginger (the apparent antagonist), who at first seems all-powerful and threatening, Sugar Plum (the real antagonist), and last but not least Clara's deceased mother Marie, who lives on in the characters' memories. This change of perspective on female genealogy, power and agency shows distinct recoding in relation to earlier Disney films and their stereotypical gender constructions (cf. Davis 2006 and 2014).The portrayal of Clara, with her rejection of traditionally feminine attributes and her emphasis on choice and agency, was welcomed by critics.[11] With respect to Disney's typical gender constructions, Sugar Plum's appearance is interesting as well: dressed in pink frills and glitzy gowns, with a towering hairdo, and a high-pitched voice on the verge of dissonance, she caricatures the "hyper-heterosexual" (Putnam 2013, 147) ideals of female beauty also reproduced by Disney. Widely held character expectations—for instance, that beauty equals good—are thwarted by the film. Appearances can be deceiving, and not only in the case of Sugar Plum: the considerably older Mother Ginger, who initially seems threatening and has the 'masculine' attributes of boots, pants and a whip—in Disney movies, usually a sign of female characters' malevolence (ibid., 148)—proves to be a positive figure who fights actively at Clara's side.

---

[11] *The Guardian's* cinema reviewer Cath Clark wrote: "With this sumptuous ballet-lite live action retelling of *The Nutcracker*, Disney is having its feminist mince pie and eating it. The heroine here, fiercely independent and brave, follows the Disney-princess-gone-rogue template set by Emma Watson in *Beauty and the Beast*." https://www.theguardian.com/film/2018/nov/01/the-nutcracker-and-the-four-realms-review-keira-knightley. Accessed: 23. November 2020.

Last but not least, diversity is featured in the casting: Clara's godfather Droßelmeier and Captain Hoffman are played by African Americans (Morgan Freeman and Jayden Fowora-Knight respectively), and ballet dancer Misty Copeland, first soloist of the American Ballet Theater in New York, also appears in the movie. This can be inferred as Disney's response to the criticism repeatedly levelled at it for its stereotypical portrayals of race, class and gender (cf. Condis 2015; Tomkowiak 2017). But in spite of these progressive casting choices and the alterations made to character design and the narrative, closer examination of the characters and their performances reveals that the claim that Disney is now employing paradigm-breaking conventions does not, in fact, hold water.

For example, Clara is now endowed with attributes traditionally considered masculine: curiosity, inventiveness, an affinity for science, intelligence, courage and a fighting spirit, all of which enable her to pass the tests she undergoes (albeit not without the help of Philip the 'nutcracker'). But merely reversing gender attributes is just another way of remaining imprisoned by the same binary framework; moreover, Clara's rebellion against the role assigned to her, for all the encouragement she gets to be true to herself, just seems to be a passing phase. In this regard, the film follows a time-honoured narrative from girls' literature, where female characters who at first seem unconventional and boyish are guided on a path to traditional femininity.[12] True, Clara initially refuses to conform to the traditionalist ideas of her father, who attaches importance to (dress) order and social appearance: when he tries to introduce Clara to bourgeois society and her proper gender role at the Christmas party by offering to dance with her, she refuses. Yet after Clara's return, despite the fact that hardly any time has passed, the film closes with this very scene as they dance together after all. This reconciliation with her father, signified by their dance, goes beyond the father-and-daughter relationship—it indicates that Clara has found herself and her place in the 'real' world, that she can now develop her strengths and rise to the expectations placed on her. The tension created by the spectacle of a female who deviates from the social norm (especially in the nineteenth century) is resolved in the movie's happy ending.

Michael Macaluso, referring to the Disney film *Frozen* (2013), whose protagonists Elsa and Anna were celebrated by critics and social media alike as feminist heroines, argues "that the film instead advances *postfeminist* characteristics and sensibilities that displace or replace feminist ideas or entangle them with anti-feminist sentiments [...]" (2016, 73).[13] The figure of the "postfeminist Princess" (ibid.), where emphasis is placed on individualism, agency and choice, can be read as a fairy-tale embodiment of the "top girl" identified by McRobbie (2010). She criticises the 'neoliberal' notion behind the rhetoric of empowerment that claims

---

[12] Regarding this narrative pattern of the *Backfischroman* (teenage girl novel), see in a historical context Wilkending 1990.

[13] By using the term *postfeminist*, Macaluso is referring to Judith Butler. Regarding its differentiation and for a discussion of the term, see Gill 2017.

that women can do anything by themselves if they only want to, that social structures are fading and that political demands for equality consequently seem obsolete or outdated.[14]

Such postfeminist discourses are also evident in the supposedly feminist design used in the scenes already discussed in the *Nutcracker* film. And when we consider the other female characters, by no means are they free from references to the generational or gender orders established in previous Disney films. In particular, the domineering Sugar Plum figures as the embodiment of "female wickedness [...] rendered as middle-aged beauty at its peak of sexuality and authority" (Bell 1995, 108). Clara's deceased mother Marie, on the other hand, joins the ranks of idealised and sentimentalised mother figures (cf. Haas 1995, 196–197): her concern for her daughter endures beyond her death, and she guides Clara's process of self-discovery with her own legacy. Even the transgressive depiction of the colourful, operetta-like Land of Sweets, with all its baroque costumes and exaggerations, is not so much a carnivalesque sabotaging of gender roles as it is a feminisation or queer coding of the fairy-tale-like, theatrical characters.[15] Hawthorne, the ruler of the Land of Flowers, is also overdrawn with humorous effects as a baroque figure and the two guardian figures who protect the palace in the middle of the realms are similarly portrayed with a bearing so feminised that they slide into risibility.

Disney's retelling of the nutcracker stories thus relies on a tried-and-true image strategy: the film takes up current negotiations of gender and diversity without fundamentally recoding them.[16] The seemingly progressive production with its outstanding aesthetics also participates in current genre developments. With its delight in opulent settings, be it steampunk London or the mechanical ballet of the magical land, the film has the earmarks of extravaganza cinema—a star-studded, globally marketable, intended blockbuster (Stiglegger 2017, 9)—the sort of product that typifies the current fantasy film.

References

Primary Sources

Books

Hoffmann, E.T.A. (1983): *Die Serapionsbrüder. Gesammelte Erzählungen und Märchen in vier Bänden*, ed. Monika Wurmdobler, vol. 1, Frankfurt/M.: Insel [[1]1819]

---

[14] Regarding criticism of this figure in youth literature and especially in speculative fiction, cf. Kalbermatten 2020.

[15] Comparable tendencies can also be found in Disney's remake of *Beauty and the Beast* (2017).

[16] A comparable approach is taken by the film *The Princess and the Frog* (2009), cf. Tomkowiak 2017, 134–135.

Hoffmann, E.T.A. (1987): Nußknacker und Mausekönig. In: *Kinder-Märchen. Von C.W. Contessa, F. de la Motte Fouqué, E.T.A. Hoffmann* [¹1816], ed. Hans-Heino Ewers, Stuttgart: Reclam

Hoffmann, E.T.A. (1886): *The Serapion Brethren,* translated by Alexander Ewing, vol. 1, London: George Bell

Films

Hallström, Lasse/Joe Johnston, dir. (2018): *Nutcracker and the Four Realms.* Walt Disney Studios Home Entertainment. DVD

Secondary Sources

Bell, Elisabeth (1995): Somatexts at the Disney Shop. Constructing the Pentimentos of Women's Animated Bodies. In: *From Mouse to Mermaid. The Politics of Film, Gender, and Culture*, eds. Elisabeth Bell/Lynda Haas/Laura Sells: Bloomington [et al.], 107–124

Bell, Elisabeth/Lynda Haas/Laura Sells, eds. (1995a): *From Mouse to Mermaid. The Politics of Film, Gender, and Culture.* Bloomington [et al.]

Bell, Elisabeth/Lynda Haas/Laura Sells (1995b): Introduction: Walt's in the Movies. In: *From Mouse to Mermaid. The Politics of Film, Gender, and Culture*, eds. Elisabeth Bell/Lynda Haas/Laura Sells. Bloomington [etc.], 1–6

Brandstetter, Gabriele (1997): Transkription in Tanz. E.T.A. Hoffmanns Märchen *Nußknacker und Mausekönig* und Marius Petipas Ballett-Szenario. In: *Jugend. Ein romantisches Konzept?* Ed. Günter Oesterle, Würzburg, 161–179

Cheu, Johnson, ed. (2013a): *Diversity on Disney Films. Critical Essays on Race, Ethnicity, Gender, Sexuality and Disability*, Jefferson

Cheu, Johnson (2013b): Introduction: Re-casting and Diversifying Disney in the Age of Globalization. In: *Diversity on Disney Films. Critical Essays on Race, Ethnicity, Gender, Sexuality and Disability,* ed. Johnson Cheu, Jefferson, 1–7

Clark, Cath (2018): The Nutcracker and the Four Realms review—a festival of winter schmaltz. https://www.theguardian.com/film/2018/nov/01/the-nutcracker-and-the-four-realms-review-keira-knightley). Accessed: 23. November 2020

Condis, Megan (2015): Applying for the Position of Princess: Race, Labor, and the Privileging of Whiteness in the Disney Princess Line. In: *Princess Cultures. Mediating Girls' Imaginations and Identities*, eds. Miriam Brunell-Forman/Rebecca C. Hains, New York [et al.], 25–44

Davis, Amy M. (2006): *Good Girls and Wicked Witches. Women in Disney's Feature Animation.* Eastley

Davis, Amy M. (2014): *Handsome Heroes and Vile Villains. Masculinity in Disney's Feature Films.* Bloomington

Dettmar, Ute (2019): Kinder- und Jugendliteratur und Populärkultur: Eine Beziehungsgeschichte. In: *Spielarten der Populärkultur. Kinder- und Jugendmedien im Feld des Populären* eds. Ute Dettmar/Ingrid Tomkowiak. Frankfurt, 17–38

Dettmar, Ute (2020a): „Toller Schnack, toller Schnack"—E.T.A. Hoffmanns Nußknacker und Mausekönig (1816) im Medienwechsel. In: *Schauplatz der Künste—Bild und Text im Kinderbuch. Festgabe für Carola Pohlmann*, eds. Julia Benner/Barbara Schneider-Kempf/ Sigrun Putjenter, Würzburg, 149–161

Dettmar, Ute (2020b) Spuren verwischen. Alexandre Dumas' père *Geschichte eines Nussknackers* (1844) als Palimpseste. In: „Bring me that horizon". Neue Perspektiven auf

Ästhetik und Praxis populärer Literaturen und Medien, eds. Brigitte Frizzoni/Christine Lötscher, Zürich, 33–42

Ewers, Hans-Heino (1987): Nachwort. In: Kinder-Märchen. Von C.W. Contessa F. de la Motte-Fouqué, E.T.A. Hoffmann, ed. id., Stuttgart, 327–350

Freud, Sigmund (1999): Das Unheimliche [1919]. In: Sigmund Freund: Gesammelte Werke. Chronologisch geordnet, 12. Band, Frankfurt/ M., 249–268

Genette, Gerard (1993): Palimpseste. Die Literatur auf zweiter Stufe, Frankfurt/M.

Gill, Rosalind (2017): The affective, cultural and psychic life of postfeminism: A postfeminist sensibility 10 years on. In: European Journal of Cultural Studies, Vol. 20(6), 606–626

Giroux, Henry A./Grace Pollock (²2010). The Mouse that Roared: Disney and the End of Innocence, Rowman & Littlefield Publishers. ProQuest Ebook Central, https://ebookcentral. proquest.com/lib/senc/detail.action?docID=500835

Goldhammer, Antonia (2018): Filmkritik—"Der Nussknacker und die vier Reiche." Disney und Tschaikowsky im Pas-de-deux. https://www.br-klassik.de/aktuell/br-klassik-empfiehlt/film/der-nussknacker-und-die-vier-reiche-film-kritik-100.html. Accessed: 23. November 2020

Haas, Linda (1995): "Eighty-Six the Mother." Murder, Matricide, and Good Mothers. In: Bell, Elisabeth/Lynda Haas/Laura Sells, eds (1995a): From Mouse to Mermaid. The Politics of Film, Gender, and Culture. Bloomington [etc.], 193–211

Hutcheon, Linda/Siobhan O'Flynn (2013): A Theory of Adaptation. London [etc.]

Kalbermatten, Manuela (2020): "The match that lights the fire." Gesellschaft und Geschlecht in Future-Fiction für Jugendliche. Zürich

Kremer, Detlev/Andreas B. Kilcher, ed., (⁴2015): Romantik. Stuttgart

Kümmerling-Meibauer, Bettina (2012): Kinder- und Jugendliteratur. Eine Einführung. Darmstadt

Limbach, Gwendolyn (2013): "You the Man, Well, Sorta": Gender Binaries and Liminality in Mulan. In: Diversity on Disney Films. Critical Essays on Race, Ethnicity, Gender, Sexuality and Disability, ed. Johnson Cheu, Jefferson, 115–128

Lötscher, Christine (2017): Teenagernöte im Freilichtmuseum. Die Märchenspielfilmreihen ‚Sechs auf einen Streich‘ (ARD) und ‚Märchenperlen‘ (ZDF). In: Märchen im Märchenwechsel. Zur Geschichte und Gegenwart des Märchenfilms, eds. Ute Dettmar/Claudia Maria Pecher/Ron Schlesinger, Stuttgart, 309–326

Macaluso, Michael (2016): The Postfeminist Princess. Public Discourse and Disney's Curricular Guide to Feminism. In: Disney, Culture, and Curriculum, eds. Jennifer A. Sandlin/Julie C. Garlen, London, 73–86

McRobbie, Angela (2010): Top Girls. Feminismus und der Aufstieg des neoliberalen Geschlechterregimes, eds. Sabine Hark/Paula-Irene Villa. Wiesbaden 2010

Neumann, Gerhard (1997): Puppe und Automate. Inszenierte Kindheit in E.T.A. Hoffmanns Sozialisationsmärchen Nußknacker und Mausekönig. In: Jugend. Ein romantisches Konzept? Ed. Günter Oesterle, Würzburg, 135–160

The Nutcracker and the Four Realms. https://en.wikipedia.org/wiki/The_Nutcracker_and_the_Four_Realms. Accessed: 23. November 2020

Putnam, Amanda (2013): Mean Ladies: Transgendered Villains in Disney Films. In: Diversity on Disney Films. Critical Essays on Race, Ethnicity, Gender, Sexuality and Disability, ed. Johnson Cheu, Jefferson, 147–162

Schmaus, Marion (2015): Nußknacker und Mausekönig. Ein Weihnachtsabend (1816). In: E.T.A. Hoffmann-Handbuch. Leben, Werk, Wirkung, eds. Christine Luboll/Harald Neumeyer, Stuttgart, 100–103

Sells, Laura (1995): "Where Do the Mermaids Stand?" Voice and Body in The Little Mermaid. In: From Mouse to Mermaid. The Politics of Film, Gender, and Culture, eds. Elisabeth Bell/Lynda Haas/Laura Sells, Bloomington [et al.], 175–192

Stemmann, Anna (2019): Bild-Text-Dynamiken in digitalen Kulturen: Memes als Baustein der Populärkultur. In: Schnittstellen der Kinder- und Jugendmedienforschung, eds. Ute Dettmar/Caroline Roeder/Ingrid Tomkowiak, Stuttgart (Studien zu Kinder- und Jugendliteratur und -medien; 1), 135–149

Stiglegger, Marcus (2017): Märchenfilm und Filmmärchen. Der beschwerliche Weg zum Happyend. In: *Märchen im Märchenwechsel. Zur Geschichte und Gegenwart des Märchenfilms*, eds. Ute Dettmar/Claudia Maria Pecher/Ron Schlesinger, Stuttgart, 1–11

Tomkowiak, Ingrid (2017): Capture the Imagination—100 Jahre Disney-Märchenanimationsfilme. In: *Märchen im Märchenwechsel. Zur Geschichte und Gegenwart des Märchenfilms*, eds. Ute Dettmar/Claudia Maria Pecher/Ron Schlesinger, Stuttgart, 121–141

Wilkending, Gisela (1990): Mädchenliteratur von der Mitte des 19. Jahrhunderts bis zum Ersten Weltkrieg. In: *Geschichte der deutschen Kinder- und Jugendliteratur*, ed. Reiner Wild, Stuttgart, 220–250

Zipes, Jack (1995): Breaking the Disney Spell. In: *From Mouse to Mermaid. The Politics of Film, Gender, and Culture*, eds. Elisabeth Bell/Lynda Haas/Laura Sells, Bloomington [et al.], 21–42

Zipes, Jack (2011): *The Enchanted Screen. The Unknown History of Fairy-Tale Films*, New York

ASPECTS OF CULTURAL HERITAGE

Walt O'Disney and the Little People

Playing to the Irish-American Diaspora

Emer O'Sullivan

Abstract *Darby O'Gill and The Little People*, Disney's 1959 live-action Irish-themed family film, features Irish folklore in the shape of leprechauns, banshees and other supernatural figures. The company had their eye firmly on the market of twenty million Irish Americans, and the extensive pre-publicity for this transatlantic ethnotypical film included Walt Disney embracing a diasporic Irish identity by presenting himself as 'half Irish.' He also claimed to have deployed actual leprechauns in the film. Through an imagological, cultural discourse analysis lens, this paper examines the paratextual and textual performances and representations of Irishness in *Darby O'Gill* in the context of Irish-American culture and its popular traditions. It asks why, contrary to Disney's hopes, it did not enjoy the success of other notable US Irish-themed films of the era, and probes the Irish involvement in and reception of Disney's 'Irish' film.

Introduction

The film which was released in 1959 as *Darby O'Gill and the Little People* was a long time in the making. Walt Disney started work on an "Irish-themed project" (McManus 2017, 192) in 1945, kick-started by "an unsolicited original story treatment entitled 'The Little People'" (ibid).[1] One of its most striking features is Disney's level of staged personal involvement with the heritage, the theme

---

[1] In his PhD thesis, *Darby O'Gill and the Construction of Irish Identity*, Brian McManus (2017) did pioneering work in the Disney archives to reconstruct the making of the film.

E. O'Sullivan (✉)
Leuphana University Lüneburg, Lüneburg, Germany
e-mail: emer.osullivan@uni.leuphana.de

© The Author(s), under exclusive license to Springer-Verlag GmbH, DE, part of
Springer Nature 2022
U. Dettmar and I. Tomkowiak (eds.), *On Disney*, Studien zu Kinder- und
Jugendliteratur und -medien 9, https://doi.org/10.1007/978-3-662-64625-0_8

and the making of the film. After introducing *Darby O'Gill and the Little People* and using an approach grounded in imagology whose aim is to deconstruct ethnotypes, or stereotypes applied to groups that are primarily perceived and characterised by their ethnicity (cf. Leerssen 2016), this article will engage with the discursive construct of 'Irishness' and its representation in the context of Irish America by analysing the film and identifying how it situates itself in the corresponding intertextual tradition. It will pay special attention to the extensive paratexts which present Disney's ethnicity as his motivation and special qualification to produce an 'Irish' film, as well as the leprechauns in the film—small wily, trickster fairies from Irish folklore—as authentic, living beings. It will show how, by using a range of ethnotypical elements, by employing Self-Other oppositions, and by engaging intertextuality with tropes from popular culture in the Irish-American diaspora, the film both explicitly and implicitly presents Irishness for an American audience of Irish descent. Although Disney is notorious for appropriating cultural traditions from all over the world, first denounced in the influential study by Richard Schickel as someone who "always came as a conquerer [...] with know-how instead of sympathy and respect for alien traditions" (Schickel 1968, 227), his presentation of Irishness has so far been absent from scholarship which engages with his appropriation of folklore.

Disney had hoped the film would be a box-office hit, especially in cinemas in the major centres of Irish America, but it did not enjoy the resounding success of other notable US Irish-themed films of the era, reasons for which will be considered here. This will be complemented by a brief account of how Irish audiences responded then and respond now to the representation from an external, diasporic perspective. In conclusion, I will ask how Disney's appropriation of Irish heritage can be assessed in relation to his appropriation of cultures and stories from all around the world.

Darby O'Gill and the Little People (1959)

Darby O'Gill (played by Albert Sharpe), an elderly Irish caretaker on Lord Fitzpatrick's estate in the small town of Rathcullen, is a roguish character more interested in poaching rabbits and telling stories in the local pub about his encounters with leprechauns than doing his job. He is replaced by a younger man, Michael McBride (Sean Connery),[2] who falls in love with Darby's daughter Katie

---

[2]Connery, a Scotsman, was then a relatively unknown actor. It was this film that brought him to the attention of Albert R. Broccoli, who subsequently cast him in his most famous role as James Bond. One of Connery's talents which can be heard in the film but wasn't later exploited by Broccoli or others, is his singing. See https://www.youtube.com/watch?v=eTwmjOySDjA.

Walt O'Disney and The Little People
117

(Janet Munro). In a series of comic misadventures, Darby is captured by the leprechauns, but manages to trick and kidnap their King Brian (Jimmy O'Dea) in order to get the three wishes a leprechaun must grant if captured by a human being. The dramatic climax of the film occurs when Katie is fatally injured, and a banshee—a female spirit who heralds the death of a family member—summons the *cóiste bodhar*, or death coach. Darby demands his third and final wish from King Brian, which is that he himself should be taken instead of Katie. King Brian grants it and offers to join him for part of the way. He then tricks Darby into making a fourth wish, in the knowledge that if he makes more than three, the fourth negates all the previous ones. So, King Brian saves Darby's life, Katie recovers, marries Michael and all ends happily.

The live-action film was directed by Robert Stevenson; Lawrence Edward Watkin wrote the script, adapted from the literary fairy tales of the Irish American Herminie Templeton Kavanagh.[3] Peter Ellenshaw pushed Disney's special effects "to the next level" (Kyra 2010), using forced perspective to trick the eye into seeing an average-sized actor playing a tiny leprechaun, and having normal sized sets built for Darby and large ones for the leprechauns. The film was not shot on location in Ireland, but at the Burbank Disney Studio in California.

Darby O'Gill displays many of the features associated with Disney movies. It is a family film which addresses both an adult and a child audience, and it has a bit of something for everyone: humour, sentimentality, romance and some horror. It also includes the all-pervasive family theme with special focus on the father-child relationship. When the leprechaun asks the widower Darby what he wants most of all, it is that his daughter Katie should be happy. And he is prepared to die in order to save her.

The entertainment value of the film is clearly founded in the adversarial relationship between Darby and King Brian. Their encounters, in which they try to trick and outdo each other with music, songs and repartee, are well-paced comic scenes which are still enjoyable today, in contrast to the dated and clichéd romantic and village scenes. The interaction between the Irish actors Sharpe and O'Dea makes the magic and their significant difference in size believable.

---

[3] Herminie Templeton Kavanagh (1861–1933) was born in England to an English mother and an Irish father. The family emigrated to the USA when she was eleven. As a writer "she expresses a wholly Irish-American ethnic identity" (McManus 2017, 73).

A Film for Irish America

Darby O'Gill and the Little People was made for an Irish-American audience; this intention is manifest on both explicit and implicit levels. It is at its most (cynically) explicit in a document circulated in the publicity department at Burbank before the film's release:

> Unlike previous campaigns, *Darby O'Gill* will have a ready-made market potential of 20 million Irish-Americans. Special attention will be paid to these people with shamrocks in their eyes. Their numbers alone could carry the picture to big box-office earnings (Quoted in McManus 2019).[4]

More implicit is the way in which Irishness is staged (and sold) in the paratextual material, and how its representation in the film itself chimes with the traditions and expectations of the specific Irish-American audience.

Staging (and Selling) Irishness in the Paratexts

The promotional material for the film focuses on two selling points: the Irishness of Walt Disney, and the actual existence of leprechauns. Irishness is taken here to be a discursive construct of an ethnic identity based on features taken to be characteristic of an essential Irish identity. In the article "How I Met the King of the Leprechauns," published in *Walt Disney's Magazine* in February 1959, Disney[5] introduces himself as a member of the Irish diaspora and recounts his childhood dream to travel to Ireland to meet a real leprechaun:

> Being half Irish myself, I learned about the Leprechauns of Ireland while I was still a small boy on our farm at Marceline, Missouri. I began to believe in Leprechauns, then, because some of my relatives had pretty convincing stories to tell about the magic powers of these Little People, and the tricks they could play when angry.
>
> So, I promised myself that one day, after I had grown up, I would go to the land of the Leprechaun myself, and meet one in person. The opportunity finally came last year when we decided to use real Little People instead of cartoon imitations in a movie we were planning (Disney 1959).

Walt Disney's paternal grandparents were indeed Irish-born immigrants to the US. But until this film, Disney's ethnicity hadn't featured in any significant way. "Walt was an American through and through, but he always had a fondness for the stories of Ireland and its people … especially the little ones," explains a special 2011 St.

---

[4] A shamrock, a sprig of young clover, was purportedly used by Saint Patrick to explain the Holy Trinity, with a leaf each representing the Father, the Son and the Holy Spirit. It is commonly used as a symbol of Ireland.

[5] The article was credited to Disney but was actually written by unit publicist John Conner (cf. McManus 2017, 284).

Patrick's Day tribute on the Disney website (Lowery 2011). This fondness is staged as the defining feature of his Irishness when it came to making and publicising *Darby O'Gill and the Little People.* The only thing Disney stopped short of when reinventing himself as an Irishman, was to rename himself 'Walt O'Disney.'

A forty-nine-minute television special, *I Captured the King of the Leprechauns* (Keller/Stevenson 1959), broadcast in May 1959, presents an extensive fiction-alised account of the making of the film. It features Disney himself and the two Irish actors Sharpe and O'Dea, blends footage from *Darby O'Gill* with new foot-age shot partly in Ireland and partly on the *Darby* set, and is framed by a con-versation between Walt Disney and the American actor Pat O'Brien, also known as "Hollywood's Irishman in Residence" (Takacs 2021). Disney wants his advice, because "there's nobody more Irish than Pat O'Brien" (Keller/Stevenson 1959, 00:01:10) and, after much chat and a bit of singing, O'Brien gives Disney his blessing to go to Ireland to capture a real leprechaun for his film.

The leprechaun has occupied a key position in Irish-American popular culture since the late-nineteenth century; its popularity has had a "monopolising effect […] on an Irish-American understanding and appreciation of Irish folklore and culture" (McManus 2017, 278). Leprechauns were especially present in American popular culture since the Broadway hit musical *Finian's Rainbow* in 1947, starring Albert Sharpe, who would later play the title role in *Darby O'Gill.*

Disney and his team made the trip to Ireland in November 1946, where they received extensive support from the Irish Folklore Commission both during and long after this trip. The Commission was set up in 1935, a little more than ten years after Ireland gained its independence from the UK, to promote Irish folklore in an academic fashion. The leprechaun—and its association with stereotypes of the colonial era—"might have been seen as a deviation from that work" (Tracy 2010, 58), and the folklorists tried to interest Disney in one of the great Irish heroic sagas instead. But in vain. The archivist Bríd Mahon wrote in her memoir: "[N]o; nothing but leprechauns would do the man who had set his heart on meet-ing one and had travelled across the Atlantic in the hope that his wish might come true" (Doohan 2017).

Although Disney passed over the material of the Irish folklorists, he "cannily incorporated them into his origin myth of the *Darby O'Gill* film" (Taaffe 2016) in the form of "an elderly scholar" (Disney 1959) who tells Disney the story of how the leprechauns came to Ireland. This story is not based on any academic sources, but on a literary fairy tale by Herminie Templeton Kavanagh (1903), and its Irish-American perspective is clearly evident. In the story, the leprechauns chose to live in Ireland because it was the "place most like heaven," and because they wanted to live among people fond of dancing and singing, and who were poor: "[W]e like to have them poor, for when a man gets rich there's no fun in him at all" (Keller/Stevenson 1959, 00:13:27–00:13:32). As it was only from a distance "that the poverty of the old country could be imagined with such fond nostalgia" (Taaffe 2016), this is clearly a tale from the Irish-American diaspora. Contrasting the poverty of the 'homeland' with the implied prosperity of the diaspora is a Self-Other opposition common in ethnotypical discourse (cf. Leerssen 2016, 17). It presents a purportedly typical feature of a hetero-image or image of the other ('they are poor') against the implied background of how it differs from an auto-image or image of the self ('we are prosperous'). This particular opposition also has the stabilising function of serving to legitimise and validate the emigration of the Irish Americans. The 'old scholar' directs Disney to Darby O'Gill who brings him to meet King Brian, and when Disney tells him "I'm making a film about Ireland. The real thing" (Keller/Stevenson 1959, 00:22:30–00:22:44), King Brian graciously agrees to come to Hollywood with one hundred and fifty leprechauns to make it possible.

The myth that Disney recruited real leprechauns for his film becomes the mainstay of the publicity campaign. John Conner of the publicity department wrote in summary of a meeting in March 1958:

> Walt expressed great enthusiasm for attempting to keep the DARBY O'GILL publicity campaign on the fanciful side […]. He made it clear he understands that, of course, no one among the press would be entirely taken in by any pretense that actual "Leprechauns" will be used in our cast, but suggested we do our utmost to keep the newsmen with us in a tongue-in-cheek campaign where our "Little People" are concerned (quoted in McManus 2017, 281–282).

A final paratext which kept up the myth is the title card in the film, a personal statement in celtic font by Walt Disney himself thanking the leprechauns for their cooperation, and bearing his familiar trademark signature (see Fig. 1). Disney was obviously prepared to go to great lengths to preserve his audience's suspension of disbelief. His own 'belief' in the leprechauns was sold as part of his 'Irish'

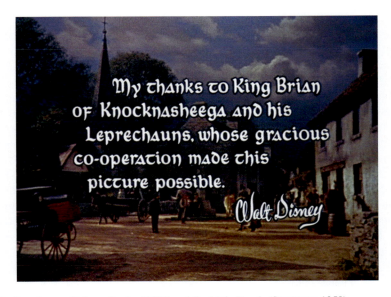

Fig. 1 Opening credit from *Darby O'Gill and the Little People* (Stevenson 1959)

identity, but it was also in line both with the company's business strategy that extolled "the virtues of the imaginary as an escape from the limits of the 'real'" and Disney's own "fascination with, and belief in, pre-modern cultures of enchantment" (Tracy 2010, 46).

Irishness in Darby O'Gill and the Little People

The way in which Irishness is discursively constructed and represented in the film itself is, next to the paratextual strategies, a further implicit indication of the addressed audience and its expectations. The film is grounded in backward-looking images of Ireland which mirror the tendency in twentieth-century American popular culture to encourage the Irish American "to envisage contemporary Ireland as exactly the same as the land from which their ancestors set sail" (McManus 2017, 202).

The setting of the film is the 'quaint,' pre-modern Irish village of Rathcullen, introduced as a timeless idyll in the opening shots. Geese, cows and horses move slowly across the sparsely populated village square, in its centre a huge stone Celtic cross. The two significant buildings are the Catholic Church and the pub (see the background in Fig. 1). A large estate owned by a mainly absent, titled landlord, would seem to situate the film before 1922, in pre-independent Ireland, but no political or social markers are referenced. Temporal signifiers in clothing, appearance and means of transport—Lord Fitzpatrick's extravagant mutton chop sideburns, the women's long woollen skirts and shawls, the horse-drawn carriage—seem to point to the mid- to late-nineteenth century. The simple, poor conditions of the Irish who, in the film are what imagology calls the *spected* or the group represented (cf. O'Sullivan 2011, 4), again serve as an implicit contrast to the modern comforts of diasporic Irish America, the *spectant* through whose perspective the spected are cast.

The folklore, especially the purported Irish 'belief' in the existence of leprechauns, implies a proximity of the Irish to the 'pre-modern cultures of enchantment' which fascinated Disney. This ethnotypical element of Irishness is closely connected to the romantic, Ossianic image of the 'Celt.' Emotional rather than rational, removed from practical reality, the Celts were seen as "visionary, often endowed with second Sight, prone to superstition; with a rich, often fantastical imagination full of fairies and miracles" (Leerssen 2007a, 123).[6] These characteristics featured largely in the work of authors of the Irish Renaissance at the end of the nineteenth century, especially in the poetic vision of William Butler Yeats, and

---

[6] Similarities on structural and contextual levels between the image of the Celtic and that of (other) colonially dominated nations have been noted by critics (Leerssen 2007a, 123).

were adopted by authors of American Celticism such as Kavanagh. Hollywood's tendency to cast Ireland as a whimsical rather than worldly place follows in this tradition.

An ethnotype with a literary tradition in the film is that of the Irish *rogue hero*. This flawed but ultimately positive figure is clever and mischievous, but can also be noble and brave (cf. McManus 2017, 42). It is a positive spin on the century-old trope of the *Stage Irishman*, drunken, stupid and violent, a demeaning figure of fun created for English theatre audiences as a counterpart to the idealised Englishman. By emphasising character traits that signalled political incompetence, the English, from the twelfth century on, stressed Irish inferiority as a justification for the English Crown's claim to supremacy over Ireland, and cast their "hegemonial expansion as a civilizing mission" (Leerssen 2007b, 191). The Irish dramatist Dion Boucicault (1820–1890) 'wrote back' by reinventing the Stage Irishman as "drunken, clever, and charming" (Cullingford 1997, 287).

The language of the film, apart from some phrases in the Irish (Gaelic) language, is Hiberno English, or Irish English with exaggerated use of accent (*brogue*) by the non-Irish actors and supposed Irish characteristics in speech. One of these is the cliché *top of the morning*, an archaic phrase formerly used throughout Great Britain and Ireland which mid-twentieth century American film makers mistakenly "picked up as an Irish colloquialism" (TaliesinMerlin 2021), as in the title of the film *Top O' the Morning* (1949). It is, therefore "an American Irish film stereotype based on an archaism" (ibid.).

The late 1940s and early 1950s saw a number of popular Hollywood romantic comedies set in Ireland: *The Luck of the Irish* (dir. Henry Koster, 1948), *Top O' the Morning* (dir. David Miller, 1949) and *The Quiet Man* (dir. John Ford, 1952), which won two Academy Awards and was one of the top ten highest-grossing films domestically that year. *Darby O'Gill* seeks to place itself in the tradition of these films by using music and elements of folklore which originate in them rather than in Disney's research in Ireland. When the leprechauns in *Darby O'Gill* claim that their copious gold and jewel possessions were recovered from ships of the Spanish Armada wrecked off the Irish coast in 1588, it is a piece of information taken directly, as McManus shows, from *The Luck of the Irish*. And the polka they dance to, *The Rakes of Mallow*, features prominently on the soundtrack of *The Quiet Man*; it would therefore have been familiar to and popular amongst Disney's targeted audience (cf. McManus 2017, 311). The intertextual origin of these elements shows how Irish-American films generated and perpetuated their own specific Irish folklore and images of Irishness; Disney aligned his film intertextually to these, and, given their huge success, it was not unreasonable for him to be optimistic about its prospects. He aimed *Darby O'Gill* at the same audience, the one "with shamrocks in their eyes" (McManus 2019). But, as McManus says, "he missed" (ibid.). Why did he miss, and is *Darby O'Gill* to be written off as an unsuccessful excursion by Disney to 'the homeland'?

Reception of *Darby O'Gill*

Reception in the USA

Darby O'Gill received mixed reviews in the US. The direction, special effects, music and acting was praised. *The New York Times* called it an "overpoweringly charming concoction of standard Gaelic tall stories, fantasy and romance" (Weiler 1959), but *The Monthly Film Bulletin* found "all attempts at Irish charm [...] pretty synthetic." Audiences were not accommodating, particularly when it came to the heavy Irish accents (cf. Motamayor 2019), and Disney had the film redubbed for reissue, also replacing Gaelic dialogue with English (cf. Samson 2008). Disney himself believed the film would have been more popular if the better-known actor Barry Fitzgerald, whom he originally wanted to cast, had played the title role (ibid.).

Brian McManus points to the paratexts to explain the lack of success. The popular Irish-themed films of the 1940s and 1950s utilised what is known as the 'return narrative,' a "diasporic wish-fulfilment fantasy" (2019), in which the male Irish-American protagonist grapples with a major problem which can only be solved by returning to "the homeland" (ibid.). Disney also utilises this popular narrative, not in *Darby O'Gill*, but in the promotional film in which he himself becomes the Irish American with a problem: he desperately needs real leprechauns. And he finds a solution by returning to the 'homeland.' However, this publicity campaign obviously did not persuade twenty million Irish Americans to go to see the film, and McManus believes that Disney may have mis-assessed his audience: in the diasporic fantasy of many Irish Americans, leprechauns belong firmly in the Celtic Twilight of a pre-modern Ireland, so Disney's tales of King Brian and his leprechauns "travelling over to glamorous, urbane and [...] modern California to star in a Hollywood film may have proven too bizarre to be borne" (ibid.).

Was that the end of *Darby O'Gill and the Little People*? It is one of the lesser-known Disney films and it is barely named in major studies of Disney's films (cf. McManus 2017, 20–21). However, the film does enjoy a certain degree of popularity in the US today, with several recent websites and blogs devoted to its analysis, many of which include positive comments and memories by viewers who enjoyed it as children (cf. Lane 2013; Samson 2008; Fanning 2019; Motamayor 2019; Foley 2020; Baia/Blake 2021; Walker 2015; Kyra 2010; Starkey et al. 2020). Viewing the film has become a ritual for many Irish Americans, especially on St. Patrick's Day. In the 2008 St. Patrick's Day list of ten great Irish movies by the review-aggregation website *Rotten Tomatoes*, *Darby O'Gill* turns up as the third most popular, and as one of the few Irish-themed movies that has a one hundred percent score on their "Tomatometer" (Rotten Tomatoes 2021). Now that the film has been divested of the tall tale surrounding its genesis, people can apparently enjoy it.

Reception in Ireland

The American critic Doug Walker who positively reviewed *Darby O'Gill* in 2015 finished by apologising to the Irish, saying they probably saw it differently from Americans. This sparked a great number of responses from Irish viewers saying that wasn't the case: "Irish guy here, no we are not offended. This movies [*sic*] great!" (Walker 2015). But that is only one side of the reception in Ireland. It is seen by many as the quintessential representation of 'Oirishness' and a touchstone for Paddywhackery.[7] In a much-quoted anecdote, the casting director for the Irish-American film *The Secret of Roan Inish* (dir. John Sayles, 1994) noted "'DOG' next to certain actors' names [...] [S]he said it stood for 'Darby O'Gill' meaning that that actor tended toward a stage-Irish character, especially when an American is looking at them" (Quoted in Tracy 2010, 45).

When *Darby O'Gill* was released in 1959, relatively newly-independent Ireland was, on the one hand grappling, "sometimes hesitantly, and sometimes ineptly, with its role or place in the modern world" (Fallon 1998, 2). On the other, Irish culture as a historical, mythological artefact with its associations of anti-material-ism and whimsy was a hugely popular export article, making the relatively young country a heritage attraction. But rather than being the victims of theme-parking, the Irish were complicit in this packaging of their culture, a complicity which was, historically, often dictated by economic circumstances.[8]

From the outset, the tourist industry was vital to the Irish economy, and post-war Ireland worked to position itself as a tourist destination for American visitors. The Irish, with dollars in their eyes, very much wanted to attract the (Irish) Americans with shamrocks in theirs, and played up to the American gaze. Recognising the potential economic benefits for the country, the Department of External Affairs cooperated with US companies who filmed in Ireland. The exasperation of contemporary Irish critics at the kinds of Irish-themed films being turned out by Hollywood is evident in a review of John Ford's *Three Leaves of a Shamrock* (1957) in the *Evening Herald* of June 1st, 1957:

> It parades about every theatrical and cinematic cliche and absurdity—in both dialogue and action—that has ever been perpetuated against the country [...] I fail to see how the makers of this film can possibly hope to realise their dream of putting Irish on the film map, encourage tourism, or help to acquire for the nation the badly-needed international recognition of growing maturity and progressiveness that would be of such enormous advantage to our critical economy (Quoted in Irish Film & TV Research Online 2006).

---

[7] *Oirish* is a term used to describe anything exaggeratedly Irish, and is associated with the tourist cult that paints Ireland as the land of shamrocks, blarney stones and leprechauns. *Paddywhackery* is the stereotyped portrayal of Irish people.

[8] Irish children's literature in English, for instance, was mainly published in Britain and the USA before the 1980s. This often forced authors to conform to 'foreign' expectations of Irishness (cf. O'Sullivan 2005, 57–59).

Darby O'Gill had its world premiere in Dublin on June 24th, 1959 with screenings in the US a few days later. Disney was greeted in Dublin Airport by six pipe bands, and was joined by the president of Ireland, Sean T. O'Kelly, for a special screening of *Darby O'Gill* attended by hundreds of under-privileged children from hospitals and orphanages (cf. Samson 2008). This was followed by a lavish state reception for the actors and Irish dignitaries, all with widespread coverage in the Irish media. Disney was feted by Ireland with an eye to reception on the other side of the Atlantic.

The critic Fintan O'Toole talks about the "strange unease" (2009) that *Darby O'Gill* still induced in Irish culture fifty years on, and refers to legends about famous Irish actors and politicians who picketed the film's launch in Dublin due to what they felt was ridiculous stereotyping of the Irish people. However, there is no record of any such protests. O'Toole thinks the Irish

> would like to think that we kicked up a fuss about *Darby O'Gill*, that we found it deeply offensive. I don't think we did. A Dublin workshop for people with disabilities, in an early example of merchandising, churned out Darby O'Gill dolls. When Jimmy O'Dea, one of the film's stars and an immensely popular figure, got married later in 1959, he had, on top of his three-tiered wedding cake, a little Darby O'Gill leprechaun. There's not much evidence that Irish people regarded him as a traitor to the race (Ibid.).

The Irish ambivalence was also evident at the sixtieth anniversary of the film in 2019. Slated by a critic in *The Irish Times* as "the notoriously icky Oirish fantasy" (Clarke 2019), the anniversary was nonetheless celebrated in Ireland with special screenings and exhibitions like *From Ireland to Hollywood:* Darby O'Gill and the Little People*: The World Premiere*, and talks about the making of the film, with Jimmy O'Dea's godson showing memorabilia from the film, including the original leprechaun suit (cf. Magnier 2019).

This anniversary coincided with the film being made available on the Disney + streaming platform, with the on-screen content warning Disney appended to a number of their films: "This programme is presented as originally created. It may contain outdated cultural depictions." Irish responses to these outdated depictions range today between offence and nostalgia, tempered by irony. In a documentary on Irish cinema by Donald Taylor Black, contemporary Irish filmmakers, who only since the late 1980s have been in a position to tell Irish stories themselves, reminisce about having seen Hollywood 'Irish' films in their childhood; they found the "bad impressions of being Irish people" very funny (Black 1995). Some criticisms are laid-back: although *Darby O'Gill* "must surely be one of the cringiest cases of cinematic paddywhackery that's ever been committed to celluloid, it's really more of a colourful fantasy, and is only as offensive as we allow it to be" (Wasser 2020). The postmodern use of ethnotypes in popular culture (the comedy-drama series *Emily in Paris* [Netflix 2020] is a prime example), encourages a type of ironic viewing unencumbered by outrage. Even the historical, demeaning stereotype of the Stage Irishman is now alive and well and present in many Irish self-presentations in a comic, ironic mode (cf. Leerssen 2016, 23). All

126   E. O'Sullivan

of this permits a kind of relaxed, amused enjoyment of *Darby O'Gill* in Ireland today which wouldn't have been possible in the late 1950s.[9]

Conclusion

Disney staged his own diasporic Irish identity in the service of *Darby O'Gill*, and he employed tropes and elements of Irishness then dominant in Irish America such as the idyllic, timeless setting, the familiar 'rogue hero' figure, Irish music and dance, exaggerated Irish English, and above all else, in his origin myth, purportedly authentic leprechauns. The film (and the 'folklore' in the paratexts) was based on Irish-American literary fairy tales, and aligned intertextually to the hugely popular post-war US Irish-themed films. Disney aimed *Darby O'Gill* at the same audience who guaranteed their success. Ultimately, he was intent on selling an entertaining story to Americans for massive profit. How can we assess Disney's exploitation of Irishness in light of his notorious exploitation of disparate native traditions from all around the world, of his lack of "respect for alien traditions" (Schickel 1968, 227)? Was the tradition that Disney exploited actually an alien one?

The source for the leprechaun folklore was Irish-American literary fairytales, the authority on Ireland in the paratexts the American Pat O'Brien, 'Hollywood's Irishman in Residence.' These were not elements of an alien tradition for Disney, but part of diasporic Irish-American culture, a hybrid culture (cf. Smith/Leavy 2008) which developed in Irish immigrant communities in the USA and has been maintained over generations.[10] The relationship between the construction of Irishness in an emigration context and in the homeland is never as simple as the Self-Other binaries commonly found in imagological studies, for while diasporic images are often informed by (sometimes anachronistic) auto-images of the homeland, they can also have a feedback effect in helping to define the 'homeland.' Declan Kiberd (1996) has shown how the definition of 'Ireland' was shaped in some ways by its diaspora, and the complexity of the relationship is also illustrated by the complicity of the Irish in the widespread commodification of Irishness (cf. Negra 2006). Discussing identity constructs in a diasporic or global context within a traditional imagological framework reveals what Zrinka Blažević has called imagology's "unforgettable theoretical sin [...,] its implicit fostering of the so-called container model of culture, which presupposes that cultures are ethnically and socially homogeneous entities with firm and impermeable boundaries"

---

[9] See, for instance, the satirical account of how *Darby O'Gill* predicted 9/11 (Waterford Whispers News 2016).

[10] When Americans are asked to report their ethnic backgrounds in the USA today, Irishness, once a socially stigmatised ethnic category, is now overreported. Diana Negra sees the category as increasingly serving "as the ideal guilt-free white ethnicity of choice" (2006, 11).

(2014, 356). Blažević argues for a new, transcultural imagology which adopts a heterogenising approach to properly account for creole, hybrid and translocal notions of culture.

The issue at stake here is not so much that Disney's product was Irish American, but that he sold it as an original, genuine Irish article. "I'm making a film about Ireland. The real thing" (Keller/Stevenson 1959, 00:22:30–00:22:44), was his claim, and he went to untold lengths to insist on its veracity. *Darby O'Gill* poses the question of perspective, and the external, American perspective on Ireland in the film is particularly manifest in the title of the love song, sung by Michael (Sean Connery) to Katie, called *Pretty Irish Girl*. If, in an Irish film set in Ireland, both characters were Irish, their nationality or ethnicity would be the unmarked form, and would not need to be made explicit. Marking the national adjective makes it evident that the film's perspective wasn't, ultimately, an Irish one.

References

Primary Sources

Black, Donald T. (1995): *Irish Cinema—Ourselves Alone?* Poolbeg Productions
Disney, Walt (1959): How I Met the King of the Leprechauns by Walt Disney. In: *Walt Disney's Magazine*, Vol. IV, No. II, 4–7. http://thehistoryofdisney.blogspot.com/2011/04/how-i-met-king-of-leprechauns-by-walt.html. Accessed: 13. March 2021
Kavanagh, Herminie Templeton (1903): *Darby O'Gill and the Good People*. Chicago: Reilly and Lee
Keller, Harry/Robert Stevenson, dir. (1959): *I Captured the King of the Leprechauns*. Walt Disney's Wonderful World of Color, Season 5, Episode 26
Stevenson, Robert, dir. (1959): *Darby O'Gill and the Little People*. Walt Disney Productions

Secondary Sources

Baia, Dion/J. Blake (2021): Darby O'Gill and the Little People, 1959. http://saturdaysleepovers.podwits.com/2020/03/13/darby-ogill-and-the-little-people-1959/. Accessed: 13. March 2021
Blažević, Zrinka (2014): Global Challenge: The (Im)Possibilities of Transcultural Imagology. In: *Umjetnost riječi*, Vol. 58, No. 3–4, 355–367
Clarke, Donald (2019): Disney Has Done the Right Thing on Its Past Offences. In: *The Irish Times*, 30.11.2019. https://www.irishtimes.com/culture/disney-has-done-the-right-thing-on-its-past-offences-1.4097953. Accessed: 13. March 2021
Cullingford, Elizabeth (1997): National Identities in Performance: The Stage Englishman of Boucicault's Irish Drama. In: *Theatre Journal*, Vol. 49, No. 3, 287–300. https://doi.org/10.1353/tj.1997.0070
Doohan, Claire (2017): 'It's a Wonderful World of Love, Laughter, and Leprechauns': University College Dublin Library Cultural Heritage Collections Blog. https://ucdculturalheritagecollections.com/2017/06/14/its-a-wonderful-world-of-love-laughter-and-leprechauns/. Accessed: 13. March 2021

Fallon, Brian (1998): *An Age of Innocence. Irish Culture, 1930–1960.* Dublin

Fanning, Jim (2019): Find Out About 007's Lucky Break and Other Magical Facts from *Darby O'Gill and the Little People.* D23. The Official Disney Fan Club. https://d23.com/8-magical-facts-about-walt-disneys-darby-ogill-and-the-little-people/. Accessed: 13. March 2021

Foley, Brendan (2020): Disney Deep-Cuts: Two Cents Film Club Finds Gold with DARBY O'Gill and the LITTLE PEOPLE (1959). The Cinapse. https://cinapse.co/disney-deep-cuts-two-cents-film-club-finds-gold-with-darby-ogill-and-the-little-people-1959-618e4541c7a. Accessed: 13. March 2021

Irish Film & TV Research Online (2006): RISING OF THE MOON, THE THREE LEAVES OF A SHAMROCK. Accessed: 13. March 2021. https://www.tcd.ie/irishfilm/showfilm.php?fid=56661

Kiberd, Declan (1996): *Inventing Ireland. The Literature of the Modern Nation.* London

Kyra (2010): The Special Effects of "Darby O'Gill". http://darbyogill-casestudy.blogspot.com/2010/09/special-effects-of-darby-ogill.html. Accessed: 13. March 2021

Lane, Jim (2013): Luck of the Irish: Darby O'Gill and the Little People, Part 1. Jim Lane's Cinedrome. https://jimlanescinedrome.com/luck-of-irish-darby-ogill-and-little-2. Accessed: 13. March 2021

Leerssen, Joep (2007a): Celts. In: *Imagology. The Cultural Construction and Literary Representation of National Characters. A Critical Survey,* eds. Manfred Beller/Joep Leerssen, Amsterdam [et al.], 122–123

Leerssen, Joep (2007b): Irish. In: *Imagology. The Cultural Construction and Literary Representation of National Characters. A Critical Survey,* eds. Manfred Beller/Joep Leerssen, Amsterdam [et al.], 191–194

Leerssen, Joep (2016): Imagology: On Using Ethnicity to Make Sense of the World. In: *Iberic@l, Revue d'études ibériques et ibéro-américaines*, No. 10, 13–31

Lowery, Paula S. (2011): I'll Always Be Irish – Walt Disney and the Emerald Isle: In Observance of St. Patrick's Day, Our Consulting Historian, Paula Sigman Lowery, Offers This Tribute to Walt's Relationship with Ireland. https://www.waltdisney.org/blog/ill-always-be-irish-walt-disney-and-emerald-isle. Accessed: 13. March 2021

Magnier, Eileen (2019): Donegal Celebrates 60th Anniversary of Darby O'Gill. RTÉ. https://www.rte.ie/news/ulster/2019/1011/1082660-darby-ogill/. Accessed: 13. March 2021

McManus, Brian (2017): Darby O'Gill and the Construction of Irish Identity. PhD Thesis, Trinity College Dublin. School of English. http://www.tara.tcd.ie/handle/2262/82823. Accessed: 13. March 2021

McManus, Brian (2019): The Making of Darby O'Gill and the Little People: Walt Disney Aimed the Film at Americans with 'Shamrocks in Their Eyes'. He Missed. In: *The Irish Times*, 22.06.2019. https://www.irishtimes.com/culture/film/the-making-of-darby-o-gill-and-the-little-people-1.3928432. Accessed: 13. March 2021

Motamayor, Rafael (2019): Revisiting 'Darby O'Gill and the Little People', Disney's Bizarre Trip to the Emerald Isle Starring a Young Sean Connery. Film blogging the reel world. https://www.slashfilm.com/darby-ogill-and-the-little-people/. Accessed: 13. March 2021

Negra, Diane (2006): The Irish in Us: Irishness, Performativity, and Popular Culture. In: *The Irish in Us: Irishness, Performativity, and Popular Culture*, ed. Diane Negra, Durham, 1–19

O'Sullivan, Emer (2005): Comparative Children's Literature. London

O'Sullivan, Emer (2011): Imagology Meets Children's Literature. In: *International Research in Children's Literature*, Vol. 4, No. 2, 1–14

O'Toole, Fintan (2009): How 'Darby O'Gill' Captured an Ireland Rapidly Fading. In: *The Irish Times*, 27.06.2009. https://www.irishtimes.com/news/how-darby-o-gill-captured-an-ireland-rapidly-fading-1.793541. Accessed: 13. March 2021

Rotten Tomatoes (2021): Darby O'Gill and the Little People (1959). https://www.rottentomatoes.com/m/darby_ogill_and_the_little_people. Accessed: 13. March 2021

Samson, Wade (2008): The Magic of Darby O'Gill. Mouseplanet. https://www.mouseplanet.com/8252/The_Magic_of_Darby_OGill. Accessed: 13. March, 2021

Schickel, Richard (1968): *The Disney Version. The Life, Times, Art and Commerce of Walt Disney*. New York

Smith, Keri E.I./Patricia Leavy (2008): *Hybrid Identities. Theoretical and Empirical Examinations*. Leiden

Starkey, Trevor et al. (2020): Darby O'Gill and the Little People (That D+ Show Ep. 3). That Nerdy Site. https://thatnerdysite.com/2020/01/21/darby-ogill-and-the-little-people-that-d-show-ep-3/. Accessed: 13. March 2021

Taaffe, Carol (2016): Walt Disney and the Little People. (First published as "Walt Disney and the little people. On the rise of the leprechaun". In: *The Dublin Review*, Vol. 61, Winter 2015–16). http://caroltaaffe.com/walt-disney-and-the-little-people/. Accessed: 13. March 2021

Takacs, Bill (2021): Pat O'Brien: Mini Biography. IMDb. https://www.imdb.com/name/nm0002285/bio. Accessed: 13. March 2021

Tracy, Tony (2010): When Disney Met Delargy: Darby O'Gill and the Irish Folklore Commission. In: *Béaloideas*, Vol. 78, 44–60

TaliesinMerlin (2021): What Is the Origin of the Phrase "Top ofthe Morning to You"? Language & Usage Stack Exchange. https://english.stackexchange.com/questions/51427/what-is-the-origin-of-the-phrase-top-of-the-morning-to-you. Accessed: 13. March 2021

Walker, Doug (2015): Darby O'Gill and the Little People - Disneycember. Channel Awesome. https://www.youtube.com/watch?v=n7aiWK8cwuY. Accessed: 13. March 2021

Wasser, Chris (2020): From Darby O'Gill to Far and Away: The Worst Depictions of Ireland on the Big Screen. In: *Irish Examiner*, 17.03.2020. https://www.irishexaminer.com/lifestyle/arid-30988397.html. Accessed: 13. March 2021

Waterford Whispers News (2016): Chilling: Did Darby O'Gill Predict 9/11? Waterford Whisper News. https://waterfordwhispersnews.com/2016/03/09/chilling-did-darby-ogill-predict-911-3/. Accessed: 13. March 2021

Weiler, H. A (1959): The Little People. In: *The New York Times*, 07.01.1959. https://www.nytimes.com/1959/07/01/archives/the-little-people.html. Accessed: 13. March 2021

From the Old World

Disney's Transformation of European Cultural Heritage in *Fantasia* (1940)

Ludger Scherer

Abstract Disney's animated films continue to exercise an enormous impact on children's media, both in the USA and in Europe. In this context, not only traditional European fairy tales underwent transformation when Disney adapted them for the screen, but classical myths from Greco-Roman antiquity were also profoundly Americanised in the animated family films. *Fantasia* (1940), Disney's experimental feature film, puts eight animated segments in dialogue with European music from the Baroque to the contemporary era, all episodes dealing with the cycle of nature and human attempts to control it. Another recurrent motif in *Fantasia* seems to be a problematic veiled eroticism, especially visible in the transformations of European pictorial heritage and antique mythological figures. Focusing on central episodes, this chapter examines some aspects of the manifold 'Disneyfication' of European texts, myths, arts and music in the film, an endeavour between creative artistic reinvention and cultural appropriation.

Introduction: Americanisation and 'Disneyfication'

To understand the immense cultural impact the United States exerts on the globalised world, it might be helpful to recall some historical aspects of American society, especially in the field of culture. The former colonies, once liberated from European domination, urged to form an independent civilisation of their own—out of the Nothing they left when they eradicated the Native Americans. Nevertheless, this American independence was created by and for immigrants from the Old World who carried their cultural backgrounds with them, along with their religious beliefs which were mostly Puritan. An orientation towards European heritage remained a strong feature of American culture, but developed a peculiarly transatlantic character. The influences from Europe were widely adapted and transformed to fit the New

---

L. Scherer (✉)
University of Bonn, Bonn, Germany
e-mail: l.scherer@uni-bonn.de

© The Author(s), under exclusive license to Springer-Verlag GmbH, DE, part of Springer Nature 2022
U. Dettmar and I. Tomkowiak (eds.), *On Disney*, Studien zu Kinder- und Jugendliteratur und -medien 9, https://doi.org/10.1007/978-3-662-64625-0_9

World's mass culture, which was dominated by the ideals of populism and progress (cf. Nunoda 2013, 33). As immigration continued, motivated not only by poverty in Europe but also by the ideological conflicts that arose with fascism, an influx of art and artists from contemporary Europe kept a steady stream of Old World culture flowing into American society. In the American melting pot, however, the majority of immigrants quickly lost their linguistic and cultural roots, amalgamating some aspects of their backgrounds in the emerging civilisation. Thus classical and modern European tradition tended to be homogenised in its reception, and works of art underwent a process of alienation. Individualism may be a strong value in the 'Land of the Free', but freedom and standardisation are just two faces of the same phenomenon, for the narrow limits of 'common sense' constrain diversification, and thus presume (self-)censorship. As a result complex themes and thoughts undergo simplification, even infantilisation, unique features become effaced and standards of the dominant culture become more and more generalised, leading eventually to cultural appropriation of foreign or minority intellectual property. American culture began to turn away from European art in the effort to create an independent cultural identity of its own. Increasing cultural self-confidence was fostered by the success that American Jazz music and Hollywood movies found in Europe, and after a period of mutual cultural transfer which occurred in the 1920s (cf. Kletschke 2011, 170), US imperialism began to include the cultural field. This tendency intensified after World War II and culminated in a reversal of cultural domination: the post-war era saw the "Americanisation of Europe" (Allan 1999, 105), which put the former colonies in a hegemonic position vis-à-vis the now weakened continent of origin. This historical development might even be considered an act of payback, the consequence of the inferiority complex and the anxiety of influence that America possessed. The US underwent a form of psychological regression, as American popular culture went from an Oedipal conflict with its mother-lands and father-cultures back to an anal phase of infantile humour: buttocks and cute baby animals began to abound in printed cartoons and animated film, as can be seen in the following analysis of *Fantasia* (cf. Armstrong [et al.] 1940).

Amidst the cultural climate of the first decades of the twentieth century, Walt Disney, with his marvellous intuition about the average taste, put his entrepreneurial ability to the service of commercialising his (and others') ideas. According to his biographers, Disney's attitude can be described as "anti-intellectualism" (Wood 2015), and he was rather uneducated and untrained in the field of 'high culture' (cf. Barrier 2007, 155). His approach to cultural tradition, especially European literature, myth, music and art, involved extensive transformations in order to make it suitable to the American public he had in mind—which means simplification and infantilisation. By commoditising cultural artefacts, Walt Disney (among others) not only built an entertainment empire but also profited from the symbolic capital of culture, in the process appropriating the very European heritage he both admired and despised.

Disneyfication is the term often applied to the cultural process of transformation that can be identified in commodity films produced by the Disney studio. The notorious *Disney formula* consists of a simplified story told as a musical comedy,

From the Old World 133

containing a happy ending, featuring formulaic one-dimensional characters representing heterosexual patriarchal stereotypes, and focusing on technical innovation and visual artistry (cf. Clancy 2006; Scherer 2020, 168; Stone 1981; Wasko 2001, 114; Wood 2015; Zipes 1995; Zipes 1996, 6–7). This framework will serve as a heuristic basis for the following interpretation of *Fantasia*.

Fantasia: **Story and Structure of a 'Masterpiece'**

After the successful release of Disney's first animated feature film, *Snow White and the Seven Dwarfs* (1937), the expanding Disney Studio worked on several animation projects simultaneously. Out of this intense period of distracted creativity and "splintered [attention]" (Barrier 2007, 147), which also included the construction of a new studio at Burbank (cf. Barrier 2007, 158–160; Kothenschulte 2020, 148–155), came the animated feature films *Pinocchio* (premiere on February 7, 1940), *The Reluctant Dragon* (June 20, 1941, a promotional studio tour movie mixing live action and animation), *Dumbo* (October 23, 1941) and *Bambi* (August 9, 1942). Of course, one must not forget *Fantasia*, Walt Disney's most experimental movie (cf. Kothenschulte 2020, 121), which premiered on November 13, 1940 in New York. This ambitious feature film, with an original length of 126 min, had been in production since 1937 under the working title "Concert Feature" (Barrier 2007, 142). This title reflected its basic conception, to combine 'highbrow' classical music with 'lowbrow' animation in order to popularise the former and to elevate the latter. As Disney put it, speaking of his "most exciting adventure": "At last, we have found a way to use in our medium the great music of all times and the flood of new ideas which it inspires" (quotation from Culhane 1987, 9). The didactic intention, to popularise classical music, represents but one side of the project, the other being to demonstrate the artistic dignity of animated films beyond comical cartoons. This was a dual attempt to "bridge the gap between the elite and the common spectator" (Nunoda 2013, 34). Animation started in January 1938 and was finished by November 1940, just in time for the premiere (cf. Culhane 1987, 22). In the meantime, the concept had changed, and the feature film had been re-baptised *Fantasia* by autumn 1938 (cf. Barrier 2007, 143). In order to furnish the best acoustics for the classical music, Disney had his department develop a multichannel sound system he called "Fantasound" (Culhane 1987, 19; cf. Kletschke 2011, 72–76; Telotte 2008, 36). The high costs of this technological innovation was borne not only by the studio for developing it, but also by the theatres which had to install it in order to be part of the exclusive road-show release of the film, and this contributed to *Fantasia*'s initial financial failure (cf. Eliot 1994, 165–166). In addition Disney had to give up his original plan to alter the film at every new release, replacing old sections by new ones. Some of the already produced items, including Debussy's *Clair de lune*, Wagner's *Valkyries*, and a baby ballet, are described by Allan (1999, 263–267), with sketches pictured by Kothenschulte (2020, 142–147).

When discussing a *Disney* motion picture it is, of course, important not to ignore the hecatomb of collaborators, in this case beginning with Ben Sharpsteen, responsible for supervising production, and the story directors Joe Grant and Dick Huemer, to name but a few of the many artists involved in this expensive $2.28 million production. In general, working for the Disney studio often entailed frustration, and the hard work of many artists remained uncredited (cf. Clancy 2006; Zipes 1995, 38). Disney, being an entrepreneurial capitalist with a paternalistic attitude (cf. Barrier 2007, 160; Allan 1999, 91), tried to prevent independent labour unions from forming in his studio, which led to a protracted strike in 1941 (cf. Barrier 2007, 163–173; Eliot 1994, 168–183; Kothenschulte 2020, 121). Story meeting notes from the studio archives describe Disney as "impatient and irascible" (Barrier 2007, 155), using a quite vulgar language. Nevertheless, Disney's leading position as the creative centre of his empire and the "editor of ideas" (Barrier 2007, 155) was crucial. The studio's successful working formula, however, especially during the production of *Fantasia*, can be described as "distributed authorship" (Fernandez 2017, 61), where Disney selected the appropriate artists and distributed work, but all the time controlled the whole project (cf. Clancy 2006) and evaluated the creativity of the animators in a competitive climate.

Walt Disney claimed that "music has always played a very important part since sound came into the cartoon" (quotation from Culhane 1987, 13). Indeed, he had experimented with synchronising music and animation before in his *Silly Symphonies* (1929–1939), a series of widely acclaimed short cartoon films which included the famous *Skeleton Dance* (1929) animated by Ub Iwerks, and *Three Little Pigs* (1933), the cartoon that combatted the Great Depression of the 1930s with its song *Who's Afraid of the Big Bad Wolf?* (cf. Kothenschulte 2020, 50–63). *The Band Concert* (1935), the first *Mickey Mouse* short film in colour, displayed a high level of artistry in its animation of classical music, in this case Rossini's *William Tell* overture. In general, it is obvious that Disney's "company has harnessed art, music, and technology to craft high commercial, family-friendly movies" (Wills 2017, 31). In 1937 Disney planned a "musically more ambitious short" (Barrier 2007, 141) based on Paul Dukas's symphonic poem *The Sorcerer's Apprentice*, buying the rights as early as July 1937 (cf. Barrier 2007, 142). The same year, Disney met Leopold Stokowski (1882–1977), the conductor of the Philadelphia Orchestra who was well-known in Hollywood; his contribution to *Fantasia* was invaluable. According to Stokowski's memories, it was a fortuitous encounter in a Los Angeles restaurant (cf. Barrier 2007, 142; Culhane 1987, 15; Eliot 1994, 160) that eventually led to his proposing a 'fantasia' feature film (cf. Culhane 1987, 18; Eliot 1994, 160), and the intense collaboration with Disney, who declared that he was "greatly enthused over the idea and believe[d] that the union of Stokowski and his music, together with the best of our medium, [...] should lead to a new style of motion picture presentation" (quotation from the *Walt Disney Archives* in Barrier 2007, 142). Stokowski, a British musician with a Polish father working in the US, shared Disney's spirit of showmanship and, most of all, his addiction to the anti-elitist American way of life. As he once declared, with the "quickening influence" of *Fantasia*, "culture is no longer an esoteric religion guarded by a few high priests" (quotation from Allan 1999, 94). Stokowski and Disney seemed to be ideal partners in the production of this new kind of animated concert feature film, even if Disney had to admit his nearly complete ignorance and dislike of classical music: "I never liked this stuff" (quotation from Culhane 1987, 29). Obviously, Disney sensed the opportunity to present himself as a real artist by collaborating with 'highbrow' musicians to create a "new type of entertainment" (quotation from Culhane 1987, 16). Disney's own artistic ambitions, together with his ability to entertain the public and to profit from the arts, seemed to converge in this project.

There is a debate about whether Mickey Mouse, the animated character that its creator and his American audience chiefly identified with (cf. Culhane 1987, 80), was present right from the beginning of the project. Deems Taylor (1885–1966), a well-known musician and music critic at the time who introduces each animated segment in *Fantasia*, affirmed that "it all began as a search for a starring vehicle for Mickey Mouse" (quotation from Culhane 1987, 13). Most of the studies and biographies about Walt Disney follow this version, declaring *The Sorcerer's Apprentice* "a sort of super Silly Symphony" (Barrier 2007, 141) and thus the nucleus of the future *Concert Feature* film (cf. Allan 1999, 122; Eliot 1994, 160). Culhane, however, supports the contradictory contemporary testimony of Disney's long-term collaborator Sharpsteen, who affirmed that "there was no such thing" (quotation from Culhane 1987, 13). In any case Sharpsteen's recollection is at odds with the essential role that Walt Disney assigned to his protagonist Mickey Mouse from the start—he is said, in fact, to have rejected Stokowski's proposal to create "an entirely new personality for this film" (quotation from Culhane 1987, 96), for instance. Setting aside this irresolvable conflict of memories, one can nonetheless say that both Disney's experience in combining music with animation and the decision to give Mickey Mouse the starring role were important factors in the genesis of *Fantasia*.

Fantasia consists of a multimedia program in which eight animated short films are bound together by live action sequences. These live action sequences feature on the one hand Deems Taylor, the master of ceremonies, who (acting rather "stiffly" [Allan 1999, 98]) introduces the segments and provides information on the music and the animated stories. On the other hand there is Leopold Stokowski (exuberantly conducting the Philadelphia Orchestra), whose silhouette frames the animated parts. Following the concept of a concert feature, the film starts with a curtain opening on a backlit stage with members of the orchestra gathering and tuning their instruments. The programme is made up of a variety of European classical music from the Baroque to the contemporary era:

- *Toccata and Fugue in D minor* (BWV 565) by Johann Sebastian Bach (1685–1750): originally written for the organ, this well-known piece was adapted for the orchestra by Stokowski. The animation, directed by Samuel Armstrong, shows the silhouettes of the conductor and some musicians illuminated by multicoloured lights in the *Toccata* part, then fading to semi-abstract forms of coloured clouds, waves and lights, musical shapes and signs in the *Fugue* part, and finally returning to show the conductor at the end.

- *The Nutcracker Suite* by Pyotr Ilyich Tchaikovsky (1840–1893), excerpted by the composer himself from his homonymous ballet (1892, op. 71a) and adapted by Stokowski (cf. Allan 1999, 115; Kletschke 2011, 149). The Overture is left out and the remaining musical numbers are rearranged in this order: *Dance of the Sugar Plum Fairy*; *Chinese Dance*; *Dance of the Reed Flutes*; *Arabian Dance*; *Russian Dance*; *Waltz of the Flowers*. The animation is once more directed by Armstrong, and shows fairies, mushrooms, fish and flowers dancing to the music, following the change of seasons from spring to winter.
- *The Sorcerer's Apprentice* (1897), a symphonic poem by Paul Dukas (1865–1935), based on Goethe's ballad *Der Zauberlehrling* (1797). The programmatic music was only slightly shortened by Stokowski and starred Mickey Mouse in the well-known story of the magician's apprentice who loses control of his master's trick. The music of this segment is the only one to be pre-recorded; this was done in January 1938 (cf. Culhane 1987, 16) and features a studio orchestra conducted by Stokowski. James Algar directed the animation; the sequence concludes with the famous metaleptic encounter between the silhouettes of the protagonist and the conductor, congratulating each other on their performances (see Fig. 1).
- *Rite of Spring* by Igor Stravinsky (1882–1971), the only then-living composer, was rearranged by Stokowski from the original ballet *Le sacre du printemps*, which had a scandalous premiere in Paris in 1913. Stravinsky came to visit Disney's studio in December 1939 while the segment was in production (cf. Culhane 1987, 20, 117) and approved the work (cf. ibid., 29; Kothenschulte 2020, 133), but years later criticised what he saw as an abuse of his music (cf.

Fig. 1 *The Sorcerer's Apprentice*: Symbolic handshake between the arts of music and animation (Armstrong [et al.] 1940, 00:37:47). Screenshot

Schickel 2019, 259). The story of the ballet deals with Russian pagan rituals and culminates in a girl's suicidal sacrificial dance. Disney chose instead to depict the early history of the earth, from the planet's formation to the extinction of the dinosaurs. The realistic animation, directed by Bill Roberts and Paul Satterfield, introduces the Darwinian concept of the survival of the fittest into the dominant Romantic view of nature as good, striving to combine and reconcile the two positions for the American public (cf. Brode 2004, 115–123).

- An *Intermission* sustains the illusion of a classical music concert with the orchestra leaving the stage. Only then is the art deco *Fantasia* title card shown on screen. After the musicians return and perform a short jazz improvisation, Deems Taylor introduces the anthropomorphised *Sound Track*, which visualises the various sounds it produces (see the 'dialogue' in Culhane 1987, 131).
- *The Pastoral Symphony* by Ludwig van Beethoven (1770–1827) was reduced by Stokowski from the original sixth symphony in F major *Pastorale* (1808, op. 68). Instead of Beethoven's rural scenes, the Disney segment, directed by Hamilton Luske, Jim Handley and Ford Beebe, depicts mythological figures such as unicorns, cupids, a Pegasus family, fauns, centaurs and 'centaurettes,' in an Arcadian setting, including a Bacchanal and a thunderstorm sent by Zeus.
- *Dance of the Hours*, an allegorical ballet from Amilcare Ponchielli's (1834–1886) opera *La Gioconda* (1876, libretto by Arrigo Boito). Although the music was not altered, Disney's directors T. Hee and Norman Ferguson transformed the ballet into a burlesque performance of ostriches (morning), hippopotamuses (afternoon), elephants (evening) and alligators (night), parodying classical ballet dancers and moves (cf. Bell 1995, 110). At the end, the final wanton tutti dance manages to destroy the palace's door where the scene is staged.
- *Night on Bald Mountain*, the symphonic poem by Modest Mussorgsky (1839–1881), was adapted by Stokowski along the lines of Rimsky-Korsakov's arrangement as 'fantasy for orchestra' (1886), an arrangement that had finally brought Mussorgsky's music to fame. This last segment of the film, directed by Wilfred Jackson, immediately fades into Franz Schubert's (1797–1828) song *Ave Maria* (*Ellens dritter Gesang*, D. 839, Op. 52, No. 6, 1825), arranged by Stokowski for the orchestra. The first part depicts the satanic Chernobog, the black god of Slavic mythology, summoning spirits, witches and restless souls to Bald Mountain, where a demonic Witches' Sabbath takes place, until church bells at dawn force the evil spirits to withdraw. A procession of pilgrims holding lighted candles, accompanied by Schubert's *Ave Maria* (with a new text in English), crosses a cathedral-shaped forest, and the film ends with the image of the rising sun, the interreligious symbol of hope and victory of life over death and evil.

An animated feature film of this segmented nature naturally ran the risk of lacking coherence and connection. In fact, critics did not fail to notice *Fantasia*'s disjointed episodic structure (cf. Allan 1999, 92; Eliot 1994, 162; Stein 2011, 73). Nevertheless, it is possible to identify some overlapping motifs and major themes. First, it is worth noting that the pre-existing classical music is what sets the rhythm of the animation and inspires the imagery of the film's micro-stories. However, the historical or mythical context of the music, as well as its own storytelling, was widely ignored and supplanted by the quite personal imagination of the Disney artists. On the level of content, the first major theme is the passing of time, from the hours of the day (*Dance of the Hours*) and the seasons (*The Nutcracker Suite*) to vast geological epochs (*The Rite of Spring*), but also, on a small scale, in the events of a day in the countryside (*The Pastoral Symphony*) or during a Sabbath's night (*Night on Bald Mountain*). Time is presented in a "natural order" (Allan 1999, 97), with the change of the seasons recalling the cycle of life, including death and rebirth. Despite his inclination to (technological) progress and modernisation, Disney's concept of time seems to adhere closely to the idea of an everlasting cycle found in ancient myth, and perhaps this subconsciously led him to create a mythological setting for Beethoven's *Pastoral Symphony*. The second major theme is "authoritarian figures reasserting order" (ibid.) and dominating the natural forces. The conflict between these two forces—the cycle of nature and the *homo faber* trying to control it—is palpable in many scenes. The element which best represents the fluid and ubiquitous power of nature is water, omnipresent in every segment of the film, from the creation of life on earth (*The Rite of Spring*) to the threat it presents to the clumsy *Sorcerer's Apprentice*'s life. Complementing the water is the sun: In the segments from Bach to Schubert, it functions as a mythical symbol of beauty, hope and victory of life over evil forces; in *The Rite of Spring* segment, on the other hand, it is also a natural power hostile to life, and plays a part in the extinction of the dinosaurs (cf. ibid., 101).[1]

There is another recurrent motif in Disney's experimental film worth noting: a tendency to "overt sexualisation of imagery" (Harrington 2014, 77). Animals and mythological creatures are shown in veiled erotic images that nevertheless do not exceed the limits of (self-)censorship. Female fairies and 'centaurettes' are depicted (partly) naked, animals like fish are eroticised (see *The Nutcracker Suite*)—even anthropomorphised mono-cells are shown kissing (Armstrong [et al.] 1940, 00:48: 57) in the story of evolution that accompanies *The Rite of Spring*. This maniacal but subdued eroticism seems quite at odds with the description of Walt Disney as "prudish" (Barrier 2007, 156), but in fact it fits all too well with the predominant puritan attitude in America, where the hypocritical censoring of nudity engenders sexual repression and ironically leads to the production of public imagery that over-sexualises bodies. For an animated feature film dealing with classical music to contain such ambiguous eroticism is, to say the least, peculiar. Superficially justified as a reference to classical 'nude' art, this pseudo-transgressive tendency is more likely due to the commodification of beauty, where beauty seduces the public's eyes and thereby acclimatises them to the unusual classical music they are about to hear: In a word, sex sells. This "'Disney' way of

---

[1] In Willis's interpretation of *Walt Disney's Los Angeles Suite*, the sun stands for God and authority, while the spontaneous power of water has to be controlled by human "rationalization" (1987, 92)—like the Los Angeles "policy of water imperialism" (ibid., 91).

From the Old World   139

conveying sexuality and sensuality in a family-friendly form" (Harrington 2014, 84) will receive intermittent discussion in what follows.

Music for the Masses: Transformation of European Cultural Heritage in *Fantasia*

Disney, in his intent to entertain the (paying) public by offering them this new combination of classical music and animation, was simply extrapolating from his own position of ignorance: "We simply figured that if ordinary folk like ourselves could find entertainment in these visualizations of so-called classical music, so would the average audience" (quotation from Culhane 1987, 10). Disney's evident contempt of 'so-called classical' music—in favour of all-American average mass culture—as well as his premise that visualisation of such music could be entertaining, will now be considered.[2]

Apart from the music, *Fantasia* abounds with art, literature and myths from Europe. Different European sources are "absorbed" (Allan 1999, 91), and many European or immigrant artists collaborated, at times, on the production of the film. In this chapter, I will focus on two examples, *The Sorcerer's Apprentice* and *The Pastoral Symphony*, mentioning only briefly the other segments of the film.

The dominant artistic style in *Fantasia* is European art deco, itself an eclectic style combining arts and industry. Its influences can be identified in most of the eight segments (cf. ibid., 103), especially in the background landscapes and designs of the Tchaikovsky, Beethoven and Ponchielli episodes, as well as in the opening Bach section.

The semi-abstract animated shapes that accompany the *Toccata and Fugue in D minor* testify to Disney's hesitance about whether or not to depict abstract images in a mass culture film. The result was a feeble compromise. Originally, Disney was quite interested in European abstract art, such as colour organs, especially Thomas Wilfred's *Clavilux*, Charles Blanc-Gatti's abstract colour music film *Chromophonie* (1939), and above all Oskar Fischinger's (1900–1967) abstract films, like the award-winning *Komposition in Blau* (1935). In fact, Fischinger was employed by Disney in November 1938 to work on the *Fantasia* animation, but

---

[2] Disney's contempt for highbrow classical music was not overturned by his *Fantasia* experience, as one can clearly observe in his later feature film *The Parent Trap* (Swift 1961). Americanising the famous children's novel *Das doppelte Lottchen* (1949) by Erich Kästner, the Disney movie inserts—as usual—a musical performance by the reunited twins. On this occasion, the cool California girl Susan interrupts the piano concert of her Boston-raised sister Sharon, declaring Beethoven's fifth symphony to be too boring (Swift 1961, 01:34:58). The following song *Let's Get Together* the twins perform in teenage harmony, however, is a simple Rock'n' Roll tune, and the choice by no means respects Susan's proposal to "compromise" (ibid., 01:35:06), to combine their musical skills and traditions in order to create something new. Again, the banal Hollywood formula wins a point, and European music is dismissed as a dull elitist intermezzo.

he left after one year, frustrated by the opposition he encountered from Disney, who wanted "something realistic" (quotation: ibid., 112) instead of pure abstract art, and from the hostile senior animator Cy Young (cf. ibid., 113; Culhane 1987, 37; Fernandez 2017, 33–37; Kletschke 2011, 102–103). Consequently, Fischinger disclaimed his collaboration on what he called "the most inartistic product of a factory" (quotation from Allan 1999, 113) and even accused Stokowski of having stolen his ideas about animating Bach's *Toccata and Fugue* (cf. ibid., 111; Kletschke 2011, 103). Notwithstanding his efforts to distance himself from the film, *Fantasia*'s first section preserves some of Fischinger's spirit and ideas (see some sketches in Culhane 1987, 42–43; Kothenschulte 2020, 122–123). In addition to these artistic difficulties, the rather simply animated images of the *Fugue* section suffer from a "lack of technological sophistication" (Allan 1999, 99) in relation to the later segments of the film.

European inspiration is also evident in the segment that follows, *The Nutcracker Suite*, on which the English artist Sylvia Holland worked for the story development (cf. ibid., 118; Culhane 1987, 57; Kothenschulte 2020, 134). Apart from Holland, other artists of European origin employed by Disney include Kay Nielsen and Vladimir Tytla, who worked on *Night on Bald Mountain* (cf. Culhane 1987, 181–197; Allan 1999, 162–165). European art also exerts a decisive influence on the abundant animated fairies responsible for the change of the seasons. These slim figures are clearly influenced by the popular fairies that appeared in paintings and drawings by the Pre-Raphaelites and by Richard Doyle and Gustave Doré, for instance (cf. ibid., 116–117). Their elegant movements, as seen in the acts of distributing dewdrops, colouring leaves and dancing on ice, are perfectly synchronised with Tchaikovsky's music. Remarkably enough, the fairies are depicted naked, surrounded and often covered by a halo of light (Armstrong [et al.] 1940, 00:14:21–00:14:38; Kletschke 2011, 150), but their feminine bodies are adolescent and androgynised. They are slender girls with extremely long legs, and their small breasts lack nipples (Armstrong [et al.] 1940, 00:23:51 and 00:26:44; Culhane 1987, 56–57, 64–67). These figures, like the cupids and other figures in the *Pastoral Symphony*, appear infantilised, reduced to an asexual state of naked innocence, "made safe by their infantile appearance and the magical setting" (Harrington 2014, 79). Disney and his animators are, it seems, more interested in their buttocks (Armstrong [et al.] 1940, 00:15:01 and 01:16:43, 01:21:38–01:21:40 for the cupids), in what Schickel calls an "explicit statement of anality" (2019, 256). From European androgyne fairies to American Barbie figures, the transatlantic journey of infantilisation has been a long one. In contrast to the nude but skinny fairies, the curvy Arabian fish of the next sequence move erotically and exchange flirtatious gazes in their underwater veil dance (Armstrong [et al.] 1940, 00:19:39–00:21:58; Culhane 1987, 61 for sketches and human models), imagery that would have been censored if drawn as human figures. Strangely enough, the mushrooms performing the comic 'Chinese' dance in this section became key figures in the successful 1969 re-release of *Fantasia*. Advertised as the 'ultimate trip', the film seemed to anticipate the decade's enthusiasm for drugs. *Fantasia*'s rediscovery thus fostered a reinterpretation of the film in the light of camp aesthetics (cf. Brode 2004, 16–19).

The Sorcerer's Apprentice: Mickey Mousing an 'Old Story'

The programmatic music of Paul Dukas's scherzo for orchestra *L'apprenti sorcier* (1897) became not only the very core of the *Fantasia* project, but also the most famous segment of the film. Such was its success that the sequence was reprised in unaltered form in the sequel *Fantasia 2000* (Hahn 1999). The visualisation of the well-known legend begins with the usual introduction by Deems Taylor, who insists that the music tells a "definite story" of a certain age: it is "a very old story" which "goes back almost 2,000 years" (see the introduction in Armstrong [et al.] 1940, 00:27:44–00:28:36; Taylor's text in Kletschke 2011, 125). The introduction thus leaves out the fact that Dukas's composition is itself a "translation of one medium into another" (Culhane 1987, 79), as it was based on Goethe's ballad *Der Zauberlehrling* (1797). More problematically, the introduction makes no mention of how clearly Dukas identified with the literary source of his music. Instead, Taylor merely evokes a diffuse ancient story, perhaps out of ignorance (cf. Kletschke 2011, 126). Since Dukas's scherzo refers to Goethe only through its title and the enclosed texts, the music in itself, with its "lack of lexical specificity" (HaCohen 2016, 42), evidently does not tell a concrete story, but only provides atmosphere, accents and tempo (cf. Kletschke 2011, 127) as a base for Disney's animators. Thus Taylor's introduction, by disingenuously claiming that the animation gives a faithful visual interpretation of Dukas's music, conceals more information than it actually gives.

The first written testimony of the 'old story', the literary theme of the Sorcerer's Apprentice (cf. Bönisch-Brednich 2014; Kalitan 2012; Zipes/Frank 2017), can be found in a story by the second-century satirist and rhetorician Lucian of Samosata (120—after 180 CE), whose dialogue *The Lover of Lies* (Φιλοψευδής) contains an internal story told by the character Eucrates about his old master Pancrates and his magic trick of making a piece of wood come to life. Goethe's notorious ballad, with its clear moral message, tells the story from the prospective of the *Zauberlehrling* who learns to act humbly in the presence of magic. The old magician, however, does not humiliate the young apprentice to punish his curiosity—these aspects will change in Disney's animated film.

Fantasia was not the first film to adapt the theme of the *Sorcerer's Apprentice*: it was Sidney Levee's black and white short *The Wizard's Apprentice* (1930), which also used Dukas's music as a soundtrack. Disney's version is clearly indebted to the Levee film (cf. Zipes 2017, 59). The *Mickey Mouse* episode in *Fantasia*, far from being a mere "comic adaptation of Goethe's mediocre poem" (Zipes 2011, 98), has complex levels of signification, and the protagonist is not acting out of "impatience" (Labbie 2015, 106, whose entire text is completely confused and unfounded). At the beginning of the sequence, we see Mickey carrying heavy buckets of water upstairs (Armstrong [et al.] 1940, 00:28:56) while the magician conjures a bat, then a butterfly, out of a skull (ibid., 00:29:40). From the start, the cute protagonist—with whom the public is supposed to identify—seems frightened by his master's tricks (ibid., 00:29:44) as well as attracted by the phallic Sorcerer's hat (ibid., 00:29:55), a symbol of magical power. An expressionistic play of shadow figures allows us to witness Mickey sneaking to the hat as the old wizard mounts the stairs (ibid., 00:30:02). Mickey puts the magical hat on, but unlike Lucian's protagonist he does not put clothes on the broom. Merely using hand movements, Mickey successfully conjures the broom to provide the water the apprentice had been forced to carry. In the meantime, he dreams a dream of universal power, depicted as an *ecstasis* (ibid., 00:32:25), where his soul leaves his sleeping body. High on a rock over the ocean, he conducts the stars and the waves (ibid., 00:32:25–33:37), imitating, caricaturing and competing with Stokowski conducting the orchestra. This dream of infantile all-mightiness comes to a wet end when he suddenly awakes, realising that the cave has been filled with water by the all-too-busy broom. Mickey soon becomes aware that the magical servant is unstoppable, so he strikes it with an axe—this act of violence is depicted only in silhouette (ibid., 00:34:22). Of course, the pieces of wood are resurrected into an army of brooms, a plot development that, by multiplying the number of infernal servants, exceeds the conception found in Lucian's and Goethe's texts. This nightmare of broom mass power recalls films by Leni Riefenstahl (cf. Allan 1999, 125). Complementing the musical crescendo, the animation shows Mickey failing at successive attempts to stop the brooms, until finally, desperately clinging to the master's magical book of spells that he is not able to use properly, the apprentice perishes in a maelstrom of water (Armstrong [et al.] 1940, 00:36:27). At this moment, the sorcerer returns to the cave, divides the water like a biblical patriarch (ibid., 00:36:43) and saves his apprentice. Anything but amused, he rewards Mickey's contrite smile with a frown (ibid., 00:37:09), takes his hat back and chases Mickey out with his broom (ibid., 00:37:33).

The music's role in relation to the animation here is what HaCohen calls "generation", that is the music in the film is "perceived as instigating action and change, and [...] lending movement" (2016, 36). *Mickey Mousing*, the term used to describe a film technique wherein music is matched to movement (cf. Wills 2017, 34–35), does not merely mean that film music imitates the images. In general, it refers to a more complex audiovisual relationship where the musical and visual synchronisation renders perception a simultaneous phenomenon (cf. Kletschke 2011, 129–132). In the case of *Fantasia,* Dukas's music, in itself a musical transformation of Goethe's ballad, generates the imagery through its rhythm and sound effects; Disney musicians amplified the sound effects by adding percussion sounds to the original score. As a result, Dukas's music and Disney's images interact in such a way that the music appears, in an ambiguous auto-reflexive way, to be at once the consequence and the trigger of the visual action (cf. Kletschke 2011, 137). Taking advantage of the "openness" (HaCohen 2016, 42) of Dukas's composition, Disney followed the story of the *Sorcerer's Apprentice* but developed it in his own way, using a more generalised type of *Mickey Mousing*: Music and images are synchronised in a complementary manner and thus create a surplus beyond the mere comic effect (cf. Kletschke 2011, 139).

Despite the slapstick elements, the episode also has "more serious implications" (Zipes/Frank 2017, 60). Disney, the master of animation, is impersonated here in a double self-portrait: He is Yen-Sid—Disney spelled backwards (cf.

Allan 1999, 99; Zipes/Frank 2017, 61)—the sinister looking magician, raising his eyebrow to show his disapproval (Armstrong [et al.] 1940, 00:37:09; see the anonymous caricature of Disney in Culhane 1987, 200). Like the master animator Yen-Sid creates beautiful images (the initial butterfly) with hand movements, like him he controls his magical realm, acting like a mighty (not quite biblical, but entrepreneurial) patriarch, and treating his apprentices (employees) like slaves. His final smile is depicted as more malicious than benign, and he seems quite satisfied with the lesson of "humiliation" (Zipes/Frank 2017, 62) he has just given his young apprentice. Disney's paternalistic authority makes it clear that in his cartoons and in his studio, "magic, or creativity, is reserved for the wizard" (Willis 1987, 88). This "master-servant dialectic" (Zipes/Frank 2017, 60) is reflected and complicated, however, by the fact that Disney's favourite animated character and alter ego is, of course, Mickey Mouse, to whom he concedes a short ecstatic dream of unlimited power, "having a spectacular lot of fun without being malicious" (Disney quoted in Culhane 1987, 84–96). By caricaturing the movements of a conductor, Disney seems to permit the animators to caricature his own position in a moment of creative and economic all-mightiness—whether purposefully or inadvertently resulting in self-directed irony it is hard to tell. The dominance of the autocratic magician is acknowledged in the apprentice's final "submission" (Zipes/Frank 2017, 62), but Mickey's dreams of conducting the whole universe with his hands suggest the ambitions of a younger generation of artists who cannot be controlled forever. Disney's Oedipal anxiety of influence meets with his nightmares of being overrun by collaborators (the army of brooms) he is no longer able to command—and his fear would later be realised in the 1941 studio strike. Disney, like Mickey Mouse, "has unleashed forbidden forces" (Allan 1999, 123) by trying to dominate and exploit his army of creative artists. There is much of Disney's personal obsessions depicted in this magical episode with "real music [of] consciousness" (HaCohen 2016, 47–48); the animated cartoon in this manifestation has evolved into something far more complex than the initial *Silly Symphony*. One final point: the central importance of the Mickey Mouse section in *Fantasia* is evident in the metaleptic handshake between protagonist and conductor. Pictured in silhouettes at the end of the segment, the pair congratulate each other on their respective performances (see Fig. 1), thus symbolising the reconciliation between high and popular culture desired by Disney.

The Pastoral Symphony: Classical Music and Hollywood 'Centaurettes'

One of Disney's—and in consequence his animators'—favourite expressions when describing their conception of their animated figures is perfectly illustrated in this episode: "cute" (Barrier 2007, 156; Wood 2015). The Pastoral segment had been initially designed to accompany music for the ballet *Cydalise et le chèvre-pied* (1915/1923) by the French composer Gabriel Pierné (cf. Kletschke 2011, 167), which dealt with an encounter in the park of Versailles between members of the seventeenth century court and mythological figures. By the time Disney expressed dissatisfaction with this music (cf. Allan 1999, 138), the mythological setting inspired by the ballet had already been developed, and a great part of the animation already completed. The final version has since been criticised as "an American idea of comic mythology" (Allan 1999, 137) resulting from Disney's "unsophisticated sense of humour" (Barrier 2007, 156), which even contains racist and sexist elements. Moreover, Disney's artist did not draw directly on Greco-Roman antiquity, but mediated through subsequent periods of classicism and popularised versions, including contemporary films dealing with the classical tradition (cf. Kletschke 2011, 171). As late as in 1939, Disney opted for Beethoven's music instead of Pierné's, a decision to which Stokowski objected because of the segment's mythological approach. "This is a nature symphony", he pointed out (quotation from Allan 1999, 145). But Disney overruled this objection, despite its grounding in musical expertise, and instead stressed how beneficial his imagery would be to the German composer's renown: "I think this thing will make Beethoven" (quotation from Allan 1999, 139). In his usual introduction, Taylor explicates the mythological setting in so much detail that one might wonder if Disney thought the audience had ever heard of Greek mythology before (Armstrong [et al.] 1940, 01:09:23–01:10:45). To make sure the average American public could appreciate the quite long (twenty-two minutes according to the table in Clague 2004, 93) and complex segment, the master of ceremonies mentions all the "fabulous creatures" (quoted in Kletschke 2011, 167) the spectators are about to meet, naming every god involved from Zeus and Vulcan to Iris, Apollo, Morpheus and Diana.

Beethoven's sixth symphony in F major, entitled *Pastoral-Sinfonie oder Erinnerungen an das Landleben*, was composed in 1807/1808. It was inspired by an Austrian countryside and referred to rural leisure activities. Despite this quite programmatic musical content, Disney's artists continued to imagine a candy-coloured Arcadian setting at the foot of Mount Olympus, populated by cute, often infantile mythological figures. The imagery, profoundly indebted to European art from Baroque to art deco, created a "blending of the old world and the new" (Allan 1999, 146).

The Pastoral Symphony consists of five movements, to each of which Beethoven gave an evocative title. The first movement, entitled *Erwachen heiterer Empfindungen bei der Ankunft auf dem Lande* (Awakening of cheerful feelings on arrival in the countryside), Allegro ma non troppo, becomes *Mount Olympus* in Disney's version (see Culhane 1987, 133, for Disney's titles). The animation depicts cheerful games played among multicoloured baby unicorns (Armstrong [et al.] 1940, 01:11:25), little fauns playing diegetic music (ibid., 01:11:29) and winged horses, Pegasus and his entire family, "[i]mproving on the Greek", as Disney claimed in 1938 (quotation from Allan 1999, 137). The group includes the usual baby animal which initially still has to learn how to fly but finally manages to keep his tail up, literally, by himself (Armstrong [et al.] 1940, 01:13:03)—an infantile symbol perfectly suited to the American dream. While Pegasos is a figure that originates in classical mythology, Disney invented for him a family, not to mention an entire species of 'Pegasi'—thus providing the creature with a social context that conformed to Disney's ideology, where the average American family stands as the only possible form of social and moral existence. After an elegant flight in the Greek landscape, the winged horses land in the water swimming like swans (ibid., 01:14:11) to meet their fellow animals.

The second movement, entitled *Szene am Bach* (Scene by the brook), Andante molto mosso, is transformed into *Centaurs and Centaurettes*, continuing Disney's ambition to 'complete' a lone mythological figure with a partner or family. As a matter of fact, the female centaurs, baptised 'centaurettes' in *Fantasia*, are not an American invention but were known in antiquity, although they appeared less commonly in the mythology than the males. Ovid, for instance, in his *Metamorphoses* (XII.405) mentions the famous 'Hylonome', who is pictured in a second-century mosaic (see Fig. 2) in the company of Venus. In the hands of Disney's animators these female creatures become the principal (love) interest. They are paired off with the males in matching colours, just as you might find in standard Hollywood depictions of high school beaus with their sweethearts. Unlike the 'Pegasi', which are pictured as a multicoloured equine family with a black stallion and a white mare as the loving parents of four different children, the colour-coding of

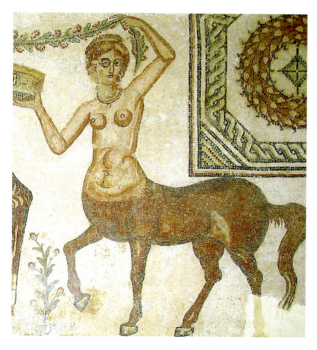

Fig. 2 The centauride Hylonome on a second-century Roman pavement mosaic in Tunisia (https://commons.wikimedia.org/wiki/File:Mosaico_con_centauresse.jpg)

the (quasi-human) centaur couples implies that "the difference between human and animal societies is racial purity" (Willis 1987, 92). At the beginning of the movement, the beauties are taking a bath in the brook and getting fashionably dressed, like contemporary American dream girls about to rendezvous with their counterparts. Following the ancient Greek pictorial tradition, the female centaurs are depicted bare-breasted, but only in the first scenes by the brook, when they are partly covered by water (Armstrong [et al.] 1940, 01:15:44–01:15:55), resembling "saccharine girls" (Culhane 1987, 140). Shortly after leaving the protective element of innocence (see Fig. 3), they cover their nipple-less breasts with garlands, in accordance with the hypocritically puritan *Hays Code* of self-censorship (cf. Allan 1999, 142; Schickel 2019, 255–256). The Hollywood starlets shaped as 'centaurettes' then busy themselves with their toilette, assisted by naked but asexual cupids (Armstrong [et al.] 1940, 01:16:12–01:17:30), whose presence is inspired by the vogue for babies in American movies of the time (cf. Kletschke 2011, 167–168). Afterwards, they glance at the arriving male objects of desire and start performing a sort of pseudo-lascivious mating dance on a catwalk. They end by choosing to match the colour of their partners, like good heterosexual couples. Two remaining individuals, sighing in loneliness, are soon brought together by the cupids' diegetic flute music (Armstrong [et al.] 1940, 01:19:50–01:21:20). The alluded scene of romance, however, is concealed when prudish cupids close

Fig. 3 A Disney 'centaurette' provoking controversial reactions because of her bare breasts (Armstrong [et al.] 1940, 01:16:05). Screenshot

From the Old World

an arbitrary curtain over the couple. Only one of them glimpses the presumed love scene when he spies through the curtain slit, thus showing his buttocks to the audience, the part of the infantile body Disney's film is obsessed with. Significantly enough, the cupid's buttocks transform into a red heart (ibid., 01:21:38–01:21:40), symbolising the anal concept of love that reigns in *Fantasia* (cf. Schickel 2019, 256).

Although the film's centaurs had originally been inspired by European artists like Franz von Stuck and Arnold Böcklin (see sketches by Albert Hurter in Allan 1999, 140–141), the eroticism of the model has vanished completely. Their female partners, the 'centaurettes', also inspired by European artists like von Stuck and Heinrich Kley (cf. Allan 1999, 143), are problematic in many ways: Fred Moore, the episode's animation supervisor, was famous for the pin-up girls he designed (see sketches in Culhane 1987, 139, 144). These American Lolitas, however, are a bad fit for the antique setting. With their "beautiful faces and voluptuous breasts", they are far from representing what the Disney artists claimed to be a "Golden Age of Greece reborn" (quotation from Allan 1999, 139). As Harrington points out, this "Disneyfication of Greek myth results in uncanny and hyper-sexualised figures" (2014, 80). Apart from an anachronism that leads to "the weirdest blend of classicism and Americanism" (Schickel 2019, 256), the underlying sexism has been widely criticised. Setting aside the hypocritical objections of puritanical religious fanatics at the sight of female bare breasts, the behaviour of the Hollywood starlet 'centaurettes' conforms to a gender stereotype that reduces women to mere Freddy Moore girls. In other words, they are superficial pseudo-seductive objects of male desire, sexualised beings but lacking sexual markings—a kitschy reminder of the "soft pornographic" (Allan 1999, 147) sculptures and painting of the Victorian age. The figures, evoking the appeal of 1940s American teenage girls, are thus an odd mixture of British and American puritanism.

In addition, there are racist elements in the 'centaurettes' episode that the Disney corporation has only partly censored in subsequent releases. Originally, two black 'centaurettes' were depicted waiting on their 'non-black', that is white-coded, fellows (see the original images in Clague 2004, 100–101). These images were edited in the 1969 edition, and then beginning with the 1980 release, magnified in such a way as to cut from view the black slave "picaninny centaurettes" (Clague 2004, 99; see the result in Armstrong [et al.] 1940, 01:16:23) while still retaining the uncut soundtrack (cf. Clague 2004, 102; Kletschke 2011, 175). But in the next scene, two black, zebra-striped 'centaurettes', shown accompanying Bacchus and depicted in a visibly more sexualised way than the others, remain unaltered (Armstrong [et al.] 1940, 01:22:37).

Beethoven's third movement *Lustiges Zusammensein der Landleute* (Merry gathering of country folk), Allegro, is transformed into the burlesque *Bacchanal*. The segment stars Bacchus, who has degenerated into a baby-shaped dipsomaniac. In this guise he more resembles the drunk Silenus of European pictorial tradition than the Greco-Roman god of wine (see sketches in Culhane 1987, 146–147; Procopio 2016, 7). While all the mythological creatures are collaborating on the vintage, Bacchus enters, riding on his equally drunk and "dim-witted" (Allan

1999, 146) baby unicorn donkey (Armstrong [et al.] 1940, 01:22:37). Without stopping to drink, he participates in the bacchanalian dances of the centaur couples, chasing the 'centaurettes' who mockingly provoke him, and whose prudish garlands are at risk of flying away because of their frolicking movements (ibid., 01:23:31). Bacchus eventually kisses his donkey instead of the female objects of his infantile desire, mocked by the 'centaurettes' (ibid., 01:24:23). Silly and innocuous as his behaviour may seem, there are nevertheless elements of sexual and social transgression that seem to require punishment (Clague 2004, 103). This occurs in the part that follows.

This fourth movement, entitled *Gewitter, Sturm* (Thunder, Storm), Allegro, by Beethoven and *The Storm* by the Disney artists, depicts Zeus chasing Bacchus with lightning bolts forged by Vulcan (ibid., 1:25:41),[3] while all the mythological creatures hide from the tempest. One young 'centaurette' is pictured in a curious manner, shying away from jumping over a high hedge in order to escape, but finally managing to discipline herself with a stick just as a rider on horseback might do. The scene thus comically plays on the double nature of the semi-human creature (ibid., 1:25:05) as well as on the fulfilment of the American dream.

While the dynamics of the animation are well-suited to the music, the moral message surrounding this fortuitous punishment remains unclear. When Zeus first makes his appearance gazing through the clouds, there is no sign of moral indignation; rather, his sardonic smile expresses a sort of sadistic pleasure at the prospect of gratuitously demonstrating his absolute power (ibid., 1:25:01). Granted, it is possible to interpret the intrusion of the father of the gods here as an example of paternal discipline, born from the obligation to limit the transgression of his children and the other infantile creatures—in other words to grant "indulgence within the paternal confines" (Harrington 2014, 80). And yet, the scene seems an exercise in disproportionate punishment: Zeus's unbridled hurling of a measureless quantity of lightning bolts far exceeds what is necessary to stop an innocuous bacchanal. The supreme god's actions would be more fit for defending Olympus from attacking Giants, such as in the episode recounted by Ovid in his *Metamorphoses* (I.154–155). If there was a didactic purpose to his actions, it had no success whatsoever, for Bacchus instantly restarts to drink from a puddle of wine formed in the deluge (Armstrong [et al.] 1940, 01:27:03), while Zeus goes to sleep in the clouds (ibid., 1:27:35) and nature recovers from the storm.

The fifth movement, *Hirtengesang. Frohe und dankbare Gefühle nach dem Sturm* (Shepherd's song. Cheerful and thankful feelings after the storm), Allegretto, called simply *Sunset* in *Fantasia*, depicts a parade of benign Greco-Roman gods restoring peace and harmony on earth. The rainbow, a biblical symbol of reconciliation, which Iris draws on the sky serves as a playground for the baby unicorns and cupids (ibid., 01:29:29); Apollo/Helios brings back the sun in

---

[3] It might be of some interest that Disney mixes up the Greek and Roman names for the gods without any criteria—another evidence of his ignorance and of the mediated reception of the Greco-Roman mythology in popular culture.

his chariot (ibid., 01:30:37); at sunset, a female Morpheus covers the Arcadian landscape with her veil of sleep (ibid., 01:31:09); and finally, as Taylor informs his audience ahead of time (Armstrong [et al.] 1940, 01:31:45–01:32:11), Diana, "using the new moon as a bow, shoots an arrow of fire that spangles the sky with stars" (quoted in Kletschke 2011, 167).

As a final addendum on gender aspects, it is of some interest that in the concluding *Night on Bald Mountain* episode the evil spirits dancing in the flames are depicted naked (Armstrong [et al.] 1940, 01:49:31–01:49:32), and the ugly, scary harpies are shown bare-breasted, with conspicuous red nipples (ibid., 01:51:01–1:51:02, see Fig. 4). This imagery exemplifies the demonisation of adult sexuality in Disney films, and sharpens the contrast with the immature eroticism of his adolescent female figures (cf. Allan 1999, 142–143). Nudity remains problematic in American movies, especially in the Disneyfied ones.

Disney's *Fantasia* was not universally acclaimed at its premiere. In addition to the initial box office failure, the critical response to *Fantasia* was quite mixed, not to say negative (cf. Allan 1999, 92; Barrier 2007, 162; Culhane 1987, 30; Schickel 2019, 260). This frustrated Disney's artistic ambitions. Music critics expressed disappointment and anger (cf. Luckett 1994, 219–224), some of them, asserting that classical music and film were fundamentally incompatible, "attack[ed] the

Fig. 4 Explicit picture of an evil harpy in *Night on Bald Mountain* (Armstrong [et al.] 1940, 01:51:01). Screenshot

film simply on the basis that the music was not meant to be visualized" (Telotte 2008, 37). Film critics, adopting different criteria, were more positive (cf. Luckett 1994, 224–229). The critical reception in 1940 also reflected contemporary concerns about the boundary between high and low arts; for example, Disney was accused of showing no "respect for the integrity of the forms [of high culture] he was seeking to make over" (Schickel 2019, 258). Horace English advanced another fundamental but well-founded objection: he criticised Disney's "central intention to weld into one significant, artistic whole the music and the visual forms which are suggested by the music" (1942, 27). English argued that music was strictly individual, and Disney's subjective imagery would yield "distraction [and] annoyance" (1942, 31). Later releases eventually established the aura that the film was a 'masterpiece', in particular the 1991/1992 video release, which advertised *Fantasia* as a rare, nostalgic piece of art (cf. Luckett 1994, 231–236). Disney, deeply embittered by the criticism (cf. Platthaus 2007, 74), ceased experimenting with 'high art', namely classical music (cf. Culhane 1987, 30), admitting: "Oh *Fantasia*! Well, we made it and I don't regret it. But if we had it to do all over again, I don't think we'd do it" (quoted in Schickel 2019, 253). While Disney was regarded as part of the avant-garde in the 1920/1930s (cf. Telotte 2008, 37), *Fantasia*, his experimental film of transition, seems to be "the culmination of film's earlier history rather than a technological window into the future" (Fernandez 2017, 82)—notwithstanding the commercial success of the long-selling film.

Conclusion: 'Disneyfication' of European Culture

The universal cultural impact of American movies, especially Disney's animated feature films—an impact so great that European children nowadays most likely first come in contact with texts from their own cultures via re-imported American movies—is but the complement of the earlier transformation of European culture by the US cultural industry. Despite the commercial success of the Disney formula, many of his commodity films have been criticised for the explicit and implicit ideological content they transmit. In *Fantasia*'s case, countless works of European art, literature and music were absorbed and adapted by studio artists. The result was a "'Disneyfied' form of high culture" (Wills 2017, 33). The transformation entailed a competitive kind of indebtedness, as American artists strove to surpass the European culture from which they borrowed. *Fantasia*'s Americanisation of European classical music witnesses an "uneasy mixture of reverence for and rejection of the film's sources in the Old World" (Allan 1999, 98). It was the result of a "compromise", as Disney himself described it later (quoted in Barrier 2007, 162), even an "uneasy compromise between elements of high and low culture" (Nunoda 2013, 32). The other side of the coin, however, is that Disney's American film could be viewed as a vehicle for preserving and redistributing European art—it could also represent a kind of memorial to European

From the Old World

culture (cf. Kletschke 2011, 171). This argument is reminiscent of the threefold meaning contained in Hegel's central dialectical term *aufheben*, which connotes *tollere*, *conservare* and *elevare* all at the same time. With *Fantasia*, however, any semantic subtlety is questionable: Disney may preserve memories of European culture, but he does so only in a quite reduced, deeply transformed and disrespectful manner—and any cultural elevation is not in sight. After all, *Fantasia* is representative of a transitional period in the American (movie) culture; it stands on the threshold between intercultural exchange and cultural hegemony.

References

Primary Sources

Armstrong, Samuel [et al.], dir. (1940): *Fantasia*. Walt Disney Productions. DVD München 2017
Hahn, Don, dir. (1999): *Fantasia 2000*. Walt Disney Pictures. DVD München 2018
Swift, David, dir. (1961): *The Parent Trap*. Walt Disney Productions. DVD München 2012

Secondary Sources

Allan, Robin (1999): *Walt Disney and Europe. European Influences on the Animated Feature Films of Walt Disney*. Sidney
Barrier, Michael (2007): *The Animated Man. A Life of Walt Disney*. Berkeley
Bell, Elizabeth : Somatexts at the Disney Shop. Constructing the Pentimentos of Women's Animated Bodies. In: From Mouse to Mermaid. The Politics of Film, Gender, and Culture, eds. Elizabeth Bell / Lynda Haas / Laura Sells, Bloomington, 107–124
Bönisch-Brednich, Brigitte (2014): Zauberlehrling. In: *Enzyklopädie des Märchens*, Vol. 14, Berlin, 1178–1181
Brode, Douglas (2004): *From Walt to Woodstock. How Disney Created the Counterculture*. Austin
Clague, Mark (2004): Playing in 'Toon: Walt Disney's *Fantasia* (1940) and the Imagineering of Classical Music. In: *American Music*, Vol. 22. No. 1, 91–109
Clancy, Susan (2006): Disney, Walt. In: *The Oxford Encyclopedia of Children's Literature,* ed. Jack Zipes, Oxford. https://www.oxfordreference.com/view/https://doi.org/10.1093/acref/9780195146561.001.0001/acref-9780195146561-e-0883?rskey=hURyLn&result=861. Accessed: 8. June 2021
Culhane, John (1987): *Walt Disney's Fantasia*. New York [[1]1983]
Eliot, Marc (1994): *Walt Disney: Genie im Zwielicht*. München
English, Horace B. (1942): *Fantasia* and the Psychology of Music. In: *The Journal of Aesthetics and Art Criticism*, Vol. 2, No.7, 27–31
Fernandez, Daniel (2017): The Sorcerer's Apprentices: Authorship and Sound Aesthetics in Walt Disney's Fantasia. Boca Raton
HaCohen, Ruth (2016): Between Generation and Suspension: Two Modern Audiovisual Modes. In: *The Oxford Handbook of Sound and Image in Western Art*, ed. Yael Kaduri, Oxford, 36–60
Harrington, Sean (2014): *The Disney Fetish*. Herts
Kalitan, Damian (2012): In Search of the Sorcerer's Apprentice: Between Lucian and Walt Disney. In: *Journal of Education, Culture and Society*, Vol. 3, No. 1, 94–102
Kletschke, Irene (2011): Klangbilder: Walt Disneys 'Fantasia' (1940). Stuttgart

Kothenschulte, Daniel, ed. (2020): *Das Walt Disney Film-Archiv. Die Animationsfilme 1921–1968*. Köln

Labbie, Erin Felicia (2015): The Sorcerer's Apprentice: Animation and Alchemy in Disney's Medievalism. In: *The Disney Middle Ages. A Fairy-Tale and Fantasy Past*, eds. Tison Pugh / Susan Aronstein, New York, 97–113

Luckett, Moya (1994): *Fantasia*: Cultural Constructions of Disney's 'Masterpiece'. In: *Disney Discourse: Producing the Magic Kingdom*, ed. Eric Smoodin, New York, 214–236

Nunoda, Erin (2013): Fantasia and the Generic Confluence of Convention and Abstraction. In: *Film Matters*, Vol. 4, No. 1, 32–37

Platthaus, Andreas (2007): Fantasia. In: *Filmgenres. Animationsfilm*, ed. Andreas Friedrich, Stuttgart, 72–76

Procopio, Ester (2016): Dionysus or Bacchus in the Figurative Art. From Kleitias to Disney, a Journey in the Iconography of the God of Wine. In: *Operaincerta* 131 (14.7.2016). DOI: https://doi.org/10.5281/zenodo.1185225

Scherer, Ludger (2020): *Pinocchio* im Film diesseits und jenseits des Atlantiks. In: *Märchenfilme diesseits und jenseits des Atlantiks*, ed. id., Berlin, 153–194

Schickel, Richard (2019): *The Disney Version. The Life, Times, Art and Commerce of Walt Disney*. New York [¹1968]

Stein, Andi (2011): *Why We Love Disney. The Power of the Disney Brand*. New York

Stone, Kay F. (1981): Disney, Walt. In: *Enzyklopädie des Märchens*, Vol. 3, Berlin, 701–704

Telotte, J.P. (2008): *The Mouse Machine. Disney and Technology*. Urbana [et al.]

Wasko, Janet (2001): *Understanding Disney. The Manufacture of Fantasy*. Cambridge [et al.]

Willis, Susan (1987): Fantasia: Walt Disney's Los Angeles Suite. In: *Diacritics*, Vol. 17, No. 2, 83–96

Wills, John (2017): *Disney Culture*. New Brunswick, NJ.

Wood, Naomi J. (2015): Disney, Walt. In: *The Oxford Companion to Fairy Tales*, ed. Jack Zipes, Oxford. https://www.oxfordreference.com/view/https://doi.org/10.1093/acref/9780198605096.001.0001/acref-9780198605096-e-219?rskey=rhsnsh&result=222. Accessed: 8. June 2021

Zipes, Jack (1995): Breaking the Disney Spell. In: *From Mouse to Mermaid. The Politics of Film, Gender, and Culture*, eds. Elizabeth Bell / Lynda Haas / Laura Sells, Bloomington, 21–42

Zipes, Jack (1996): Towards a Theory of the Fairy-Tale Film: The Case of *Pinocchio*. In: *The Lion and the Unicorn*, Vol. 20, No. 1, 1–24

Zipes, Jack (2011): *The Enchanted Screen. The Unknown History of Fairy-Tale Films*. New York

Zipes, Jack / Frank, Natalie, ed. (2017): *The Sorcerer's Apprentice. An Anthology of Magical Tales*. Princeton NJ.

ICONIC CHARACTERS AND NARRATIVES

Music in Their Bones

Play, Music and Materiality in Disney's Dancing Skeleton Films

Julia Benner

Abstract Dancing skeletons figure prominently in a number of animated films produced by Disney, starting with *The Skeleton Dance* (1929). As integral characters in animated film, dancing skeletons are like actors yet are also both playing musicians and playable toys. Due to their acoustic and visual qualities, they are particularly well suited to highlighting cinematic innovations as well as the advantages, potentials and possibilities of film. By animating the dead, skeleton films demonstrate the wonders of animation. Early Disney films show skeletons in undifferentiated groups. They make use of the sound of bones and stress their overall importance for the making of music, highlighting several (pop)musical practices. Later films such as *The Nightmare Before Christmas* (1993) and *Coco* (2017) individualise the skeletons and make meta-cinematic comments on previous films. Skeleton films can thus be read as filmic palimpsests and as animated films about animation, but they also show the integration of different folkloristic backgrounds and festivities as well as subcultural elements into pop culture.

Skeletons have been dancing in animated films since their early days. Their essential qualities, together with historical correlations, led to their great popularity and frequent appearance from the early silent film era to the first decade of the talkies. For The Walt Disney Company, skeletons were ideal characters to demonstrate the synchronisation of sound and picture and the many possibilities of the new medium of sound film. It is no exaggeration to say that skeletons literally form the skeleton of early animation.

In the following, I will explain why skeletons are particularly well suited to highlighting cinematic innovations as well as the advantages, potentials and possibilities of film. To illustrate this, I will first discuss the significance of skeletons in the early phase of film and highlight the special features of these characters. After

---

J. Benner (✉)
Humboldt-University, Berlin, Germany
e-mail: bennerju@hu-berlin.de

© The Author(s), under exclusive license to Springer-Verlag GmbH, DE, part of
Springer Nature 2022
U. Dettmar and I. Tomkowiak (eds.), *On Disney*, Studien zu Kinder- und
Jugendliteratur und -medien 9, https://doi.org/10.1007/978-3-662-64625-0_10

that, I will turn to the dancing skeletons in the animated Disney films *The Skeleton Dance* (Disney 1929b), *The Haunted House* (Disney 1929a), *The Nightmare Before Christmas* (Selick 1993) and *Coco* (Unkirch 2017),[1] which I will analyse from the perspective of materiality, by examining the musical instruments shown in the films and their historical and (sub)cultural backgrounds.

Seeing Skeletons

Apparently, many pioneering filmmakers thought that nothing could showcase the wonders of animated film better than moving skeletons. Indeed, these films clearly demonstrate that in cinema everything is possible, even the resurrection of the dead (cf. Westfahl 2005; Leeder 2017; Nitsche 2015; Räuber 2019). From the medium's very beginning, animated skeletons appear prominently, e.g. in Louis and Auguste Lumière's *Le Squelette Joyeux* (1897), Frederick S. Armitage's *Davey Jones' Locker* (AM&B 1903), George Albert Smith's *The X-ray Fiend* (1896), Segundo de Chomón's *Satan s'amuse* (1907) as well as George Méliès's *Escamotage d'une dame chez Robert-Houdin* (*The Vanishing Lady*, 1896), *Les Rayons X* (1898) and *Le Monstre* (1903). Among these films there are numerous examples of dancing skeletons, such as in *Skeleton Dance: Marionettes* (Edison 1898) and *L'antre des Esprits* (Méliès 1901) (Westfahl 2005; Merritt/Kaufman 2016, 5; Leeder 2017; Räuber 2019, 50). All in all, given that spiritism and gothic novels were *en vogue* in the Victorian Era, and many craved the new, the sensational and the impossible, the general popularity of the fantastic and the morbid in the period's filmmaking does not seem unusual. What stands out as exceptional, however, is the frequent use of skeletons.

In different cultural artefacts and across different media, skeletons mainly appear as allegorical figures of death, and dancing skeletons in particular are typically associated with the *danse macabre* (The Dance of the Dead), which has been a frequent motif in Western art and culture since the Middle Ages (cf. Oosterwijk/ Knöll 2011). In the nineteenth century, skeletons also figured prominently in popular forms of entertainment that Leeder calls "haunted or haunting media" (2017, 3). Shows given by magicians and illusionists, magic lantern performances and phantasmagoria often transformed ideas of the *danse macabre*. Traces of these performances can be found in silent films (cf. ibid., esp. 146). In the live performances, skeletons

---

[1] There are several other animated but non-dancing skeletons in Disney films (e.g. the Army of the Dead in *The Black Cauldron*, 1985). Disney's competitor Max Fleischer also made skeleton dances. In the *Betty Boop* film *Minnie the Moocher* (1932), for which Cab Calloway provided the music, skeletons appear as background dancers and singers. They can also be found in *Betty Boop's Museum* (1932). Hermann-Ising's *Hittin' the Trail for Hallelujah Land* (Warner Bros., 1931) includes a scene heavily influenced by *The Skeleton Dance* (cf. Merritt/Kaufman 2016, 56).

were usually depicted as ghosts, devils or women; films rationalised their ability to move either with magic or with X-rays. Filmic skeletons dance frantically and remove their limbs, spook on a ship or in a horror cabinet, are made to vanish or are brought back to life by a magician. Continuing the traditions of earlier media and performances, the silent films thus rely on transformations, disappearances, projections and other horror tropes and ghost story plots, emphasising visual effects.

In addition, the discovery of X-rays by Wilhelm Conrad Röntgen in 1895 may account for the popularity of skeletons in particular (cf. ibid., esp. 145–172). Around the turn of the century, fascination with X-rays was significant, as cultural artefacts such as trading cards demonstrate (cf. Thomas/Banerjee 2013, 59–72). Leeder even writes about a "skeleton vogue" of the late nineteenth century (2017, 137). The luminescence of X-rays was reminiscent of ghosts and there were many raunchy cartoons about the possibility of revealing a nude body or a bodily secret. X-rays provided a glimpse inside the body, changed the perception of it and reminded us of its mortality. In response, early skeleton films played with the possibilities of making a body visible. They were both humorous and spooky and can partly be understood as intermedial references to earlier performances and traditions that helped to familiarise the viewer with the new medium. Moreover, they challenged viewing habits and the question of the ontological status of what was presented.

Skeletons remained popular during the next few decades and "[b]y the 1920s, skeleton-dancing acts, like comic skeleton and dancing songs, were staples as novelty entertainment," as Merritt/Kaufman (2016, 5) point out. It is therefore unsurprising that dancing skeletons also feature prominently in Disney films, namely in *The Skeleton Dance* (1929), *The Haunted House* (1929), *Fantasia* (Algar/Armstrong 1940),[2] *The Nightmare Before Christmas* (1993) and *Coco* (2017). All of these Disney films are united by their focus on music and on pre-Christian beliefs or festivities that continue to be viable today. As will become apparent, the films integrate folkloristic traditions into modern narratives about pop music and performance art.

---

[2] In *Fantasia*, skeletons can be seen in the episode *Night on Bald Mountain*. They appear to be a spirit army that is commanded by the giant demon or God Chernabog to Bald Mountain, where a Walpurgis Night or Saint John's Night scene takes place. (The character Chernabog is based on an evil Polabian Slavic God that is called Tschernebog, Chernobog, Czarnobóg or Czernebog, Czorneboh, cf. Vollmer 1859, 403–404). The sequence shares some characteristic elements with the previous films, but the skeletons do not form the core of the episode. Moreover, they are almost transparent and have silent bodies, as their dances do not produce diegetic sounds. The episode *Night on Bald Mountain* is therefore less a skeleton dance than a dance of the witches or a Witches' Sabbath. However, even though the skeletons in *Fantasia* do not actively participate in the making of music, they function—as their counterparts in the earlier films do—as visualisers of the music. These skeletons are almost immaterial, which corresponds with the airiness and lightness of the strings of Modest Petrowitsch Mussorgski's *Night on Bald Mountain* and contrasts with the fire. In this way, the skeletons also contribute to the innovation of 'Fantasound' which is often called a milestone in the history of sound film (cf. Telotte 2008; Kerins 2011, esp. Chapter 6; Moen 2019, 180–186; Hanson 2019, 36–40).

In this article I will examine several dancing skeletons that appear in Disney films, focusing on the interplay between body and music and on markers of identity. It is important to note the special features of skeletons: the skeleton does not have a body in the sense that is usually discussed in body culture studies, gender studies or even in fantasy/monster studies, where the body is understood as a structure of a living human being. A skeleton is the framework of a body and therefore only a part of it. As the skeleton of a living person can only be seen with the help of X-rays, skeletons are strongly associated with death. Even though experts can very often determine a person's sex, ethnicity, age and even social class from a skeleton,[3] the layperson sees only a set of human bones. Consequently, the skeleton can be described as a cadaver stripped of all distinguishing identity markers. Real-life skeletons are of course inanimate, still, stiff and silent. In contrast, films show them as animate and flexible. The skeleton films discussed in this article play with the possibilities of animated skeletons: limbs are detached and skulls roll, the skeletons appear and disappear, shrink and expand, fly and rattle with their bones. Most importantly, the skeletons in the Disney films not only dance, but also produce sounds: they make music. Thus, the assemblage of bones that forms a skeleton is essentially an instrument predestined to become a medium for visualising music.

The Dead Must Dance. Skeletons in Animated Disney Films of the Early Sound Era

Early animated sound film in particular made heavy use of skeletons. All of the classical animated shorts—*Betty Boop*, *Toby the Pup* and *Flip the Frog*—contain dancing skeletons. These films highlight the synchronisation of music and the new Mickey Mousing[4] technique: music exaggerates the movements or vice versa, while the high and low of the music correspond with the up and down movements of the characters (cf. Kaul 2015).

Between 1929 and 1940,[5] The Walt Disney Company released several films featuring skeletons. In addition to the various advantages, discussed in the previous section, that skeletons brought to the filmic medium, the recycling of scenes or sequences that had already been produced might explain the comparatively strong presence of dancing skeletons during this early, experimental period.[6] Moreover, as we shall see, these skeletons have decisively musical qualities. Three Disney shorts feature skeletons: *The Skeleton Dance* (1929), *The Haunted House* (1929)

---

[3] All of these categories or markers of difference should be regarded as a spectrum.

[4] New in film.

[5] The last film, *Fantasia*, is not part of this analysis. See footnote 2.

[6] The films also borrows from earlier Disney productions (cf. Merritt/Kaufman 2016, 7).

and *The Mad Doctor* (Hand 1933); only in *The Mad Doctor* the skeletons don't dance. All of the films start with a storm and depict several well-known elements of ghost stories or nineteenth-century gothic fiction.

The Disney film that introduces (dancing) skeletons to the animated sound film universe is *The Skeleton Dance*. Released on 22nd August 1929, it is also the first short of the *Silly Symphonies* and thus plays a central role in the development of Mickey Mousing (cf. Kaul 2015), which was introduced a year before with *Steamboat Willie* (1928). In *The Skeleton Dance*, several skeletons dance boisterously under a full moon in a graveyard until the sun rises and they must return to their tombs. While this rather simple plot is, as Ross Care and others have noted, based on the poem *danse macabre* by Henri Cazalis that the composer Camille Saint-Saëns used for his tone poem (cf. Merritt/Kaufman 2016, 7), the composer Carl W. Stalling is said to have had the idea to make an animated skeleton dance. In an interview, he pointed out that he had been fascinated by a moveable cardboard skeleton that would "'dance' when kids pulled and jerked at each end of the string" (2008, 423).

With *The Skeleton Dance,* Walt Disney wanted to create "a musical novelty" (quoted from Merritt/Kaufman 2016, 5): the pictures were drawn after the music was composed in order to match them symbiotically. When writing the musical scores, Stalling "juxtaposes the melody of Edvard Grieg's 'March of the Dwarfs,' reorchestrated for xylophone, with vernacular musical strings and Saint-Saëns' 'Danse macabre'" (Merritt/Kaufman 2016, 8; cf. Gabler 2006, 129), which is based on the poem *Égalité-Fraternité* by Henri Cazalis. The cartoons synchronise the steps and beats of the skeletons with the drumbeats, and the characters use their own bones to play music, producing an overall effect in which percussive diegetic or *on* music is synchronised with *off* music. The skeletons are both the dancers and the musicians: with their movements, they create the music they are dancing to, underlining the possibilities of the synchronisation of sound and movement (cf. Telotte 2008, 30–31).

The undead dance a foxtrot, but they discard the formal foxtrot for a combination of line dance formations, *Pas de deux*, round dance and Charleston. Hans Emons describes the film as an "absurdes ballet noir" (2012, 90). The skeletons' dance aims for comic effects and is reminiscent of vaudeville and clown theatre as well as of folklore or children's dances. Instead of dancing the couple's dance, the foxtrot, the skeletons rely on different group dance styles, which gives the overall impression of a collective, reminiscent of the last line of Cazalis's poem: "Et vivent la mort et l'égalité!" (quoted in Retzlaff 2012, 513). Not only do the skeletons act alike, they also look the same. It seems impossible to tell their erstwhile skin colour, gender or age.

On closer inspection, it becomes apparent that the skeleton can be read as what Sammond calls "vestigial minstrels," as characters "carrying the tokens of blackface minstrelsy in their bodies and behaviors yet no longer immediately signifying as such" (2015, 3). This is suggested by stereotypes such as overlarge mouths and certain gags. More importantly, the film draws on a set of corresponding musical traditions: many characteristic features of what is known as Mickey Mousing had been used before in minstrel and vaudeville shows (cf. Brennan 2020, 28–30; Sammond 2012). As skeletons possess no instruments apart from their own bones, the dance is a decisively percussive one. Percussive dances originate in the Pattin' Juba (or hambone), a dance performed by slaves who were not allowed to play the drum (cf. Brennan 2020, 12–16). It "referred to musical drumming on the body using hands and feet" (ibid., 13) as is shown in *The Skeleton Dance*. Juba dances were combined with elements of Irish step dances and performed in minstrel shows, where "[t]he primary rhythm instruments were tambourine and bones" (Winans 1996, 142), and vaudeville acts, where entertainers addressed the audience directly. This can also be found in the film (cf. Merritt/Kaufman 2016, 7). These dances later evolved into the Charleston (cf. Holloway 2005, 52), also visible in the film, especially in the 'knocky knees' motif. Minstrel and vaudeville shows combined comic elements with the juba dance. This also plays an important role in the film and adds contrapuntal comedy to the otherwise spooky scenario. Thus, *The Skeleton Dance* picks up on a number of well-established musical and dance styles that were largely popular in live shows in the late nineteenth and early twentieth century. Moreover, Grieg's *March of the Dwarfs* links the film to music of the Romantic era, emphasising the setting that is reminiscent of a ghost story. A favourable reading, like that of Merritt and Kaufman, would thus hold that African-American and European musical traditions are harmoniously brought together: "The Symphonies revelled in a musical openness ahead of its time, a non-hierarchical approach in which all genres of music were considered equal" (2016, 8).

Four months after *The Skeleton Dance*, Disney and Ub Iwerks's short film *The Haunted House* was released (2nd December 1929), which contains several scenes obviously borrowed from the earlier film. Like *The Skeleton Dance* and many other animated skeleton shorts, *The Haunted House* starts with a storm, proleptically evoking the rattling of bones. Mickey sees the house that, on closer inspection, does not inspire confidence. An anthropomorphised tree, resembling the tree in *The Skeleton Dance*, pushes him into the building, which locks the little mouse inside. A swarm of bats flies towards the fictive camera, again reminiscent of the earlier film. The haunted house also frightens Mickey via standard horror tropes such as flickering light, an enormous spider, strange sounds and creeping shadows. Mickey encounters a large, cloaked, death-like figure that commands him with its deep voice to play the piano. Seven skeletons and the hooded figure begin to dance. The sequence features dance-crazed skeletons that play with different body parts—their ribs, head, feet and arms—as well as with the brickwork and the radiator. Not only the bones of the skeletons, but also the haunted house itself, are included in the making of music. All in all, the music-making seems more complex, as the skeletons' drumming technique has evolved. They use sticks and are accompanied by Mickey. As in many vaudeville shows, the musical act now consists of a drummer and a piano player.

In comparison with the minimalistic plot of *The Skeleton Dance*, *The Haunted House* is more complex. This is mainly due to the presence of a protagonist, Mickey, who encounters a problem and gets into a dangerous situation. Without

Mickey, the viewer would not be able to perceive any markers of difference among the skeletons. Yet Mickey clearly marks the gender of the cloaked skeleton. When the death character urges him to play, the mouse responds with "Yes, ma'am" (Disney 1929a, 02:29–02:51),[7] thus marking Death clearly as a woman. There are many different depictions of Death as a woman (cf. Guthke 1999), but in *The Haunted House* this trope, again, refers to the earlier film, where skeletons were predominantly portrayed as female (cf. Leeder 2017, 138). Moreover, the paradoxical gender assignment of female to a large, deeply voiced masculine physique is meant to be surprising and funny; the humour derives from the inversion of gender stereotypes. A similarly humorous effect produced by the same kind of gender paradox can also be found in minstrel shows (cf. Morris 2007, 4–7; Gerstner 2017). In *The Haunted House*, the character in question is singled out as larger, clothed and female. She is also given a voice and she dances by herself, which marks the beginning of the individualisation of skeletons in Disney films. If we read Mickey as a vestigial minstrel character, the cloaked skeleton can be interpreted as a *white* lady.

Like the silent movies, *The Skeleton Dance* and *The Haunted House* transfer older forms of entertainment to the new medium of sound film, but while the silent films concentrated on the play between the visible and the invisible, the cartoons starring skeletons focus on popular musical traditions. Whereas *The Skeleton Dance* shows de-individualised skeletons and a simple, raw (often called *primitive*) musical performance, *The Haunted House* presents a band consisting of a lead singer (Death), a piano player and several percussionists who use the haunted house as a drum set. *The Skeleton Dance* and *The Haunted House* show the development of popular African-American music from juba dancing slaves to jazz. It is, however, significant that the musical performances lack an audience, and are thus non-commercial. They take place in a secluded area, where the dead make music to entertain themselves. In both shorts, the bones of the skeletons play a key role in the musical performance: The secret of the skeletons' success in early sound film lies in their bones.

The Skeleton's Dance Fatigue: *The Nightmare Before Christmas*

After *Fantasia*, dancing skeletons are absent for a long time from Disney productions. Films released after 1940 show many dances—from ballet in *Make Mine Music* (1946) to swinging felines in *Aristocats* (1970)—but hardly any skeletons

---

[7]This encounter is echoed in several animated shorts released shortly after: In *Betty Boop's Museum* (1932) a large skeleton commands Betty to sing for a group of skeletons. The number also involves a skeletal line dance formation and a piano player. In Ub Iwerks's *Flip the Frog in Spooks* (1932), Flip meets a skeleton in a haunted house and addresses the figure—like Mickey—with "Yes, ma'am." The skeleton has, again, a very deep voice and wears a top hat.

and no dancing skeletons at all. This boneless period lasted until the horror genre gained popularity in books and TV series for children[8] and the gothic subculture became more important, and it ends with the filmic celebration of Halloween and the skeleton in *The Nightmare Before Christmas* (1993). Tim Burton and Henry Selick's stop-motion film[9] went on to become a cult film in the Gothic scene, as it emphasises many aspects that are central to the subculture, such as the favouring of the macabre and the melancholic, the colour black, highly individualised and theatrical fashion, and of course gothic literature, horror and dark romanticism. Halberstam even calls *The Nightmare Before Christmas* a "brilliant example of what happens when a narrative is gothicised" (1995, 22). But even though it is easy to see how the plot, visual characteristics and lyrics are informed by this aesthetic, the musical style has very little in common with the music produced by bands usually considered gothic. Like the earlier films, *Nightmare* thus combines elements of different (sub)cultures.

As the leader of the Halloween festivities, the "Pumpkin King" Jack Skellington is the most celebrated character in Halloweentown, the home of Halloween. The inhabitants look up to him, and one boy, Barrel, even dresses up like a skeleton, commenting self-referentially on the tradition. The fact that Jack is a skeleton highlights the importance of skeletons for the celebration. Moreover, his name not only draws attention to his skeletal body, but also to the close connection between Jack and Halloween. Unlike the Jack in the Irish legend, however, the Jack in *The Nightmare Before Christmas* does not trap Satan, who claims that it is time for him to die; instead he traps Santa Claus ("Sandy Claws") in order to take over Christmas.

As American Halloween traditions were highly influenced by ghost and horror stories and vice versa (cf. Rogers 2002), it is not surprising that *The Nightmare Before Christmas* shares many characteristics and motifs with the earlier shorts, including screaming cats, haunted houses, graveyards and bats. In fact, the film can be read as an homage to or parody of earlier skeleton movies. As is typical for skeletal characters, Jack can remove his limbs, and he does so in order to throw a bone for his ghost dog Zero (*NBC*, 11:20–11:40). Furthermore, the objects that the mad scientist Dr. Finklestein studies are none other than X-rays (19:00–19:25).

The Nightmare Before Christmas can thus be understood as a film about skeleton films: it is a meta-skeleton film. However, there are important differences regarding the depiction of skeletons: First of all, the bones of the skeletal characters are not directly involved in the making of music. Even though Jack sings a number of songs and is the main source of music in the film, his bones do not function as instruments. The only visible instruments are those of the three street musicians. Accordion, bass and saxophone are not considered to be classical bone

---

[8] E.g. *Funnybones* (1992), *Masters of the Universe* (1987)/ *H-Man and Masters of the Universe* (1983–1985), Angela Sommer-Bodenburg's *The Little Vampire* (book series (1979–2015) and several TV shows and films), *Skeleton Warriors* (1994–1995), *Round the Twist* (1989–2001).

[9] Tim Burton and Mike Johnson's *Corpse Bride* (2005) is also noteworthy. In this stop-motion animated film roughly based on a Russian folktale, a number of skeletons sing and dance to the song *Remains of the Day*. The scene picks up on a number of dance and music-playing motifs.

instruments and usually do not contain any bones.[10] However, the instruments in the film possess a clear skeleton aesthetic: The accordion looks like a large fishbone, the sax is shaped like a vertebral column of a snake, and the double bass is a coffin with non-functional bones on top of the scroll.

The second difference is that Jack does not dance frenetically. His elegant movements and grand gestures are aestheticised and synchronised to the music, giving them a dance-like quality that is reminiscent of opera and musical theatre. As Smith notes, Jack has an "Astaire-like grace" (2018, 88). Yet because *The Nightmare Before Christmas* absorbs well-known images from skeleton films and Halloween, the absence of explicit dancing on Jack's part is significant. The melancholy master of ceremonies is restless, discontented and longs for novelty, as the Halloween routine presented both in the earlier films and in Halloweentown has become an unbearable monotony. In Tim Burton's poem, which provides the storyline for the film, Jack emphasises that he is tired of dancing: "And my feet hurt from dancing those skeleton dances" (Burton 1993, 01:28–01:33). Skeleton dances are thus presented as an integral part or standard of Halloween films and festivities. The absence of explicit dancing in the film, then, can be read both as a symptom of Jack's Halloween fatigue and as the result of its excessive use in films.

Thirdly, unlike the films that preceded it, *The Nightmare before Christmas* equips Jack Skellington with a story, feelings and an identity, as is signified by his possession of a name. This sets him apart from the other humanoid skeletons found in *The Nightmare Before Christmas* and previous films, which are identical to each other and are thus not individualised.[11] Jack himself is a strikingly artificial character. For one, he is impossibly lean; he is overdrawn, depicted as even skinnier than a real skeleton, and contrasts harshly with the extremely round Santa Claus. According to Ingrid Tomkowiak, the film (like many other Disney movies) celebrates its love of detail and the aura of products that are "made by hand" (2019; cf. also Smith 2018, 88). By emphasising their artificiality, the film invites us to perceive the characters as puppets or toys. It is, furthermore, remarkable that Jack, unlike the earlier skeletons, wears clothes—a striped tailcoat and a frill collar. This decidedly eccentric clothing traditionally connotes someone male, formal and very old fashioned, marking Jack out as upper class. Jack is not a background dancer, but rather the star of the show and (most of the time) a solo performer. In his self-centred songs, the skeleton displays and articulates his emotions, as apparent from some of the titles, like *Jack's Lament* and *Poor Jack*. In the words of David McGowan:

> While the earliest film of the Silly Symphonies series, *The Skeleton Dance* (1929), foregrounded the synchronicity between characters' movements and musical effects, later instalments experimented with music as an additional means of developing emotion. (2016, 5–6)

---

[10] Bones are sometimes used in keyboards and bone glue is used for double basses.

[11] There are, however, two types of skeletons: the skeletons in Halloweentown and the skeletons in the Bogeyman's cave.

The merry, percussionist collective of dancing skeletons found in the earlier Disney films has been converted, in *The Nightmare Before Christmas*, into a melancholy individualist singer. But it is not until *Coco* that the skeleton explicitly becomes a pop star.

The Skeleton as Pop Star: *Coco*

The plot of the 3D, computer animated film *Coco* (2017), directed by Lee Unkirch and produced by Darla K. Anderson, revolves around twelve-year old Miguel Rivera, who is born into a family of shoemakers but aches to become a Mariachi. Against his family's wishes, Miguel wants to play at the festivals. To make this dream come true, he steals a guitar from the mausoleum of his idol Ernesto de la Cruz. This results in a voyage to the land of the dead, where Miguel learns his family history and discovers that de la Cruz is actually an evil fraud who murdered Miguel's real grandfather, Héctor, in order to steal both his songs and his guitar.

In *The Nightmare Before Christmas*, there is only one individualised skeletal character among other halloweenesque inhabitants. *Coco* now shows a whole society consisting of skeletons. Consequently, the figures in *Coco* must be individualised in order to tell them apart. In the afterlife, skeletons are easily distinguished by their clothes, hair and size, a feature that is sometimes exploited for comic effect. The slightly overweight Tía Rosita is literally heavy-boned in her skeletal form, for example. Taken together, *The Nightmare Before Christmas* and *Coco* illustrate that skeletons become more and more individualised over the course of time in Disney film. This phenomenon may be due in part to the development of cinema itself (and the concomitant lengthening of a film's running time) as well as to increasing tendencies towards individualisation in Western society. Moreover, with regard to *Coco*, the folkloristic background is particularly important to the individualisation of skeletons in the narrative, for the film is based primarily on the Mexican tradition of the *Día de Muertos*, the Day of the Dead (cf. Riofrio 2019; see also Martín-Rodríguez 2019). The earlier skeleton films, by contrast, have narrative and folkloristic traditions originating primarily in northern Europe: *The Skeleton Dance* is reminiscent of the *danse macabre*, *The Haunted House* recalls horror or ghost stories and *The Nightmare Before Christmas* is a spooky inversion of Clement Clarke Moore's famous poem. In fact, the earlier films are often called Halloween films, even though they only begin to refer to Halloween in the 1930s (Skal 2002, 157), with shorts such as Toby the Pup's *Halloween* (1931) and Betty Boop's *Halloween Party* (1932).[12] Unlike these earlier films, *Coco* instead looks to

---

[12] In 1937 *The Skeleton Dance* was also made into a more halloweenesque colour variant called *Skeleton Frolic* (Columbia) that features a large pumpkin. It also includes non-bone instruments such as a contrabass.

Hispanophone folktale traditions, as its title invokes not only the name of Miguel's grandmother but also a traditional bogeyman-like character that scares naughty children.

As in Halloween, skeletons play a major role in the Día de Muertos festivities, which are mostly regarded as a fusion of pre-Hispanic with Spanish beliefs and traditions. Like Halloween decoration, Day of the Dead decoration is commercial as well as seasonal and often meant to be humorous (Brandes 1998, 188). However, in real life as well as in the skeleton films, the decorations look strikingly dissimilar: while the early shorts and *The Nightmare Before Christmas* were dominated by black and white, sinister and spooky, *Coco* shows an electrifying richness of colour. This corresponds with different traditions surrounding death and festivities that take place around the 1st of November.

Coco also presents skeletons and skulls as essential parts of festive decoration by showing many inanimate skeletons that all look similar and appear practically everywhere: in the form of *papel picados*, paintings, murals, toys and, of course, *calaveras* (sugar skulls). Only after that, the viewer encounters actual moving skeletons and these skeletons are highly individualised. This individualisation of skeletons in the land of the dead corresponds with the traditions of the Día de Muertos:

> […] throughout the republic [there is] an enormous variety of skeleton toys of all sizes and plastic materials, with the skeleton displayed as naked or clothed, holding a recognizable object like a pipe or musical instrument, and usually giving some indication of age, gender, occupation, and the like (Brandes 2006, 43).

In the film, however, it is not the decoration that is individualised, but rather the characters. They refer back to Día de Muertos traditions, where festive skeleton puppets are moveable and have ludic functions. The skeletons thus indicate once again that they were created from the idea of actual toys.

In *Coco*, source and score music as well as the original songs from the soundtrack refer to Mexican music or fusion like Cumbia, Son Jarocho or Mariachi (cf. Riofrio 2019; Castro 2018, 35). The film also involves a lot of skeletal dancing, including the traditional dancing of the *zapateado*. The steps and clapping of the skeletons are often audible, but they are not in the foreground, since another instrument is highlighted in the movie: the guitar, or more precisely, the iconic guitar of the Mariachi star Ernesto de la Cruz. While many musical instruments—including bone instruments such as a donkey's jaw bone (*quijada*)—can also be seen in the film, the guitar is the most important instrument and is central to the plot. Because of an old photograph that shows his grandmother Coco and the headless body of his unknown grandfather who carries this special guitar, Miguel thinks that his idol de la Cruz is his ancestor. This leads him to steal the guitar from de la Cruz's mausoleum. By playing a chord on the iconic instrument, Miguel is transported to the land of the dead. Again, despite the fact that the guitar is not a classical bone instrument,[13] this particular guitar is closely connected to

---

[13] Bridges are often made of bones.

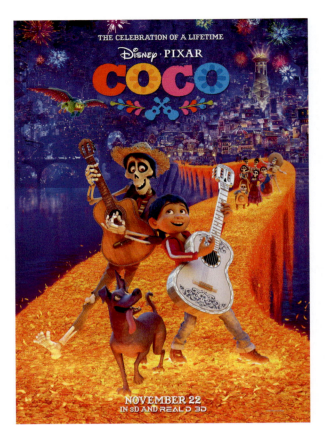

Fig. 1 *Coco*. Film poster. (©Disney)

skeletons through its design, as it is made to resemble a skeleton (Fig. 1). Through its visual appearance and narrative function, the skeletal guitar connects the land of the living to the land of the dead.[14]

The border between these lands looks like a real-life modern border, with a customs station and an ID check: the characters are scanned and compared with photographs placed on the *ofrendas* (home altar), because only the deceased who have a family to put up their photos are allowed to cross to the land of the living.[15] X-rays are taken to compare the skeletons with the photos and verify their identity. The X-ray scanners cannot be tricked, as becomes evident when Héctor tries to

---

[14] The importance of the guitar is further stressed by de la Cruz's pool, which is shaped like the instrument.

[15] In terms of space, a marigold bridge connects these lands.

pass as Frida Kahlo. In the early days of film, X-rays were used to make skeletons visible. But after more than a century of animated skeletons, *Coco* now playfully reverses the process and uses X-rays to identify the fleshed-out body of the skeleton as represented in a photograph.

Conclusion

Skeleton dances can be read as a meta-cinematic reference to the medium's ontological status: film transforms still or inanimate pictures into living or animate, moving, pictures. The process suggests a strong analogue with skeletons and Dances of the Dead (cf. Nitsche 2015, esp. 11; Wells 1998, 10; Smith 2018; Leeder 2017). This idea can be attributed to Sergei Eisenstein; in the 1940s, he wrote about Disney films and found that "Disney provided direct grounds and material for an analysis of the 'survival' of animism and totemism in modern consciousness and art" (Kleimann 1988, xi):

> The animated drawing is the most direct manifestation of ... animism! That which is known to be lifeless, a graphic drawing, is animated. *Drawing as such*—outside an object of representation!—is brought to life. But furthermore and inseparably, the subject—the object of representation—is also animated: ordinary lifeless objects, plants, beasts-all are animated and humanized" (Eisenstein 1988, 43).

He concludes: "The very idea, if you will, of the animated cartoon is like a direct embodiment of the method of animism" (ibid., 44).

Skeleton films can be understood as celebrations of animation itself. Early silent films exploited the visual characteristic features of skeletons (fantastic and X-ray themes) and thus focused on making the invisible visible and vice versa. But Disney's early sound films also made use of the sound of bones, focusing on the interplay between pictures and sound. In both cases, the skeleton becomes a visual object that helps exemplify the innovations and potentials of the medium. It is also striking that skeleton films reference older performance art and "haunting or haunted" media as well as previous skeleton films. Their status as intermedial palimpsests not only becomes evident in the frequent use of typical ghost story or horror tropes, but especially in the recurrent references to X-rays and the various dance numbers.

Disney films featuring dancing skeletons moreover show how animated movies adapt festivals and folklore, and transform old tales and legends into modern ones, combining typical Hollywood plots with folkloristic aspects from different cultures. The films are (retrospectively) connected with celebrations that take place around the 1st of November: Halloween, Samhain, All Saints' Day, All Hallows' Eve and the Day of the Dead. All of these festivities are concerned with the border between the world of the living and the world of the dead, again hinting at the art of (re)animation.

In addition, the films can be connected to the *danse macabre*, but this connection becomes weaker over time. The connection between *The Skeleton Dance* and the *danse macabre* is relatively stable, as the music and the plot by Camille Saint-Saëns refer to Dance of the Dead traditions. Also, as in the Dance of the Dead, in *The Skeleton Dance* all are equal and the skeletons dance back to their graves. Yet the skeletons do not dance with mortal human beings—they only dance with other skeletons. Thus, the dancing skeletons in the short films have a different function: they do not appear to kill and remind us of our own mortality, they come alive to entertain. This is further stressed by the connection that films beginning in the 1930s made between skeleton dances and Halloween, and which is finally made explicit in *The Nightmare Before Christmas*. As time went on, skeletons in film underwent increasing individualisation and emotionalisation, corresponding to the development of pop music and its ethos. No wonder, then, that skulls appear in every second music video and are generally found in many pop cultural artefacts. In the films, the skeleton is essentially a musician and an entertainer, and can be understood as the embodiment of music. Skeletons make music with their bones, a trope that references the materiality of the oldest instruments as well as juba dances and minstrel shows. This connection is so strong that even later diegetic instruments are aesthetically skeletonised, retrospectively suggesting the importance of bones for the music and the earlier skeleton dances. This emphasises the bodily aspects of music. In the earliest skeleton dance sound film, *The Skeleton Dance*, the skeletons are shown as a de-individualised collective of dancers. A skeletal musical group then follows in *The Haunted House*, and finally, we have a solo performer in *The Nightmare Before Christmas*. In *Coco*, the skeleton musician is further presented as a pop star. Not only do the skeletons become more individualised over time, but the playfully designed instruments do as well.

Looking at the materiality and use of skeletons in Disney films, it becomes evident that skeletons are there to "play" in both senses of the word: they are playing musicians and playable toys. Stalling's idea for *The Skeleton Dance* came from a cardboard toy, *The Nightmare Before Christmas* stresses the artificiality of its gothic puppets and the skeletons in *Coco* derive from the moveable toys used in The Day of the Dead decoration. Overall, skeletons have a prominent place in animated films due to their acoustic and visual qualities as well as their particular significance for (pop) cultural practices.

References

Primary Sources

Algar, James/Samuel Armstrong [et al.], dir. (1940). *Fantasia*. Special edition (2010). Disney. Blu-ray

Burton, Tim (1993): *The Nightmare Before Christmas*. Read by Christopher Lee. Extra in: The Nightmare Before Christmas, dir. Henry Selick. Disney. Blu-ray

Disney, Walt, dir. (1929a): *The Haunted House*. Walt Disney Studios. https://www.youtube.com/watch?v=3hoThry5WsY. Accessed: 22. April 2021

Disney, Walt, dir. (1929b): *The Skeleton Dance*. In: Silly Symphonies: The Historical Animated Classics. Walt Disney Productions/Buena Vista Home Entertainment. DVD

Hand, David, dir. (1933): *The Mad Doctor*. Walt Disney Productions. https://www.youtube.com/watch?v=LPW70q4w5pw. Accessed: 22. June 2021

Selick, Henry, dir. (1993): *The Nightmare Before Christmas*. Disney. Blu-ray

Unkirch, Lee, dir. (2017): *Coco*. Walt Disney Pictures/Pixar Animation Studios. DVD

Secondary Sources

Brandes, Stanley (1998): Iconography in Mexico's Day of the Dead: Origins and Meaning. In: *Ethnohistory*, Vol. 45, No. 2, 181–218

Brandes, Stanley (2006): *Skulls to the Living, Bread to the Dead. The Day of the Dead in Mexico and Beyond*. Malden, MA

Brennan, Matt (2020): *Kick It. A Social History of the Drum Kit*. New York

Castro, Elizabeth (2018). When Coco Feels like Home: Film as Homenaje. In: *Harvard Journal of Hispanic Policy*, Vol. 30, 33–38

Eisenstein, Sergej M. (1988): *Eisenstein on Disney*, ed. Jay Leyda. Transl. Alan Upchurch. London [et al.]

Emons, Hans (²2012): *Für Auge und Ohr: Musik als Film. Oder die Verwandlung von Kompositionen ins Licht-Spiel*. Berlin

Gabler, Neal (2006): *Walt Disney. The Triumph of the American Imagination*. New York.

Gerstner, Frederike (2017): *Inszenierte Inbesitznahme: Blackface und Minstrelsy in Berlin um 1900*. Stuttgart

Guthke, Karl Siegfried (1999): *The Gender of Death: A Cultural History in Art and Gender*. Cambridge

Halberstam, Judith [Jack] (1995): *Skin Shows. Gothic Horror and the Technology of the Monster*. Durham [et al.]

Hanson, Helen (2019): *Hollywood Soundscapes. Film Sound Style, Craft and Production in the Classical Era*. New York

Holloway, Joseph E. (²2005): "What Africa Has Given America": African Continuities in the North American Diaspora. In: *Africanisms in American Culture*, ed. Joseph E. Holloway, Bloomington, 39–64

Kaul, Susanne (2015): Totentanz und Zeichentrick. Filmkomik in Walt Disneys *The Skeleton Dance*. In: *Mit dem Tod tanzen: Tod und Totentanz im Film*, ed. Jessica Nitsche, Berlin, 31–46

Kerins, Mark (2011): *Beyond Dolby (Stereo). Cinema in the Digital Sound Age*. Bloomington/Indianapolis

Kleimann, Naum (1988): Introduction. In: *Eisenstein on Disney*, ed. Jay Leyda. Transl. Alan Upchurch, London [et al.], iv–xii

Leeder, Murray (2017): The Modern Supernatural and the Beginnings of Cinema. London

Martín-Rodríguez, Manuel M. (2019): The Best Mexican is a (Day of the) Dead Mexican. Representing Mexicaness in U.S. Animated Films. In: *Latinx Ciné in the Twenty-First Century*, ed. Frederick Luis Aldama, Tucson, 355–381

McGowan, David (2016): "And They Lived Happily Ever After???!" Disney's Adaptation of *Snow White and the Seven Dwarfs* (1937) and Fleischers' *Gulliver's Travels* (1939). In: *It's the Disney Version! Popular Cinema and Literary Classics*, eds. Douglas Brode/Shea T. Brode, Lanham [et al.], 1–12

Moen, Kristian (2019): *New York's Animation Culture. Advertising, Art, Design and Film, 1939–1940*. Cham (Palgrave Animation)

Merritt, Russell/J.B. Kaufman, (2016): *Walt Disney's Silly Symphonies. A Companion to the Classic Cartoon Series,* Glendale, Cal.

Morris, Linda (2007): *Gender Play in Mark Twain. Cross-dressing and Transgression.* Columbia, Miss. [et al.]

Nitsche, Jessica (2015): Wie der Film den Totentanz re-animiert. Eine Einleitung. In: *Mit dem Tod tanzen. Tod und Totentanz im Film,* ed. Jessica Nitsche, Berlin

Oosterwijk, Sophie/Stefanie Knöll, ed. (2011): *Mixed Metaphors. The Danse Macabre in Medieval and Early Modern Europe.* Newcastle upon Tyne

Räuber, Laura (2019): *Todesbegegnungen im Film. Zuschauerrezeption zwischen Zeichen und Körper.* Diss. Bielefeld

Retzlaff, Jonathan (2012): *Exploring Art Song Lyrics. Translation and Pronunciation of the Italian, German, and French Repertoire.* Oxford [et al.]

Riofrio, John D. "Rio" (2019): (Re)Animating the Dead: Memory, Music, and Divine Justice in Coco. In: *Latinx Ciné in the Twenty-First Century,* ed. Frederick Luis Aldama, Tucson, 382–404

Rogers, Nicholas (2002): *Halloween: From Pagan Ritual to Party Night.* New York

Sammond, Nicholas (2012): "Gentleman, please be seated": Racial Masquerade and Sado-masocism in 1930s Animation. In: *Burnt Cork. Traditions and Legacies of Blackface Minstrelsy,* ed. Stephen Johnson, Amherst [et al.], 164–190

Sammond, Nicholas (2015): *Birth of an Industry. Blackface Minstrelsy and the Rise of American Animation.* Durham [et al.]

Skal, David J. (2002): *Halloween. The History of America's Darkest Holiday.* Minola NY.

Smith, Susan (2018): The Animated Film Musical. In: *Media and Performance in the Musical. An Oxford Handbook of the American,* eds. Raymond Knapp/Mitchell Morris/Stacy Wolf, Oxford [et al.] 2018

Stalling, Carl (2008): Carl Stalling Master of Cartoon Music: An Interview. In: *Music in the USA. A Documentary Companion,* ed. Judith Tick, Oxford [et al], 421–427

Telotte, J.P. (2008): *The Mouse Machine. Disney and Technology.* Urbana [et al.].

Thomas, Adrian M.K./Arpan K. Banerjee (2013): *The History of Radiology.* Oxford

Tomkowiak, Ingrid (2019): „It's all made by hand". Ästhetik und Inszenierung des Handgemachten in. Animationsfilmen. In: *Spielarten der Populärkultur. Kinder- und Jugendliteratur und -medien im Feld des Populären,* eds. Ute Dettmar/Ingrid Tomkowiak, Berlin [et al.], 405–424

Vollmer, Wilhelm (²1859): *Vollständiges Wörterbuch der Mythologie aller Völker. Eine gedrängte Zusammenstellung aus der Fabel- und Götterlehre der Völker der alten und neuen Welt.* Stuttgart

Wells, Paul (1998): *Understanding Animation.* London [et al.]

Westfahl, Gary (2005): Skeletons. In: *The Greenwood Encyclopedia of Science Fiction and Fantasy.* Themes, works, and wonders, Vol. 2, ed. id., Westport, Conn. [et al.], 722–742

Winans, Robert B. (1996): Early Minstrel Show Music 1843–1852. In: *Inside the Minstrel Mask. Readings in Nineteenth-Century Blackface Minstrelsy,* eds. Annemarie Bean/James V. Hatch/ Brooks McNamara, Hanover [et al.], 141–162

"Taxing the Heart and Soul Out of the People"

Disney's *Robin Hood* (1973) as Conservative Fable

Anika Ullmann

Abstract The *Robin Hood* myth is remembered via its hero's actions: stealing from the rich to give to the poor. Despite socialist tendencies implied by the Robin Hood ethos, the myth and most of its retellings favour the reactionary over the revolutionary. This is especially obvious in Disney's *Robin Hood* (1973). This article reads the movie as conservative political-economic fable. Semantics of stability and instability, expressed by the collection, theft and return of taxes establish a conservative vision of a prospering society—a vision that connects the *Robin Hood* myth to sentimental Disney populism.

There is a constant to how the *Robin Hood* myth is reproduced in different media and contexts. Seal, in his conceptualisation of "The Robin Hood Principle," states: "Despite many local adaptations and inflections, at the core of the facts and fictions surrounding outlaw heroes remains the belief that he, or very occasionally she, robs the rich to give to the poor" (2009, 69). The *Robin Hood* myth is defined by its ahistorical mythical core.[1] It is remembered as a story about financial movements and societal relations. Literary and cinematic retellings reflect and solidify the centrality of wealth exchange in the name of charity in the conceptualisation of

---

[1] Levi-Strauss in *The Structural Study of Myth* notices that there is an ahistorical aspect to myth, "an everlasting pattern" (Lévi-Strauss 1955, 430), which relates to the meaning of the myth (434).

A. Ullmann (✉)
Leuphana University Lüneburg, Lüneburg, Germany
e-mail: anika.ullmann@gmx.de

© The Author(s), under exclusive license to Springer-Verlag GmbH, DE, part of Springer Nature 2022
U. Dettmar and I. Tomkowiak (eds.), *On Disney*, Studien zu Kinder- und Jugendliteratur und -medien 9, https://doi.org/10.1007/978-3-662-64625-0_11

Robin Hood heroism.[2] James Meek in his 2016 *London Review of Books* lecture *Robin Hood in a Time of Austerity* even claims that Robin Hood is "the first and often the only political-economic fable we learn" (n. p.). Political programmes, like the Robin Hood tax, further perpetuate this pattern when they use the outlaw's name as shorthand for tax regulations focused on the redistribution of wealth.

Although fables are usually learned in childhood, Meek contends that *Robin Hood* is "not a children's story, although it is childlike" (ibid.).[3] This statement requires critical assessment. Connections between the *Robin Hood* myth and children's literature have been repeatedly noted by *Robin Hood* scholars (cf. Brockman 1982, 1983; Couch 1999; Petzold 1995; Dobson/Taylor 1997; Carpenter 2008). Indeed, it is an adaptation addressed to children that presents itself as especially potent as political fable: the Disney animated film *Robin Hood* (1973) by Wolfgang Reitherman. Probably, due to the movie's triple stigmatisation as Disney version, object of popular culture and subject of children's media, academic discourse on *Robin Hood* often ignores the Disney version or relegates the title to an enumeration of further examples. However, with its cast of anthropomorphised animals and its focus on the core of the myth it offers a "brief account of animal life [...] which serves as an example that teaches about the human social order" (Schuster 2014, 137), a move which is typical for the Aesopian-style fable. The cultural efficacy of the 'Disneyfication' of literary sources, its manifestation as *Disney folklore*, combined with the movie's concentration on the memetic, highly reproductive element of the myth, further heighten its power to spread a political message.

In 2015 a *Buzzfeed* post recast Disney's *Robin Hood* with Trump as Prince John and Elizabeth Warren, the prominent fighter for a 'wealth tax,' as Robin Hood (cf. Professor Fox [n. p.]). This interpretation, however, ignores the actual values that the movie propagates. Andrew Lynch notes that its "depiction of taxes is more conservative [....] The sufferings of the honest poor of the story stand for the economic damage done to the private sector by central taxation" (2012, 33). In doing so, the movie resembles the assessment of the myth and its retellings in recent media and political discourse. Reviewing the 2018 movie adaptation with

---

[2] This ahistorical pattern only appeared in the late sixteenth and early seventeenth century and is connected to the protagonist's social status. Knight asserts in *The Politics of Myth*, "Robin Hood never stole from the rich to give to the poor until he was transformed from a yeoman into a lord" (Knight 2015). Though the late fifteenth/early sixteenth century *Gest of Robyn Hode* (the first arrangement of *Robin Hood* ballads into a longer *Robin Hood* poem) mentions at its end that he "dyde pore men moch god" (Knight/Ohlgren 2000, 148), Robin's charitable efforts are never narrated in the *Gest*. *Robin Hood* ballads and retellings that relate to the ballads as hypotexts are tales of trickery, disguise, fights (against enemies or to make new friends) and tests of moral character. Stealing from the rich with the distinct purpose to give to the poor is seldom more central to his escapades than paying the ransom for King Richard or helping the honourable.

[3] For a discussion of child appropriateness and the Disney *Robin Hood* version (Reitherman 1973), see Harty 2012.

Taron Egerton, Steve Rose of *The Guardian* remarked that despite Robin Hood's public image as "a Marxist guerrilla, a left-leaning populist—or perhaps even as a progressive-taxation radical" (2018 [n. p.]), the *Robin Hood* myth can offer a very Republican vision of societal justice. Republican Texas Senator Ted Cruz in that vein asserted in a debate with Bernie Sanders in 2017:

> Robin Hood was robbing the tax collectors, who were collecting too much taxes from the working men and women, and taking it for the rich. [...] And Robin Hood is saying, "Tax collectors: stop hammering people who are struggling, who were laboring in the fields who are working, stop taking it to the castle to give out to your buddies" (cited in Beavers 2017 [n. p.]).

In the realm of Republican politics *Robin Hood* boils down into a fable about taxes. The rich have morphed into Big Government robbing its—not poor but hardworking—citizens. This notion is already present in Ayn Rand's *Atlas Shrugged* (1957), a favourite novel of modern-day Republicans. Rand, a personal acquaintance of Walt Disney, has her character Ragnar Danneskjöld question the way Robin Hood is remembered:

> It is said, that he fought the looting rulers and returned the loot that had been robbed, but that is not the meaning of the legend which has survived. He is remembered, not as a champion of property, but as a champion of need, not as a defender of the robbed, but as a provider of the poor. (1957, 534)

It is the difference between *robbed* and *poor*, between a focus on *wrongful dispossession* and *charity* which is also central to the construction of Robin Hood's heroism in Disney's *Robin Hood*.[4]

The goal of this article is to offer a close reading of Disney's *Robin Hood* as a conservative political-economic fable. Doing so requires the interpretation of a narrative gap. The movie's happy ending begins with the narrator's explanation that King Richard came back and "straightened everything out" (Reitherman 1973, 01:17:36). At this point a time jump between the climax of the movie and this conclusion has opened an ellipsis. The narrative is split into two parts, one in which England suffers under the rule of Prince John and one in which it flourishes again under the rule of its King. The concrete steps that lead from crises to prosperity are left out. The characterisations of Prince John and Robin Hood via the semantics of stability and instability, of renewal and change, enable the viewers to interpret the ellipsis and fill the absence with a conservative vision of a healing society. It is a vision that connects the *Robin Hood* myth to Walt Disney's political views and makes visible the applicability of the myth for a depiction of sentimental Disney populism (cf. Watts 1995, 96–97).

---

[4] For more on Rand and capitalism see Collins 2003.

Prince John—A Dangerously Unstable Circus Master

Disney's *Robin Hood* depicts a dynamic society and thematises the interdependencies between government and subjects that come to play in it. It opens, in the tradition of classic Disney movies, with a story book that links the narrative to its intertextual roots.[5] Here the *Robin Hood* formula as it developed in the sixteenth century sets the stage for an economy out of balance: The king is absent on a crusade, and the "greedy and treacherous" (Reitherman 1973, 00:21) Prince John has seated himself on the throne. Robin Hood is introduced as the people's "hope," who "rob[s] from the rich, to feed the poor" (ibid., 00:31). The fight for resources as the movie unfolds follows the Republican understanding of the myth. The government is comprised of the greedy Prince John, Sir Hiss, his treasurer, and the Sheriff, his tax collector. Governmental action is limited to the task of tax regulation and collection,[6] which is reflected in the movie's semantics of space. Scenes in the castle interior exclusively show Prince John and his servants in relation to and surrounded by money. Every room in the castle is used as storage space and therefore has lost most of its functionality. When he delivers his tax collection, the Sheriff (ibid., 51:50–52:05) only needs to walk a few steps down the castle's main hallway to reach Sir Hiss's desk. The placement of the treasurer as receptionist creates the impression that there is only one main purpose for entering the castle: to deliver taxes. Shown inside his throne room, Prince John is seated on a wooden throne that stands directly in front of the fireplace. The distance between the throne and the fireplace hints at the fact that this ruler does not give audiences or dispense justice, as there literally is no space that would offer his subjects the

---

[5] Allusions to elements that have become fixed points in retellings can be found throughout the movie. The quarterstaff fight between Robin and Little John, described in the seventeenth century ballad *Robin Hood and Little John*, over who gets to cross a stream first (cf. Knight/Ohlgren 2000, 476–485), is mentioned in the song *Oo-De-Lally*. The friends arrive at a crossing over stream. Both cordially bow to each other, each, in a reversal of the well-known scene, offering the other the opportunity to cross the stream first (cf. Reitherman 1973, 03:47–03:53). The archery competition, a mainstay of Robin Hood adaptations, which is already present in the *Gest* in the late fifteenth/early sixteenth century (Knight/Ohlgren 2000, 125–127) is also included. The animated film further hints at the ballad *Robin Hood Rescues Three Young Men* from the eighteenth century. Here Robin approaches the Sheriff disguised as a beggar to thwart executions (cf. ibid., 514–518).

[6] The fight for resources in *Robin Hood* retellings is generally more complex. Firstly, the exclusivity of the king's deer in the king's forest is a topic for dispute. Many versions of the tale even posit that the crime of shooting a king's deer is the reason for Robin Hood or one of his men becoming an outlaw (cf. Knight/Ohlgren 2000, 508–510, Mopurgo 2012, 26–27). Adaptations that present Robin Hood as a nobleman (e.g. Robin of Locksley or Robert, Earl of Huntington) turned noble outlaw, a common theme from the late sixteenth century onwards, also centre on the fight over land, property or title. This aspect features prominently in most popular Robin Hood cinematizations, among them *Robin Hood* (Dwan 1922) with Douglas Fairbanks, *The Adventures of Robin Hood* (Curtiz 1938) with Errol Flynn, *Robin Hood: Prince of Thieves* (Reynolds 1991) with Kevin Costner and *Robin Hood* (Bathurst 2018) with Taron Egerton.

possibility of coming before the throne to voice grievances. No furniture is visible aside from two tables to the left and right of the throne, both holding money (ibid., 58:50). The royal bedroom, shown during the climax of the film (ibid., 01:08:30), likewise, aside from two beds, lacks furniture, but is filled with bags of gold coins. Only one room in the castle is an exception to this rule: Maid Marian's (ibid., 26:16–27:00). Rugs, a plate with fruit, chairs and a closet create an atmosphere of comfort and functionality. The absence of money in her room establishes the rule that taxes and a liveable standard of life are mutually exclusive.

This single-purposed state power is repeatedly portrayed as a mixture of the silly and the dangerous, a duality that is perfectly reflected in the names of the Sheriff's subordinates, two vultures called Trigger and Nutsy. Prince John is characterised as immature, his propensity to cry for his mother and suck his thumb being public knowledge (ibid., 24:52). In addition, the regent is prone to angry outbursts and violent behaviour. It is thus only fitting that Little John instinctively exclaims: "It's only a circus!" (ibid., 09:22–09:24), when he sees the royal procession, come to Nottingham to collect taxes, arrive in the forest.

Yet, as becomes clear from the start, this 'circus' can punish and kill. The royal procession through the forest consists of heavily armed guards in armour. Scores of large rhinos with halberds, elephants, hippos, and crocodiles populate public royal events. Their presence stands in contrast to the vulnerability of the townspeople. Robin Hood and the inhabitants of Nottingham are almost exclusively depicted as small furry animals. The physical disparity reaches its peak in the portrayal of the executioner, who enters the archery tournament scene to behead Robin Hood. Glowing, demonic red eyes peer out of a black mask. The rhinoceros's upper body and his axe fill the whole screen. The absence of any other objects in the frame as well as the upward camera angle make it impossible to measure the size of the approaching threat, but the impression of enormity is effectively created (ibid., 42:08–42:17). Additionally, the military animals do not have any individual features. While even the many bunny children of the bunny family are in different shades of white and wear different coloured shirts, the rhinos, hippos and elephants all look alike. Together they comprise an abstract oppressive force. In line with the unstable nature of the government, this uniform mass of jungle animals (ibid., 13:56–14:06, 44:36–45:35, 01:12:08–01:12:20) thrice turns into a stampede in the movie and uncontrollably destroys objects, each time hurting either the king and/or his followers.

Robin Hood—Force of Stability and Reproduction

In this time of uncertainty Robin Hood is established as a source of stability. This is marked by three major differences from Prince John and his government: the way in which Sherwood Forest is depicted, the performances of age which are presented and the association of Robin Hood with the reproductive, heteronormative-futuristic message of the movie.

Prince John lives behind stone walls in dysfunctional rooms. Robin dwells on a clearing in the forest. His home has no walls yet is highly functional and homey. Tree branches serve as hooks for pots and substitute for washing lines. In the middle a campfire hearth is set up, and a table stands close by. Notable is the absence of luxury. Most *Robin Hood* ballads and retellings portray Robin Hood's camp as an alternative court (cf. Green 1956, 25), where the outlaw is king among his merry men. There the men feast on the king's deer, drink ale (cf. ibid., 90; Knight/Ohlgren 2000, 47) and indulge in rituals of masculinity. These features are explored to their fullest in Howard Pyle's 1883 retelling for young readers. As MacLeod remarks, the mode of the narration is "adolescent, male, idealistic, violent" (2000, 45). It tells the story of a "jokey, competitive band of brothers with no regular occupations, no families and no dull responsibilities" (Ibid.). Nothing is left of this in the Disney version. The stew Robin and Little John prepare is unpalatable. Even the townsfolk's celebration in the forest lacks indulgences like food or drinks. The space of the clearing is also marked as grown-up. The scene opens with Little John wearing an apron and hanging up the washing, while Robin is cooking and dreaming of Maid Marian. Staff fights, archery matches and brotherly brawls are replaced by domestic duties and talk of marriage. This rather grown-up domesticity stands in contrast to Prince John's childish, vengeful and greedy personality.

These two aspects ultimately feed into the depiction of Robin Hood as romantic hero and his role as future husband and father, which in the movie are intertwined with the stability of society in Nottingham. Even before Maid Marian is mentioned for the first time, Robin is linked to the logics of reproduction and procreation. After the Sheriff steals the little bunny Skippy's birthday present, Robin replaces the stolen penny with a bow, an arrow and his own hat. Though the "hat is too big" (Reitherman 1973, 19:27) as his sister remarks, Maid Marian and Lady Kluck later have no problem recognising, in the young bunny's new outfit, the "notorious Robin Hood" (ibid., 22:39). When the children go on to play-act Robin Hood's heroism in a preview of events to come, Skippy takes the role of the outlaw who fights Prince John, played by Lady Kluck, and rescues Maid Marian. This enactment serves two functions. In line with what Seal calls the 'Robin Hood principle,' it alludes to the survival of outlaw heroism as a cultural script, one that can be performed again and again by different generations in different contexts (cf. Seal 2011, 172). It also underscores Skippy's role as a future Robin Hood. While climbing onto Robin and Marian's wedding carriage at the end of the movie Skippy explains: "Robin Hood's gonna have kids. So somebody's gotta keep their eye on things" (Reitherman 1973, 01:18:28–01:18:32). Thus, without even fathering a child, Robin, in the first minutes of the movie, already creates a child that later fulfils the symbolic value of the CHILD[7] in reproductive, heteronormative futurism. This CHILD, Lee Edelman explains, "endows reality with [the fantasy

---

[7] The capitalised CHILD in Edelman's text refers to the symbolic child.

of] fictional coherence and stability, which seem to guarantee that such reality, the social world in which we take our place will still survive when we do not" (2004, 34). This promise of a perpetuation of things as they are also defines the love story between Robin and Marian. Cooking in the clearing in the forest, Robin is dreaming of Maid Marian, whom he, as was established in the scene before by Maid Marian herself, has not seen for seven years, yet still loves. The domesticity of the clearing and this depiction of faithfulness show that in Disney's *Robin Hood* "the love story" has not "been used to 'tame' the hero," as Lynch claims (2012, 40). Comparable to Green's retelling, where Robin is outlawed in the course of his wedding to Maid Marian, which causes the ceremony to be disrupted, we are confronted with a love story that is on pause, as long as England is ruled by an unjust leader. Their relationship is then seamlessly reactivated in the tournament scene. Significantly, it is while Prince John's military sinks into chaos that Robin asks Marian to marry him. Their normative fantasy of marriage, honeymoon and a family is a stable counter-script to the situation created by the government (Reitherman 1973, 44:00–44:54). Taking the display of its heteronormative reproductive futurist logic even further, the movie contains two marriage scenes. The first is after the lovers flee from the tournament into Sherwood Forest. Here Robin puts a makeshift ring on Marian's finger. The act's repetitive nature is underscored by the text of the extra-diegetic song *Love*: "Life is brief, but when it's gone love goes on and on. Love will live. Love will last. Love goes on and on and on" (ibid., 47:45–48:15). This symbolic marriage, in the final scene, turns into church-sanctioned matrimony. Notably, Robin Hood's reproductive potency is increased by the fact that he is the only one in Nottingham who is shown to populate and thereby stabilise the future. The families of Nottingham either lack children or a parent. In the case of the bunny family, which is very fertile but fatherless, it requires Robin to stand in as a substitute in order to make Skippy a part of the heteronormative future that stabilises the society of Nottingham. He will also, during the climactic fight, risk his own life to save the bunny baby Tagalong (ibid., 01:13:13– 01:13:33). Moreover, Skippy's sister will, in the second marriage scene, catch Marian's bouquet (ibid., 01:18:47), thereby becoming the bride-to-be and thus also a future part of a reproductive, society-stabilising unit.

Giving (Back) to the Poor/Robbed

Prince John's reign is defined by the instability of the government itself and the society it creates; Robin Hood by the way his actions as outlaw and romantic hero (re)establish stability. As taxation defines the relationships between government and subjects and drives the story forward, the contrasting forces of Prince John and Robin Hood clash in a financial tug of war over the flow of money between rich and poor. In the opening minutes of the movie Prince John rides in his golden carriage, surrounded by bags of gold. "Taxes! Taxes! Beautiful, lovely taxes! [...] To coin a phrase my dear councillor: Rob the poor, to feed the rich" (ibid.,

06:20–06:39), he exclaims, as he lets coins rain through his heavily bejewelled fingers. The reversal of the signature Robin Hood ethos straightaway establishes Prince John as Robin's total opposite. As the movement of money changes direction, Prince John also positions himself as the actual outlaw, a thief, not a regent, who *robs* from his subjects instead of lawfully collecting taxes. The Prince's criminal tax collection intersects with his role as usurper, who, as the dialogue in the carriage unveils, has tricked his brother, the rightful king, into going on a crusade. On the visual plane this is expressed by Prince John's inability to properly wear King Richard's crown, which is too big for him and constantly slides off his head. Robin, in line with the general image of outlaw heroism, is thus established as the lawful agent, forced to become an outlaw by an unjust system and charged with the role of re-establishing justice. Consequently, shortly before they rob Prince John's carriage, Robin announces that it is "collection day for the poor" (ibid., 05:40), which is directly categorised as "sweet charity" (ibid., 05:45) by Little John.[8]

The movie repeatedly draws a connection between tax policy and societal welfare. Central to this is the sequencing of the scenes. The village of Nottingham, Prince John establishes during his carriage ride, is "the richest plum of them all" (ibid., 06:53). It is thus implied that the inhabitants of Nottingham are, in fact, not poor per se, but because of Prince John's tax policy. This is a departure from the predominant perception of the fight over resources in *Robin Hood* narratives. Seal explains:

> The right—assumed where it does not exist—of all members of a society to a reasonable share of its riches and access to its resources, is integral to the rationale of outlaw heroism. Robin Hood's levelling of the wealth disparities of medieval England echoes again and again through the lives, deaths, legends and literature of bandit after bandit. (2011, 175)

The Disney version, however, does not advocate "fundamental notions of equity" (ibid.). The principles of the redistribution of wealth are abandoned for the principles of status quo. Robin the fox does not steal from the rich and give to the poor, he steals from the rich and gives *back* to the *momentarily* poor, or, to refer to the logic of Rand's *Atlas Shrugged*, the *robbed*. Directly following the introduction of Prince John as *robber*, the effects of his criminal activities are displayed. Narrator Alan-a-Dale, the minstrel, stands inside Nottingham and explains the situation as visual cues are given: "what with taxes an' all, the poor folk of Nottingham were starving to death" (Reitherman 1973, 14:45–14:53). In the background a village is shown. Desaturated brown, beige and grey colours dominate the colour palette. The subsequent shots guide the viewers through a village where normal life has stopped. No one is on the street aside from the *criminals* in the stocks. Shops have

---

[8]The Sheriff of Nottingham also mirrors the Robin Hood character. Although the Sheriff insists on the lawfulness of his actions, declaring that, "they call me a slob, but I do my job" (Reitherman 1973, 16:49–16:52), the wolf gets constructed as a criminal, since he acts lawfully in an unjust system.

closed. Houses have been boarded up and abandoned. Holes in a roof hint at a lack of money for necessary repairs. Furthermore, the causality between taxes and this social crisis is announced on wooden signs that read "tax dodgers," "tax sale" and "tax auction." These are visible in front of characters and buildings, turning the whole town into a billboard for the impact of taxes on the economy and village life.

Tax regulations, the beginning of the movie makes clear, are the reason for societal imbalance and chaos. Poverty here is an effect, not a precondition. The Sheriff of Nottingham, in this context, serves as a manifestation of Prince John's destabilising power. As tax collector he directly engages with the people of Nottingham and translates royal regulations into social action. The Sheriff notably enters the movie right after the stagnation in the village is depicted and is causally linked to the social crisis. Then in quick succession he collects taxes from a sick smith, takes away young Skippy's birthday money and steals coins out of a blind beggar's cup. Via the exchange of money, the Sheriff's personality as well as the government's laws are characterised as disreputable and morally degenerate (cf. ibid., 15:35–18:08). The fact that he is a wolf marks the Sheriff as traitor, who, despite being a local, works for the Prince (cf. Lynch 2012, 39). It also highlights the greediness of the government, which *wolfs down* the people's means to survive or thrive.

Both scenes, Prince John in his carriage and the Sheriff's rounds in Nottingham, expand on the general theme of money flow. Viewers witness a cyclical process of stealing (taxes from the poor) and giving back. After Robin Hood and Little John rob the carriage, the subsequent village scene shows Friar Tuck bringing money from Robin to the sick smith, who then loses the money to the Sheriff yet again. This back and forth intensifies throughout the movie. After the song *The Phoney King of England* becomes popular in Nottingham, Prince John orders his subordinates to "[d]ouble the taxes, triple the taxes. Squeeze every last drop out of those insolent, musical, peasants" (Reitherman 1973, 52:48–52:57). Again, tax regulations and societal well-being are constructed as linked. In the scene following the prince's decision the societal crisis in Nottingham has worsened. As Alan-a-Dale remarks, Prince John "taxed the heart and soul out of the poor people of Nottingham" (ibid., 53:20–53:23). The situation is visually depicted via pathetic fallacy. Dark clouds and rain paint Nottingham in depressive greyness, and reflect, not the interior of a specific character, but the despair of an entire village. All villagers, even Alan-a-Dale the narrator himself, are in prison. The exceptional nature of the situation is underscored by the song the minstrel sings. *Not in Nottingham* is about the imbalance that was created by Prince John. "Every town," the text goes, "has its ups and downs. Sometimes ups outnumber the downs but not in Nottingham" (ibid., 53:39–53:59). Following the movie's basic narrative logic as a succession of scenes in which money is taken from and given back to the poor (who once were rich), Prince John's tax increase is again answered in kind by Robin. He breaks into the Prince's bedroom while Little John frees the imprisoned. Via a cable haulage Robin transports all the stored money into the prison cell and there back into the arms of the people of

Nottingham (ibid., 01:08:30–01:13:05). Notably, the return of the subjects' taxes coincides with them gaining their freedom, creating the impression that the "tax rebate" (ibid., 01:10:12) as Friar Tuck states, literally frees them from the shackles of oppression.

Following the robbery of the castle and the rescue of the people of Nottingham, the movie jumps forward in time. The burning castle fades out and the next scene begins back in the village in a set-up echoing the first village scene at the beginning of the movie. Nature again mirrors the state of Nottingham. This time the sky is blue, flowers are blooming and the leaves on the tree in the middle of the village are green. The houses are no longer boarded up. The timber framework and thatched roofs seem brand new. Curtains and hanging baskets decorate the windows and the exterior. Life has returned, not only to nature but to the village, in the form of investment in the town's infrastructure. Nottingham is a 'rich plum' again. Again, the minstrel informs the viewers of the cause: King Richard "straightened everything out" (ibid., 01:17:36). Although the movie at this point cuts to the imprisoned Prince John, Sir Hiss and Sheriff of Nottingham as an explanation for what "straightened out" means, it is not made explicit what concrete political action has been taken. It is possible that King Richard has re-established a tax policy that allows the people of Nottingham to simultaneously flourish and pay taxes. The conservative logic of the movie, however, makes it unnecessary to spell out King Richard's political programme or fill the ellipsis with a socialist vision of tax regulations. The logic implied by the change from taxed village, made visible by the signs at the beginning of the movie, to blooming society, represented by the flowers, is clear: the taxes are gone. Without them, the village can continue to prosper and, as Robin and Marian's wedding signifies, start to partake in fantasies of futurism once again, envisioned here as a heteronormative reproduction of sameness.

A Conservative Fable—Walt Disney and the Robin Hood Myth

In its downscaled version of the myth, and with its focus on the political-economic, the movie reveals the importance of how Robin Hood heroism is framed. In the ballads, as well as most retellings, Robin Hood's giving to the poor is a temporary activity which is embedded within a larger logic of repetition. It stops the moment the King returns, and the idea of a just system is restored. "Robin Hood, the noble robber, is not therefore a social revolutionary, he seeks restorative justice, the re-establishment of things as they used to be and ought to be," Pollard summarises referring to Hobsbawm (2004, 157). Disney's *Robin Hood* thus offers a rather good understanding of the mythical core of its literary references. Regarding Walt Disney's approach to adaptation Jill May writes critically: "He was not impressed with a book's intricate development of a universal theme. He was simply concerned with finding a good story that could be simplified and

Americanized for his audience" (1981, 466). The Disney version of *Robin Hood*, however, succeeds in offering the essence of the myth as a simplified depiction of the fight for resources, within its own reactionary vision of society.

Though Walt Disney died in 1966, the movie, however, not only continues (cf. Lynch 2012, 34) but gives new quality to the presence of Walt Disney's values in his company's productions. Rather than being merely an Americanised version of the tale, Disney's *Robin Hood* proves to be fertile ground for looking for intersections, where the myth and Disney's political views complement and reinforce each other in what Watts calls Disney's "sentimental populism" (1995, 96). This becomes obvious when Lee Artz defines what he calls the "essential Disney law": "Narrative resolution in each film," he points out, "defends and reinforces the *status quo*. Nothing is resolved until the preferred social order is in place. No one lives happily ever after until the chosen one rules" (2004, 132). The *Robin Hood* myth and Disney ideology appear, in large part, to coincide. Furthermore, Watts describes Disney as sharing a "rural opposition to urban industrial society and the 'money power'" (1995, 97). An aversion rooted in a

> Protestant work ethic, and the heritage of eighteenth-century 'republicanism' with its ideology of civic obligation. This petty bourgeois creed, suspicious of the machinery of modern finance and its cash matrix, demanded a moral valuation of labor through 'producerism' and insisted that property ownership and personal independence provided the key to citizenship (ibid., 97).

These values are echoed in the resentment toward tax collection as a threat to private property, evident in the difference between the dying and reanimated village, which is mainly represented by the decay and prospering of housing and small, self-owned businesses. They are also reflected in the difference between Prince John and King Richard, the former representing a ruler distant from the common man, the latter one who is close. Joseph Taylor notes that the *Gest* thematises the change in governmental structure in the fifteenth century. Centralisation threatened regional autonomy as it concentrated power in London, "that distant city" (2013, 320). The sheriffs, he states, "represented the Crown," they "acted as lawmen on the king's behalf—declaring outlaws, seizing property and issuing court summons" (Ibid.). These notions also reverberate in the Disney version. Prince John engages with his subjects via the sheriff as proxy. Though residing in Nottingham, he is defined by distance, a detached ruler behind thick castle walls, who threatens local autonomy and personal independence with a *jungle-esque* foreign military force. King Richard, on his return in the last scene, freely walks among his people. The military now is comprised of locals. Power, financial and military, has in many ways been given back to the locals.

Though the contexts are decidedly different, both the *Gest* and Disney's *Robin Hood*, which stands in the tradition of Walt Disney's own ideology, reflect on the relationship between citizen self-control and centralised, big (government) power.[9]

---

[9] For a more detailed analysis of the connections between the *Robin Hood* myth and populism see Rolfe 2016.

These clash in a battle between movements of restoration versus rudiments of change. In its celebration of the status quo the *Robin Hood* myth lends itself to the propagation of Republican ideals. It also allows the conclusion, that Robin Hood, in his foxy incarnation, is the quintessential *disneyesque* hero.

References

Primary Sources

Books

Green, Roger Lancelyn (Auth.) and Arthur Hall (Ill.) (2010 [[1]1956]): *The Adventures of Robin Hood.* London: Puffin Books
Morpurgo, Michael (2012): *Outlaw. The True Story of Robin Hood.* London: Harper Collins
Pyle, Howard (2016 [[1]1883]): *The Merry Adventures of Robin Hood.* San Diego: Canterbury Classics
Rand, Ayn (1992 [[1]1957]): *Atlas Shrugged.* New York: Signet

Films

Bathurst, Otto, dir. (2018): *Robin Hood.* Santa Monica, CA: Summit Entertainment
Curtiz, Michael/William Keighley, dirs. (1938): *The Adventures of Robin Hood.* Burbank, CA: Warner Bros. Pictures
Dwan, Allan, dir. (1922): *Robin Hood.* Douglas Fairbanks Pictures
Reitherman, Wolfgang, dir. (1973): *Robin Hood.* Burbank, CA: Walt Disney Animation Studios, 2013, 40th Anniversary Edition Release. DVD
Reynolds, Kevin, dir. (1991): *Robin Hood: Prince of Thieves.* Burbank, CA: Warner Bros. Pictures

Secondary Sources

Artz, Lee (2004): The Righteousness of Self-Centred Royals. The World According to Disney Animation. In: *Critical Arts.* Vol. 18, No.1, 116–146
Beavers, Olivia (2017): Bernie Calls GOP Tax Plan a 'Robin Hood Proposal in Reverse'. In: *The Hill*, 18.10.2017
Brockman, Bennett A. (1982): Robin Hood and the Invention of Children's Literature. In: *Children's Literature*, Vol. 10, 1–17
Brockman, Bennett A. (1983): Children and the Audiences of Robin Hood. In: *South Atlantic Review*, Vol. 48, No.2, 67–83
Carpenter, Kevin (2008): Robin Hood in Boys' Weeklies to 1914. In: *Popular Children's Literature in Britain*, eds. Julia Briggs/Dennis Butts/ M[atthew] O[rville] Grenby.
Collins, Michael S. (2003): Between Robin Hood and Ayn Rand: High Capitalism in the 1950s. In: *Michigan Quaterly Review, Vol. XLII, No. 2* [n. p.]. http://hdl.handle.net/2027/spo. act2080.0042.213 [permalink]

Couch, Julie Nelson (1999): Childe Hood: The Infantilization of Medieval Legend. In: *In Parentheses: Papers in Medieval Studies*, Vol. 1, 128–144

Dobson, Richard Barrie/John Taylor, ed. (1997 [[1]1976]): *Rymes of Robyn Hood. An Introduction to the English Outlaw*. Stroud, Gloucestershire

Edelman, Lee (2004): *No Future. Queer Theory and the Death Drive*. Durham [et al.]

Harty, Kevin J. (2012): Walt in Sherwood, or the Sheriff of Disneyland: Disney and the Film Legend of Robin Hood. In: *The Disney Middle Ages. A Fairy Tale and Fantasy Past*, eds. Tison Pugh/Susan Aronstein, New York, 133–152

Knight, Stephen/Thomas Ohlgren, ed. (2000): *Robin Hood and Other Outlaw Tales*. Kalamazoo, Michigan

Knight, Stephen (2015): *The Politics of Myth*. Carlton, Victoria. Kindle

Lévi-Strauss, Claude (1955): The Structural Study of Myth. In: *The Journal of American Folklore*, Vol. 68, No. 270, 428–444

Lynch, Andrew (2012): Animated Conversations in Nottingham: Disney's Robin Hood (1973). In: *Medieval Afterlives in Popular Culture*, eds. Gail Ashton/Daniel T. Kline, New York, 29–42

MacLeod, Anne Scott (2000): Howard Pyle's Robin Hood: The Middle Ages for Americans. In: *Children's Literature Association Quaterly*, Vol. 25, No. 1, 44–48

May, Jill P. (1981): Walt Disney's Interpretation of Children's Literature. In: *Language Arts* , Vol. 58, No. 4, 463–472

Meek, James (2016): Robin Hood in a Time of Austerity. In: *London Review of Books*, Vol. 38, No. 4, 18.02.2016

Petzold, Dieter (1995): Der Rebell im Kinderzimmer: Robin Hood in der Kinderliteratur. In: *Robin Hood. Die vielen Gesichter des edlen Räubers / The Many Faces of that Celebrated English Outlaw*, ed. Kevin Carpenter, Oldenburg, 65–78

Pollard, A[nthony] J[ames] (2004): *Imagining Robin Hood: The Late Medieval Stories in Historical Context*. London [et al.]

Professor Fox [i. e. Steve Jones] (2015): Robin Hood: A Presidential Recasting. In: *Buzzfeed*, 23.10.2015. https://www.buzzfeed.com/crafanc/robin-hood-a-presidential-recasting-1syvy. Accessed: 20. July 2021

Rolfe, Mark (2016): *The Reinvention of the Populist Rhetoric in the Digital Age. Insiders and Outsiders in Democratic Politics*. London

Rose, Steve (2018): How the Robin Hood Myth Was Turned on Its Head by Rightwingers. In: *The Guardian*, 22.11.2018

Schuster, Joshua (2014): The Fable, the Moral, and the Animal: Reconsidering the Fable in Animal Studies with Marianne Moore's Elephants. In: *Representing the Modern Animal in Culture*, eds. Jeanne Dubino/Ziba Rashidian/Andrew Smyth, New York, 137–154

Seal, Graham (2009) The Robin Hood Principle: Folklore, History, and the Social Bandit. In: *Journal of Folklore Research*, Vol. 46, No. 1, 67–89

Seal, Graham (2011): *Outlaw Heroes in Myth and History*. London [et al.]

Taylor, Joseph (2013): 'Me longeth sore to Bernysdale': Centralisation, Resistance, and the Bare Life of the Greenwood in A Gest of Robyn Hode. In: *Modern Philosophy*, Vol. 110, No. 3, 313–339

Watts, Steven (1995): Walt Disney: Art and Politics in the American Century. In: *The Journal of American History*, Vol. 82, No. 1, 84–110

Jack Sparrow—the Ultimate Adventurer

Aleta-Amirée von Holzen

Abstract When Disney dared to bring a pirate movie to theaters in 2003, Captain Jack Sparrow rather unexpectedly sailed brilliantly into the hearts of the audience. Although a pair of young lovers were the main characters, Jack Sparrow, played by Johnny Depp, stole the show from everyone. Sparrow stands out from all the other characters: He is contrasted with the young and still idealistic couple, with cursed pirates and also with the representatives of social order. The character draws much of his fascination from the fact that he oscillates between different binary pairs, which marks him not least as an adventurer. This article argues that Jack Sparrow is the epitome of the adventurer—representing an almost ideal (though perhaps sometimes exaggerated) embodiment of the concept of the adventurer as described by German philosopher Georg Simmel in 1911.

Captain Jack Sparrow—there is hardly a name which rings as much with the fascination of epic pirate adventures as the main character of Disney's five-part blockbuster film series *Pirates of the Caribbean*. His only rivals may be Long John Silver and Captain Hook, who also owe their fame at least in part to classic Disney films: *Treasure Island* (1950) and *Peter Pan* (1953). Unlike these two characters, however, Jack Sparrow is not based on a pre-existing fictional character. *Pirates of the Caribbean—The Curse of the Black Pearl* (Verbinski 2003) was rather inspired by the Theme Park Ride at Disneyland in Anaheim, California. Contrary to expectation—the pirate movie as a genre had been considered dead for years—the first film was such a smashing success that the story was subsequently expanded into a trilogy: *Dead Men's Chest* (Verbinski 2006) followed, then *At World's End*

A.-A. von Holzen (✉)
Schweizerisches Institut für Kinder- und Jugendmedien SIKJM, Zurich, Switzerland
e-mail: aleta-amiree.vonholzen@sikjm.ch

© The Author(s), under exclusive license to Springer-Verlag GmbH, DE, part of Springer Nature 2022
U. Dettmar and I. Tomkowiak (eds.), *On Disney*, Studien zu Kinder- und Jugendliteratur und -medien 9, https://doi.org/10.1007/978-3-662-64625-0_12

185

(Verbinski 2007).[1] A few years later, the series was continued with a fourth—*Stranger Tides* (Marshall 2011; cf. Pfister 2012)—and a fifth instalment—*Salazar's Revenge* (Rønning/Sandberg 2017). Among a lot of other spectacular features, the series owes a part of its success to the scene-stealing performance of actor Johnny Depp in the role of Captain Jack Sparrow. Although plot-wise Will Turner (played by Orlando Bloom), a young blacksmith, and his love interest Elizabeth Swann (Keira Knightley), the governor's daughter, are the main characters in the first film, Johnny Depp garnered an Oscar nomination for his performance (in a leading role) and ended up being the only main character to star in all five films.

In his unique way, somewhere between genius and madness, Jack Sparrow represents the concept of the adventurer in a close to ideal, sometimes even exaggerated way, as I will show in this essay.[2] For this purpose, I will mainly draw on Georg Simmel's reflections on adventure and the adventurer and focus on the trilogy, as Jack is characterised in great detail in the first three instalments and does not fundamentally change in the subsequent films.

Adventure as a Combination of Change and Necessity

German philosopher Georg Simmel tried to fathom what gives distinction to the concept of adventure in his essay *The Adventure* (first published in 1911, see also Kalbermatten 2011, 13–16). In contrast to other experienced events (e.g. a sea voyage), the adventure is an "incomparable experience," according to Simmel (1959, 233). As a "total experience of the present" (Best 1980, 113), it is an experience of extraordinary intensity. It lies beyond the daily routine of our life and yet seems connected to life's centre—it contains "necessity and meaning" (Simmel 1959, 231, 233). Adventure is a synthesis between "external accidents" and "inner necessity" (233). This synthesis can be useful for grasping a basic narrative trope in adventure literature. The element of chance can manifest itself in a myriad of different ways, but in the end the bad guys are most likely defeated and the good guys are happy. In literary adventures, the necessity mentioned by Simmel is not necessarily clear at the beginning of the story, but has to be grasped from the way the story ends (cf. Wulff 2004, 13). What may appear to be a coincidence at the beginning turns out to be necessary for the narrative structure to unfold. In *PotC* 1, for example, one of the huge coincidences is that Jack, of all people, saves Elizabeth from drowning at the beginning, thus is thrown into prison and, furthermore, is the only prisoner who cannot escape during the attack of the *Black Pearl*, so that he—as literally the only person who can bring Will to Elizabeth—virtually 'waits' for Will in prison.

---

[1] In this article the film titles are abbreviated as *PotC* and numbered consecutively.

[2] This article is based on the author's earlier work published in German (von Holzen 2007 and 2009).

In contrast to the predictable monotony of everyday life, uncertainty is adventure's basic requirement (cf. Simmel 1959; Hügel 2003; Best 1980; Wulff 2004). It is uncertain if and when an adventure will occur, what dimensions it will take, and how it will end (cf. Klotz 1979, 14). However, the unpredictable not only holds the risk of failure but also the potential for success (cf. Hügel 2003, 91). In genre literature, adventure generally has a positive connotation, for there is rarely a negative outcome for the daring adventurer. The "professional adventurer," in the words of Simmel, "makes a system of life out of his life's lack of system" (1959, 233).

As a popular trope, the adventurer is characterised by qualities that correlate with adventure. While Will and Elizabeth are not yet adventurers at the beginning of the narrative, Jack as a pirate clearly leads the life of one.

It should be noted that Simmel speaks of the adventurer only in the masculine form—at the time his text was written, adventure literature rarely featured female adventurers; furthermore, a female adventurer often connoted liberal sexuality (for the male adventurer, Simmel acknowledges this connection by mentioning Giacomo Casanova as a real-life example, cf. 1959, 233). Thus a female adventurer was seen as an even more disreputable character than her male counterpart (as is sometimes implied by the word 'adventuress'). Since this paper is about Jack Sparrow, I will refer to the adventurer as a *he*, but I would like to make clear that the concept—for at least the last few decades—is readily transferable across gender boundaries. For example Elizabeth in the *PotC* trilogy is without doubt also an adventurer (cf. von Holzen 2007).

Activity and Passivity: The Seizure of Opportunity

An adventurer is characterised by initiative and activity. At the same time, he cannot escape having an element of passivity, since he cannot create the uncertainty or randomness of adventure himself. Therefore, he needs an opportunity for adventure to present itself, which he in turn must seize: "Adventure has the gesture of the conqueror, the quick seizure of opportunity [...]" (Simmel 1959, 235). Although he must to a certain extent surrender himself to fate, he meets fate with activity. In the words of Fritze/Seesslen/Weil: "The adventurer is the human who does not want things only to happen to him, but wants to happen himself" (1983, 15, my translation). For example, in *PotC* 1, the bored governor's daughter Elizabeth Swann, in accordance with her social position, could allow herself to be killed in the pirate raid at Port Royal—instead, she demands to speak to the pirate captain (Barbossa) and thus seizes her chance for adventure. Although she represents the damsel in distress in the first film, she does not wait for rescue but always tries to act.

Within an adventure, the adventurer also needs opportunities to find ways to pass his trials successfully. This 'seizure of opportunity' is reflected in Jack Sparrow's firm belief in the 'opportune moment,' a certain sequence or coincidence of events that enables a person to carry out a particular action.

The adventurer moves "between what we conquer and what is given to us" (Simmel 1959, 234–235). The result is a "coexistence of conquest, which owes everything only to its own strength and presence of mind, and complete self-abandonment to the powers and accidents of the world, which can delight us, but in the same breath can also destroy us" (ibid., 235). The adventurer's action is actually often a *re*action. Thus, *PotC* 1 is also ultimately not a self-initiated adventure for the three main characters; and even though Jack has been waiting for his chance for ten years and always seeks adventure, he also reacts to events—Elizabeth falls into the water, he rescues her not knowing that this would bring him an important piece of information and the chance to finally win back his beloved ship, the *Black Pearl*. In addition to physical prowess, the adventurer also needs presence of mind and quick reflexes—which often includes impressive skills in negotiating—in order to survive the dangers in one piece and bring the adventure to a happy and successful end. For the combination of activity and passivity as a characteristic which distinguishes the adventurer from other literary figures Klotz uses the term charisma, understood on the one hand as a (passive) gift of grace, on the other as an (active) charm that allows him to win friends and defeat enemies (cf. 1979, 15).

Self-confidently Walking the Fine Line between Genius and Madness

On a conceptual level, the adventurer's main characteristic is his (heightened or even exaggerated) self-awareness (Hügel 2003, 92). It is both a condition and a consequence of his relation to the world. According to Simmel, "the adventurer of genius lives […] at the point where the course of the world and individual fate have, so to speak, not yet differentiated from each other" (1959, 236–237), which means that he believes in being able to influence fate with his actions. Jack's belief that he can influence the course of the world is revealed, for example, in one of the few serious conversations he has with Will Turner in *PotC* 3. Will is in a dilemma—he cannot decide whether to save his relationship with Elizabeth or save his father by killing Davy Jones and taking his place as captain of the *Flying Dutchman* himself. Jack's advice is: "Avoid the choice altogether. Change the facts" (Verbinski 2007, 01:22:56).

Simmel further explains that, contrary to everyday life, the adventurer in his "typical fatalism" risks all on the "hovering chance, on fate and the more-or-less" (1959, 236). The adventurer behaves towards unpredictable events as if he were certain about their outcome: "For this reason, to the sober person adventurous conduct often seems insanity; for because, in order to make sense, it appears to presuppose that the unknowable is known" (ibid.). Jack's behaviour upon his arrival in Port Royal in *PotC* 1 exemplifies this: He drifts into the harbour on the mast of his sinking boat at the precise moment his boat finally sinks. The scene is especially memorable because Jack does not in the slightest seem to be impressed by his unusual predicament; with a totally straight face he sets his foot on the jetty, transforming the ridiculousness of the scene into elegance.[3] Jack embodies the "'sleepwalking certainty' with which the adventurer leads his life" precisely because he considers the unpredictable to be "the premises of his conduct" (ibid., 237).

Remarkably, in previous Hollywood pirate films every protagonist sooner or later is told that he is crazy, which emphasises the unusualness and improbability of his deeds. With Jack Sparrow, however, 'crazy' becomes his defining characteristic: he perpetually oscillates between genius and madness. The fact that Jack constantly balances between these two traits, even if at times he seems on the brink of disaster, makes him one of the most unique and impressive characters in pirate film history. The deliberate oddity of his appearance and whimsical behaviour, such as slightly staggering (on land), makes him seem eccentric. This is further emphasised by attributes like the compass which doesn't point north. An oft-cited scene sums up Jack's character early in *PotC* 1, when Will says: "This is either madness—or brilliance" and Jack gives a telling answer: "It's remarkable, how often those two traits coincide" (Verbinski 2003, 00:43:30). In fact, Jack's plan proves to be brilliant: His scheme succeeds because they first pretend to capture the *Dauntless* (the Navy's largest ship), misleading commodore Norrington's men, so that they can sail off on the *Interceptor* (the fastest ship). When the main mast breaks on Beckett's ship as a result of Jack's actions in *PotC* 3, an officer articulates the question in the audience's mind: "Do you think he plans it all out or just makes it up as he goes along?" (Verbinski 2007, 01:12:16). The admiration of Jack's enemy mirrors the audience's fascination with him. It is scenes like this that illustrate the adventurer's "sleepwalking certainty" (Simmel 1959, 237).

Jack's oscillation between madness and genius is sustained throughout the series and culminates in an equally striking exchange in *PotC* 3: to Cutler Beckett's exclamation, "You're mad!", Jack counters, "Thank goodness I am,'cause if I wasn't, this would probably never work." But he actually manages a spectacular exit from Beckett's ship onto the *Black Pearl*, which is already sailing away, whereupon he doubles down: "And that was even without a single drop of rum!" (Verbinski 2007, 01:11:25–01:11:50).

The adventurer's genius as well as his madness is expressed in his trademark, a self-confident laugh or smile, which he does not lose even when in the greatest danger. It may rather indicate his nonchalance or even a certain skepticism towards the world (Fritze/Seesslen/Weil 1983, 33).[4] For example, Jack smiles—incomprehensibly, to the other characters—when he jumps over the railing into the sea at the end of *PotC* 1. For him this is a calculated risk, because he surmises, based on a clue (the parrot), that the *Black Pearl* is nearby and will fish him up.

---

[3] As Steinhoff points out, the scene alternates between staging him as a hero and as an anti-hero (cf. 2011, 45; see also Zhanial 2020, 60).

[4] Simmel explains further: "[…] to him whom the unlikely is likely, the likely easily becomes unlikely" (1959, 236). The same laughter is often found distorted and with a bitter undertone in the villainous pirate, who embodies an adventurer in a negative fashion. In *PotC* 1, this applies to Barbossa (who becomes more positive in *PotC* 2/3).

The adventurer dares a lot because he can accurately assess his abilities and trusts that he can recognise and take advantage of opportunities as they arise. An adventurer may doubt the world at times, but never himself. With boldness and daring, he accomplishes the improbable. Jack is the character with the most prominently displayed ego, whose behaviour at times even hints at delusions of grandeur, as when he insists on being called *Captain*, which becomes a running gag. He himself stresses his identity[5] as *Captain Jack Sparrow* several times as an explanation when the probability of his deeds (be they in the future or in the past) is doubted: "You forgot one very important thing. I'm Captain Jack Sparrow" (Verbinski 2003, 01:13:40). Jack's identity seems to represent the unlikely. That he shows up in the pirates' cave in *PotC* 1 repeatedly is not "not possible" but "not probable," as Jack explains to Barbossa at one point (ibid., 01:40:30).

When Will, Elizabeth, Barbossa and his crew bring Jack back from Davy Jones' Locker in *PotC* 3, here, at the latest, it becomes clear that his presence is indispensable for the adventure in the series. The first thing they do is tell him everything that's wrong and why he's urgently needed. His mere presence seems to open up possibilities for action and to bring a certain unpredictability into play. When the world of adventure is threatened with extinction from two sides (Davy Jones as mythical threat and Cutler Beckett as representative of a trading company and globalism), Jack, as the personification of adventure, must save the threatened freedom—even though he himself is not really comfortable with this.

Negotiating for Profit

In each film, Jack proves to be the one to tip the scales at the end to prevent the looming disaster. When he is presumed dead at the end of *PotC* 2, his comrades lament his loss by acknowledging this trait:

Will	[...] The *Pearl*'s gone. Along with its captain.
Gibbs	Aye. And already the world seems a bit less bright. He fooled us all right to the end. But I guess that honest streak finally won out. To Jack Sparrow!
Ragetti	Never another like Captain Jack.
Pintel	He was a gentleman of fortune, he was.
Elizabeth	He was a good man. (Verbinski 2006, 02:12:13–02:12:38)

Jack's uniqueness, his being an adventurer ("gentleman of fortune") and ultimately his acting as a "good man" are emphasised. Of course, no one except Elizabeth knows that Jack's heroic sacrifice (letting himself be swallowed by the Kraken) was not a voluntary action. Thus, when he returns in *PotC* 3, the game

---

[5] Zhanial analyses the ongoing play with Jack's identities and fragmentation throughout the series (2020, 70–78).

starts anew. Again it seems questionable whether he will decide to do the right thing. His intentions are repeatedly doubted by the other characters due to the fact that time and again he seeks to benefit himself; sacrificing himself or taking action for others when it is not absolutely necessary is not his forte. Nevertheless, in *PotC* 1 he saves Elizabeth from drowning (because the two soldiers standing beside him can't swim). Apart from this incident he constantly seems to be pursuing his own agenda, sometimes in a rather dishonest manner. Thus Jack embodies—and to a greater extent than the protagonists in classic pirate films from the 1950s— the merchant adventurer. This subtype of the adventurer, as described by Nerlich (1977), Best (1980) and Hügel (2003), is based on English merchants from the late Middle Ages who did not belong to any guild and sold cloth on their own account. Characters who correspond to this subtype weigh the risks of their actions and try to keep them as low as possible. They calculate their chances and seek (monetary) profit. This sets Jack (and the other pirates) apart from Will and Elizabeth (and the other young lovers in the subsequent films). When there's no prospect of profit Jack won't budge an inch, as he explains to Will in his prison cell in *PotC* 1: "Well, if you're intending to brave all, hasten to her [Elizabeth's] rescuing and so win fair lady's heart, you'll have to do it alone, mate. I see no profit in it for me" (Verbinski 2003, 00:41:30). Will's offer to free him is accepted only after he has reassured himself of the quality of the goods, so to speak: that Will is indeed Bootstrap's son and therefore is able to lift the *Black Pearl's* curse. There is one more among Jack's prevailing character traits that can be linked to the merchant adventurer. He tries to avoid physical combat and prefers to negotiate with his adversaries (and sometimes even with his fellow comrades) although he masterfully fights and shoots when necessary. This adds to the uniqueness of his character. In *PotC* 2 he declares: "Why fight, when you can negotiate? All one needs is the proper leverage" (Verbinski 2006, 01:58:00). In this scene, however, Jack discovers in an ironic twist that his leverage is missing, and his plan is foiled. His negotiations actually fail several times (Zhanial 2020, 62), and it is in *PotC* 1 as well as in *PotC* 2/3 that 'mistakes' from past deals catch up with him. Regardless, scenes involving negotiations provide Jack with the opportunity to show his cleverness.

But because he keeps his cards close to his chest, he also arouses suspicion. When he asks Will to wait for the opportune moment in *PotC* 1, the latter reproaches him suspiciously: "When's that? When it's of greatest profit to you?" (Verbinski 2003, 01:08:18). Jack is never completely transparent about his plans, possibly because they are not fixed and he adapts them according to the situation at hand—because the *seizure of opportunity* that marks the adventurer cannot be planned in advance. He does not commit himself to any side (or so it seems). When Elizabeth sees Jack, who has turned into a ghostly skeleton, fencing with Barbossa, she asks: "On whose side is Jack?" Will can only ask back: "At the moment?" (ibid., 01:55:14). Zweig aptly describes the somewhat ambiguous position of the adventurer:

He is not loyal, not a model of right behavior. Quite the contrary, he fascinates because he undermines the expected order. He possesses the qualities of the "hero": skill, resourcefulness, courage, intelligence. But he is the opposite of selfless. He is hungry; "heightened," not as an example, but as a presence, a phenomenon of sheer energy. [...] They [the heroes who are not heroes at all] share the qualities of the "moral" hero, but one: they are not loyal, nor are they disloyal. The question simply does not arise for them. Their loyalty is directed towards the turns and chances of their own destinies. We call such a hero an *adventurer*. (1974, 35–36)

Jack would not be an ideal adventurer, however, if he were really concerned with profit. His material objective is the *Black Pearl*,[6] which in turn symbolises an intangible item: "What the *Black Pearl* really is, is freedom" (Verbinski 2003, 01:33:45). Of course, for an adventurer, and even more so for a pirate, his unboundedness is a central requirement. For the adventurer is constantly on the move; to stand still would mean the end of his life as an adventurer (cf. Hügel 2003, 94). Therefore adventurers are, like Jack, "escape artists" (Zweig 1974, 60) who do not allow themselves to be permanently bound—this is true for Jack in matters of love as well as loyalty. Jack declares this himself in *PotC* 3 before the pirate council, when he counters Barbossa's accusation that he is always running away: "I have only ever embraced that oldest and noblest of pirate traditions: [...] We must fight—to run away" (Verbinski 2007, 01:43:31). Of course, his flexibility allows him to even override this maxim on occasion, namely in the final sea battle against Beckett's armada. As he explains to Gibbs: "Never actually been one for tradition" (ibid., 02:23:19). This flexibility—or mobility—is probably the very basis of his unpredictability, and in this his ability to influence events in a crucial way is rooted.

Accordingly, immobility represents a particular hell for an adventurer, as Jack experiences in Davy Jones's locker: There is a dead calm; the *Black Pearl* is stuck in a wasteland. In addition, the numerous alter egos deny him the opportunity to stand out from those around him, and thus they deny him his individuality.[7]

Following His Own Rules

Another pivotal point is the adventurer's own set of rules and guiding principles. As Hügel (2003, 93) emphasises, their specific content is not that important, only that he follows them. Still, they usually correspond more or less to a common code of honour (cf. Wulff 2004, 20; Fritze/Seesslen/Weill 1983, 33). The pirate is also characterised, on a conceptual level, by adherence to his own set of rules; the pirate thus can be seen as another subtype of the adventurer, one who is both

---

[6] Steinhoff notes that the *Black Pearl* is the real damsel in distress for Jack in the film series (2011, 52–53).

[7] Although Jack flirts with immortality multiple times, he deliberately misses the opportunity each time because it would ultimately rob him of his mobility.

hyperbolic and twisted into negative (see Seesslen 1996, 91). In his radical form, as described by Hofmann (2003, 337), the pirate is a dissolute, anarchic figure: he indulges in cruelty and debauchery; he is greedy, hungry for booty and hedonistic to an extreme degree (see also Christen 2004, 68). In pirate literature, it is usually the antagonistic pirate who fits this description; so too does the cursed Captain Barbossa, the pirate villain of *PotC* 1 (although the curse prevents him from experiencing the pleasures he seeks, because he feels nothing). Inspired by real-life examples, fictional pirates possess and abide by their own set of laws. In *PotC* the audience hears only a few concrete rules of the Pirate's Code, but it exists (and, as is hinted in *PotC* 3 with the thick volume in the Code Keeper's possession, may contain a whole collection of rules, or, as the pirates in *PotC* 1 say, guidelines). Jack's own maxims, however, do not refer to the Pirate's Code: "The only rules that really matter are these: What a man can do and what a man can't do" (Verbinski 2003, 00:47:30). This rule offers much room for interpretation and once again hints at the adventurer's activity and passivity. Jack does not really deny the validity of the pirate rules, but implies that they can be overridden if necessary. The adventurer correspondingly does not necessarily fight against the social conventions of the world he's travelling in, but simply ignores them (Hügel 2003, 97).[8] For example in *PotC* 1 Jack's crew includes a woman, Ana Maria, even though Gibbs mentions that this is believed to be bad luck. The adventurer follows his own rules not only in his actions, but often also in the way he moves and performs his actions, with exuberance, in a rollicking manner or with a staggering gait like Jack.

Jack also displays an 'unpiratical' preference for non-violence on several occasions, e.g. when he implores Will in *PotC* 1 to stand aside, because the bullet in Jack's pistol is not meant for Will. Sticking to one's own rules is often associated with being crazy, but it also gives the adventurer the advantage of surprise. Jack also uses the adventurer's 'own rules' in *PotC* 3, when he breaks the custom of the pirate lords to always vote only for themselves in the election of the pirate king—without violating the code. By voting for Elizabeth to be king, Jack accomplishes the improbable (even Captain Teague, the Code Keeper, had thought the election of a pirate king to be most unlikely) while achieving his own ends. When Will learns that Elizabeth has become king, he speculates: "Maybe he [Jack] really *does* know what he is doing" (Verbinski 2007, 01:52:58).

Because he stands apart from both 'ordinary' and cursed pirates, Jack, as an ultimately good pirate, is blatantly given the status of an adventurer. By establishing his own rules, the adventurer deliberately separates himself from the world he lives in and thus, in a sense, sets himself apart. The adventurer must take a "step out of the dominant order" ("Schritt aus der Ordnung," Best 1980, 9) to constitute himself. This step leads into a space of adventure that offers the adventurer an opportunity for "self-assertion of the individual" ("Selbstbehauptung des

---

[8] Jack's character also blurs gender boundaries: see Steinhoff 2011.

Individuums") and where he is totally in his element (Hügel 2003, 96; see also Kalbermatten 2011, 17–41). In *PotC,* this space of adventure stretches between two poles against which the adventurers, the good pirates, must hold their own: on the one hand, there are the villainous pirates, elevated to a supernatural level; on the other, there is a civilian world similar to the courtly palaces in classic pirate movies (see Christen 2004, Seesslen 1996). Compared to the genre classics from the 1930s to the 1950s, the modern pirate movies have (since 1983) established a significant change in the genre's plot structure that is also adopted by *PotC.* In the end, the good pirate is not rewarded with rehabilitation and is not (re)integrated into society (marriage and recognition of his merits).[9] Pirates are allowed to be pirates, as an end in itself. The pirate world thus undergoes a change in status: it enables adventure (as before), but being a part of this world may now be worth striving for. Piracy as an adventure thus is no longer in need of justification, which becomes clear by the end of the *PotC* 3 at the latest. The protagonists remain pirates beyond the end of each film, and Jack (just like his counterpart Barbossa) already sees a new adventure on the horizon.

Full Circle

What makes Jack Sparrow the ultimate adventurer? In addition to everything discussed thus far, one aspect of *PotC* has not yet been addressed: genre hybridity and intertextuality, often named as characteristics of postmodern narrative. Elevating (mostly) villainous pirates to a supernatural level may, in this case, accentuate the adventure's extraordinariness. The *PotC* series has an abundance of references to other pirate films (cf. Zhanial 2020). In addition, *PotC* repeatedly celebrates self-references (cf. Horst 2004, 99; Traber 2004; Zhanial 2020): memorable lines are picked up several times, but are used by a different character or in a completely different situation. As Traber maintains, in *PotC* 1 the film's motifs are presented with irony and are repeatedly reflected upon. Here, too, Jack's role is crucial: his character is tied to various stories with questionable, to say the least, validity (cf. Zhanial 2020). Sometimes they turn out to be a sailor's yarn, but sometimes they are even surpassed by the 'truth.' Jack is the one character who is aware of being narrated. He plays with his reputation and the expectations others have of him. As Zhanial points out, in *PotC* 4 Jack also acknowledges the possibility of receiving immortality not as a supernatural extension of life, but in living on as a story (cf. ibid., 76–78). "Again and again, the other characters comment on and discuss Sparrow's absurd behavior. Again and again they activate their knowledge of pirate stories and have to adapt it to the perceived reality [...]" (Traber 2004, 401, my translation). In a way, *PotC* creates a somewhat perpetual circle

---

[9] Instead, characters from *PotC*'s 'courtly world' (Will, Elizabeth, and, at the end of *PotC* 3, also the two soldiers Murtogg and Mullroy) become adventurers themselves—they become pirates.

of self-reference, and this applies to adventure as well. Perhaps, on the narrative level, this circle of constantly rearranged and pastiched elements also mirrors the constant mobility that is crucial for the adventurer (and even more so the pirate, who lives on the ocean)—for example, the pirate song from the trilogy can be read as symbolising the cyclical nature of pirate life. By keeping the adventurer perpetually in motion, the story of the adventurer is never finished either (cf. Hügel 2003, 95).

The adventurer as a narrative trope represents a "total figure" (Klotz 1979, 17) whose grandiosity rejects claims to being a true-to-life portrait (cf. Kalbermatten 2011, 40). In contrast to the genre heroes of nineteenth century literature (e.g. Old Shatterhand, see ibid., 28–40), in the twenty-first century, such a character, in order not to appear anachronistic, can no longer work without ironic 'refractions.' For Zhanial, Jack is a "particularly apt example of a postmodern character" (2020, 62), not least because he oscillates between madness and genius. His "seemingly insane actions" (ibid.), paired with his occasional clumsiness, infuse his character with hilariousness[10] (cf. ibid.), he is hero and comic relief rolled into one (cf. Traber 2004, 400). This, on the surface, contrasts and lessens his *grandezza* (and casually shows that adventure takes place "in a world of toil and labour" [Hügel 2003, 94, my translation]). His well-orchestrated oscillation—his constant movement—between multiple binary pairings (self-interest and selflessness, male and female etc.) also prevents him from becoming a hero. But perhaps in particular because 'Captain' Jack Sparrow manages to integrate these contradictions in his amazing, peculiar personality, he, who is adventure personified, remains a larger-than-life character.

References

Primary Sources

Verbinski, Gore, dir. (2003): *Fluch der Karibik* [= *Pirates of the Caribbean—The Curse of the Black Pearl*]. 3-Disc Special Edition. Walt Disney Pictures/Jerry Bruckheimer Films. DVD

Verbinski, Gore, dir. (2006): *Pirates of the Caribbean—Fluch der Karibik 2* [= *Pirates of the Caribbean—Dead Man's Chest*]. Walt Disney Pictures/Jerry Bruckheimer Films. DVD

Verbinski, Gore, dir. (2007): *Pirates of the Caribbean—At World's End*. Walt Disney Pictures/Jerry Bruckheimer Films. DVD

Marshall, Rob, dir. (2011): *Pirates of the Caribbean—Stranger Tides*. Walt Disney Pictures/Jerry Bruckheimer Films. DVD

Rønning, Joachim/Sandberg, Espen, dir. (2017): *Pirates of the Caribbean—Salazar's Revenge*. Walt Disney Pictures/Jerry Bruckheimer Films. DVD

---

[10] Because of the combination of grandiosity and clumsiness and his willingness to negotiate, Steinhoff, among others, sees Jack as a trickster figure (cf. 2011, 46–47); Zhanial emphasises that he can also be seen as a response to uncertainties in the age of information (cf. 2020, 69). Indeed, the scriptwriters mention being inspired by the trickster motif (Elliott et al. 2004, 00:36:30, 01:04:28).

Secondary Sources

Best, Otto F. (1980): *Abenteuer—Wonnetraum aus Flucht und Ferne. Geschichte und Deutung.* Frankfurt/a. M.

Christen, Matthias (2004): Der Piratenfilm. In: *Filmgenres. Abenteuerfilm,* eds. Bodo Traber/ Hans J. Wulff, Stuttgart (RUB; 18404), 66–77

Elliott, Ted/Terry Rossio/Stuart Beattie/Jay Wolpert (2004): Audio Commentary. In: *Fluch der Karibik* [i.e. *Pirates of the Caribbean—The Curse of the Black Pearl*]. 3-Disc-Special-Edition. Disney, Buena Vista Home Entertainment. DVD

Fritze, Christoph/Georg Seesslen/Claudius Weil (1983): *Der Abenteurer. Geschichte und Mythologie des Abenteuer-Films.* Reinbek bei Hamburg (Grundlagen des populären Films; 9)

Hofmann, Felix (2003): Pirat. In: *Handbuch Populäre Kultur. Begriffe, Theorien und Diskussionen,* ed. Hans-Otto Hügel, Stuttgart [et al.], 334–339

Horst, Sabine (2004): *Orlando Bloom. Ein Porträt.* Berlin (Stars!; 11)

Hügel, Hans-Otto (2003): Abenteurer. In: *Handbuch Populäre Kultur. Begriffe, Theorien und Diskussionen,* ed. Hans-Otto Hügel, Stuttgart [et al.], 91–98

Kalbermatten, Manuela (2011): „*Von nun an werden wir mitspielen.*"*Abenteurerinnen in der phantastischen Kinder- und Jugendliteratur der Gegenwart.* Zürich

Klotz, Volker (1979): Abenteuer-Romane. Sue, Dumas, Ferry, Retcliffe, May, Verne. München [et al.]

Nerlich, Michael (1977): Zur Begriffsgeschichte von „Abenteuer". In: *Weimarer Beiträge. Zeitschrift für Literaturwissenschaft, Ästhetik und Kulturtheorie,* Vol. 23, No. 8, 160–171

Pfister, Eugen (2012): "What did you say your occupation was?—I'm a grog-swilling, foul-smelling pirate!" Das Piratenbild in ‚alten' und ‚neuen' Medien. In: *Schrecken der Händler und Herrscher. Piratengemeinschaften in der Geschichte,* eds. Andreas Obenaus/ Eugen Pfister/Birgit Tremml, Wien, 248–269

Seesslen, Georg (^{3}1996): Totenkopf und weiße Segel: Der Piratenfilm. / Pirate's Gold. In: *Abenteuer. Geschichte und Mythologie des Abenteuerfilms,* ed. id., Marburg (Grundlagen des populären Films), 91–117, 247–251

Simmel, Georg (1983): Das Abenteuer. In: id.: *Zur philosophischen Kultur. Über das Abenteuer, die Geschichte und die Krise der Moderne. Gesammelte Essays.* Berlin, 13–26

Simmel, George [sic] (1959): The Adventure. In: *The Partisan Review,* Vol. XXVI, No. 2, 231–242

Steinhoff, Heike (2011): *Queer Buccaneers. (De)Constructing Boundaries in the Pirates of the Caribbean Film Series.* Berlin (Transnational and Transatlantic American Studies; 10)

Traber, Bodo (2004): Fluch der Karibik. In: *Filmgenres. Abenteuerfilm,* eds. id./Hans J. Wulff, Stuttgart (RUB; 18404), 399–402

von Holzen, Aleta-Amirée (2007): "A Pirate's Life for Me!" Von *The Black Pirate* bis *Pirates of the Caribbean*—Abenteuerkonzepte im Piratenfilm. Zürich (Populäre Literaturen und Medien; 1)

von Holzen, Aleta-Amirée (2009): Abenteurerkonzepte im Hollywood-Piratenfilm. In: *Schweizerisches Archiv für Volkskunde,* Vol. 105, 153–169

Wulff, Hans J. (2004): Einleitung. Grenzgängertum: Elemente und Dimensionen des Abenteuerfilms. In: *Filmgenres. Abenteuerfilm,* eds. Bodo Traber/Hans J. Wulff, Stuttgart (RUB; 18404), 9–30

Zhanial, Susanne (2020): *Postmodern Pirates. Tracing the Development of the Pirate Motif with Disney's Pirates of the Caribbean.* Leiden [et al.] (Contemporary Cinema; 8)

Zweig, Paul (1974): *The Adventurer.* London

IMMERSIVE EXPERIENCE, REFLEXIVE ENGAGEMENT

From Anaheim to Batuu

Fan Tourism and Disney's *Star Wars*: Galaxy's Edge as Transmedia Playground

Lincoln Geraghty

Abstract Recent additions to Disney's portfolio such as *Star Wars* and the Marvel Cinematic Universe have not only expanded their storytelling potential but also inspired new theme park experiences that attract fans. The *Star Wars*: Galaxy's Edge attraction is a full-scale immersive experience containing rides, eateries and shops that draw directly from the fictional universe of the science fiction franchise. Fans engage with Disney cast members performing as various characters such as Darth Vader, making the fictional and fantastic a little more real and tangible. Rides offer immersive experiences and new characters guide you through your journey. This chapter examines the transmedia narratives within Galaxy's Edge, arguing that the fan tourist experience is an integral component of Disney's development of the *Star Wars* story. As fans seek more realistic interactions with fictional texts, Disney offers a transmedia playground that helps to grow the *Star Wars* universe and bring it to life.

In 2015 Disney announced they would be building a new themed area inspired by the *Star Wars* franchise in both Disneyland and the Disney World Resort. Anaheim and Orlando would become home to a new part of the fictional galaxy far, far away. The attraction, called *Star Wars*: Galaxy's Edge, is set in the outpost settlement of Black Spire on the frontier planet of Batuu. It opened in both parks in 2019. Based on characters and settings from the movie world of *Star Wars*, Galaxy's Edge seeks to extend the transmedia story by including a new planet, culture and characters, but it would still link directly with the established story. Bob Iger, former CEO of Disney, underscored this connection to the well-established narrative in his speech announcing plans at the 2015 D23 Disney Convention: The new area will be "occupied by many inhabitants; humanoids, aliens and droids … the attractions, the entertainment, everything we create

---

L. Geraghty (✉)
University of Portsmouth, Portsmouth, UK
e-mail: lincoln.geraghty@port.ac.uk

© The Author(s), under exclusive license to Springer-Verlag GmbH, DE, part of Springer Nature 2022
U. Dettmar and I. Tomkowiak (eds.), *On Disney*, Studien zu Kinder- und Jugendliteratur und -medien 9, https://doi.org/10.1007/978-3-662-64625-0_13

will be part of our storytelling. Nothing will be out of character or stray from the mythology" (cited in Prudom/Zumberge 2015). Disney's intention to build a theme park area that draws directly from the *Star Wars* universe highlights the continued importance of transmedia storytelling in twenty-first century media entertainment franchises. It also highlights how physical sites and the desire to create immersive experiences add significantly to the storytelling potentials still offered by global media corporations to fans and consumers.

Considering this, the chapter will interrogate how important the theme park attraction is in developing and expanding transmedia storytelling. It also will look at how Disney has managed the *Star Wars* brand since purchasing the property in 2012. Lastly, it examines the role of place and space in identifying as a *Star Wars* fan in the twenty-first century. By visiting Galaxy's Edge, fans are able to appreciate the *Star Wars* storyworld and create affective connections with props, rides and themed sets when passing through the theme park attraction. In studying this phenomenon, it is important to look beyond the intellectual boundaries of tourism, media and cultural studies and integrate methods and approaches across those disciplines. Therefore, in this chapter I revisit the figure of the *flâneur*, the passionate wanderer emblematic of nineteenth century literary culture, to provide a conceptual framework through which to understand how fans relate to, interact with, and pass through spaces of popular culture. Tracking the fan as *flâneur* allows us to form a more intricate picture of how fans relate to their objects of fandom and understand the relationship between communities and individuals, texts and geographies, fan tourism, transmedia storytelling and immersive theme park experiences.

Disney's *Star Wars*

Star Wars is a prime of example of contemporary transmedia storytelling and a modern media franchise. The story and brand are both spread out across multiple media platforms and paratextual commodities, driven by the central narrative story arc of the ongoing battle between the forces of good and evil: Jedi versus Sith or Rebellion versus Empire. *Star Wars* can be seen as a "commercial supersystem of transmedia intertextuality," a phrase coined by Marsha Kinder (1991, 3) in her analysis of the children's media franchise *Teenage Mutant Ninja Turtles*. Building on this, Henry Jenkins (2006), Marc Steinberg (2012) and Colin B. Harvey (2015) have each discussed the phenomenon of transmedia storytelling, a strategy informing the creation and development of megamedia franchises like *Star Wars* through the dispersal of one story across multiple media outlets. Both transmedia storytelling and media franchising contribute to how Hollywood builds on its filmic output, ensuring longevity and financial success well beyond the first iteration of a text. For Derek Johnson, where "transmedia storytelling suggests cultural artistry and participatory culture, 'franchising' calls equal if not more attention to corporate structure and the economic organization of that productive labor" (2013, 33).

In this chapter, I want to broaden Johnson's discussion of the relationship between transmedia storytelling and media franchising to analyse how Disney's theme park experience adds to the narrative storyworld of *Star Wars*.

Disney purchased Lucasfilm in 2012, thus becoming copyright owner of every film and television series, character and creature ever created by George Lucas. Later, in 2014, Disney announced that the canon would be reset in order to make the six original movies and *The Clone Wars* and *Star Wars Rebels* animated television series "immoveable objects" in the narrative universe (The Legendary). Novels and comics that had provided fans with an *Expanded Universe* of stories and characters over many years were sidelined. New stories and texts would originate, underscoring Disney's strategy to rebuild *Star Wars* wholesale for a new generation. In anticipation of the release of *Star Wars: Episode VII—The Force Awakens* (2015), this decision can be interpreted as a means to clear the slate, delete previously established characters such as Luke and Leia's Jedi offspring so as to introduce the likes of Rey and Kylo Ren (Ben Solo). As a corporate author of *Star Wars* post George Lucas, Disney is keenly aware that it has to extend the franchise for future storytelling whilst playfully engaging with its past. New toys, associated merchandise like books and guides, video games, in addition to the films and television series, all contribute to a complex narrative network of *Star Wars* texts. These work in tandem to underscore the pre-eminence of the new Disney strategy and recycle the mythic saga of the Force. Yet, at the heart of this textual network are well-established and iconic characters and scenarios upon which Disney continually place tremendous narrative importance. Thus, this chapter also highlights the interconnected nature of corporate production, fan consumption and transmedia world-building in the contexts of Disney's most recent addition to the franchise: the Galaxy's Edge theme park attraction.

The transference of characters and narrative across different media platforms is emblematic of transmedia storytelling. Jenkins (2006, 334) defines this as "stories that unfold across multiple media platforms, with each medium making distinctive contributions to our understanding of the world." Each revisioning of the story adds another level of meaning, enhances the original and makes a distinctive contribution to the *Star Wars* universe. For Jenkins, "the core aesthetic impulses behind good transmedia works are world building and seriality" (2009). This statement describes *Star Wars* quite well, before and after Disney. But what defines Disney's transmedia strategy following the acquisition is how it strove to rebrand and re-establish canon in the lead up to *The Force Awakens*. It recycled the world built by George Lucas and added to it through the serialisation of new spin-off novels, animated and live-action television series on its Disney+ streaming service, and blockbuster movies. William Proctor and Matthew Freeman (2016) described this as an example of the "transmedia economy" of *Star Wars*. Within this economy, new characters can flourish and new stories can develop in a world recognisably *Star Wars* but also separate from the primary texts like the original movies. In these contexts I would argue that the theme park experience offers new potentials for transmedia storytelling because it becomes an immersive space for both Disney and fans to add more depth and detail to the ever-expanding fictional universe.

Building the Franchise

Modern media conglomerates such as Disney seek to maintain their brands through strategies epitomised by the media franchise. Branded lines rely on corporate ownership, management and protection of culture as intellectual property. In the case of *Star Wars*, this means Disney protects its asset through copyright and manages it so as not to dilute the brand or risk alienating the target audience. The realignment of the *Star Wars* canon after 2014 signalled their intention to assert their rights as owner of the franchise and protect the brand from alternative versions—such as the Expanded Universe of *Star Wars* as depicted in the novels and comics published continuously since 1978 (cf. Hidalgo 2012, 227–228). Franchises exploit these strategies in service of consolidation and conglomeration, bringing the property under tighter control so as to prevent the brand from fading or its message from becoming confused. This affords the promise of synergy, where the same content can dominate across markets and generate more income. For Kristin Thompson synergy is about "selling the same narrative over and over in different media" (2003, 82): in other words, Disney promoting *Star Wars* on its ABC network of television channels, in its theme parks and through its chain of high street stores. However, according to Johnson (2013, 68), this reduces the franchise to a selling machine, where business structures are purely about the marketing of the same product regardless of form and content. *Star Wars* is a narrative, evidently very marketable, but the story in its various incarnations and media specific formats requires careful consideration and development. As a transmedia narrative *Star Wars* requires Disney to look outside of its own corporate structures to enlist creative talent who can drive and extend the property beyond Disney's established network reach.

Franchises are built to reflect the corporate structure that bore them, but they are also influenced by changes in the wider media and entertainment industries. Johnson (2013, 68–69) argues that the decline of mass production in Hollywood of the 1970s and '80s meant that studios had to search for niche markets to promote their movies. The blockbuster film turned franchise thus grew out of the need to stimulate renewed interest in film as a form of entertainment. Before Disney purchased Lucasfilm it had originally partnered with them to create Star Tours, a *Star Wars* themed motion simulator attraction at several of its theme parks. Debuting in 1987, Star Tours featured familiar characters such as R2-D2 and C-3PO and added new ones including Captain Rex—a droid who would pilot you through numerous space battles on the simulator screen. This was the first attraction based on non-Disney licensed IP and would become one of its most iconic and popular until it closed for a massive overhaul and technical update in 2010. Working with George Lucas and Industrial Light & Magic, Disney's imagineers created an attraction that combined specially produced film footage, animatronics and new characters, thus turning the previously screen-based transmedia *Star Wars* storyworld into a physical and immersive live experience. Modern media franchises built on social partnerships between big corporations and creative companies strike a balance between 'sameness and difference,' between source and elaborations. Johnson (2013, 107) argues that differences between the two allow for creative input, negotiating production identities in using intellectual property shared across multiple networks. Modern franchises work where texts and paratexts, resources and ideas, cross between franchisor and franchisee—in this case Disney and Lucasfilm: "The world in play in franchised production offers a shared creative context in which many different individuals and communities can draw resources and contribute in kind" (Johnson 2013, 109). Thus, while transmedia narratives are based on Jenkins' concept of *world building*, franchises that develop through creative social partnerships partake in *world-sharing*: "worlds once built, become shared among creative stakeholders working in and across multiple production sites" (ibid., 108–109). In 2011, Star Tours: The Adventures Continue opened in Disney theme parks across the world. Updated to include more content drawn from the expanding world created by Lucas, the attraction went 3D and continued to bring the story to life through immersive storytelling.

As media conglomerates grew in the 1990s, due to the relaxing of laws which prevented large-scale corporate ownership, synergy became one way of utilising new networks of production and dissemination. Janet Wasko, in her comprehensive analysis of the Walt Disney Company, its brand and multiple media outlets, points out that partnerships with other companies were central to its economic success. From the 1950s, Disney took part in synergistic cross-media promotion, connecting films, television and theme park. In creating Disneyland, the company worked with thirty-two companies that either sponsored attractions at the park or helped build them (cf. Wasko 2020, 176–178). Indeed, it is this formula that provided the foundation, first for Disney to work with Lucasfilm to create Star Tours and bring the *Star Wars* brand into the corporate fold, then to go further by purchasing the rights to *Star Wars* so as to steer that product in a particular direction. Wasko (ibid., 2) refers to the Disney Company's expansion as an entertainment business going from universe to multiverse: Disney, by buying rival companies and acquiring established intellectual properties, has gone beyond just focusing on what it is known for, but is also working to build other franchises across sports, film, television and comics. *Star Wars* is now one universe within the Disney multiverse; the films, television series and animation provide the narrative framework that Disney can incorporate into its own fantasy world: the theme park.

Fan Tourism and Disney's Galaxy's Edge

In describing different kinds of touristic gaze—the vision that occurs when travelling—John Urry refers specifically to the "mediatised gaze." (2002, 151) Able to extend engagement with media texts like television shows and films by inhabiting the spaces associated with them, tourists become part of the text: "Those gazing on the scene relive elements or aspects of the media event" (ibid., 151). For Matt Hills, being in the place matters more than just watching it on the screen because it allows fans access to extratextual pleasures and affords them the opportunity to reinterpret the text since *"the media cult cannot be entirely reduced to metaphors of textuality"* (2002, 145). Seeking out locations allows fans to extend their relationship with media: "Cult geographies also sustain cult fans' fantasies of 'entering' into the cult text" (ibid., 151). Similarly, Cornel Sandvoss asserts, "The physical places of fandom clearly have an extraordinary importance for fans" (2005, 61). These mediated tourist locations can be open to the public, made significant because of the types of media that are associated with that space; or they can be private, made special by the rituals and performances in which fans participate. Therefore, it is not simply being there that counts. What fans do or how they act in the space seems to make fan tourism unique and personally valuable. Stijn Reijnders has developed this idea of fans transforming real places through their imaginative engagement with space and text by applying Pierre Nora's concept of *lieux d'imagination* (places of the imagination). He argues that places of the imagination "are not so much concerned with collective memory, as collective imagination. *Lieux d'imagination* are physical locations, which serve as a symbolic anchor for the collective imagination of society. By visiting these locations, tourists are able to construct and 'validate' a symbolic distinction between imagination and reality" (2011, 8). Further, Reijnders outlines how fans, using their imagination, seek physical and material references to their favourite media texts (ibid., 114). In this way, Disney's Galaxy's Edge attraction—based on the transmedia narrative of *Star Wars* – has become a place of the imagination. Fans who walk through the attraction do not just imagine the *Star Wars* storyworld, they can live it and return home with a part of it thanks to the merchandise and memories collected whilst in that space. Much like how the *flâneur* embodies the city as they walk through it, *Star Wars* fans can live the transmedia narrative, carefully created and nurtured over decades, as they explore the theme park attraction.

The *flâneur* is personified by the act of "passing by" (de Certeau 1984, 97)—walking, wandering, window shopping in the city. This act of urban exploration has a triple "enunciative" function: the pedestrian appropriates the "topographical system" through the process of walking and learning the city; they act out the city by following routes in and around the multiple spaces; and through this movement the pedestrian creates relations between different spaces, connecting the city in multiple ways. Thus, by walking the *flâneur* "enunciates" or "speaks" the city, articulating the space through the route they take and what they visually take in (ibid., 97–98). For Urry, the nineteenth century *flâneur* was the forerunner to the twentieth century tourist: once "able to travel, to arrive, to gaze, to move on, to be anonymous, to be in a liminal zone," now by taking photographs and making videos to post online afterwards, they are about "being seen and recorded, and of seeing others and recording them" (2002, 126–127). Similarly, when fans pass through mediated spaces, taking photos and posting videos on YouTube to preserve the moment and celebrate their fandom, they are *enunciating* or *speaking* their fan identity. Fans perform, communicate and remember mediated spaces of popular culture. The space is documented, for both personal and public benefit, and as a result their fandom is on display. The Galaxy's Edge theme park

From Anaheim to Batuu

attraction personifies this aspect of the fan as *flâneur*: they enunciate their fandom through movement around spaces and taking photographs.

Scholars of the theme park experience highlight the performative aspects of being on site: from interacting with rides and animatronic characters, consuming themed food and drink,[1] wearing branded clothing, and engaging with employees playing a role or character. Indeed, the Disney theme parks are renowned for the important role the employees, called "cast members" (Urbanski 2018, 262), play in making visitors feel immersed and part of the Disney experience. In her autoethnographic study of being a *Star Wars* scholar and fan in Disneyland, Heather Urbanski discusses the importance of performance and play on behalf of both cast members and fans: "The Disney Parks, with their focus on story-based experiences enacted by cast members for and with guests, is a space for fandom performance of many kinds" (ibid.). She goes on to argue that fan performance enables a sense of community, continuing the experience well after it has ended. Through sharing memories of both the franchise and attraction post visit, fans are able to extend their interaction with it. The videos posted online, which review the rides, show the merchandise and explain what you can do in Galaxy's Edge, are examples of fans enunciating their fandom and replaying their felt experience. Marie-Laurie Ryan reminds us that the theme park is designed to be "an environment in which you can literally take your body with you into worlds of the imagination" and as such it "stands as a testament to the postmodern fascination with the playful spirit and protean nature of the carnivalesque" (2001, 288–289). So, just as Galaxy's Edge encourages fans to play in the imagined transmedia world of *Star Wars*, it also encourages fans to linger and play in that world by sharing their experiences through stories and videos—the performance does not stop. Galaxy's Edge thus becomes a liminal space, making *Star Wars* more tangible for fans able to situate themselves in the text when posing and photographing their experience.

For the *flâneur* the process of exploring and making connections—the journey—is important, but so too is the notion of place and the search for a place to rest: "To walk is to lack a place. It is the indefinite process of being absent and in search of a proper [place]" (de Certeau 1984, 103). Fans of *Star Wars* are similarly in a search of a special location where they can connect to what they enjoy. Disney's theme park location becomes a site of popular veneration; strange and familiar, it nonetheless becomes home to fans looking for a physical connection to what is usually ephemeral, temporal and unreal. Just as scholars have argued that the *flâneur* walks through unfamiliar spaces, they have also argued that walking masters those spaces, making them familiar and permanent. Rob Shields describes the *flâneur* as being in a constant state of appropriation, mapping and remapping the city through repeated touring. This transforms the streets from the unknown to the mastered, and the city becomes the *flâneur*'s to control and manipulate: "The gaze of the flâneur is thus part of a tactic to appropriate not only

---

[1] See the chapter by Natalie Borsy in this volume.

the local, physical spaces of the city as one's own 'turf' […] but also to participate in the popular sense of empire, to master and even revel in the 'emporium'" (Shields 1994, 74). Further, Stefan Morawski says the *flâneur* is "a kind of tourist at home" (1994, 184), someone who is both homeless and at home when travelling through space—occupying spaces not of their own yet made so through imitation and through being present. In the Galaxy's Edge attraction you can personalise your experience so as to make it yours through a number of activities and specific things to do: go to the Black Spire Outfitters to buy apparel to dress like the citizens of Batuu; create your own custom droid in Mubo's Droid Depot; and build your own lightsaber in Savi's Workshop. These are extra things fans can do and pay for, but they also add to the customised sense of owning something important once they have returned home. Those fans who seek repeated pleasure in revisiting familiar spaces not only create a sense of home, they create a sense of ownership. The space is theirs and thus what takes place and is made in it is highly emotive and personal.

Discussions of fan tourism have suggested that a specific mediated site is made special when fans believe that there is an intrinsic value in visiting it; fans are drawn to physical sites that make their fandom more real, whereas to non-fans those sites are ordinary and everyday. While a theme park is not everyday in that sense, the attractions it offers are shared and appreciated by everyone. Galaxy's Edge caters to fans of *Star Wars*; thus being a fan and having certain fan knowledge of the fictional universe only adds to the immersive experience that Disney has imagineered. Imagineering was a term coined by Walt Disney himself, a combination of the words imagination and engineering, which he used to describe the processes of creating and designing his theme parks around the world. The term does not just refer to the idea of creating a uniform theme for the park or attractions within, but rather it also incorporates the technologies and story elements that combine to create a fully immersive experience, from ride to park to hotel to shops and open spaces. Sabrina Mittermeier considers the creative uses for imagineering in her comprehensive study of Disney theme parks, arguing that all the forms of technology used (such as music, film, virtual reality, animatronics, touch screens, transportation and simulators) are engineered: "The purpose of all these is the immersion of the visitor into the venue and the story or information it tries to convey" (2021, 5). In Galaxy's Edge we see two specific imagineered rides that not only bring the experience of Batuu to life for fans but also tie into the transmedia story of the *Star Wars* universe. Smugglers Run is a simulator ride where guests can pilot the Millennium Falcon like Han Solo and Chewbacca—fans can therefore role play as those characters as if in the films. *Star Wars: Rise of the Resistance* is another ride that tells more of a story, this time from the more recent films, and it also uses the same actors playing their roles; like Smugglers Run this ride fills in gaps in the wider narrative and extends the transmedia story. The fan becomes central to the ongoing saga and thus their visit takes on important meaning beyond simply enjoying a day out at the park. As I have been suggesting, the fan as *flâneur* makes a space important through the act of walking around and passing through it. For de Certeau spaces become liberated, broken free of meaning when explored by the *flâneur* (cf. 1984, 105). The original meaning and significance of a place like Disneyland transforms when fans enter into and interact with the imagineered space of Galaxy's Edge, becoming actors in the developing transmedia story of *Star Wars*.

With such an array of rides and interactive attractions to visit in Galaxy's Edge, fans are able to achieve a tangible and comprehensive mastery of the frontier outpost of Black Spire on Batuu, like the *flâneur* of old as they explore the city. Visiting provides a foundation for new fans to learn about the creatures and characters of the *Star Wars* universe and encourages existing fans to go deeper into the mythos and reaffirm their fandom. Speaking about Galaxy's Edge before it opened, Rebecca Williams argued that its construction "signals a further shift toward the desire for a completely immersive theme park experience, one that is designed to appeal both to fans of the franchise and also the Parks themselves" (2019, 142). I would agree that in imagineering Galaxy's Edge, Disney has both *Star Wars* fans and general theme park fans in mind. The shops for food and merchandise refer to elements in the wider transmedia story but they are also targeted at bringing people into the fold with toys, clothing and other souvenirs that serve as introductions to becoming a fan through consumption. Indeed, Williams goes further by linking the concept of *haptic fandom* to the fan experience in the immersive spaces of the theme park (cf. ibid., 144). The things people touch, smell, taste and hear in these spaces build a sensory experience that brings fact and fiction, real life and fantasy closer together. In the Galaxy's Edge fictional outpost of Black Spire on the planet Batuu, the smells and tastes are brought to life through the food available there, but the sets and props on display also add to the haptic experience fans desire. If one is not a fan of *Star Wars* before visiting, then the lived experience of the attraction could be repeated if they were to watch the films and TV series, or read the books to find out more about the universe they have just inhabited. For returning fans, those who know the *Star Wars* universe very well, Williams' concept of *spatial transmedia* helps us to understand the importance of Galaxy's Edge in extending the story to which fans were originally drawn. She argues that fans have to be physically in spaces based on mediated texts, to make meaning and add to their already detailed appreciation of the transmedia narrative. Transmedia, therefore, is not just about storytelling, it is also a kind of experience built over time and over many physical interactions: "Transmediality in the theme park is not only often resolutely rooted in specific places and, therefore, physical experiences of an extended storyworld, it is also frequently a more organic and fan-led process" (Williams 2020, 12). In the case of Disney's Galaxy's Edge, going back repeatedly to such a rooted space is about piecing together the *Star Wars* storyworld and building a world that exists off the screen. Media fans change the meaning of places and spaces through the act of passing through and between them (like the *flâneur*) but they also become fans of specific media texts because they had the physical experience of being there and participating in the rituals of performance and pilgrimage associated with those spaces.

Conclusion

In this chapter I have outlined how *Star Wars* fan tourism is about passing through Disney's Galaxy's Edge theme park attraction and finding meaning in the act of being present, taking photos and performing as a fan within that imagineered space. As this happens, multiple identities are revealed, fan identities are transformed over time, and memories of the transmedia storyworld become important signifiers of fandom. As I have argued elsewhere, fan spaces are imagined, real and unreal, constructed and natural, subverted and official, consumed and constructed, creative and hierarchical (cf. Geraghty 2014). They can be known through traditional tourism, such as visiting a city filming location, but at Galaxy's Edge they are made more personal for fans because of the transmedia storyworld created by Disney. What fans can do and buy in particular locations is also important. Spaces can become fan spaces because they are designated as such, or they can be constructed specifically to attract a fan audience. What fans do in these media tourism sites contributes to their fan identity; it can reaffirm their fandom and make them fans of new media texts after exploring the site in more detail. Applying the concept of the *flâneur* to Disney's Galaxy's Edge theme park attraction, I have argued that *Star Wars* fans both construct and are constructed by the physical environment in which they travel.

Like the *flâneur*'s walks through the city, taking in the sights, sounds and people, the *Star Wars* fan travels to Galaxy's Edge to view, take in and interact with the rides, cast members and other fans. Fan tourism is therefore an act of *passing through* space, characterised by physical movement between familiar spaces and venerated places of popular culture. We see this happening in the transmedia space of the theme park attraction where fans travel around and between rides and exhibits that are familiar to them because they know the *Star Wars* story so well. But fan tourism is also about *passing as* a fan, as in the case of the fans who dress up or create custom droids and lightsabers that they will take home as souvenirs. In theme park fandom we see how the site, rides and experiences serve to create an immersive space where fans engage with the story and visual icons of the *Star Wars* narrative. At the same time, they can connect with imagineered elements via simulators, themed restaurants and role-playing cast members. Just as the *flâneur* masters the city through walking, *Star Wars* fans can master Galaxy's Edge through the appropriation and exploration of their fan identity. Lastly, the fact that Galaxy's Edge is just one newly built section of an historic theme park that attracts millions more than just *Star Wars* fans suggests that transmedia fandom is also about *passing from* one fandom to another: transitioning from Anaheim via Main Street to Batuu via other rides, worlds and attractions. In walking through the city, the *flâneur* fractures space and creates new meanings within it. Likewise, those fans that travel to Galaxy's Edge move between levels of fandom as they pass through. A non-fan of *Star Wars* can gain an appreciation of the franchise— its core characters, story and cultural significance—and at the same time long-term

From Anaheim to Batuu

fans can immerse themselves in a world they have sought to make more real. Fans and non-fans perform and take on aspects of fandom related to that specific place; doing so helps the shift between contrasting fan identities and brings the transmedia story of *Star Wars* to life.

References

de Certeau, Michel (1984): *The Practice of Everyday Life*. Berkeley

Geraghty, Lincoln (2014): *Cult Collectors. Nostalgia, Fandom and Collecting Popular Culture*. London

Harvey, Colin B. (2015): *Fantastic Transmedia. Narrative Play and Memory Across Science Fiction and Fantasy Storyworlds*. Basingstoke

Hidalgo, Pablo (2012): *Star Wars. The Essential Reader's Companion*. London

Hills, Matt (2002): *Fan Cultures*. London

Jenkins, Henry (2006): *Convergence Culture. Where Old and New Media Collide*. New York

Jenkins, Henry (2009): The Aesthetics of Transmedia: In Response to David Bordwell (Part Two). In: *Confessions of an Aca-Fan: The Official Weblog of Henry Jenkins*. http://henryjenkins.org/2009/09/the_aesthetics_of_transmedia_i_1.html. Accessed: 6. April 2021

Johnson, Derek (2013): *Media Franchising. Creative License and Collaboration in the Culture Industries*. New York

Kinder, Marsha (1991): *Playing with Power in Movies, Television and Video Games. From Muppet Babies to Teenage Mutant Ninja Turtles*. Berkeley

The Legendary Star Wars Expanded Universe Turns a New Page (2014). In: *Merchandise*. http://www.starwars.com/news/the-legendary-star-wars-expanded-universe-turns-a-new-page. Accessed: 6. April 2021

Mittermeier, Sabrina (2021): *A Cultural History of the Disneyland Theme Parks. Middle Class Kingdoms*. Bristol

Morawski, Stefan (1994). The Hopeless Game of *Flânerie*. In: *The Flâneur*, ed. Keith Tester, London, 181–197.

Proctor, William/Matthew Freeman (2016): *"The first step into a smaller world": The Transmedia Economy of Star Wars*. In: *Revisiting Imaginary Worlds: A Subcreation Studies Anthology*, ed. Mark J.P. Wolf, New York, 223–245

Prudom, Laura/Marianne Zumberge (2015): 'Star Wars' Themed Land Coming to Disney Parks; Harrison Ford Visits D23 Expo. In: Variety. https://variety.com/2015/film/news/d23-star-wars-land-disneyland-1201571059/. Accessed: 6. April 2021

Reijnders, Stijn (2011): *Places of the Imagination. Media, Tourism, Culture*. Farnham

Ryan, Marie-Laure (2001): *Narrative as Virtual Reality. Immersion and Interactivity in Literature and Electronic Media*. Baltimore

Sandvoss, Cornel (2005): *Fans. The Mirror of Consumption*. Cambridge

Shields, Rob (1994): Fancy Footwork: Walter Benjamin's Notes on *Flânerie*. In: *The Flâneur*, ed. Keith Tester, London, 61–80

Steinberg, Marc (2012): *Anime's Media Mix. Franchising Toys and Characters in Japan*. Minneapolis

Thompson, Kristen (2003): *Storytelling in Film and Television*. Cambridge

Urbanski, Heather (2018): The Kiss Goodnight from a Galaxy Far, Far Away: Experiencing *Star Wars* as a Fan-Scholar on Disney Property. In: *Star Wars and the History of Transmedia Storytelling*, eds. Sean Guynes/Dan Hassler-Forest, Amsterdam, 253–263

Urry, John (2002): *The Tourist Gaze*. London

Wasko, Janet (2020): *Understanding Disney. The Manufacture of Fantasy*. Cambridge

Williams, Rebecca (2019): From Star Tours to Galaxy's Edge: Immersion, Transmediality, and "Haptic Fandom" in Disney's Theme Parks. In: *Disney's Star Wars. Forces of Production, Promotion, and Reception*, eds. William Proctor/Richard McCulloch, Iowa City, 136–149

Williams, Rebecca (2020): *Theme Park Fandom: Spatial Transmedia, Materiality and Participatory Cultures*. Amsterdam

Consuming Disney

Image Cultivation, Indoctrination and Immersive Transmedia Storytelling in Disney Cookbooks

Natalie Borsy

Abstract Fictional cookbooks promise immersive, transmedial gateways to fictive worlds through culinary means. Cookbooks in general are also powerful educational devices that both reflect and shape cultures. Disney, too, has sought very early to physically integrate its 'magic kingdom' into the world and minds of its consumers, as is most evident in its various parks and resorts but also in its cookbooks. The cookbooks not only reproduce Disney's iconography, but also its ideology, which is both physically realised and incorporated in the recipes. The cookbooks give insight into Disney's overt self-referentiality and self-image as artistic innovator and as global, inclusive producer of wholesome, inter-generational media texts. They exemplify the 'Disneyfication' of daily familial commensality and of rites of passage in people's personal lives. Additionally, recipes shed light on the dynamic relationship between franchises, fans and texts. Here one can observe how the 'Disney curriculum' (Sandlin/Garlen Sandlin, Jennifer A./Julie C. Garlen (2016): Introduction. Feeling Disney, Buying Disney, Being Disney. In: Disney, Culture, and Curriculum, eds. id. New York [et al.], 1–26) can also be appropriated and re-shaped.

"Do you want to Build a Snowman … Cheese Balls?" Upon reading this one might stumble over the transition from the iconic song *Do You Want to Build a Snowman?* to the cheese dish that is featured in the *Disney Frozen Cookbook & Cookie Cutters Kit* (Disney Enterprises 2016, 26). Those who are familiar with *Frozen* (2010) might remember that the song refers to princess Anna's attempts to draw her sister Elsa, the snow queen, out of self-imposed seclusion. Later in the story the much-beloved snowman sidekick Olaf is magically brought to life to embody the playfulness and love that Elsa has denied herself during her childhood. So now the user of the cookbook gets a chance to build his or her very own

---

N. Borsy (✉)
University of Zurich, Zurich, Switzerland
e-mail: natalie.borsy@uzh.ch

© The Author(s), under exclusive license to Springer-Verlag GmbH, DE, part of Springer Nature 2022
U. Dettmar and I. Tomkowiak (eds.), *On Disney*, Studien zu Kinder- und Jugendliteratur und -medien 9, https://doi.org/10.1007/978-3-662-64625-0_14

sentimentally coded snowman: "Design your own special snowman friends, built from 'snowballs' made from cheese! Then decorate and watch them melt away as you eat them" (ibid., 26). One might find it macabre to build a snowman friend only to gobble him up right away. Yet again, those who recall Olaf's belief, that some people are worth melting for, might come to view the consumption of Snowman Cheese Balls as the devotional act of love that Olaf's melting represented in the film. Thus, a simple cheese ball recipe mimetically reproduces fictive characters that upon consumption represent the film's—and Disney's—emphasis on the power and beauty of familial bonds, childhood and love.

It would be too easy to dismiss Disney cookbooks as a crude means to increase revenues in the company's flourishing merchandising sector. That view would neglect the pleasure that fans derive from the immersive potential of expanding stories (cf. Jenkins 2007). Even though transmedia franchises are often a requisite precondition for the creation of fictional cookbooks, they are not its sole driving force. There is a great number of fictional cookbooks based on popular literature, films, series and computer games that are unlicensed, sometimes self-published fan productions; there are also fan authors of fictional cookbooks who, over time, professionalised themselves and are now commissioned to write recipes—this happens to be the case for one of the authors of *Star Wars Galaxy's Edge. The Official Blackspire Outpost Cookbook* (2019), Chelsea Monroe-Cassel. Not only are these cookbooks based on works of fiction but they can also exhibit varying degrees of fictionality themselves. The mechanisms underlying these cookbooks are in fact very complex. Recipes are embedded discourses (cf. Leonardi 1989, 340) and as such they shed light on the dynamic relationship between franchises, fans and the text; *fictional* recipes also raise fundamental questions about fictionality, material aesthetics, transmediality, reader response and of course, the cultural impact of popular media and food upon its consumers.

These claims may seem bold, but the fact that we are dealing with a combination of cooking literature and the Disney corporation should help to substantiate it: Cookbooks are usually educational, non-fiction books that represent but also shape cultures (cf. Bower 1997, 5). Employing literary strategies (cf. Leonardi 1989), they tell stories of families, communities and nations. Janet Floyd and Laurel Forster find that recipes.

> evoke the elaborate scene of home, and the contentious arena of domestic politics and family values. In their different appearances, they are also persistently drawn into cultural debates around health and purity, about lifestyle and individualism, and into definitions of the national past, present and future. (Floyd/Forster 2003, 1–2)

Or as Arjun Appadurai succinctly put it: cookbooks are "revealing artifacts of culture in the making" (Appadurai 1988, 22).

Enter Disney, a company with unprecedented cultural impact on the Western entertainment landscape that has, over the years, become an increasingly manifest part of individuals' everyday life and identity. I will not go into detail on Disney's broad product range and general conceptions of family, childhood, gender, class, American exceptionalism etc. (cf. Watts 1997, Wasko 2001) at this point. I do want to highlight Jennifer Sandlin's and Julie Garlen's idea of Disney as being part of a 'big' curriculum that permeates culture in public and private spaces both through formal and informal educational experiences (cf. Sandlin/Garlen 2016, 3). Drawing on Mike Budd and Max Kirsch, they describe how Disney's cultivation of its image as merely being family-friendly fun and wholesome entertainment makes it almost impossible to criticise the company (cf. Budd/Kirsch 2005, 2–3). Hence, the emphasis on happiness and pleasure helps to influence these various forms of education and obscure obvious signs of this influence at the same time.

Similarly, fictional cookbooks are a potent combination of informal, private, everyday education and pleasurable, transmedial entertainment. Through cookbooks, fictive worlds materially extend from page and screen into the kitchens and bellies of media consumers; in that way, fans physically incorporate texts (cf. Tippen 2018, 19) and to some degree also social and biophysical systems and ideologies that are represented in them (cf. Tigner/Carruth 2018, 1). Thus, Disney cookbooks give insight into the company's self-referentiality, self-image as artistic innovator and global, inclusive producer of inter-generational media texts that both delight and educate. They also shed light on the 'Disneyfication' of daily familial conviviality, and of rites of passage in people's personal lives.

Incorporating Corporate Identity

"'I think all artists—whether they paint, write, sing or play music, write for the theater or movies, make poetry or sculpture—all of these are first of all pleasure givers.'—Walt Disney" (Garofalo/Meyer 2003, 8). This is how Ira L. Meyer's preface in *Disney Recipes. From Animation to Inspiration* (2003) starts off. In that way, Meyer reproduces the rhetoric of 'innocent,' pleasurable entertainment, and at the same time aligns his culinary art with that of the animators, or more precisely, with that of the aggrandised Walt Disney. Similarly, editor Marcello Garofalo outlines both the memorability and semantics of food and scenes depicting the preparation, consumption and sharing of food in Disney movies, often making reference to similar scenes from famous Hollywood classics such as *Casablanca* (1942), *Citizen Kane* (1941) and *Gone with the Wind* (1938) (cf. ibid., 10–11). The message is clear: Disney movies don't come second to Hollywood productions; they are memorable works of art in and of themselves, and food is linked to their memorability. Food becomes a digestible mnemonic device.

The introduction makes a point of emphasising the inclusiveness of both the films and the recipes with regard to nationality and age. The authors praise the "international and multicultural flavor" of the book, as there is "practically no historical period or geographical area [...] that is not in some way represented in the Disney filmography" (ibid., 16). The cookbook embodies the "far-reaching ideal" that "fantasy and creativity extend well beyond national borders" (ibid., 16–17). And faithful to Disney's credo that it offers entertainment for the whole family, the authors pay particular attention to adding recipes that are "sure to be a hit amoung

[sic] the young and the young at heart," in order to make cooking "a family activity, a way to spend quality time with the little ones" (ibid., 17). The inclusion of children is also reflected in the recipes, which offer suggestions as to how "little hands" (ibid., 81) may help in the preparation of the dishes. Beyond the simple claim of giving pleasure, the introduction in fact spotlights Disney's deep-seated ideology.

The recipes, too, are a culinary tribute to the opus, artistry and philosophy of the Disney studios. The films referenced not only include the major feature-length "masterpieces of today's computer animation" (ibid., 16), but also early hand-drawn shorts like those in the *Silly Symphonies* series (1929–1939). Each recipe is attributed to film characters, designed to represent their respective cultural contexts; sometimes dishes that were shown or mentioned in the movies are reproduced. For instance, there is a recipe for "Mushu's Egg Rolls and Juk" (ibid., 32–33) which is partially featured in *Mulan* (1998), or "Peg Leg Pete's Seared Swordfish with Mint Bread-Crumb Sauce" (ibid., *100–101*), which alludes to the stuffed swordfish that Mickey uses to defeat Peg Leg Pete in *Shanghaied* (1934). The recipe headnotes not only contain descriptions of the dishes but also provide context by describing the characters and scenes that inspired them. And rather than depicting the finished dishes, the recipes show sketches and film stills of the characters. The archive sketches especially help to underline the craft of film animation, something that has been a source of fascination for decades (cf. Watts 1997, 165). But they also suggest the alignment of this craft with the culinary arts; the steps for making a dish are presented alongside the varying stages of film animation. And indeed, one might go even further and argue that the cooking and eating of a dish, the transformation from raw to edible, external to internal, dead to life-sustaining is also a kind of animation. Eventually, both film and dish are consumed, both containing Disney's history and ideological context, the two becoming one in the consumer's body (cf. Tippen 2018, 19; Tigner/Carruth 2018, 1).

Cooking and Living in the Image of Disney

Of course, a significant number of Disney cookbooks are typical examples of licensing and merchandising. *The Disney Princess Cookbook* (2013), for instance, is part of the *Disney Princess* franchise and toy line. *Disney. The Simple Family Cookbook* (2018) belongs to the bestselling *Simplissime* cookbook line and thus expands its clientele to children. Insight Editions, the publisher of *Entertaining with Disney. Exceptional Events. From Mickey Mouse to Moana!* (2019) and *Star Wars Galaxy's Edge. The Official Black Spire Outpost Cookbook* (2019), offers a wide selection of Disney products besides the cookbooks, including elaborate pop-up books, art books and model sets. The appeal of these books mainly centres on the characters, to whom the recipes are attributed. However, this time the link between dish and character is constituted on a mainly (material) aesthetic, iconographic level, rather than on the heavily contextualised narrative level that we saw in *Disney Recipes*. Rather than connecting the dish with Disney's opus, these cookbooks focus on domestic settings and how children, families and grown-up Disney fans can integrate Disney into their private lives.

The *Disney Princess Cookbook*, for instance, uses form, texture and colour scheme to cite the princesses and their stories. The recipe for "Ham and Cheese Biscuit Braids" (Disney Princess 2013, 36–37, see Fig. 1) is embedded in a decorative frame that matches the colour of Rapunzel's dress. The recipe's headnote makes reference to Rapunzel's artistic talent, which is supposedly also apparent in her cooking. An illustration depicts her making a huge dough braid, her long golden hair flowing beneath the work surface. While the dish itself was not part of the story, the reference is obvious. The biscuit braid can be braided just like Rapunzel's magical hair and even has the same colour. Those who know the film *Tangled* (2010) well might also remember a scene where Rapunzel's hair really does get braided, enabling her to move freely without getting entangled in her surroundings. This recipe thus operates both via visual correspondence and implicit, iconotextual (cf. Wagner 1996) references to the film. As with *Disney Recipes*, with *The Disney Princess Cookbook* one can symbolically consume part of the princess, turning her into a bodily reality (cf. Lötscher 2014, 59, 61). Unfortunately, this consumption has a somewhat bitter aftertaste. Dominated by pink, the book reproduces binary gender stereotypes, also reflected in instructions that address only girls (cf. Disney Princess 2013, 13).

On a different note, Disney's iconography can also be appropriated. Faithful to the principle of simplicity, Jean-Francois Mallet's *The Simple Family Cookbook* reduces contextual framings to a minimum. The book dispenses with recipe headnotes and places character illustrations and food photography next to each other without comment, leaving it up to the cookbook user to draw the connections. While most recipes correspond with the cultural background of the characters— Moussaka for Hercules, Saltimbocca for Pinocchio etc.—others correspond only on a visual level, such as the recipe for "Beauty's Bouquet of Roses," where the finished appetiser resembles the symbolically charged rose from *Beauty and the Beast* (1991) [see Fig. 2]. One might argue that examples like the rose recipe are misrepresenting the story—after all, it was to the Beast that the enchanted rose belonged, and it was rather a sinister reminder of the impending permanence of his curse. In the introduction Mallet admits that he, unlike his daughters, is not particularly familiar with Disney characters, but the characters give him the opportunity to get the children to eat vegetables that they normally might not like. For him, the aim is to provide healthy, balanced food that is prepared and eaten together (cf. Mallet 2018, 5). In this way, Mallet reproduces Disney's approach to activities for the whole family, while appropriating Disney's characters and its family friendliness for his own nutritional agenda.

Finally, aesthetics can also be used to emulate Disney's role as entertainer and provider of pleasure and magic. *Entertaining with Disney. Exceptional Events. From Mickey Mouse to Moana!* (Croushorn 2019) is a guide to Disney-themed parties, such as a "*Cinderella* 'Stroke of Midnight' New Year's Eve Party" (ibid.,

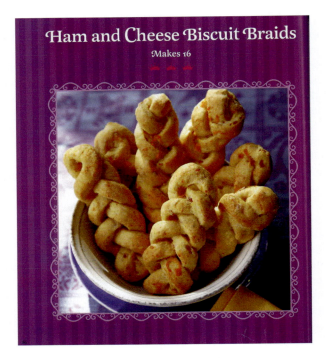

Fig. 1 Rapunzel's edible braid. In: Disney Princess 2013, 36–37.

Fig. 1 (continued)

Fig. 2 Beauty's Bouquet of Roses. In: Mallet 2018, 19.

10–25) or a "*The Little Mermaid* Bridal Shower Brunch" (ibid., 74–89). The intended users, young upper-middle class adults, are depicted throughout the book. Each party suggestion includes a menu, decoration and games or party bags, all making use of the iconography of the relevant films. The *Cinderella* party decoration and food, for instance, is glittery and light blue, just like Cinderella's ballgown (see Fig. 3). Since the book is officially licensed, it also offers downloadable templates for invitation cards and decorative elements that depict Disney characters and other recognisable elements from the films. The aesthetic 'Disneyfication' and homogenisation of cyclical, personal events is in itself remarkable, but the author's justification for it is even more so:

> Who says Disney is just for kids? Not us! […] Disney transcends age, delighting the youngest kid to the most sophisticated adult. And adults love to entertain.
>
> When it comes to entertaining, the experts always start with a theme—one that complements and enhances the event you're celebrating, bringing a little extra magic to a special occasion. And no one does magic like Disney. Hosting a Disney party is a great way to get everyone into a fun, festive mood, infusing your party with a special atmosphere of joy, romance, and nostalgia. (ibid., 7)

Fig. 3 Cinderella 'Stroke of Midnight' New Year's Eve Party. In: Croushorn 2019, 13.

These comments are testament to the fact that Disney is such a prevalent part of people's lives that, even after they grow up, they reflect the feelings that the movies have evoked in them—the pleasure and nostalgia—and *consciously* use it to frame personal milestones. In doing so, these consumers demonstrate the success of Disney's curriculum, as well as their own awareness of it. They understand the power of Disney's iconography so well that they are able to apply it.

The Happiest Kitchen on Earth

The various Disney parks and resorts also play a pivotal role in integrating food into Disney's curriculum. The parks have served themed dishes and pursued the idea of physical immersion from the very beginning. Additionally, they demonstrate an acute awareness of the power that sensory experiences have. Scent outlets, so-called Smellitzers (cf. Franko 2020), are installed throughout the premises and attractions, enhancing the experience and making a visit more memorable. It is a well-known fact that memory can be heightened with the help of sensory

Consuming Disney 219

input, especially through smell and taste[1]; this is a fact also explored in Disney's *Ratatouille* (2007), where food critic Anton Ego is overwhelmed by childhood memories when he takes a bite of the eponymous dish. Unsurprisingly then, there are several cookbooks that are based on the different foods served in the parks and resorts.

The earliest example of Disney cookbooks is *Cooking with Mickey Around Our World* (1986) which comprises the "MOST requested recipes"—as promised in the subtitle—from the various parks and resorts. Dedicated to the "guests, without whose requests this book would not exist" (The Walt Disney Company 1986, n.p.) the book is allegedly the result of bottom-up petitions from dedicated fans who enjoyed the food during their Disney experience. The subtitle implies a practice that usually occurs in private and informal contexts, between friends and family who invite each other to dinner. Like a good host, Disney generously complies and shares the recipes in a practical ring-bound format that enables domestic cooks to use the book without difficulty.

While the framing of the book may be informal and domestic, the recipes reflect American conceptions of international foods as it was and still is presented in the parks' and resorts' culinary palette: Luao Chicken from the Polynesian Village Resort, authentic Kartoffelsalat from the Germany Showcase in EPCOT, Sherry Trifle as served in the Rose & Crown Pub & Dining Room. The focus rests more on cultural variety and less on the immersive experience of Disney's narrative worlds. In this respect the cookbook follows the idea of EPCOT as a permanent world fair, the American 'disneyfied' melting pot of the world's nations. The phrase "*Our World*" in the title also stresses that this particular vision of international variety has been subsumed into the world created by Disney, so that, by means of this culinary transaction, it becomes the guests' world too. Furthermore, Disney makes no secret of the book's commercial nature. After the recipes, there is a chapter titled *Order*, with a selection of licensed Mickey Mouse dinnerware, complete with prices, order numbers, shipping charges and order forms (see Fig. 4). The cookbook thus performs a complex balancing act between the private domestic sphere of free exchange on the one hand, and commodified globalism as envisioned and marketed by the Disney corporation on the other.

This informal exchange of recipes can also happen between the guests themselves. Only recently, another cookbook dedicated to the Disney Parks was published 'unofficially' by a true Disney disciple:

> As a child who grew up in Anaheim Hills, California, ASHLEY CRAFT could recite the Star Tours ride by heart and navigate the park without a map, and fell asleep to the sound of Disneyland fireworks each night in her bedroom. After two internships at Walt Disney World and many, many more visits to the Disney Parks, Ashley is now one of the leading experts on Disneyland and Walt Disney World. (Craft 2020, blurb)

---

[1] Psychologist John A. Robinson calls this phenomenon "autonetic consciousness" (Robinson 1978, 237).

Fig. 4 Cooking with Mickey. In: The World Disney Company 1986, 294.

We learn that Craft, now an adult and mother, no longer lives in California and cannot take regular trips to the parks. That "privilege," as she puts it, "really isn't [feasible] for the average family either" (ibid., 14). To keep Disney in her life she started to re-create "that magic at home" (ibid., 15). The result was a blog dedicated to Disney Park-inspired foods and, following upon the blog's success, the "Guide to the Happiest Kitchen on Earth" (ibid., title page) came into being. The goal of the cookbook is "to help you transform your own kitchen into a world Walt Disney himself would be proud of" (ibid., 31), to offer tastes "worthy of a certain mouse" (ibid., 16). The driving forces behind the book's creation are apparently manifold: there is the wish to re-create the 'Disney magic,' but also the acknowledgment that there exist economic disparities that enable some but exclude others from experiencing the magic first-hand. The cookbook thus presents itself as a democratising vehicle that aims to share this privilege through culinary means, while meeting standards as envisioned by the genius patriarch Walt Disney himself, alternately embodied by The Mouse.

Consuming Disney

A brief glance at the chapter *The Disney Cook's Essentials*, however, will quickly call the inclusionist premise into question. Among the many equipment essentials are blenders, electric pressure cookers, food processors, stand mixers and even shaved ice makers, all of which are expensive and rather luxurious tools for the average household (ibid., 33–45). Those who want to taste the magic according to such prescriptive and high-flying standards would still have to be very privileged. One might argue, as Carrie Helms Tippen does, that this cookbook, like others, might be more invested in the imagining of the food and the places from where they come than in putting the recipes into practice (Tippen 2018, 10). But even then, it is a culinary fantasy that tastes of privilege.

Particularly interesting is Craft's autobiographical and historical approach to the recipes. Firstly, they vividly illustrate what Sandlin and Garlen (2016) observe: Craft is the perfect example of an individual who has been exposed to Disney's manifold forms as a cultural force and formal as well as informal educator. A strong nostalgic connection to Disney-related childhood memories leads to work experience in their internship program. To the knowledge acquired in formal training Craft adds the layman's expertise of a being frequent visitor herself, and she duly frames the entire book with insights from her many visits: all the contextualising markers are explicitly linked to the parks. And most notably, Craft is very proud of her personal connection with Disney: she advocates unreservedly for the many achievements of the corporate imperium.

Secondly, Craft aims to use both her own and Disney's histories to legitimise her claim to culinary authority. According to Tippen a recipe's authenticity must be established: it is an "informally agreed upon set of signs, symbols, certificates, badges, and strategies" (Tippen 2018, 15) and one way to mark a recipe as authentic is to frame it with origin narratives, whether (auto)biographical or historical. The cookbook's introduction starts off with a history of the parks and the role that food has played in them. Craft includes quotations from newspaper ads and contextualises the novelty of luxurious snacks and treats in post-Depression America. The recipes themselves are meticulously attributed to specific parks, restaurants and food stalls, and each is prefaced with an informative as well as advertising headnote. For example, the recipe for Pork Belly Skewers, which are served in Disneyland's Adventureland, is introduced this way:

> Have you ever taken a Pork Belly Skewer aboard the Jungle Cruise? It's like dinner and a show! Trainee Jungle Cruise Skippers are given a packet of jokes dozens of pages long to study in preparation of their job. […] Whip up these savory skewers for your next meal and challenge your family to come up with their own jokes worthy of the Disneyland cruise (Craft 2020, 65).

Here, Craft demonstrates what Peter Naccarato and Kathleen Lebesco term culinary capital. Following Pierre Bourdieu, they understand food practices as markers of status and cultural authority. With rising awareness of issues like sustainability, healthiness, quality, and artisan-produced food, food and food practices have become information dense (Naccarato/Lebesco 2012, 8–9). The above headnote not only provides the informational context that firmly grounds the dish in

Disney's Adventureland park attraction, but it also offers a glimpse behind the scenes that Craft as a former employee can legitimately offer. For Craft, having that knowledge and offering it to a general public gives her authority, which, in turn, gives her pride. Craft's and Disney's histories intermingle in the making of this book. On the one hand the book illustrates how successful Disney's curriculum is; on the other Craft demonstrates how she has employed the curriculum to her own advantage, as she turns Disney into a positively valued part of her identity—and a source of income.

Culinary Immersion—Journeying across Transmedial Borders

So far we have seen how food functions as an adaptation of Disney's stories and their characters, or how it recalls and reproduces the menu of the parks and resorts. While the stories thus far discussed, and the ideologies they embody, are represented in aesthetic and culinary terms, they nonetheless do not add further narratives to the fictive worlds to which they refer. Henry Jenkins, however, points out that the appeal of transmedial engagements with popular texts lies in the expansion of the narrative story-universes, enabling fans to revisit and, more importantly, to discover *new* aspects of the fictive worlds (cf. Pietschmann/Völkel 2020, 95; Jenkins 2007). The cookbooks discussed previously are indeed transmedial *engagements* with Disney products, but they are not transmedial *storytellings* in the conventional sense. The final example I'd like to discuss is both.

Star Wars Galaxy's Edge. The Official Black Spire Outpost Cookbook was published in 2019 by Insight Editions, which eloquently presents Jenkins's observation as a selling point in its promotional video. In the video it claims to be a company with an "in-world approach" that gives fans "the ultimate visual and tactile experience," that creates an "immersive experience for its readers that is authentic, beautiful and engaging" (Inside Editions 2015, 00:23–00:41, 02:10–02:23). Obviously, a cookbook is the perfect fit for this material aesthetic strategy, as it extends the tactile experience from the handling of the book to the application of its content. The in-world approach of this book spans not only the material aesthetic design, but also the narrative and contextual framing.

The book is expensively designed, with hardcover binding and full-page, full-colour photographs of meticulously staged dishes. The depicted food is sometimes served on rusty metal grids, surrounded by laser sword handles and tools, reflecting the look of battle-worn spaceships. Other times it is arranged on earthen kitchenware, amid ferns and outlandish-looking plants, referencing diegetic jungle planets and moons that were featured in the movies, such as Dagobah and Endor (see Fig. 5). The recipe instructions are not printed on a white glossy surface but on seemingly yellowed and stained paper that often has unidentifiable marginalia in a font that is similar to those in fantastic contexts. The design both grounds

Fig. 5 Dagobah Slug Slinger. In: Monroe-Cassel 2019, 146.

the dishes and the book itself in the fantastic world of *Star Wars*. It seems to be a genuine artefact that has somehow made its way into the hands of the reader. The book is thus turned into a magical threshold object (cf. Lötscher 2014, 16–17), bridging the fictive and the real world.

The book's status as a threshold object is also emphasised in the narrative framing. The book introduces the Artiodac (an alien species) Strono Tuggs, alias Cookie, as the originator of the recipes. An illustrated portrait of Cookie accompanies his introduction, in which he tells the reader how he came to be a cook in the Black Spire Outpost. Mainly alluding to other characters and events from the *Star Wars* movies that Disney produced after it acquired Lucasfilms in 2012, Cookie, who was never featured in the films, narratively grounds himself in the story and adds new details to it. Through Cookie's narration we learn that the recipes are the result of his extensive travels throughout the galaxy. He explains: "I always try to leave a little piece of my kitchen behind on every world I visit. And that's what you're holdin' in your hands right now" (Monroe-Cassel/Sumerak 2019, 11). Cookie's rhetorical use of the apostrophe elicits a presence effect (*Präsenzeffekt*, cf. Gumbrecht 2004, 33) that draws attention to the materiality of the book; the reader is encouraged to believe that this is indeed a material part of the fictive world.

Like the photographs, the recipes are attributed to specific locations and customs, and are associated with various canonical side characters. The recipe headnotes are filled with stories and anecdotes, adding to the fictive world and creating a dense context. For instance, a recipe for Gruuvan Shaal Kebab (ibid., 112–113, chicken-vegetable skewers) tells a story set in the Takodana castle, which was first introduced in *Star Wars Episode VII: The Force Awakens* (2015) as a neutral meeting place for all sorts of shady characters, due to the strict prohibition imposed by its owner on discussion of politics and war. In the film, the castle is one of the linchpins in the heroine's journey and is destroyed by the First Order in the ensuing battle. Cookie, who had been the castle's residing cook, explains that this dish was once banned because the required skewers could be used in fights. The culinary anecdote that focuses on the long-maintained neutrality of the castle, then, contrasts with the referenced canonical battle that brought Cookie to the Black Spire Outpost in the first place.

Incidentally, the Black Spire Outpost has also found its way into material reality. The book was published alongside the opening of the new Disneyland Park attraction *Star Wars: Galaxy's Edge* in Anaheim, California.[2] The new attraction features several dining areas, such as Oga's Cantina, Ronto Roasters, and Docking Bay 7 Food and Cargo, the place where Cookie's food freighter is located (cf. Star Wars Galaxy's Edge). All of these locales are introduced in the cookbook (Monroe-Cassel/Sumerak 2019, 12–25), featuring illustrations that match the actual park decor (see Figs. 6 and 7). A peek in the park's menu reveals many dishes and drinks that are also included in the cookbook, such as Kat's Kattle Corn (ibid., 43), Fried Endorian Tip-Yip (ibid., 97) and Dagobah Slug Slinger (ibid., 147). The book and the park complement each other in working to provide a sense of total immersion, the former by bringing a piece of the fictive world into the readers' homes, and the latter by letting them step into the recreated world itself. Book and park both enable fiction and reality to converge in the bellies of Disney's consumers.

A Recipe for Disney Magic

As stated in the beginning, a recipe is an embedded discourse. Like a story it is exchanged by a giver and a receiver, and it is shaped by this exchange (cf. Leonardi 1989, 340). More than other types of texts it is obliged to explicate and authenticate its content. The instructions must be clear, the result should match the intent. As such, recipes are most revealing as objects of investigation on the dynamics between givers and receivers and their respective contexts and motivations.

---

[2] On *Star Wars: Galaxy's Edge* cf. Lincoln Geraghty's chapter in this volume.

Consuming Disney 225

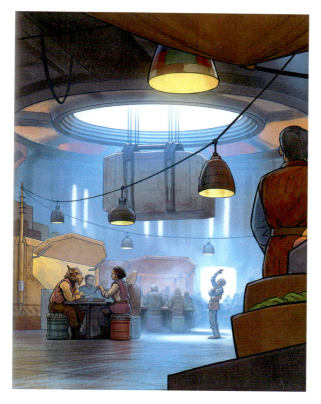

Fig. 6 Docking Bay 7 Food and Cargo. In: Monroe-Cassel 2019, 17.

Fig. 7 Docking Bay 7 Food and Cargo. In: *Star Wars*: Galaxy's Edge.

The Disney curriculum is overtly put into action only to be self-consciously appropriated by its subjects. This is common for recipes: always to be changed according to the context and taste of its user, and most cookbooks encourage precisely that. And though one might be tempted to ignore this mechanism in the face of a corporation whose efforts to indoctrinate its consumers are so obvious, it is still a given fact when one returns to the recipe/story analogue. Even in enthusiastic attempts to reproduce the Disney magic exactly, to make it as 'intended,' the recipe is transformed over and over again.

A look at the Disney recipes reveals many such transformations, exchanges and crossovers: between animation and the culinary arts; between private, domestic and commodified, corporate spheres; between generations; between consumers and producers; between autobiography and corporate history. And between texts and bodies, fiction and reality. I would argue that this is where the real magic happens.

References

Primary Sources

Craft, Ashley (2020): *The Unofficial Disney Parks Cookbook*. New York, London [et al.]: Adams Media

Croushorn, Amy (2019): *Entertaining with Disney. Exceptional Events. From Mickey Mouse to Moana!* San Rafael CA.: Insight Editions

Disney Enterprises (2016): *Disney Frozen Cookbook & Cookie Cutters Kit*. London: Chronicle Books

Disney Princess (2013): *The Disney Princess Cookbook*. Glendale CA.: Disney Press

Garofalo, Marcello (ed.)/ Ira L Meyer (2003): *Disney Recipes. From Animation to Inspiration*. New York: Disney Editions

Inside Editions (2015): Inside Inside Editions. In: Youtube.com, https://www.youtube.com/watch?v=LAD5fF1SaXU&feature=emb_logo. Accessed: 10. February 2021

Mallet, Jean-François (2018): *Disney. The Simple Family Cookbook*. London: Ilex

Monroe-Cassel, Chelsea/Marc Sumerak (2019): *Star Wars. Galaxy's Edge. The Official Black Spire Outpost Cookbook*. San Rafael CA.: Insight Editions

Star Wars: Galaxy's Edge. In: www.disneyworld.disney.go.com, https://disneyworld.disney.go.com/destinations/hollywood-studios/star-wars-galaxys-edge/. Accessed: 26. November 2020

The World Disney Company (1986): *Cooking with Mickey around our world. Walt Disney World's MOST requested recipes* [Orlando FL.: Walt Disney Co.]

Secondary Sources

Appadurai, Arjun (1988): How to Make a National Cuisine. Cookbooks in Contemporary India. In: *Comparative Studies in Society and History* Vol. 30, No. 1, 3–24. https://www.jstor.org/stable/179020

Bower, Anne (1997): Bound Together: Recipes, Lives, Stories, and Readings. In: *Recipes for Reading. Community Cookbooks, Stories, Histories*, ed. Anne Bower, Amherst MA., 1–14

Budd, Mike (2005): Introduction: Private Disney, public Disney. In: *Rethinking Disney: Private Control, Public Dimensions*, eds. Mike Budd/Max H. Kirsch, Middletown CT., 1–33

Floyd, Janet/Laurel Forster (2003): The Recipe in its Cultural Contexts. In: *The Recipe Reader. Narratives, Contexts, Traditions.*, eds. id., Lincoln [et al.], 1–11

Franko, Rachel (2020): Turn on those Scent Memories: We're Bringing You the Top Nine Smellitzer Scents at Walt Disney World. https://allears.net/2020/03/04/turn-on-those-scent-memories-were-bringing-you-the-top-nine-smellitzer-scents-at-walt-disney-world/. Accessed: 12. February 2021

Gumbrecht, Hans Ulrich (2004): *Diesseits der Hermeneutik. Die Produktion von Präsenz.* Frankfurt a. M.

Jenkins, Henry (2007): Transmedia Storytelling 101. http://henryjenkins.org/blog/2007/03/transmedia_storytelling_101.html. Accessed: 26. November 2019

Leonardi, Susan J. (1989): Recipes for Reading. Summer Pasta, Lobster à la Riseholme, and Key Lime Pie. In: *PMLA* Vol 104, No. 3, 340–347

Lötscher, Christine (2014): *Das Zauberbuch als Denkfigur. Lektüre, Medien und Wissen in zeitgenössischen Fantasy-Romanen für Jugendliche.* Zürich

Naccarato, Peter/Kathleen Lebesco (2012): *Culinary Capital.* London [et al.]

Pietschmann, Daniel/Sabine Völkel (2020): Transmediales Erzählen. In: *Handbuch Kinder- und Jugendliteratur*, eds. Tobias Kurwinkel/Philipp Schmerheim. https://doi.org/10.1007/978-3-476-04721-2_12, 95–104

Robinson, John A. (1978): Autobiographical Memory. In: *Aspects of Memory I: The Practical Aspects*, eds. Michael Gruneberg/Peter Morris. London, 223–251

Sandlin, Jennifer A./Julie C. Garlen (2016): Introduction. Feeling Disney, Buying Disney, Being Disney. In: *Disney, Culture, and Curriculum*, eds. id. New York [et al.], 1–26

Tigner, Amy L./Allison Carruth (2018): *Literature and Food Studies.* New York/London

Tippen, Carrie Helms (2018): *Inventing Authenticity. How Cookbook Writers Redefine Southern Identity.* Fayetteville

Wagner, Peter (1996): Introduction. Ekphrasis, Iconotexts, and Intermediality—the State(s) of the Art(s). In: *Essays on Ekphrasis and Intermediality*, ed. id. Berlin [et al.], 1–40

Watts, Steven (1997): *The Magic Kingdom.* Columbia MO.

Wasko, Janet (2001): *Understanding Disney. The Manufacture of Fantasy.* Malden MA.

The Social Aesthetics of Family Space

The Visual Heritage of Disney in a Swedish Amusement Park

Anna Sparrman

Abstract Disneyland's 1955 Main Street is inspired by Walt Disney's childhood on hometown street. Today, Disney Main Street has become a visual, cultural and historical heritage, and its aesthetic is visible in the architecture of American outlet villages, shopping malls and leisure parks all over the world. The Swedish amusement park Liseberg is one example of a place that reflects its influence. Initially this project set out to use visual documentation to explore the transference of Disney Main Street to a local context. In the course of this endeavour, however, its aim became to take on board an approach that can twist and challenge the settled, consensus view that Disney Main Street is an infantilising construct. So, the chapter begins by facing its own challenge: how to say something new about the well-trodden ground of Disney Main Street. This is resolved via the premise that methods enact the topics we research. The chapter will thus demonstrate that it is possible to avoid taking on the assumptions of earlier research in discussing Disney Main Street. This is achieved by discussing Main Street with family ethnography and the concepts of pure and impure critique (Illouz 2007). What emerges is a more ambiguous and complex interpretation of both Main Streets and their visitors.

Introduction

So, I set out to write about Disney's iconic American *Main Street* (Fig. 4) and how it has travelled from Disneyland in Anaheim California, USA, across the world to non-Disney theme and amusement parks. My idea was to say something about what happens when Disney Main Street becomes *Storgatan* (Main Street) in the Swedish amusement park Liseberg and what happens when Main Street appears in a local context. I set out to investigate issues of inclusion and exclusion, the moral

---

A. Sparrman (✉)
Linköping University, Linköping, Sweden
e-mail: anna.sparrman@liu.se

© The Author(s), under exclusive license to Springer-Verlag GmbH, DE, part of Springer Nature 2022
U. Dettmar and I. Tomkowiak (eds.), *On Disney*, Studien zu Kinder- und Jugendliteratur und -medien 9, https://doi.org/10.1007/978-3-662-64625-0_15

229

Fig. 1 Knott's Berry Farm, Buena Park, California. Photo courtesy of Orange County Archives. https://www.knotts.com/blog/2020/april/the-history-of-knotts-berry-farm. Accessed: 3. May 2021

ordering of the street and what the social aesthetics (cf. MacDougall 1999, 2006) of the street can tell us about family spaces. My aim was to use photographs from a visual documentation of Liseberg amusement park made by me and a research team before opening hours as part of the project "Culture for and by children: A visual ethnographic study of Children's museums, theme parks, amusement parks and Science Centres".[1]

I say "this is what I set off to do," because the endeavour turned out to be more challenging than I had expected. It is not as if it is impossible to discuss and relate the two Main Streets. As a matter of fact, it turned out that someone had already done it (cf. Strömberg 2007, 2016). The amount of research written on Disney Main Street and how it has expanded beyond the first Disneyland park (1955) was also a revelation to me (cf. Bartling 2004; Freitag 2017; Salamone/Salamone 1999). It made me curious as to why so many researchers, including myself, are so preoccupied with Disney Main Street.

In reading up on the history of Disneyland's Main Street I learned that Walt Disney was inspired by his own childhood main street from the early 1900s, Kennedy Avenue in Marceline, Missouri (cf. Francaviglia 1996, 1995). Then again, this was not his only inspiration. He had also looked at pre-existing full-scale versions of Main Streets, the early Knott's Berry Farm Main Street from the 1940s (Fig. 1) and Yesterday's Main Street at the Chicago Museum of Science from 1943 (cf. id. 1995).

---

[1] Financed by the Swedish Research Council 2010–2014, Dnr 2009–2384.

The Chicago street was part of a museum exhibition while Knott's Berry Farm looked more like today's Open-Air Museums.

Just like the Disneyland Main Street all these streets intermingle history and fiction to fill gaps between the *then*, the *now* and the *future* (cf. Watson/Waterton 2010). None of the places, not even the street in the Chicago Museum, is an authentic historical place. Rather, the visual reconstruction is used to create a feeling for the past and how it could have felt to be there. Main street becomes what Watson and Waterton (2010) describe as a mix between performing arts, science and, let me add, 'visual proofs' of emotions, memories and dreams (cf. Sparrman 2011).

The problem I ran into when setting out to write this text was that most research conducted on Disney Main Street follow similar patterns. They explain how Disney Main Street has become an archetype (cf. Francaviglia 1996), travelling across amusement and theme parks, and how it is used in community planning (cf. Bartling 2004; Jansson 2017; Salamone/Salamone 1999) and to model outlet villages, shopping malls (cf. Strömberg 2007) and ski resorts. They talk about the process as a *Disneyfication* in the sense that it involves a perceived romanticisation and infantilisation not only of the US but the whole world (cf. Bryman 2004). Most of the research start off with both implicit and explicit criticism of the various Disney Main Streets. There is criticism of neo-liberal management and capitalism (cf. Rojek 1993; Moser 2017), and the discussion is rife with comments about the tension between the real and the unreal—how the innocence, cleanliness and reassuringly (cf. Marling 1997) colourful street architecture conceal a dirty, or real, backstage (cf. Rojek 1993; Salamone/Salamone 1999). Most striking of all is that the voices of visitors are generally absent. As pointed out by David Cardell and me (cf. Cardell 2013, 2015; Cardell/Sparrman 2012), the majority of the research on theme parks and amusement parks discuss imaginary visitors which makes it possible to create a coherent picture of Main Street.

Research methodologies are neither neutral nor unproductive. Each and every method should, rather, be perceived as enacting the very topic we are researching (cf. Law 2004; Law/Urry 2003; Sparrman 2014). To study Main Street and Storgatan through park maps, documentary photography, biographical knowledge about Walt Disney, interviews with management or through visual documentation, is to breed a certain type of methodology and knowledge. It is striking that I, who have experience from the way children and families make use of theme and amusement parks, set off to study Disney Main Street in the same way as other research has. I more or less fell into condemning Liseberg Storgatan's similarity to Disneyland Main Street by wondering why on earth Sweden should need to look like the US. The approach, however, did make me uncomfortable, and I started to ask myself where this criticism came from and whose criticism it was. It turned out that the methodological difficulties I experienced had to do with feeling that I had nothing new to say about the street, and this realisation helped me re-think my approach by trying to explore the street beyond fixed patterns and coherencies (cf. Law 2004).

The result is a new aim: to see if avoiding the assumptions made by earlier research can lead us to talk about Disney Main Street in a different way. This necessitates an approach that is reflective and suggestive in nature rather than argumentative, and an exploratory rather than explanatory mode (cf. Mol 2002).

Framing the Topic

In the research project "Culture for and by children," a visual documentation was made of Liseberg with the help of museum preservation/documentation guidelines for buildings. The Liseberg documentation was made by five researchers before opening hours. We made visual documentations of all buildings, spaces, rides, attractions and signs. We delved into what makes a place for children a place for children (cf. Sparrman et al. 2016). The documentation was logged and saved as archival material and a few images have been used in research publications.

The obvious likeness between Storgatan and Disneyland Main Street in the documentation was what gave me the idea to do a visual study of the two streets. After looking at the documentation photographs again I searched Disney Main Street online and was easily able to find visual similarities between Disneyland and Storgatan buildings, such as in Fig. 2 and 3.

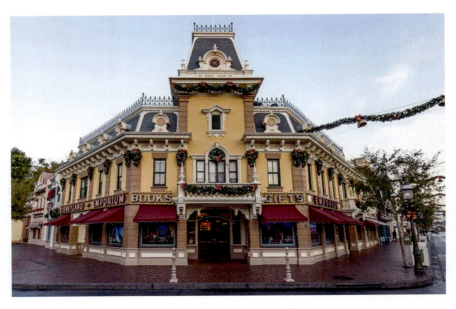

Fig. 2 Disneyland Main Street. https://insidethemagic.net/2020/09/main-street-disneyland-guide-ba1mmb/. Accessed: 30. March 2021

The Social Aesthetics of Family Space

Fig. 3 Liseberg Storgatan. Visual documentation 3–4 May, 2012

The buildings in the two places have a similar colour scheme. Both are colour coordinated so that complementary colours match darker bases with lighter trims (cf. Francaviglia 1996). The roofs and the decorations have commonalities as do the surrounding streets. The scale of the buildings and the language of the signs differ though. As does the organisation of the respective streets. At Disneyland visitors enter Main Street and the entire park through a Victorian-style brick train station (Fig. 4). After passing through the station visitors are positioned at one end of Main Street. From there they have a direct line of sight to Sleeping Beauty's medieval-style castle, looming in the distance at the other end of the street. All visitors to Disneyland must walk through Main Street twice, once when entering and a second time when leaving the park.

At Liseberg, on the other hand, you can avoid Storgatan altogether, as the street is situated in the middle of the park (Fig. 5). The street makes a straight line and can be entered from two directions. At one end there is a wooden building that looks like a train station; at the other is a small open area. So, what can be said about this? There are differences and similarities. This is where my troubles started.

Fig. 4 Disneyland Main Street. https://insidethemagic-119e2.kxcdn.com/wp-content/uploads/2020/09/Screen-Shot-2020-09-03-at-9.13.53-AM.png. Accessed: 3. May 2021

Fig. 5 Liseberg Storgatan. http://www.betaschool.eu/wp-content/uploads/2017/07/20170521_112647.jpg. Accessed: 3. May 2021

The Social Aesthetics of Family Space

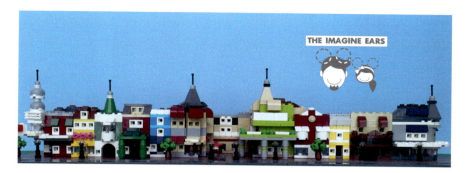

Fig. 6 Lego Disney World Main Street made and presented by "The Imagine Ears". https://imagineearsblog.files.wordpress.com/2018/02/lego-main-st-side.png?w=1324. Accessed: 3. May 2021

In the online search for Disney Main Street I encountered some other visual depictions of the street. On the blog "The Imagine Ears,"[2] created by a father and his daughter, a Lego version (Fig. 6) of Disney World Main Street was presented, accompanied by the words:

> The Imagine Ears features the DIY projects, adventures, and thoughts of a father and daughter who use a shared love of all things Disney to create memories together through encouraging her interests in architecture, design, Imagineering, while exploring history and science.[3]

Another blog caught my attention: "Disney Mamas: Real Mamas. Real Families. Real Disney,"[4] created by the "Disney fan from birth" mama Lin. In 2016 she shared her insights on the architecture of Disneyland Main Street.[5] She describes and highlights the differences between the Main Streets in Disneyland and in Disney World and also points out the differing architectural heritage of the respective buildings (Fig. 7).

Lin questions the idea, without citing any sources, that Main Street is based on Walt Disney's own childhood street. She argues instead that Walt wanted to create a Main Street in "Anywhere, USA" and that he was also inspired by Harper Goff's ideals (cf. Francaviglia 1996).[6] Blogs like these made it obvious that ordinary people—not just scholarly researchers—engage with Disney Main Street in their

---

[2] https://imagineears.blog/2018/02/19/lego-disney-magic-kingdom-main-street-right-side/. Accessed: 30. March 2021.

[3] https://imagineears.blog/2018/02/19/lego-disney-magic-kingdom-main-street-right-side/. Accessed: 30. March 2021.

[4] http://disneymamas.com/. Accessed: 30. March 2021.

[5] http://disneymamas.com/disney-architecture-main-street-usa/. Accessed: 3. May 2021.

[6] http://disneymamas.com/disney-architecture-main-street-usa/. Accessed: 30. March 2021.

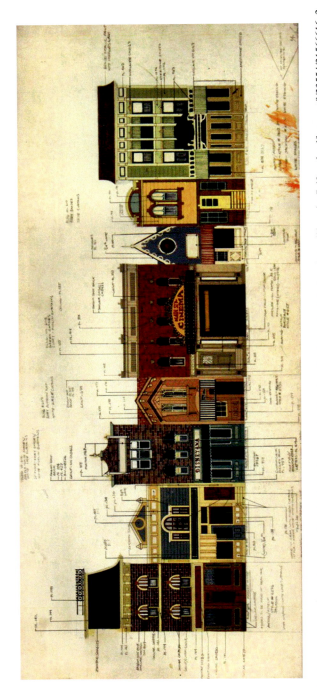

Fig. 7 Disneyland Main Street, 1991. Original elevation drawing by Imagineer Kim Irvine. https://dygtyjqp7pi0m.cloudfront.net/i/23554/21566616_2.jpg?v=8D212D21C9DD880. Accessed: 3. May 2021

The Social Aesthetics of Family Space   237

Fig. 8 Eksjö North Storgatan, part of the national interest Eksjö wood town. Photographer: Bengt A Lundberg, Swedish National Heritage Board (CC BY). https://kringla.nu/kringla/objekt;jsessionid=3F2E4498C4E20D573F6D05F361AFCA50?filter=province=sm&filter=serviceOrganization=ra%FF%FF&antal=72&sokFlik=1&referens=raa/kmb/16001000305884. Accessed: 3. May 2021

everyday lives. These are just two examples of family encounters. It became obvious just as mama Lin points out, that every Disney park has its own Main Street; Tokyo, Hong Kong and Paris,[7] and of course Liseberg. Instead of talking about *the* Main Street, visual expressions of Main Street always have been and still are multiplying across Disney parks, across continents and across non-Disney theme and amusement parks, all looking like each other without being exact copies. Not even the Disney corporation has only one Main Street (cf. Francaviglia 1996).

For example, even though Liseberg's Storgatan resembles Disneyland Main Street in some ways, it is also modelled on Swedish architecture. Storgatan was planned and built during the 1980s after a large park fire. An architectural firm was recruited to create the street (cf. Strömberg 2007, 2016). For inspiration the architects visited eight Swedish turn-of-the-century small towns[8] that had wooden houses still preserved (e.g. Fig. 8).

Storgatan is modelled on these Swedish wooden houses but are not exact replicas (cf. Strömberg 2007). The idea was to have Storgatan work as an image of the good life as it was in Sweden 1923. Not being an exact copy either of Disney or Swedish houses, the street is described in similar terms as Disney Main Street: it is seductive, dreamlike, nostalgic; it is an idealised bourgeois small town that gives a deceptive feeling of belonging (cf. id. 2016). When preparing the street, Liseberg

---

[7] http://disneymamas.com/disney-architecture-main-street-usa/. Accessed: 30. March 2021.
[8] Sigtuna, Norrtälje, Eksjö, Vaxholm, Alingsås, Kungälv, Marstrand and Haga in Gothenburg.

management had direct contact with Disney's management (cf. id. 2007). These differences are the result of Liseberg management wanting to distance itself from Disney, to avoid an Americanisation and hyper-commercialisation (cf. ibid.). This glimpse of selectivity shows how likeness and difference are intertwined and how likeness is probably not always the key ingredient. It is enough to create a recognisable likeness and then add your own touch. Just like in the "Disney mamas" and "The Imagine Ears" blogs mentioned above.

Critiquing Disney Main Streets and Liseberg Storgatan

The point is that there is a variety of Main Streets out there. The question is how to think critically about it without falling into platitudes. Earlier I promised to return to and reflect on the uniformity of the research on Disney Main Street. I am not alone in my observation of the repetitiveness of the critique. Alan Bryman (2004) stresses the difficulty of discussing Disney neutrally. Disney has, he argues, become an icon of a superficial product. As a result even critical analysis is not thoroughly pursued. Instead, the analysis itself has become simplified, as commentary on trivialisation, sanitisation and sentimentalisation, are repeatedly restated with the result of each time reinstating that very reputation. This simplification is what Bryman calls *Disneyfication*. To avoid this simplification when discussing Disney, Bryman instead suggests that we talk about *Disneyization*. To disneyizise means to account for the spread of principles used in Disney theme parks, namely (1) theming, (2) hybrid consumption, (3) merchandising and (4) performative labour (cf. Bryman 2004). None of which, incidentally, Walt Disney was the first to employ. Disneyization is about increasing people's inclination to consume, but not through simplifying and turning Disney objects into something superficial. Instead, it is about how, for what, when and by whom the four above-mentioned principles are used.

To further Bryman's thinking I have looked to Eva Illouz (2007) to delve into the notion of productive critique more generally. Illouz works with two concepts: pure and impure critique. Her aim is to resist the paradigm of 'pure critique' often found in critical theory and employed within, for example, cultural studies. Pure critique stresses that culture either emancipates or represses, by conveying either trash or treasure (cf. ibid., 91). This position, maintains Illouz, does not benefit analysis because it leaves no question marks. Cultural expressions ought to surprise, not be efficient packages delivering clear and straightforward positions, whether they be political and/or moral. Each sphere, the social, political as well as economic, is performative and produces potentially contradictory values and images (cf. Illouz 2007). To ignore this means to subsume the cultural completely under the political. From a Disney Main Street perspective this means not straightening out what is not straight and clear, and making sure to really unpack and study the principles, beyond talking about trash or treasure.

Bryman (2004) and Illouz (2007) both criticise consumerism and capitalism. And it seems that Bryman shares Illouz's view that each one of us today is born into and lives within capitalist societies. Consumer critique can therefore, as pointed out by Illouz, no longer shoot in from the side, or from outside in. This should not obstruct critical analysis. Instead, pure critique needs to be replaced with interpretation strategies as 'cunning' as the market forces being analysed. A cunning critique of cultural expressions, Illouz states, ought to proceed from the moral criteria at work *within* the social sphere being critiqued.[9] This approach 'from within the practice,' is what Illouz calls "impure critique" (2007, 95).

Impure critique treads "the fine line between those practices which further people's own desires and needs—however distasteful these may be to us—and those practices which clearly hamper them from attaining their goals." (Ibid.) At the centre of this approach is a thick analysis of social practices (cf. Law 2004; Illouz 2007), using slow, vulnerable, quiet, uncertain and multiple methods (cf. Law 2004). There are, however, always political reasons for preferring and enacting one kind of reality rather than the other. The question is why these political reasons are important, and for whom? Concerning Disney Main Street and Liseberg Storgatan the critique ought to be closely connected to the moral criteria of the individual streets rather than defined from the side.

When research enacts, re-enacts and again re-enacts Disney Main Street as coherent and solid, it begins to seem real (cf. Law 2004). To think with *impure critique* makes it possible to account for the fact that individuals always are included in the collectivity, that the invisible are seen in the visible and the front stage in the backstage. This merging of dualities becomes important if we want to understand the complexity of Disney Main Street. Disney Main Street is only singular in theory. I want to reach out to two critical art projects to see if they can help us think differently about Disney's and Liseberg's Main Streets from the dominant perceptions.

The Ambiguity of Main Streets

Let us further the thinking around Disney Main Street with the help of two visual artists, the American Jeff Gillette and his 2010 visual arts series *Dismayland*, and the internationally-renowned 'street artist' Banksy, who created the bemusement park *Dismaland* in 2015. In his series *Dismayland* Jeff Gillette combines Disney visual principles (cf. Bryman 2004) with images from the Brazilian slum[10] (Fig. 9). His art has been described as depictions of appalling 'slumscapes' or post-apocalyptic third-world wastelands (cf. Goldner 2015).

---

[9] Here Illouz draws on Michael Waltzer's later work.

[10] https://sandboxworld.com/dismayland-by-jeff-gillette/. Accessed: 7. April 2021.

Fig. 9 Artist Jeff Gillette from the series *Dismayland*: Donald drowning. https://gasivness.wordpress.com/2010/04/18/dismayland-by-jeff-gillette/. Accessed: 22. March 2021

Figure 9 shows, I argue, a version of Disney Main Street. The gaze follows a straight line until the street disappears in the distance. There are multi-coloured houses flanking both sides of the street, reminding us of the multiple colours of Disneyland's, Disney World's and Liseberg's houses. The houses are of multiple heights and made out of wood, just like the Disneyland (cf. Francaviglia 1996) and Liseberg houses. At the end of the river, rising towards the sky and surrounded by twinkling stars, is Disney World's Cinderella castle pictured in a slight haze. The castle attracts the gaze and brings attention to the image as reflective of Disney Main Streets. This Main Street is however slightly different. The street is a river, and the buildings are not offering commodities like food or souvenirs. Instead, the houses on the left are set up on colourful consumer waste which are slowly sliding into the river. In the left-hand corner, nearly invisible, is Donald Duck lying in the water. He is impeccably dressed in his blue hat, but is struggling not to drown in the water, under the waste and from poverty.

The picture combines images from real slums in Brazil with fantasy characters and characteristics, as well as images of Main Streets from 'real' Disney parks. It also depicts a potential future, a future where Disney holds a double position. First the positive one where Disney stands for hope: Cinderella's bright castle in the distance symbolising a dream that is currently unreachable but possible to fantasise about. Then the negative, where the picture stands for capitalism and over-consumption—this is the closed shops, the leftover waste piling up and propping up the houses standing, and the toxic-looking water. The title of the series, *Dismayland*, underlines this perplexity without sentimentalising or trivialising by making the street timeless, innocent or de-racialised. Gillette visually encompasses the whole complexity of any Disney Main Street. He engages with

The Social Aesthetics of Family Space 241

the ambiguity of the street: how it simultaneously realises our need for fantasy, dreams and hopes, at the same time he reminds us how the world is unequal and how it deteriorates around us, often due to our own actions. That Gillette chooses to maintain this ambiguity and this sense of wonder in life is what renders his critique, as Illouz (2007) would say, *impure*.

Of more general importance, however, for this discussion on impure critique is the so-called bemusement park *Dismaland* by the internationally-renowned street artist Banksy. *Dismaland* was set up as a physical park from the 21st of August to the 27th of September 2015 in the British seaside town of Weston-super-Mare. The word Dismaland alludes to Disneyland as does the park's logo (Fig. 10), but in containing the word 'dismal' it speaks to the gloominess or sadness of the place. Meanwhile the term bemusement park recalls 'amusement park,' but in suggesting that bemusement or perplexity awaits the visitor, it opens up rather different expectations.

Dismaland has no Main Street. What interests me here is the effort that researchers have invested in trying to make sense of what Dismaland 'is.' It is described as a sub-genre of theme parks known as the "critical theme park" (Freitag 2017, 924), as a critique of neo-liberalist fantasies (cf. Moser 2017) and as an urban art practice (cf. Zebracki 2018).

Despite not having a Main Street, Dismaland's castle—an allusion either to Sleeping Beauty's (Disneyland) or Cinderella's (Disney World)—nevertheless had a central position for the duration of the event. The castle was a deteriorated version of its models, neither clean nor shiny nor colourful. It was as if the potential backstage of Disneyland had swapped places with the clean, colourful façade of the front stage. Is this what the purist critique (cf. Illouz 2007) is asking for

Fig. 10 Banksy's logo for his/her theme/amusement park *Dismaland*. https://www.nme.com/news/music/various-artists-713-1222604. Accessed: 3. May 2021

when it criticises Disney Main Street? The visitors meet "reality at every corner" in Dismaland, writes Keith Moser (2017, 1026), in reference to events inside the park such as miniature motorboats containing destitute refugees, a structure that enabled visitors to climb up a nuclear cloud tree house, and a mini 'Gulf' course (see also Freitag 2017).

Even though Dismaland was different from, for example, Disneyland, commentators still used the same genre of pure critique to criticise Banksy. It was said that yes, on the one hand, Dismaland 'is' a public piece of art, but on the other, it is still not really street art (cf. Zebracki 2018). Because art and commodities like T-shirts and a Dismaland catalogue were sold in the park, reflecting the same capitalist strategy as Disney, Banksy was not critical enough of neo-liberalism (cf. Moser 2017). Again, the impure research critique leaves out the visitor perspective and make claims on behalf of the visitors (cf. Freitag 2017; Moser 2017; Zebracki 2018). As Illouz has pointed out (2007), it is difficult today to launch a critique of capitalism from an outside position, since each and every one of us is born into and lives life from within a capitalist system. Banksy her/himself says in an interview on the Dismaland website[11]:

> It's an experiment in offering something less resolved than the average theme park. For some reason it's been labelled as 'twisted' but I've never called it that. We just built a family attraction that acknowledges inequality and impending catastrophe. I would argue it's theme parks which ignore these things that are the twisted ones. (Quoted in Freitag 2017, 928)

Three interesting words appear in this quotation: "resolved," "twisted," and "family attraction." I want to begin by exploring the way Banksy talks about *twisted*. Banksy states that s/he/they does not see the park as twisted, but rather that it acknowledges inequalities and predicts "impending" catastrophes with no clear-cut solutions. Combined with the wish to offer something less *resolved* than the "average" theme park, Banksy's view of the park exhibition conjures up the notion of a world that does not have easy answers but rather is full of impurity and uncertainty. Does this imply, then, that a place like Disneyland gives easy answers? What seems to be at stake here is whether Dismaland is in fact truer than Disneyland.

Real Un-Real

According to the scholarship both Disneyland Main Street and Liseberg Storgatan are modelled on 'real' buildings. And visiting the parks is a real activity in the sense that you have to go there to be part of the park. Let me exemplify this with a description of a visit to Disney World.

---

[11] http://www.dismaland.co.uk. The interview cannot be found there anymore. Accessed: 3. May 2021.

The Social Aesthetics of Family Space 243

The researchers Salamone and Salamone (1999) describe in their article something that happened during one of their family visits to the park: they ran into a staff member changing costumes in a side street. They describe how these few seconds of seeing this person "brought us back to reality" (Salamone/Salamone 1999, 86). My question is: did they mean that the family had actually experienced the visit up until then as "unreal"? Annemarie Mol (1999) argues that reality is made in and through practices. Her idea is that reality never precedes mundane practices, but rather that reality is shaped within and through them. The character of reality is in this way simultaneously open and contested.

If real equals reality, reality is both inside and outside Disneyland, Liseberg, Dismayland or Dismaland. Gillette's artwork (Fig. 9) shows this in an interesting way. Subsequently it is Salamone and Salamone who enact the park visit as unreal; it is not by definition unreal. Dismaland therefore 'is' not more real than Disneyland or Liseberg; they bluntly enact different parts of the social world. Disney Main Street, in other words, can be multiply constructed. The various parks are what Mol would describe as "different realities, that coexist in the present" (1999, 79). To further this discussion let us move on to Banksy's third key concept: family attraction.

Family Attraction

The idea that Banksy aimed to create a *family attraction* fits nicely with what Walt Disney wanted Disneyland to be a place for: "[P]arents and children to share pleasant time in one another's company" (Paul Mosley 1985 quoted in Rojek 1993, 126). People of all ages, in all sorts of social groupings, are welcome, and there should be something for everyone (Hunt/Frankenberg 1990; Rojek 1993). Liseberg takes a similar approach. Families are not mentioned on the webpage; instead the place is described as "for everyone."[12]

Continuing to employ the idea that Main Streets are enacted through situated practices, then, we can say that children and families take part in these enactments (cf. Law 2004; Mol 1999). David Cardell's (2015) ethnographic child and family study of Liseberg can further our thinking about the idea of the real-unreal. His work enables us to reflect on the notion of family attractions and to interrogate previous research, for instead of streams of robotic visitors produced from imagination, he provides data from actual family visits to the park. A park visit, Cardell shows, is closely intertwined with families' everyday lives. A family visit to the park is often planned weeks, even months ahead. Money is saved to make the trip doable; some families have integrated the visit in the family budget as a recurring

---

[12] https://www.liseberg.com/about-liseberg/. Accessed: 4. May 2021.

yearly outing. The planning of park visits is then merged with other everyday matters. Cardell shows how families, when they finally arrive at the park, also bring everyday life with them. Family disagreements on what to do and not do, who should do what with whom, bribing to keep everyone happy, are routine, as well as all the other practicalities that come with being a family. Banksy picks up on these tensions in her/his/their promotion film for the park.[13] The film shows an ethnically white nuclear family visiting Dismaland. The children laugh at the horrors while the parents cry. Cardell's study shows that a rigid division between an inside and outside of the park, or the dualism of the real and unreal, does not reflect the situated family practices of actual life. When walking down Main Street, children and adults do not necessarily behave like pre-programmed robots in ways that follow the intentions of the designers. Families split up in smaller groups to ensure satisfaction for as many as possible. At times they resist what is on offer by bringing their own picnics; they do not adjust to the entire set up (cf. id. 2013, 2015; Sparrman et al. 2017). To enjoy Liseberg and/or Disneyland does not exclude one from being critical. To reflect on this point let us return to Jeff Gillette's pictures.

As a child Gillette loved watching Disney cartoons on television, and his biggest wish was to visit Disneyland. Due to an impoverished childhood this did not come true until he was a teenager, and then the visit was a disappointment (Holmes, 2016). After half an hour in the park he left disappointed (Goldner, 2015). In an online conversation with Gillette (between the 22nd of March and 9th of April 2021) I wrote a reflection on this asking if the park was not fantastical enough. Sometimes fantasy is needed to cope with life. In his adulthood Gillette has witnessed how, for children living in slums, the sense of wonderment always is intertwined with eating garbage and sniffing drugs. Gillette told me that during an artist-in-residence in Mumbai, he made visits to the Mahi-mahi slum. On one of these occasions he built a makeshift façade of a Disney castle facing the train station at the slum. When it was completed he made arrangements for a Disney-themed "kid's fun day" for children with colourful paper plates, makings of Mickey Mouse ears, serving candies and sodas. Gillette says: "it is lots of fun to give back and give a glimpse of the magic kingdom to kids that will never experience the real thing …like me!!" (Ibid.) Note that in this case "the real thing" means a visit to Disneyland, the real place of fantasy.

Maybe this is what Liseberg is also trying to accomplish in the sustainability program they offer which reaches out to families with special needs.[14] On a yearly basis Liseberg management arranges for social workers to hand out entrance tickets and visitor passes to families on long-term income support.[15] The idea is to give

---

[13] https://www.youtube.com/watch?v=V2NG-MgHqEk. Accessed: 26. April 2021.

[14] https://www.liseberg.se/hallbarhet/. Accessed: 31. March 2021.

[15] https://www.liseberg.se/hallbarhet/socialt-engagemang/socialnamnderna/. Accessed: 16. March 2021.

The Social Aesthetics of Family Space 245

the most vulnerable children the opportunity to go back to school after the summer holiday with a story of enjoyment of their own. To meet "reality at every corner," as Moser (2017, 1026) describes Banksy's Dismaland, is a privilege for the middle class, just like Disneyland, since most people can never visit either place. There are, after all, children and families who *live* the practices of Dismaland, who lack the cultural or experiential exposure to even choose whether to visit Disneyland or Liseberg. For these people there is no room in their lives to mix reality with fantasy.

The Inconsistent Consistency

Methods are powerfully productive, for they bring into being what they discover (cf. Law/Urry 2003). By unpacking what researchers have taken for granted about Disney Main Street I have identified how the method of pure critique (cf. Illouz 2007), together with the ontological stance that the real is stable and distinguishable from the unreal (cf. Mol 1999), is one that merely reproduces static images of Disney Main Street. This methodological approach can be described as imperialistic (cf. Law 2004), as it positions researchers as superior relative to people like park visitors. Visitors are not robots. Criticism is integral to visitor practices. That the imagined visitor is the foundation of pure critique becomes a hindrance for nuancing between for example Disneyland Main Streets and Liseberg Storgatan. And the nuances can be found in the implied absences when making something present (cf. ibid.). Researching Main Street without visitors, as I had originally set out to do, led me into *pure critique*. Jeff Gillette's and Banksy's reflexive, self-contradictory, paradoxical and ambiguous artworks show how critique does not need to be either emancipatory or repressive. They are both, and this is what makes them *impure critique* (cf. Illouz 2007), a non-imperialist method. This book chapter shows how it is easy to be caught in predefined research assumptions as we all live with prejudice. It is always a struggle to unpack what is taken for granted, for it means that we must challenge our own prejudices.

References

Bartling, Hugh (2004): The Magic Kingdom Syndrome: Trials and Tribulations of Life in Disney's Celebration. In: *Contemporary Justice Review*, Vol. 7, No. 4, 375–393
Bryman, Alan (2004): *The Disneyization of Society* [Electronic Resource], London
Cardell, David (2015): *Family Theme Parks, Happiness and Children's Consumption. From Roller-Coasters to Pippi Longstocking.* (Diss.) Linköping
Cardell, David (2013): Tysta Barn och Talande Robotar: Om Tema- och Nöjesparksforskningens problem och Barnstudiernas Möjligheter. In: *Nu Vill Jag Prata! Barns Röster i Barnkulturen,* ed. Karin Helander (Centrum för barnkulturforsknings skriftserie; 46), Stockholm, 141–152
Cardell, David/Anna Sparrman (2012): Enacting Money at an Amusement Park. In: *Situating child consumption. Rethinking Values and Notions of Children, Childhood and Consumption,* eds. Anna Sparrman/Bengt Sandin/Johanna Sjöberg, Lund, 115–132

Francaviglia, Richard (1995): History after Disney: The Significance of "Imagineered" Historical Places. In: *The Public Historian*, Vol. 17, No. 4, 69–74

Francaviglia, Richard V. (1996): Main Street Revisited: Time, Space, and Image Building in Small-town America (The American Land & Life Series). https://www.uipress.uiowa.edu/books/9780877455431/main-street-revisited

Freitag, Florian (2017): Critical Theme Parks: Dismaland, Disney and the Politics of Theming. In: *Continuum: Journal of Media and Cultural Studies*, Vol. 31, No. 3, 923–933. https://doi.org/10.1080/10304312.2017.1310180

Goldner, Liz (2015): Before Banksy, Painter Jeff Gillette's 'Dismayland' Took on Disney, *KCET*, 13. December 2015. https://www.kcet.org/shows/artbound/before-banksy-painter-jeff-gillettes-dismayland-took-on-disney. Accessed: 22. March 2021

Holmes, Kevin (2016): Meet the 'Slumscape' Painter Who Inspired Banksy's Dystopian Theme Park, *Vice*, 28. June 2016. https://www.vice.com/en/article/aenpng/jeff-gillettes-subversive-paintings-inspired-banksys-dismaland. Accessed: 22. March 2021

Hunt, Pauline/Ronald Frankenberg (1990): It's a Small World: Disneyland, the Family and the Multiple Re-representations of American Childhood. In: *Constructing and Reconstructing Childhood: Contemporary Issues in the Sociological Study of Childhood*, eds. Allison James/Alan Prout, London, 99–117

Illouz, Eva (2007): *Cold Intimacies. The Making of Emotional Capitalism*. Cambridge

Jansson, David (2017): The Work of Southering. In: *Southeastern Geographer*, Vol. 57, No. 2, 131–150

Law, John (2004): *After Method. Mess in Social Science Research*. London

Law, John/John Urry (2003): *Enacting the Social*, published by the Department of Sociology and the Centre for Science Studies, Lancaster University, Lancaster. http://www.comp.lancs.ac.uk/sociology/papers/Law-Urry-Enacting-the-Social.pdf

MacDougall, David (2006): *The Corporeal Image. Film, Ethnography, and the Senses*. Princeton [et al.]

MacDougall, David (1999): *Transcultural Cinema*. Princeton

Marling, Karal Ann, ed. (1997): *Designing Disney's Theme Parks. The Architecture of Reassurance*. Paris

Mol, Annemarie (2002): *Body Multiples. Ontology in Medical Practice*. Durham

Mol, Annemarie (1999): Ontological Politics. A world and some questions. In: *Actor Network Theory and After*, eds. John Law/John Hassard, Oxford, 74–89

Moser, Keith (2017): Exhuming the "Dismal" Reality Underneath Banal Utopian Signs: Banksy's Recent Parody of the Disneyfication of the Modern World. In: *The Journal of Popular Culture*, Vol. 50, No. 5, 1024–1046

Mosley, Leonard (1985): *The Real Walt Disney*. London

Rojek, Chris (1993): Disney Culture. In: *Leisure Studies*, Vol. 12, No. 2, 121–135

Salamone, Virginia A./Frank A. Salamone (1999): Images of Main Street: Disney World and the American Adventure. In: *Journal of American Culture*, Vol. 22, No. 1, 85–92

Sparrman, Anna (2011): Barnkulturens Sociala Estetik. In: *Locus*, No. 3, 25–44

Sparrman, Anna (2014): Access and Gatekeeping in Researching Children's Sexuality: Mess in Ethics and Methods. In: *Sexuality & Culture*, Vol. 18, 291–309

Sparrman, Anna/Tobias Samuelsson/Anne-Li Lindgren/David Cardell (2016): The Ontological Practices of Child Culture. In: *Childhood*, Vol. 23, No. 2, 255–271

Sparrman, Anna/David Cardell/Anne-Li Lindgren/Tobias Samuelsson (2017): The Ontological Choreography of (Good) Parenthood. In: *Doing Good Parenthood. Ideal and Practices of Parental Involvement*, eds. Anna Sparrman/Allan Westerling/Judith Lind/Karen Ida Dannesboe, London, 113–126

Strömberg, Per (2016): Et in Chronotopia Ego: Main Street Architecture as a Rhetorical Device in Theme Park and Outlet Villages. In: *A Reader in Themed and Immersive Spaces*, ed. Scott A. Lukas, Pittsburgh PA., 83–93

Strömberg, Per (2007): *Uppelvelse industrins turistmiljöer: Visuella berättarstrategier i svenska turistanläggningar 1985–2005*. (Diss.) Uppsala

Watson, Steve/Emma Waterton (2010): Introduction: A Visual Heritage. In: *Culture, Heritage and Representation: Perspectives on Visuality and the Past*, eds. Emma Waterton/Steve Watson, Farnham, 1–18

Zebracki, Martin (2018): Regenerating a Coastal Town through Art: *Dismaland* and the (L)imitations of Antagonistic Art Practice in the City. In: *Cities*, Vol. 77, 21–32

Printed in the United States
by Baker & Taylor Publisher Services